Praise for

Progressive Capitalism

"In this deeply considered and precisely detailed examination of technology's impact on the country's financial future and emotional present, Khanna presents policy initiatives that aim to bring civility back to public discourse, both online and in person, and to level the employment playing field. With both anecdotal accounts and factual evidence, Khanna champions the responsible use of technology to improve lives and unite factions."

—*Booklist*

"Khanna has a nuanced take on the tech industry and offers genuine solutions to significant problems plaguing the country.... [A] commonsense call for change."

—*Publishers Weekly*

"Just on the evidence of his new book, Ro Khanna is one of the broadest, brightest and best-educated legislators on Capitol Hill.... His book is bulging with ideas about how to transform big tech from a huge threat to liberty into a genuine engine of democracy."

—*The Guardian* (US)

"[F]ierce and compelling."

—*The National Book Review*

"Congressman Ro Khanna (D-Calif.) argues democratizing access to tech can strengthen both the economy and our social fabric with a roadmap to bridging the geographic and digital divides."

—*Fortune*

"In this passionate and inspiring book, Khanna offers a vision for creating spaces for rational exchange in digital media that do not serve first and foremost economic interests. I am impressed by the precise imagination of this well-informed politician."

—Jürgen Habermas, Professor Emeritus of Philosophy, Johann Wolfgang Goethe University of Frankfurt am Main

"Is there any dignity in digital? That's a great question to ask in the wake of the attack on the Capitol on January 6, 2021, which got a toxic assist from tech giants like Facebook. It seems more clear than ever—from misinformation to hate speech, from screen addiction to the immense wealth held by tech billionaires—that tech is working against us more than for us, as it was intended at the dawn of the internet age. It's to Ro Khanna's credit then that he is trying to change the narrative so that we can democratize the inventions that were paid for by the American people and let us all share in the wonders they are capable of delivering. If you are interested in trying to even the digital playing field as we move to even more critical technologies of the future, you should read this book to find out how."

—Kara Swisher, *New York Times* columnist and cohost of *Pivot* and host of *Sway* podcasts

"In his new book, California Representative Ro Khanna rolls out a vision to train rural as well as urban job seekers to build 'digital' roads, bridges, and other aspects of infrastructure. Calling simultaneously for effective regulation of Big Tech and protection of local communities, Khanna envisions redistributing opportunities from coastal cities to rural Middle America, bridging cultural differences, and creating a new cosmo-local culture. An exciting vision, brilliantly rendered—a must-read."

—Arlie Russell Hochschild, author of *Strangers in Their Own Land: Anger and Mourning on the American Right*

"This book is a highly principled, empirically grounded, progressive blueprint for building an inclusive society in which all Americans share a common national identity and participate in constructive dialogue. It is founded on the possibilities of sharing technology much more widely, on building the skills and capabilities of all people, and on the basic principles of inclusion and participatory democracy to chart a path to a flourishing society."

—James J. Heckman, Nobel Prize winner and professor of economics at the University of Chicago

"Congressman Ro Khanna's book, *Dignity in a Digital Age*, is both a practical and aspirational guide to the future of tech, governance, and equity. Congressman Khanna leans on critical race and gender theorists, economists, and philosophers to articulate a vision for the future of the technology sector that centers racial and gender justice and eschews the digital segregation that has defined the tech sector since its infancy. *Dignity in a Digital Age* asks the question, 'What could our country look like if we legislated and designed for marginalized people to lead the next era of Silicon Valley?' and leads its reader to a measured understanding of how our country can't afford any other alternative. Too often, the voices of people of color who've called for a radical reimagining of technology companies, their hiring and retention practices, and the products they produce, have been shouted down as too radical or their ideas too impractical. *Dignity in a Digital Age* not only amplifies those leaders, their stories, and their solutions, but provides a legislative and policy roadmap for anyone unsure of how to reach that vision."

—Kimberlé Crenshaw, cofounder of the African American Policy Forum and professor at the UCLA School of Law and Columbia Law School

"It might seem counterintuitive for a member who represents Silicon Valley to write a book on expanding technology to the middle of the country, but that is precisely why it is so important. In this 'shake the snow globe' moment, Representative Khanna makes a compelling case for place-based policymaking and how a more well-dispersed innovation economy can help rising cities thrive."

—Steve Case, author of *The Third Wave: An Entrepreneur's Vision of the Future*, chairman and CEO of Revolution, and cofounder of America Online

"In *Dignity in a Digital Age*, Khanna provides a compelling vision of how spreading opportunities in the technology revolution across America can contribute to healing the nation's wounds. Today's technologies allow workers to collaborate on projects with diverse people in disparate locations while staying rooted in their communities. This joint work has the potential to humanize differences and increase the democratic intelligence of the body politic, allowing America to live up to its founding vision."

—Charles Taylor, Professor Emeritus of Philosophy, McGill University

"Ro Khanna is a great American dreamer. His dream, powerfully presented here in personal, political, and philosophical registers, is of a twenty-first-century democracy—multiracial and multiethnic, with fair opportunity for all to participate in the extraordinary fruits of American technological innovation. Deeply rooted in values of equality, freedom, and public reason, Khanna's democracy is also rooted in places—from redwood forests to Gulf Stream waters, from diamond deserts to waving wheat fields. It is a democracy in which strong attachments to families, neighborhoods, and local communities—places that people call their homes—is married to a capacious, generous, inclusive sense of justice. This is the American democracy that my grandparents immigrated for, that my father defended on the beaches of Normandy and in the

Ardennes Forest, and that I hope my own children live in. We are in danger of losing it. But with people like Ro Khanna fighting for it, with great moral clarity and political energy, we all have reason to hope."

—Joshua Cohen, coeditor of *Boston Review* and member of faculty, Apple University

PROGRESSIVE CAPITALISM

HOW TO MAKE TECH
WORK FOR ALL OF US

RO KHANNA

SIMON & SCHUSTER PAPERBACKS

NEW YORK   LONDON   TORONTO   SYDNEY   NEW DELHI

Simon & Schuster Paperbacks
An Imprint of Simon & Schuster, Inc.
1230 Avenue of the Americas
New York, NY 10020

First Simon & Schuster trade paperback edition February 2023

SIMON & SCHUSTER PAPERBACKS and colophon
are registered trademarks of Simon & Schuster, Inc.

For information about special discounts for bulk purchases,
please contact Simon & Schuster Special Sales
at 1-866-506-1949 or business@simonandschuster.com.

The Simon & Schuster Speakers Bureau can bring authors to your live event.
For more information or to book an event, contact the
Simon & Schuster Speakers Bureau at 1-866-248-3049 or
visit our website at www.simonspeakers.com.

Interior design by Ruth Lee-Mui

Manufactured in the United States of America

1   3   5   7   9   10   8   6   4   2

The Library of Congress has cataloged the hardcover edition as follows:
Names: Khanna, Ro, author.
Title: Dignity in a digital age : making tech work for all of us / Ro Khanna.
Description: New York : Simon & Schuster, [2022] | Includes bibliographical references and index.
Identifiers: LCCN 2021041629 (print) | LCCN 2021041630 (ebook) |
ISBN 9781982163341 (hardcover) | ISBN 9781982163365 (ebook)
Subjects: LCSH: Information economy—United States. | Information technology—
Economic aspects—United States. | Information technology—Social aspects—United States. |
Economic development—United States. | Digital divide—United States. | Equality—United States.
Classification: LCC HC110.I55 K43 2022 (print) | LCC HC110.I55 (ebook) | DDC 330.973—dc23
LC record available at https://lccn.loc.gov/2021041629
LC ebook record available at https://lccn.loc.gov/2021041630

ISBN 978-1-9821-6334-1
ISBN 978-1-9821-6335-8 (pbk)
ISBN 978-1-9821-6336-5 (ebook)

For Ritu, Soren, and Zara

Contents

Foreword

BY AMARTYA SEN

W. B. Yeats worried about things falling apart when people's differences turn destructive. This can, obviously, be a cause for alarm. And yet a well-thought-out understanding of an integrated society can accommodate many useful diversities within it. Ro Khanna's beautifully written book, *Dignity in a Digital Age*, offers a graceful picture of the coexistence of disparate ways of living, allowing justice and fairness. People can jointly benefit from richly varying opportunities which can be made accessible to all, even though they come from—and have background in—many different communities.

Dignity in a Digital Age is an exciting book, written by a much admired U.S. congressman who is also an innovative social thinker. Whether we consider the future of America, or of other places, we have reason to be grateful to Ro Khanna. There is much foundational work to be done in the problem-ridden world in which we live, and it is wonderful to find a treasure trove of creative proposals to address the unique challenges of the digital age.

The technological world has been moving ahead offering potentially huge opportunities to people across the world. And yet differences in the practical possibility of making good use of technology has also on many occasions split up people in many ways, linked to their history, location, ethnicity, and inherited and acquired capabilities. Khanna is hostile to inequality but determined to promote the best possible use of opportunities for all. With adequate preparation and discernment, and being intelligently guided by democratic principles, we can move in that attractive direction. No community need be excluded from getting the benefits of new technology, which has to be a crucial component of any robust development strategy.

Will our diversity allow us to still coalesce around a common identity in the constructive way outlined by Khanna? His hope for democratic patriotism where we each have an equal opportunity to shape national culture and embrace a spirit of civility to appreciate and resolve differences is well reasoned. In the process he also draws inspiration from Frederick Douglass, the enslaved person who fought for—and achieved—freedom, and proceeded to fight inequalities of all kinds, including slavery. Our diversity, Khanna observes, allows us to harness the talents of different groups, challenging our ideas, pushing us to improve, and perhaps most important (here he quotes Douglass directly) avoiding the "arrogance and intolerance which are almost the inevitable concomitants of general conformity."

Khanna defends strongly the right of the people to move and choose their location—an issue of much contemporary relevance. However, even though migration may play a part in the realization of Khanna's vision, it is not something on which he relies. Just as people can move to technology, technology too can move to people. People need not be compelled to relocate from one place to another to reap the benefits offered by technological progress. He points out that the nature of modern technology allows its wide use in communities previously untouched by modernity or radical change. He offers ideas for facilitating constructive dialogue on digital platforms in search of mutual understanding to overcome divergent social realities.

What is important is to be guided by carefully examined human values related to the process of development. Democratic reasoning has to play a central role in examining and celebrating the opportunities that people benefit from—without their having to be personally flung across the world to make use of what exists. There will of course be much to discuss on how exactly to proceed, but that is the nature of democracy, particularly—as John Stuart Mill has taught us—when we learn to see democracy as "governance by discussion." We have reason to be grateful to Ro Khanna for the insights he presents in this splendidly written book.

Preface

Many Americans share a deep frustration with capitalism and globalization. They have seen their hometowns destroyed and their parents laid off as corporations moved high-paying manufacturing jobs offshore to China or Mexico in pursuit of profits. For decades, both political parties in America put too much faith in global markets. They paid little attention to both the things that were changing, such as the working and middle class that has lost nearly 25 percent of its wealth since 1980, and the things that will never change, such as people's attachment to place.

The ideology of the 1980s and 1990s, which encouraged training blue-collar workers for new service jobs or moving them from their factory towns and rural communities to a big city, proved unrealistic and out of touch. Many people didn't leave their hometowns, and many didn't get the promised new economy jobs. Instead, they have witnessed a brain drain in their communities as their kids have been forced to leave to pursue opportunity elsewhere. They understandably have a resentment for our nation's governing political class. The reality is that it was a colossal mistake for America to lose its production capacity. We gave up jobs that sustained local economies, that drove innovation, and that gave communities self-worth and pride.

Today, there is a recognition that we cannot just let the market dictate where jobs or capital should go. For the past forty years, America has had an unstated industrial policy, influenced by large multinationals, that concluded industry should be sent offshore for cheaper wages and higher profits. Americans will no longer stand for this. It's time for ordinary citizens to have a say in where new industry, new jobs, and new factories should be. Progressive capitalism, which I hope can be a new governing philosophy for the twenty-first century, means that it is appropriate for the government to consider community and place in defining the rules of the market. We should adopt policies that bring the industries of the future to the United States, specifically in towns that have been left out.

In short, we need a new vision that builds on our history. We need a *new economic patriotism* that calls for America to lead in creating technology—the new battery plants, the next generation of steel, advanced medicines, electric vehicles, solar panels, and even masks, auto parts, and baby formula—that will fuel this nation. America needs to *make* things again. This will require government support to champion the leading technology and build a workforce that is cutting-edge. A shining example is Intel's recent $20 billion investment in Columbus, Ohio, which is creating two new semiconductor factories and thousands of jobs. There is a new enthusiasm and energy in Columbus that transcends party, ideology, and race. The Intel investment was made possible because of the Chips and Science Act that I co-led with Senator Schumer and Senator Young. The success of this initial investment shows what we can do when business and government work together. This book makes the case for innovative policies like the Chips Act at a much larger and faster scale.

We forget that much of America's production in the twentieth century was cutting-edge from a technology standpoint. Our workers were highly skilled and trained in the tech of their day. It's now time to bring key pillars of the twenty-first-century economy home to America. We need to bet on and invest in American workers to lead the next generation of production. Investing in our workers means providing them with a free college or vocational education, advanced training in the trades, and a digital proficiency. It means giving them healthcare, the right to form a union, and childcare. These are the basics that working class people are demanding across the country. We see it in the labor movement at Starbucks and Amazon, and in the food service industry with McDonald's, Burger King, and Chipotle. If we want young people in particular to embrace capitalism—after they have seen family members lose jobs, healthcare, and housing even as they're saddled with student and medical debt—then we need to show workers that they will be compensated fairly for their work and that government is both willing and able to work on their behalf.

Progressive capitalism is about celebrating free markets for the entrepreneurship and innovation they bring, while insisting that markets must be in service of the good of local communities and, ultimately, our national community. Unfettered capitalism has robbed too many American cities of their pride and too many Americans of their dignity. It's time for a fundamental reset. It's time for us to embrace a progressive capitalism that will center the American dream again for the working class in our nation.

PROGRESSIVE CAPITALISM

1

DEMOCRATIZING THE DIGITAL REVOLUTION

After the coal industry took a hit in Eastern Kentucky, Alex Hughes's business went under. Alex found himself unemployed for nearly six months in what was the lowest period of his life. Nearly two decades earlier, Alex was stabbed in the face by a drunk stranger, and the scar still stretches across his jaw and cheek. If given the choice, Alex told me, he would prefer being stabbed again to losing the business he owned for fifteen years and going without work.

When you're unemployed, Alex explained, "No one sees you're injured." But a lack of income can be a lot more stressful than physical trauma when your family depends on you. He lost his house and car, and he worried constantly about his wife and family. Some of his unemployed friends began drinking, while others saw marriages dissolve. Unemployment leaves scars of its own. To this day, even when times are good, Alex still fears he could lose everything at any moment.

Alex never gave up searching for work, however. He comes from a proud family tradition with an *I can fix that* attitude. Alex told me, "I am certainly not the type of person that is going to sit around. There has to be something to do. Letting someone take care of me is not the thing that comes to mind." Whenever he felt dejected, he tried to think about his newborn son. "When he grows up, what's he going to think if I lay down and quit?"

Alex, now in his mid-forties, has a heavy build and a dreamcatcher tattoo on his forearm. After high school, he attended Big Sandy Community and Technical College, but stopped to provide for his daughter. At the time, he worked construction jobs, then opened a tattoo shop to make ends meet. After saving money and teaching himself about electronic equipment, he started his now defunct business installing large-format printers at offices that oversaw coal mining. Like so many small businesses in the region, it had depended on the coal economy to survive.

In 2017, while unemployed, Alex saw a television ad for the Interapt technology services program, which paid $400 a week for six months of intensive training in Apple's iOS software. Interapt was founded by Ankur Gopal, an Indian American who was born and raised in rural Kentucky and sought to bring quality tech jobs to the region. Hughes applied to the program and was accepted. He now describes it as "on the miracle level." It led to a full-time job that allows him to "have a pretty good life" and provide for his family. After finishing his training, Alex earned $42,000 per year as a basic coder, and now makes $77,000 as a lead software developer. He is responsible for managing a team which has members in Chicago and Atlanta that implements software solutions for General Electric Appliances, headquartered in Louisville, to build smart appliances including refrigerators, coffee makers, ovens, and laundry machines. Alex can schedule his own hours and feels lucky to have worked remotely every day during the pandemic.

Stories like those of Alex were on Representative Hal Rogers's mind when he invited me to visit Paintsville, Kentucky, or "Silicon Holler" as he calls it. Rogers is an eighty-three-year-old Republican who has served in Congress for forty years in the heart of Trump country. His referring to the region as Silicon Holler indicates how much Appalachian Kentucky aspires to build a tech-savvy workforce to support their broader economic ecosystem. They reject the emptiness and elitism of the mantra that all laid-off middle-aged workers or liberal arts students should now become coders. Instead, they recognize that digital wealth can sustain a wide diversity of jobs. My trip to Paintsville captured the imagination of many. Headlines followed dubbing me the "Ambassador of Silicon Valley." I suspect the interest in this story was about more than just tech jobs. It was noteworthy that people from different parts of the country like Alex Hughes and I were even talking to each other.

Alex shared with me that although he comes from some of the "whitest" parts of Kentucky, he never saw "a whole lot of divisiveness" when "people from foreign countries ended up being doctors and business owners that we all rely on." Now, a man by the name of Ankur Gopal, the son of immigrants, gave him the best opportunity of his life. He compares being a software professional to being a member of a club with its own identity, common language, and shared way of thinking. These days he receives frequent recruitment inquiries on LinkedIn. Our nation gains when people like Alex are working on distributed teams tackling common projects online.

This book imagines how the digital economy can create opportunities for people where they live instead of uprooting them. It offers a vision for decentralizing digital innovation and wealth generation to build economically vibrant and inclusive communities that are connected to each other. We need a development strategy that fosters a nucleus of tech jobs with myriad applications for different industries and local entrepreneurs in thousands of rural and underrepresented communities across our nation. The digital revolution is reshaping our economy and society, but it continues to sideline, exclude, upend, and manipulate too many in the process. My aim is to advance our democratic values by empowering all of us to direct and steer these digital forces.

Placing democratic values at the center of the twenty-first-century tech revolution is about more than unleashing untapped talent like Alex, facilitating his rise, and allowing him to support the cultural life of his hometown. It demands that we uplift service workers who face economic precarity. It requires the regulation and redesign of digital platforms to prioritize online rights and quality discourse over profits. We must make the high-tech revolution work for everyone, not just for certain Silicon Valley leaders who commodified our data while amassing fortunes and now have a disproportionate influence on our national culture and debate. This concentration of digital prosperity makes the already difficult task of becoming a functioning, pluralistic democracy harder. A key pillar of building a multiracial, multireligious democracy is providing every person in every place with the prospect of a dignified life, including the potential to contribute in and shape the digital age.

MY FAMILY'S JOURNEY

My story, as you may have guessed, is quite different from Alex Hughes's. My earliest memories are of Amarnath Vidyalankar, my maternal grandfather. I remember playing chess with him and listening to his tales about the Mahabharata, a sacred Hindu epic, and the Indian Independence movement. He was and remains a legend in our family.

My grandmother talked about the time he was in jail for four years starting in 1942 as part of Gandhi's Quit India movement that demanded an end to British rule of the subcontinent. During this period, she never spoke to him and did not know whether he was alive. Every six months or so she would send Dev, her oldest son who was barely twelve, on a train from Amritsar, where they lived, to the prison in Lahore. Dev took new clothes and my grandfather's favorite Indian sweets like halvah. The guards took the sweets and clothes, promising to give them to my grandfather. They told Dev he was doing fine, but my grandmother never knew what to believe.

Although he never did receive those sweets and clothes from the guards, my grandfather was one of the fortunate ones who made it out in good health and spirits. After India attained independence, he served as an MP in India's first Parliament in 1952. He was proud to serve as part of India's founding generation, which outlined the nation's principles for liberal democracy. My grandfather would never have conceived of the possibility that his grandson would one day serve in Congress.

The cliché rings true for me: only in America is a story like mine possible. My mother came to the United States because she fell in love with my father, who was studying chemical engineering at the University of Michigan. Their parents arranged for them to meet. My father, born a year before India's independence, traveled back to India to meet her and won her over after three dates. She and my father started their life in Bensalem, Bucks County, a suburb of Philadelphia, where my father took a job with a manufacturer of specialty chemicals. My father stayed with that same company for almost thirty years, while my mother worked as a substitute schoolteacher for special needs kids. Both benefited from the civil rights movement that opened emigration from non-European countries and America's policy of recruiting engineers and scientists to compete with the Soviets.

I was born in Philadelphia in 1976, our bicentenary. While growing up, I attended public schools and took out large loans to finish my education at some of the most elite institutions in the world. My most formative years, however, were in Bucks County. I lived in a community in Holland, Pennsylvania, that was economically mixed. We were comfortable and never lacked for anything meaningful, but we were not rich. We were careful with what we spent on clothes, eating out, cars, and tickets to games. On our street were midlevel professionals like my father and also an electrician, a nurse, a teacher, an HVAC technician, and a couple of senior executives at corporations. Our neighbors and a few families in the township became our extended family. We played Little League and touch football and watched the *Rocky* movies. We went to each other's homes for meals, had sleepovers, and celebrated holidays together.

Forty years after beginning my life in Philadelphia, I was elected to Congress to represent Silicon Valley, arguably the most economically powerful place in the world. The lure of building the future with limitless opportunity drew me to the Valley much like it drew my parents to America. When I told my family that I accepted a job offer from a tech law firm in Palo Alto, my grandmother told my mother she would now understand what it feels like to have a child move far away. Today, I represent a district that is home to Apple, Google, Intel, Yahoo, eBay, LinkedIn, and Tesla. As exciting as it is to live in a district that has hundreds of high-growth companies, I still love going back to Bucks County to visit my parents, especially with my wife and kids.

When President Donald Trump presided over a rally where the crowd chanted "send her back!" about Representative Ilhan Omar, a Muslim American woman, my office was inundated with media inquiries. The press wanted to know if I had ever been told to go back to where my parents came from, especially growing up in a county that was more than 95 percent white in the 1980s. At first, I avoided the interviews, not wanting to be tokenized just because I was a son of immigrants and a person of color. Upon further reflection, I relented. I told inquiring journalists there were occasions during a heated basketball game when some kid would shout "go back to India!"

But that is not what stands out. What I remember more is teachers like Mrs. Raab and Mr. Longo who believed in my potential more than I did. I remember Little League coaches who encouraged me to keep practicing, even though I was not a strong player. I remember local editors of the *Bucks County Courier Times* who published almost every one of my letters to the editor. And I remember neighbors like Patty Sexton who were overly proud of my amateur writing and pushed me to have a voice at local school board meetings. The people in Bucks County led me to believe that dreams are worth pursuing in America, regardless of one's name or heritage.

I also remember what America gave me. I had an extraordinary education at Council Rock High School. My father had a job that came with health care, so I did not have to worry about the cost of seeing a doctor, allergist, or dentist. I lived in a safe neighborhood and never worried about a nutritious meal. My parents had time to help me with my homework and attend most of my games, even when I sat on the bench. I had the chance to pursue as much higher education as I wanted, even if it meant taking out loans to do so.

If our nation could give the son of an immigrant such a chance at life, it has the capability to do so for every American. When you have a story like mine, you can't help but be hopeful about the American experiment.

This book is grounded on the belief that the core of my family's story should be commonplace, not exceptional. It's a very simple story, about having worthwhile job opportunities, high-quality education and health care, and better prospects for one's kids. This country has everything it needs to foster these opportunities for every American. In this new century, we can cultivate unimagined possibilities for people across our nation, if not the world.

PLACE MATTERS

From the dawn of the digital revolution, leaders have celebrated the promise of technology and globalization. They have hailed our dramatic growth in GDP and plummeting prices for consumer products. People have undoubtedly benefited from easily accessible information, better health treatments, online learning options, convenient and affordable shopping even in remote areas, and the simplification of managing bills and everyday chores. Extreme global poverty, moreover, has been cut in half, which is the fastest drop in recorded history.

Despite this remarkable progress, leaders often have suffered from the same blind spot—that *place matters*. Even as GDP and production gains soared, too many American towns hollowed out and local factories closed with manufacturing supply chains moving to China. Thousands of stores shuttered downtown, suffering a "retail apocalypse" as they were unable to compete with online giants. The businesses that *were* booming, particularly the tech industry, tended to be siloed in far-off cities. According to a 2019 Brookings report, just five U.S. cities account for 90 percent of the innovation job growth in recent decades. Other Brookings reports document our nation's economic divergence.

Nearly 50 percent of digital service jobs, they find, are in ten major metro centers. In contrast, nearly 63 of 100 largest metro regions saw their share of tech jobs *decline* this past decade. Most towns and midsize cities are disconnected from the wealth generation of the digital economy, despite having their industries and residents' lives transformed by it. In fact, those living in communities with a population of under fifty thousand, like Alex Hughes, have had stagnant job and wage growth since the Great Recession. As they struggle to gain footing in the modern era, they read every morning about the soaring revenue of tech, with Silicon Valley companies alone exceeding $10 trillion in market cap—a staggering figure of value creation in the sweep of economic history. This extreme disparity is distancing us from each other and deepening fissures in our nation.

Leading economists argue that our nation is witnessing a march toward urbanization, where select cities will be the hubs for new high-paying jobs. They point to the industrial revolution as a parallel, observing that it created similarly large disruptions yet made us better off in the long run. Let's encourage people to move to where the new opportunities will be, so the argument runs. But perhaps our politics would not be in such turmoil if we listened to more humanists for balance. Historians, journalists, sociologists, and ethnographers would have insisted we ask: What does this disruption mean for people's livelihood and identity? What does it mean for families living in the places left behind?

National policymakers, to our peril, have ignored the destabilization of local communities. For that matter, we have overlooked the extent to which Americans' sense of fulfillment is tied to where we live. In an unfamiliar age, home represents the familiar. Choosing to stay where you grow up might mean a life where extended family members meet for weekend meals, instead of one where grandchildren only see their grandparents on FaceTime. It might mean choosing love and responsibility over one's career ambitions, putting the needs of an aging parent or a special needs sibling first. Place matters to the vast majority of us—as much for certain techies in San Francisco who cannot envision leaving as for parents in rural communities who do not want to lose their children to faraway places. What about the unemployed? Is it fair or reasonable to expect people like Alex Hughes to leave their hometown and move across the country? If they want to, they should absolutely be able to. But there is a difference between leaving because of an ambition to become prosperous and leaving because your hometown is sinking into decline. A central thesis of this book is that no person should be *forced* to leave their hometown to find a decent job. That is foundational to the American promise.

This is why we need place-based policymaking that extends twenty-first-century jobs beyond the current superstar cities to overlooked communities. This book sees as flawed any economic arrangement where tech titans satisfy their consciences by depositing monthly checks indefinitely to fellow citizens living in the rest of the country. A national agenda must not simply favor the redistribution of wealth but should focus on the democratization of the value creation process itself. People do not simply want to be taken care of; they want to be agents of their own lives and productive members of society. The research expertise, new technology, collaborative platforms, digital training, and creative financing that are driving a huge chunk of prosperity in our modern economy must be broadly accessible, not confined to the coasts.

We need to seed digital jobs, which are expected to grow to 25 million by 2025 and have a median salary of more than $80,000, in geographically diverse communities customized for diverse sectors. What we learned during the pandemic is that this is entirely possible. The Covid-19 crisis shattered the status quo thinking about tech concentration. We saw that digital technology can allow millions of jobs to be done anywhere in the nation with high-speed broadband. According to a Harris poll, nearly 40 percent of respondents said that post-Covid-19 they are considering leaving city life for the suburbs or rural towns. This presents an opening for economic policies that promote decentralization to succeed. Although wealth is still likely to be concentrated in places like Silicon Valley that will remain magnets for tech enthusiasts and profit from increased digitization, we can cultivate sparkling nodes of new economic activity across our nation.

As we saw with Alex, decentralizing tech can allow more Americans to stay rooted in their communities. They can attend their hometown church or synagogue, share meals with family and friends, read the local paper even if it's online, join a service club, play in sports leagues, and support traditional industries and workers. At the same time, they can build more resilient and dynamic local economies by accessing cutting-edge digital tools, advanced training, and high-paying remote jobs. They can take risks and embrace bold opportunities without necessarily having to move. Communities can thus balance engaging with the wider world, exposing residents to new and different perspectives and activities, and providing outlets from parochial prejudices through digital platforms, while supporting institutions and events that build civic bonds, loyalty, and pride. The aspiration is to foster a meaningful digital identity that adds to participation in a shared local culture. The promise is of new jobs without sudden cultural displacement—it is a vision of restoring the economic health of a community while promising them some control over developing their way of life. If we respect that place matters while facilitating connection to broader economic ventures and social affairs, we can foster a rich plurality of American communities while softening our cultural fault lines.

BUILDING COMMON PURPOSE

The United States in 2021 has one of the deepest partisan divides in its history. It also sees a marked split between those who are college educated and those who are not, those in urban centers and rural towns, those who are white and nonwhite, and those who trace their heritage back to America's founding and those who are first-generation Americans.

The central aspiration of this book is to lessen some of the bitterness within our nation. It is my belief that increasing connectivity and digital opportunities for left-behind Americans can reduce the divisiveness and dysfunction of our contemporary democracy. This is not a cure-all by any means, but it is one of the more consequential initiatives we can undertake. Consider that 38 percent of rural white Americans and 45 percent of urban nonwhite Americans say jobs are a big problem in their community compared to only about 20 percent of whites living in urban or suburban communities. For all the punditry about rural communities caring more about cultural issues, American Enterprise Institute's Samuel Abrams analyzed survey data from 2006 to 2016 and concluded that economic concerns are consistently ranked by rural residents as among the most important to address. A jobs agenda must, of course, be broader than championing investment in technology and should not become what Dan Breznitz, author of *Innovation in Real Places*, appropriately calls "techno-fetishism," where communities are futilely chasing Silicon Valley unicorns that are solving extremely complex software problems. As Nobel Laureate Abhijit Banerjee pointedly told me, innovation in a community can also mean a new shopping center, tourism office, or business cooperative. But the multiplier effect of tech jobs, which include production, means that when they arrive tailored for the needs and talents of a local community, they bring a wide range of supporting careers, incoming revenue, and changes in organizations and processes driven by digitization that can spark new growth. It's not just about the economic data. These jobs are powerful symbols for families that have borne the brunt of stagnation, giving them hope that their kids and grandkids might have new opportunity.

Perhaps that explains why Pinckney, a small town in Michigan, decided to create the nation's first K–12 institute for cybersecurity, or Claflin University in South Carolina launched a strategic partnership with Zoom. Moreover, in an astounding *Roanoke Times* poll, 90 percent of southwest Virginia—one of the most rural areas of the state—supported Amazon opening a second headquarters in Arlington, a city on the other side of the state. That was even higher than the 72 percent of the Arlington-area urban residents who supported this initiative, which created many software jobs, and not just data or fulfillment centers.

Some Americans are understandably wary of the change that digital jobs may bring. They worry that a significant tech footprint could lead to more gadgets and sensors running their life and more isolation. Neighbors might be glued to their phones and laptops instead of engaged in community picnics and parades. Then there are concerns about the character of a community. Longtime residents fear that any outsiders who come in may be transient, indifferent to local traditions and the music and art scene. They associate outsiders with rising housing costs, increased traffic, overcrowded schools, and gentrification. A vocal minority has even pushed back against bringing the "liberal ideology" identified with tech to their communities. There is resistance to Californians, for example, who account today for "nearly 60 percent of Idaho's net migration." But concerns that Californians will bring different values and norms often dissipate when locals realize that they are "tolerant and positive" and "respect local culture." Conspiracy peddlers, nonetheless, speculate that techies settling in the heartland is all part of an insidious plot to turn red counties blue.

Most Americans understand, however, that the wealth generated from building digital capability can be spent on building community. Smaller cities and towns want to keep local hospitals and schools open, and their congregations and communities intact. It's that basic. Their main issue is vacant storefronts and declining property values that impede local investment. There is so much land in rural Ohio or Iowa that the image of the rust belt or corn belt being overrun by tech flies in the face of maps and math. The alternative to competing for these high-paying jobs is to see them go elsewhere, including migrating north to places like Toronto and Ottawa. Local leaders do not want the growing and extensive digital systems underlying their own economy to be built and owned out of state, extracting wealth.

What people recognize is that many jobs in the twenty-first century will require digital competency. Health care now involves telemedicine, just as education involves online learning; finance is inseparable from online trading, just as retail today means e-commerce and digitized warehouses; entertainment in the digital age means Netflix and You-Tube; even construction now involves digital design; manufacturing integrates robotics and digital inventories, and agriculture has moved toward precision farming. The new technology revolution is not simply the playground for app developers in San Francisco, but impacts nearly every region, occupation, and industry as they compete for customers and business.

The practical question, then, is not whether we want more or less tech, but whether we can insist that democratic values guide its development, accessibility, commitment to fairness, and boundaries. We cannot leave its evolution to an invisible hand that may foster creative brilliance and overnight billionaires but also leaves many behind, creating stark inequality both geographically and within communities with a strong tech presence. Our goal should be to help communities find an appropriate balance when it comes to tech, so they are not engulfed by it or left diminished in its wake. Our digital economy needs more equity and a better national equilibrium, which will drive greater economic prosperity for all.

I offer policy proposals to spread out the innovation economy and make it more just. At the same time, anyone who has seen Congress's performance in questioning tech CEOs is probably skeptical of lawmakers' tech competence. So we also need leadership from tech companies. This book calls for mutual responsibility, and it outlines how we can achieve it. It recognizes the trust deficit that Silicon Valley faces and offers suggestions for recentering human values in a culture that prizes the pursuit of technological progress and market valuations.

There are obvious limits to how much reimagining the digital economy can address polarization, resentment, and social alienation in our body politic. Cultural anxiety is a response not only to economic anxiety or to the fear for losing what is familiar, but also to racism that demagogues are stoking in light of the changing face of leadership and power. As Isabel Wilkerson has described in *Caste*, the United States' history contains numerous examples of white Americans inflicting cruelty on

Black Americans to maintain a racial hierarchy. Arlie Hochschild high-lighted a modern-day manifestation of this in *Strangers in Their Own Land*, which recounts the frustrations of white Americans who feel that they are "waiting in a long line stretching up a hill" that is "not moving, or moving more slowly." In the recent decades, they blame Black people and immigrants as well as "women, refugees, public sector workers" for "cutting ahead of them."

Good jobs cannot wash away this racism. But what jobs can do is give more Americans pride in restoring their communities with many impor-tant customs intact and respect as breadwinners in their families, mak-ing it harder for narratives of resentment to take hold. The idea also is to create interconnection between communities that are currently siloed off, fostering not just communication between distant Americans but in-terdependent economic growth. Remote work can expand the kind of diverse interactions and joint projects that currently take place in certain health care facilities, educational institutions, and the hospitality indus-try throughout our nation. We must be wary of any economic reduction-ist argument that does not acknowledge the need for an ongoing national reckoning with racism and sexism. But we can hope that when a person's pride and respect are linked to America's diverse demographics through online work platforms, as in Alex Hughes's case, it may lessen opposi-tion to the increasingly multiracial nation we are becoming. On the flip side, cosmopolitan techies may become less disconnected, learning to appreciate the culture, traditions, struggles, and stories of blue-collar or rural towns if they work with people who live there. And from a justice perspective, the inclusion of Black and Brown communities in the inno-vation economy is imperative to overcome the stark economic disadvan-tages that exacerbate the devaluation of their voices in our democracy.

While distributed jobs are foundational, they are just the start of what must be a broader conversation to respect dignity in the digital age. If we are going to expand the digital economy to new places, we must si-multaneously call for reforms that address the abuses of big tech. The digital economy has brought real dangers, such as surveillance, vitriol,

censorship, exclusion, and the proliferation of misinformation. I will outline principles for protecting our autonomy online and creating space for
new platforms to emerge that can improve the quality of both our markets
and public discourse. In addition, we should create digital institutions
that better link citizens to governance, providing them with an empowering alternative to merely liking and sharing social media posts. A theme
running throughout these pages is how to facilitate robust citizen participation in this new era, whether on science policy, climate policy, or
even foreign policy. I ultimately put forth a theory of *democratic patriotism* that calls for citizens to have an equal opportunity to participate in
building our national culture, which can inspire shared attachment as we
experience tensions stemming from social and demographic change. It
asks us to embrace a spirit of civility so we can appreciate and support a
plurality of local cultures, including many important customs and traditions passed down to us, as vibrant threads comprising our nation.

Each chapter of this book shares a set of stories, ideas, and policies
that will help us reach this goal as a nation, recognizing the need for mobilization, activism, experimentation, and struggle along the way. These
chapters are broken down into two main parts—the first devoted to the
twenty-first-century economy, and the second devoted to twenty-first-
century citizenship. A brief road map follows to lay out the arc of the
argument.

PART I: TWENTY-FIRST-CENTURY ECONOMY

The first part of the book focuses on jobs and the question of how to
expand technology-driven opportunities to the people and places who
have been left out of the first wave of the digital revolution. Chapter 2
looks in particular at a few rural areas of the country, picking up with
the story of Alex Hughes and the people I met when visiting places like
Paintsville, Kentucky; Beckley, West Virginia; and Jefferson, Iowa. These
regions aren't trying to become tech utopias but want to use tech to revitalize their local economy in the industries of *their* choosing while

augmenting their existing skill set and expertise. They recognize, as the writer Michael Lind astutely observes, that digitization can be a source of renewal for farming, construction, and manufacturing, in addition to bringing in new possibilities for remote work. There are also jobs in setting up a town's digital libraries, digital malls, and digital services. It no longer makes sense to speak of a stark distinction between the old and new economies. Many of these new digital opportunities do not require a college degree, or for that matter, learning how to code.

Chapter 3 extends the focus on tech equity beyond geography to race and gender. I share the experiences of Ifeoma Ozoma, a rising tech star who was subjected to retaliation at Pinterest for criticizing the company's racism. Unfortunately, Ozoma's story is common. Nearly 20 percent of computer science graduates are Black and Latino, yet they comprise fewer than 10 percent of technical employees at big tech companies. These companies are 70 percent male. Consider also that less than 3 percent of all venture capital in the United States went to Black or Latino entrepreneurs—only .32 percent to Latinas and .0006 percent to Black women. Equally problematic, the multiplier effect of tech jobs does not benefit those who live in racially segregated neighborhoods far from a city's tech center. Black and Brown communities must be participants in the wealth generation of the digital revolution. Younger generations, in particular, are tired of being consumers, early adopters, and cultural influencers only to have investors and founders reap the profits. I will argue that tech companies must do much more than appoint diversity officers and will offer fresh ideas for inclusion.

Chapter 4 confronts the reality that high-tech has disempowered many in the working class. A staggering share of high-tech gains go to software developers and executives, but far too little to the people I spoke with like Courtney Brown, an Amazon Warehouse worker, or Marcie Silva, a bus driver for a big tech company who sleeps in her car. These workers deserve respect for the physically demanding and difficult jobs they do, not condescending lectures about acquiring more "digital skills" or overcoming a "skills gap" that devalue their contributions. This era calls for an Essential Workers Bill of Rights, which I introduced with Senator Elizabeth Warren during the height of the pandemic. The framework would promise livable wages, benefits, and bargaining rights for workers. It envisions giving employees a voice in shaping automation and pushing back against intrusive surveillance and abusive supervisors—a particular challenge in a remote and distributed workplace, which makes organizing difficult. Until all workers reap the benefits of their hard work and are treated with dignity, the promise of the digital age remains unfulfilled.

Chapter 5 concludes Part I of the book by building the recommendations of the first three chapters into a larger vision for progressive capitalism. There is space in our nation's politics for pro-innovation progressives who celebrate the distinctive American ethos of starting a business in a garage and are committed to ensuring everyone has the freedom to fulfill their potential and lead a dignified life. Markets are at their best when they are truly open to everyone, allow individuals to start new ventures, and are designed to advance the public interest. Crippling them hurts the wealth generation necessary for social progress. So when I talk about progressive capitalism, I mean that our nation must make significant investments in every American and facilitate attractive and fair opportunities for them to produce value in today's economy, including the private sector.

My framework is indebted to Amartya Sen and Martha Nussbaum, two of the leading thinkers who formulated the capabilities approach. They say our society has a responsibility to cultivate the intrinsic capabilities of every person to lead the life they envision *and* to provide avenues to exercise their talents. Investments in developing capabilities, particularly early in life, unlock human potential and are also principal drivers of growth in an innovation economy. We achieve national excellence when every individual reaches their highest potential. The progressive framework for our era can be both pro-dignity and pro-growth.

PART II: TWENTY-FIRST-CENTURY CITIZENSHIP

Dignity is about more than an economic agenda. Silicon Valley has not only left many Americans out of wealth generation; certain tech companies have made profits by commoditizing them, extracting their data, and amplifying misinformation campaigns. Social media often targets the very communities that are struggling with economic decline with conspiracies and misinformation, leading to an increase in both polarization and even radicalization in our nation. We need to ask what reforms are necessary to ensure that the digital economy does not infringe on our standing as free citizens or erode our democracy.

Chapter 6 focuses on protecting our freedoms on the internet and on regulating the tech giants who have been its chief architects. The chapter starts by outlining an Internet Bill of Rights, which I created at the request of Speaker Nancy Pelosi in collaboration with Tim Berners-Lee, founder of the World Wide Web. Our list of rights protects Americans from both private firms and the government abusing their data to manipulate or surveil them. This chapter underscores the power that big tech companies wield in shaping our digital architecture, and in turn it calls for stronger antitrust protection to curb and remedy their anticompetitive practices and provide new players in different regions with a fair chance to succeed. I also suggest policies to counter tech's antidemocratic impact on local newspapers, local artists, and retail shops.

Chapter 7 turns to the internet's impact on deliberation. The internet was supposed to be the great equalizer. It launched viral movements like #MeToo, Black Lives Matter, and the Sunrise Movement, and gave voice to communities long shut out of traditional media. Yet it also spread conspiracy theories and hate far and wide, promoting violence that culminated in the Capitol attack on January 6, 2021. We need an alternative to the dominant model for social media that elevates attention-grabbing and addictive content. I argue that a well-regulated market can facilitate the emergence of multiple digital forums, including publicly backed ones, that have new structures and features to improve our public discussion. The hope is that a plurality of online discursive spaces with various guardrails against the rapid mainstreaming of violence, hate, and disinformation will, over time, strengthen our public sphere.

Chapter 8 takes up broader issues of the place for science in a modern democracy. Public confidence in science was high during the space race, but public opinion and funding have both languished despite scientific progress and literacy being more important than ever. This chapter looks at how we can broaden support for major scientific investments to tackle climate change and continue our technology leadership. And it also explores the areas of investment that will jump-start all areas of the country in the coming decades. We need a new Apollo moment to build solar plants, electric car factories, battery plants, and clean steel, and to drive breakthrough technologies such as synthetic biology. At stake is whether our democracy is capable of leading in advanced production or whether authoritarian regimes like China take the lead by constructing and exporting new technology platforms that violate dignity.

The role of technology on foreign policy is the focus of Chapter 9. The digital age has already shown that technology can be used on the one hand to combat repressive regimes and, on the other, to entrench state surveillance, censorship, and authoritarianism. Within a democracy like the United States, I argue that the digital age will give citizens beyond the Beltway a larger voice in our country's role in the world. There is concern over whether the decentralization of foreign policy would lead to "America First" skepticism of multilateralism, or to greater global engagement. But such concerns warrant more involvement of our increasingly diverse citizenry, not less democracy. The lasting question for the United States and its allies is whether pluralistic democracies can establish transnational norms and rules for dialogue on global digital platforms to respect dignity.

I conclude the book by looking back a century and a half to Frederick Douglass's "Our Composite Nationality," in which he lays out a vision for a cohesive multiracial, multireligious democracy that is shaped by his lifetime struggle for dignity. His speech, when read in conversation with Jürgen Habermas and John Rawls, who are the two political philosophers who have most influenced my thinking, offers a foundation for what I have described as democratic patriotism. It also speaks to me personally, and to the future that millions of Americans would like to see. Douglass writes: "I want a home here not only for the negro, the mulatto and the Latin races; but I want the Asiatic to find a home here in the United States, and feel at home here, both for his sake and for ours."

My belief in this vision is grounded foremost in my parents' story, stemming from the conversations they had with neighbors, the acts of kindness they received, and the dignified way they continue to live in Bucks County. It is also grounded in the people I have met around the country like Alex Hughes who have opened up to me about their dreams for themselves, their children, their hometowns, and our country. They give me hope for a future where we can be fiercely proud of our defining narratives and add to local cultural life but also embrace a shared national purpose that at minimum gives every American the freedom to thrive.

PART I

TWENTY-FIRST-CENTURY ECONOMY

2

BUILDING COMMUNITY

Alex Hughes was part of Interapt's inaugural training class, joining forty-eight other Kentuckians who lost their jobs when the coal mining economy sharply declined. Interapt trains participants in iOS software and then employs them as developers in the region for contracts all around the country and the world. It charges its clients $38 an hour compared to $21 that offshore firms bill for such services, but Interapt's workers accomplish 33 percent more work for clients in that hour, without the language barriers or time zone differences. Its workers also have less turnover compared to disgruntled college graduates in the Philippines who hold similar jobs for short stints, and Interapt was more effective during the Covid-19 pandemic, since offshore workers lacked the infrastructure for remote work.

Still, while the overall business proposition makes sense and the training has had success stories like Alex, it isn't universal. According to Ankur Gopal, the CEO of Interapt, of the company's forty-nine initial trainees, thirty-five completed the program, twenty-five received offers, and nineteen accepted positions at the company making about $40,000 a year. More than two thirds of those receiving offers did not have college degrees. Of those Interapt hired, most worked on Fortune 500 projects. Four years later, six of the nineteen are still at the Interapt making between $70,000 and $100,000 and seven moved on to other jobs, while four were let go for performance reasons and two succumbed to opioids and stopped showing up. For Alex, the training opportunity was transformational, but such programs are not magic bullets, and it's important to set realistic expectations about the number of trainees likely to end up with long-term careers.

The Interapt program is just one technology development initiative in Eastern Kentucky. Jarred Arnett led the Shaping Our Appalachian Region (SOAR) organization, which is committed to diversifying the region's economy. Arnett is tasked with figuring out how Eastern Kentucky recovers from the decline of coal jobs, which went from "15,000 to 4,000" and "within just a few years beginning in 2009." That means a loss of closer to 30,000 jobs, because one coal job supported at least two additional jobs in the region. Arnett is working to support the local timber industry, furniture business, and traditional manufacturing as part of a broader strategy. But he is blunt in assessing what it takes to hit 30,000: "That cannot be done solely upon filling every industrial park and vacant building with new businesses. This must be done in a comprehensive and diversified manner fully leveraging technology."

Arnett believes tech jobs can do for the regional economy what coal once did. He does not subscribe to an easily lampooned vision of turning all coal miners into coders and has no patience for tone-deaf lectures to unemployed workers pushing them to learn to code. Rather, he understands that many miners want to keep their jobs or do something requiring physical skill instead of sitting behind a computer. Arnett views tech as an important complement to other industries for people like Alex who want these opportunities, not a substitute. He believes the region desperately needs more jobs that can bring dollars in from outside to support local businesses, and tech can serve that function.

Remarkably, Eastern Kentucky already has three thousand people working remotely in tech-enabled jobs. No other sector has come close to creating that many new jobs in the area. Arnett understands technology is a game changer, allowing rural students to consider careers other than being "a teacher or a nurse." Arnett says, in the digital age, the "reality is that you can do whatever you want" without leaving the region's hollers.

My visit to Paintsville convinced me that an agenda for expanding access to the innovation economy is not the paternalistic brainchild of Silicon Valley or the Beltway, but what rural communities themselves champion. Arnett made it clear his organization's plan for Eastern Kentucky is "not necessarily a plan we take to D.C. and Frankfort, and say, 'Here's how you fix us.' It's more of a plan that I can take to Ashland and say here's how we fix ourselves." Arnett's plan calls to "strengthen entrepreneurial education," improve "network density" for entrepreneurs, and provide private sector "employer-led training," tech education, and affordable, high-speed internet.

What mattered most to the leaders I met in Paintsville was to shatter the myth that people in Appalachia are stuck in the past. That's a prejudice of our nation's managerial and governing elite, as I experienced directly ahead of my visit. Political consultants warned me it would be risky to travel to Kentucky and discuss the future of work: "They will simply view you as an Indian who wanted to offshore or automate their jobs." But they were wrong.

Interapt's apprenticeship program, however, was not universally celebrated. For every success story like Alex Hughes, there were disgruntled participants who abandoned jobs to enroll but failed to land a job. Jeff Whitehead, executive director for the Eastern Kentucky Concentrated Employment Program Inc., said, "Interapt's hiring results have not been what we expected, and that is unacceptable." Whitehead believes that the government should not have invested so many tax dollars in one company but should have diversified training to include "a consortium of tech employers." Interapt received nearly $2 million in grant money for the pilot to hire teachers, pay stipends, acquire facilities, and relocate employees. This amounted to nearly $40,000 per trainee—undoubtedly a high start-up cost. Ankur told me that with a few years of experience the training cost is now down to $15,000 a person, which makes it easier to scale the program and justify a return on future public investments.

It would be naive to believe bringing technology jobs to places like Eastern Kentucky will be without dispute and cultural misunderstandings. But if Arnett is correct that "technology is the economy," then what option do we have but to try? While Arnett respects Interapt's accomplishments, he says they may have overpromised by giving every participant the impression they would have a job. Political and business leaders gave Appalachians false hope in the past. Any tech to rural initiative requires local validators, deep community engagement, and an achievable timeline for deliverables. The challenge of seeding tech in Eastern Kentucky also speaks to the need for new and creative federal policies to develop digital capability in places where previous economic development efforts have failed. This chapter offers a plan for how to do that.

THE ECONOMICS OF INNOVATION

Nearly a century ago, Winston Churchill prophesied in a *Popular Mechanics* article that "wireless telephones and television" would connect people and that the "congregation of men in cities would become superfluous." He foresaw a world where "the cities and the countryside would become indistinguishable." A century later, even after the advent of the internet facilitated a whole new level of connectivity, Churchill's vision has not come about. If anything, the opposite is true.

The rise of the internet facilitated not the obsolescence of city centers but the further concentration of jobs in cities with highly educated populations. It's a paradox that defies all predictions from a century prior. The dynamics in play have been explained by Paul Krugman, a Nobel Prize–winning economist. The key, according to Krugman, is that technology makes "it possible to separate the low-value activities from the high-value activities." Most creative enterprises benefit from being concentrated, because it allows them to share ideas and networks. For instance, most venture capitalists in Silicon Valley like investing in start-ups within fifty miles not just because it's easier to monitor but because the concentration of the employee base, legal talent, university connections, and financial resources makes it easier to scale up businesses. As Krugman observed, technology has allowed companies to prioritize keeping their high-wage jobs in superstar cities with exorbitant rents and wage premiums, because they can outsource low-wage work to cheaper locations. Apple can design the iPhone in Cupertino, for instance, but assemble it in Shenzhen.

Ultimately, this has led to increased geographical inequality, as high-income and low-income jobs have been sorted into different locations. Accordingly, as reported by Brookings, 72 percent of employment growth since 2008 has taken place in cities of more than a million people. This geographic inequity is particularly alarming since, until the Covid-19 pandemic, Americans had been moving less than at any point in the previous seven decades. Fewer than 10 percent of Americans moved in 2019 compared to twice that rate in the 1940s, 1960s, and 1980s. Despite exhortations to move to where the jobs are, "there is relatively little migration" today from "low income to high income places." According to the Federal Reserve Bank of New York in 2019, almost half the participants indicated that "they were 'rooted' and preferred to stay close to family and friends." The difficulty of buying a new home in an expensive area and increased reliance on extended family for raising kids, amidst the skyrocketing costs of child care, has contributed to many Americans staying put.

In the face of this immobility, decentralizing the tech sector is even more essential. These high-paying jobs are important pathways to the modern middle class. Microsoft estimates that by 2025, there will be 149 million *new* "technology-oriented" jobs—with nearly 13 million of those additional jobs in the U.S. That means the total number of U.S. tech jobs at 25 million would be as many as the number of manufacturing and construction jobs combined, not even discounting for the many tech jobs in these traditional sectors. For all the popularity and focus on building our roads and bridges, there is no denying that digital will be a large chunk of the American economy. According to Glassdoor.com, the top seven of the fifty best jobs in America are all in tech, including front end engineer, Java developer, data scientist, product manager, DevOps engineer, data engineer, and software engineer. It may not come as a surprise that the lifetime earnings for computer science majors average more than $1.6 million, which is 40 percent higher than the average college graduate. But what is striking is that many of these digital jobs do not require a college degree, and even the *median* wage of $80,000 is nearly twice the national median.

Not all agree about the value of digital jobs. Trump's U.S. trade representative Robert Lighthizer diminishes their impact, suggesting that "Apple, Facebook, Google, and Netflix collectively employ just over 300,000" people. The problem with this argument is that it overlooks millions of tech jobs at Fortune 500 companies, consulting firms, manufacturers, and medium-sized businesses that provide pathways to the middle class. It ignores the jobs focused on building our digital infrastructure, including the need for data storage, transmission, and categorization, in both the public and private sectors. It also leaves out the thousands of other tech companies, including trillion-dollar behemoths like Microsoft and Amazon. Importantly, tech jobs are less likely to be automated because businesses will always need people to design, support, and operate software systems.

Lighthizer somewhat sarcastically dismisses the idea that former "autoworkers could be taught to code," but this issue is not so cut-and-dried. We've already seen that in traditional industries some people like Alex Hughes are enthusiastic about digital opportunities and excel in these new careers. And, for that matter, many autoworkers already have software skills since modern-day cars are basically large computers on wheels. So many of today's manufacturing jobs are hybrid tech jobs. In fact the United Auto Workers bargains to have their assembly plant workers trained in robotics and drone technology, operating programmable logic controllers (PLCs), and 3D and additive printing. Their members must know how technology works in cars, a trend that will only increase as cars become more autonomous, and they also know how to run and service complex factory equipment. Of course, not everyone can or should need to work in tech, but the range of opportunities available is nothing to scoff at.

In fact, although hybrid jobs cut across sectors and defy easy classification, the digital contribution to our GDP is roughly comparable to manufacturing when factoring in the benefits to consumers and producers. The main difference is that the digital economy is, according to Enrico Moretti, a leading economist, more "geographically clustered" than manufacturing. Imagine if manufacturing was concentrated in only Detroit and Cleveland. My father would not have worked near Philadelphia. When one considers how the disbursed gains of manufacturing led to the emergence of a strong middle class across our nation, a distributed tech model is all the more appealing. Further, the tech multiplier, per Moretti's research, is "the largest multiplier of all: about three times larger than that of manufacturing." That is, tech jobs tend to create more jobs in other sectors, as innovative companies and their employees rely on lawyers, baristas, gym trainers, hairstylists, nannies, and food service workers in addition to construction workers. Even in Silicon Valley, only 25 percent of employees work in tech.

It is no wonder, then, that cities bend over backward to compete to attract tech companies. There was more fuss over where Amazon would place its second headquarters than LeBron James's "The Decision" of what NBA team to join. U.S. states and cities spend more than $80 billion annually in subsidies to lure companies.

But the success rate of efforts to lure large investments from companies and create entire new tech hubs has been disappointing. Too often, large subsidies are used to attract a data center, satellite office, or a single tech company that then underdelivers on jobs. These investments seldom succeed in revitalizing a local economy and compromise a city's ability to fund basic services like education, health care, and infrastructure.

Many economists are skeptical not just about the use of state subsidies to create tech hubs, but also of place-based policy, which has a mixed record. As Moretti observes, "In my reading of the history of the innovation hubs," there is no example of a "deliberate policy" working that says, "We're going to create the next Silicon Valley, *there*." Like Moretti, Krugman also is cautious about place-based policymaking, pointing out countries that "tried hard to sustain lagging regions much more explicitly than we have ever had in this country" failed. Rural America, he believes, "is being undermined by powerful economic forces that nobody knows how to stop." Krugman argues that the "gravitational pull" of big cities with their capital and highly skilled workforces might be too much to overcome. He is dubious of "reviving declining regions" considering the failure of such initiatives in Southern Italy and East Germany. Krugman observes that West Germany spent nearly $1.7 trillion "in an attempt to revive the former East Germany," more than $100,000 for every resident, with meager results.

However, rural America and midsize cities have far more promise in creating the jobs of the future than declining regions in other parts of the world such as East Germany or Southern Italy, as even Krugman would acknowledge. For starters, before the Wall fell, East Germany was a completely planned economy with no entrepreneurship or economic success. The massive German capital expenditures in the 1990s in large buildings seem poorly targeted in an age of telecommuting. Southern Italy also suffers from low levels of entrepreneurship, and high rates of crime and corruption. In stark contrast, just a couple decades ago, rural America was an engine of America's economic growth. As the Economic Innovation Group, a think tank, concluded, rural America helped lead our economic recovery out of the 1990 recession. Many new businesses during that period were formed in counties with fewer than 100,000 people. These regions can come back.

America, moreover, has not spent anywhere near the Germans' $1.7 trillion investment in East Germany on specific job creation initiatives in left-behind regions. In casting doubt on the prospects for success,

Krugman fairly points out that we already transfer a large amount of resources to poorer states for their social safety net programs. But that must be coupled with out-of-the-box approaches to spur economic development. Safety net investments are essential, but declining regions also seek revitalization and private sector careers. New jobs and business opportunities capture their imagination and generate excitement.

There may be some trade-off between maximizing economic growth and geographically distributing it. Perhaps, over the short or even medium term, the highest return on a dollar is public and private investment in existing hubs of economic activity. But such an approach will not serve the goals of a functioning democracy that respects the dignity of all. Even apart from issues of fairness, our nation's long-term competitiveness depends on not abandoning entire regions, particularly the young populations therein. We do not have room to make such a mistake when competing with the population giants in Asia. Every corner of this country has people who aspire to develop unique ideas and generate wealth—and there is no reason why any region that's fallen behind should be left behind.

THE COVID-19 REALIGNMENT

After years of steadily growing economic concentration, 2020 saw a reversal. One of the unexpected side effects of Covid-19 was that it transformed the innovation economy, opening up the possibility of tech decentralization to places that have been left behind. Many tech companies realized that the quality of remote work did not decline and often improved. John Hennessy, the former president of Stanford University and current Alphabet chairman, told me that "in post-Covid-19 times further densification may not be wise" and the "online work model" during the crisis showed us that "we can live with more work online." A Harvard Business School study concluded that "skilled professionals" in "knowledge-intensive" industries were productive working remotely during Covid, and many of them will continue to do so even after the pandemic.

The proven effectiveness of online work opens bold new possibilities for distributing jobs geographically. Cisco CEO Chuck Robbins says the effectiveness of remote work during the crisis "has given us confidence that we can hire talent anywhere and have them participate productively on teams, regardless of their location." He told me research engineers still insist on being in the same space, but most other jobs can be remote.

Facebook's and Twitter's decisions to allow for "permanent remote working" garnered the most headlines, but other companies made similar decisions. Pinterest paid $89.5 million to terminate a major office space lease in San Francisco because they wanted a more "distributed workforce." Salesforce announced "the 9-to-5 workday is dead" and offered many of its employees the freedom to work from any location. Dropbox instituted a "virtual first" policy where remote work is the "primary experience" for employees and office space is only used for collaboration and team activities. Employees would have "flexibility to relocate outside of locations" where Dropbox has offices, and the company expects to "become more geographically distributed over time." Coinbase, the largest cryptocurrency exchange company with a valuation of nearly $70 billion, no longer considers itself San Francisco based but instead a "decentralized company, with no headquarters," which has allowed it to hire "more of the best people."

The trend lines are noteworthy. Over the next decade, thousands of their employees may exercise that option, triggering some amount of dispersion away from Silicon Valley. This means local communities across the country will see incoming tech talent who will be Moretti multipliers, serving as angel investors, catalysts for new start-ups, science and technology leaders, and advisors to educational institutions and local businesses. According to *The New York Times*, a Facebook group about leaving California, founded by Terry Gilliam, who lives in my hometown of Fremont, already has 33,000 members contemplating where in the country they should relocate. As of the end of 2020, rents fell by 15 to 30 percent in Silicon Valley cities because remote work made it possible for techies to live outside California. The Milken Institute found that San Francisco and San Jose fell in their 2021 rank from the top 5 to No. 24 and No. 22 for jobs and economic growth, while lower-cost-of-living areas such as Appleton, Wisconsin; Hinesville, Georgia; and Harrisburg, Pennsylvania, saw some of the biggest gains. When it comes to software engineers and information technology employees, an *Axios* analysis based on LinkedIn data concluded that during the pandemic they were more likely than before to leave Silicon Valley and Seattle and move to Philadelphia, Miami, and Atlanta. Two decades after I had made the journey from Philadelphia to Silicon Valley, there now were signs of a reverse migration back east!

The recent decentralization does not make Moretti's and Krugman's insights about agglomeration less relevant. Satya Nadella, Microsoft's CEO, cautions that most of the remote work during Covid was completed based on accumulated goodwill built up over years of in-person interactions, and it can be harder to work remotely on complex new projects without first building a strong social foundation. Nadella also highlights the importance of avoiding the burnout that may arise from working alone. I know senior tech executives who were so stressed with constant Zoom calls with no social interaction that they either quit or needed personal days offline to recover. The sheen of remote work wore off the longer the pandemic lasted. Sundar Pichai, Alphabet's CEO, emphasizes that some of the most cutting-edge work requires personal interaction, and his view is supported by a *Wall Street Journal* report indicating that remote work delayed the completion of complex projects and made employee training and mentorship harder. Google recently announced an investment of $7 billion in creating offices across the country, recognizing the need for both a distributed workforce and physical spaces to collaborate. Similarly, at the height of the pandemic in 2020, Facebook invested in 730,000 square feet of office space in New York City, observing that "physical locations are going to continue to be such a contributor to our culture." On a personal level, many of my own colleagues were eager to return to the office, get coffee or lunch with each other, and engage in team-building activities.

Indeed, after the pandemic, the pendulum may swing back, at least partially, to value common space. But that won't fully erase all the lessons that a successful year of working remotely have revealed. Google, for example, expects about 20 percent of their Silicon Valley workforce to permanently relocate to a different company hub and an additional 20 percent to work remotely full-time from any location. What is likely to emerge over time is a hybrid model, in which companies allow for a limited number of days of remote work for those employed at various regional hubs and support a widely dispersed employee network that extends to more rural communities. This may, unfortunately, have a negative impact on service jobs linked to office complexes in existing tech metropolises. It means that coffee shops and restaurants in business districts will have to adapt their business model to rely more on delivery and will have to reassess their location as well. Transportation services will have to anticipate reduced demand during commute hours and pivot to taking people to sporting games, vacations, downtowns, parks, and community events. On the positive side of the ledger, a hybrid work model creates more space to experiment with targeted, place-based policies. The key is to distribute not just midlevel tech jobs but also opportunities for local wealth creation that stem from the digital transformation of our economy.

THE VIRTUAL WORKPLACE

Telework opens the possibility of facilitating constructive interactions among employees from different regions of the nation. This is not just an anecdotal observation but supported by the academic literature. Studies suggest that virtual teams, where people participate from the "comforts of home," promote contact under conditions of relative equality and reduce prejudice. Virtual encounters diminish awareness of status symbols that are more apparent in in-person interactions, from "subtle differences in manner of dress, body language, use of personal space, and the seating positions taken in the room." With fewer hierarchy symbols, people can let down their guard and potentially overcome misunderstandings as well as appreciate different perspectives. The development of virtual and augmented reality will make it even easier for employees in different communities to interact and collaborate.

At the same time, virtual teams with diversity face significant hurdles, including issues with integration, trust, and inclusion. Many working-class perspectives, for example, will be underrepresented as their jobs are less online. MIT economist David Autor has highlighted that the class divide in the workplace is growing because there is "less and less mixing" of those with desk jobs and physical jobs as "they're no longer producing stuff jointly together." It takes thoughtful leadership and well-designed platforms to build a shared, online work culture where team members respect each other and, as importantly, are aware of exclusions and collective blind spots. Most important, employers need to allow for an exchange of political and social views instead of restricting them if the online workplace is to have social benefit. They also should foster an openness to all perspectives so that no one feels compelled to silence by company leadership to advance in their jobs. Companies that build a culture which encourages employees to get to know each other beyond just collaborating on work can help motivate performance, reduce misunderstandings and conflicts, and contribute to our social cohesion.

At its best, a healthy remote work culture can facilitate networks that begin to bridge divides. This insight crystallized for me as I corresponded with the renowned philosopher Charles Taylor. He observes, "if you're not just talking, but working together on something, a common project," you discover that "the other is not a monster" and suspicions and fears "begin to thaw." As he memorably says, engagement in difficult projects with fellow citizens increases "democratic intelligence." At a time where there are, unfortunately, few civic projects that foster understanding among different communities, we should not discount the role of the remote workplace in nurturing our basic democratic capability. For a pluralistic, modern democracy to thrive, the private and civil sectors have a critical responsibility to build community among their workforce.

If tech has a jobs multiplier, it also has the potential to have a cultural bonding multiplier where a core group of networked employees within a community can puncture stereotypes and deflate hatred.

A TWENTY-FIRST-CENTURY JOBS AGENDA

Today, particularly with the remote work model, applied technology jobs can thrive in small towns and rural areas which are much more affordable than big cities. Although few Americans work directly for big tech in digital roles, many Fortune 500 companies and traditional businesses need digital services. There are new opportunities outside of the "Big Five" working on tech support, cloud platforms, AI bots to automate business practices, digital and social media marketing, business or data analysis, Q&A testing, customer design, and marketing and sales strategies for tech products. While most of these jobs require a basic proficiency with computers, many do not require coding, which is certainly not everyone's cup of tea. It is a common misconception that anything to do with the tech sector requires people to learn a new technical language, and propagating that myth is a disservice to developing our future workforce.

Hundreds of thousands of digital jobs that were offshored can be done in rural America. According to Matt Dunne, founder of the Center on Rural Innovation, this is needed as "rural America represents 15 percent of the nation's workforce but only 5 percent of the digital economy jobs." Matt is not interested in bringing the stereotypical call center jobs that make rural communities wary at the first mention of insourcing. Call center jobs have dignity too, of course, but they often demand long hours, pay poorly, and lack upward mobility. Instead, Matt envisions communities having a base of professional, tech jobs with substantial advancement opportunities. As economics Nobel Laureate James Heckman told me, "Some of the things companies outsource to China or Taiwan, they can outsource to Peoria, Illinois." Although it is not feasible to bring entire global supply chains for tech back, we certainly should *expand* them to rural America. People in digital jobs may prefer buying a spacious house with a backyard in a rural community to paying $3,000 rent for a one-bedroom in Cupertino or a suburb of New York. Companies, in turn, may prefer to hire them in locations without huge wage premiums.

Practically speaking, we should focus first on "younger workers" for new tech credentialing and training, which, as Heckman demonstrates, has proven more successful compared to returns on training "displaced American workers in their forties" or more generally "older workers." These younger high earners could, in turn, support many traditional jobs in a community and also provide a strong tax base. There are challenges. Many of these towns are demographically older and are seeing the flight of their younger population, leaving a smaller pool to develop as a tech anchor. The reality is that urban centers with numerous tech firms attract talented employees and their spouses because they provide multiple options for modern-day careers. Nobel Laureates Abhijit Banerjee and Esther Duflo further observe it is a hard road being the "one biotech firm in Appalachia" compared to firms located in a vibrant, urban center.

Telework offers some possibility of changing these dynamics. A rural town no longer needs a small cluster of tech firms to sustain a remote, tech workforce which can today apply for opportunities in companies located anywhere. In towns of a few thousand, training even twenty-five young residents a year in good tech jobs can be a game changer and turn around the local economy. These employees and their spouses could work for a large company headquartered elsewhere, be part of setting up a satellite office locally, join a hot, high-growth start-up located anywhere, or provide tech services to the local industry such as in bio-manufacturing, timber or lumber processing, or health care. Each community will have to decide what mix is best for them. Some of the newly trained tech workers will eventually start their own businesses and can help build an ecosystem of entrepreneurialism and expertise to generate local wealth.

When it comes to midsize cities in the heartland such as Erie, Rochester, or Columbus, we should make substantial investments in technology infrastructure. This is not to say that the government can replicate the cultural magic of Silicon Valley, or that it can predict where the next Bill Gates or Jeff Bezos will locate. But by making foundational investments, like those that the federal government made in places like Silicon Valley, Boston, and Raleigh, we maximize our chances for new hubs to emerge in different industries. Even if remote work makes geography less relevant, there still are enough benefits to agglomeration for the most cutting-edge innovation work to cluster around leading research institutions.

Hubs in Erie or Columbus will help surrounding rural areas, allowing residents there to work remotely but commute occasionally to their company's headquarters. A vision of "hub-and-spoke" ecosystems across our nation, each thriving and unique, is within reach. Someone working remotely in Paintsville can travel to Lexington (two hours), someone in Jefferson to Des Moines (one and a quarter hours), and someone in Beckley, West Virginia, to Raleigh-Durham (two and a half hours). They are far more likely to take a job for a company headquartered a few hours away than one in Silicon Valley. An attractive model then, is to invest in new tech hubs in midsize cities that can be a home for high-growth businesses and combine that with talent cultivation in rural communities. This would enable a hybrid approach to remote work where employees can work from home but still drive to the office a few days a week.

But what is the best way to make such a vision possible, and how do we do so quickly and effectively? During the height of the Great Depression, Franklin Roosevelt offered a vision for "bold, persistent experimentation" to provide Americans with jobs and economic security. Tackling geographic inequality in our nation requires a similarly bold vision but one that addresses the unique dynamics of a twenty-first-century economy, recognizing what many new jobs will look like. The agenda outlined below offers proposals to help bring prosperity to rural America and midsize cities in the digital age, while also serving as an invitation for further experimentation.

DIGITAL GRANT COLLEGES

Abraham Lincoln created the land grant universities in 1862 by signing the Morrill Act, which parceled federal land out to each state that they would use to establish public universities. The purpose of these universities, according to West Virginia University president Gordon Gee, was to provide practical instruction in the agricultural and mechanical fields to prepare Americans for the new jobs created by the industrial revolution. Gee argues that the large public universities that resulted helped America emerge as the dominant twentieth-century economy. Studies show that parts of the country that were awarded land grant universities saw larger population density, more manufacturing output per worker, better-educated citizens, and higher salaries. Today, there are a total of 112 land grant institutions, located in every state, and Gee envisions these universities as the economic factories of the twenty-first century. He wants to harness them to prepare Americans for the technology revolution. For instance, places like West Virginia University, Ohio State University, and Michigan State University can focus on providing applied technical training for the hundreds of thousands of unfilled tech jobs that currently exist in the country. We should provide funding to these institutions to create digital grant colleges analogous to the space grant and sea grant colleges that exist today.

As Gee sees it, the Covid-19 crisis was a potential accelerant for virtual jobs, pushing trends and capabilities for remote work forward by ten years. More people now see the benefits of telecommuting and of living in rural communities that have a great quality of life. Land grant universities should make the most of this unique opportunity by being practical about the needed skills in a modern economy.

Gee helped me craft a proposal for the Department of Commerce to provide institutions with up to $100 million annually in digital grants to develop future-of-work programs. These programs would provide students, including adults seeking a new path, with applied technology associate or bachelor degrees as well as industry credentials and certificates.

Land grant universities would be the natural pilot grant recipients since their explicit mission focuses on serving the "industrial classes," or, in other words, working-class families. Extension programs in rural areas already exist, which primarily help farmers with the latest agricultural innovations, and these can be expanded to provide certifications in digital skills.

One of the goals of this program would also be to bring private sector expertise to job training. The tech curriculum is often lacking due to the absence of private sector consultation. Currently, 71 percent of tech talent is employed in private industry, 18 percent in the education sector, and 11 percent in the government. And in today's changing economy, it is difficult for university faculty to be nimble enough to meet industry needs without the private sector's direct participation. Jason Su, the cofounder of Whiterabbit.ai, a hot Silicon Valley AI company, shares that the biggest barrier students face today in finding a tech job is their lack of experience in "real world projects that lack textbook solutions" or industry products such as Amazon Web Services or Microsoft Dynamics. This lack of familiarity becomes apparent in interviews, and academic curriculums are insufficient for making someone job ready. With all this in mind, to receive funding under the new land grant program, universities would need to demonstrate a thorough knowledge of the needs of private industry and plan for collaborating on instruction. Heckman has demonstrated that job programs should lead to a credential "valued by employers" and have "strong links with local employers" to be effective.

Digital grant colleges can also partner with leading research universities or online education platforms to access cutting-edge content that employers view favorably. In a post-Covid world, they can pursue a hybrid model for online learning that combines interactive classroom experience with material from popular technical courses from Stanford or MIT. Online.Stanford.edu, for instance, offers classes ranging from algorithmic design to AI techniques to careers in media technology. Coursera offers six-month courses for credentials relevant to digital entry jobs, with content produced by Google, Facebook, or Salesforce and high job placement rates at a cost of a few hundred dollars per student.

Finally, the Department of Commerce should provide funding to set up remote apprenticeship or internships with tech companies. Employers like Amazon, Microsoft, or Salesforce who want to see more students trained on their software will have a particular incentive to participate. For those students who do not secure paid apprenticeships or internships, the Department would provide a stipend for tuition and living expenses.

West Virginia University's tech extension campus in the rural town of Beckley is a model for what digital grant colleges can look like. I saw firsthand the enthusiasm for fostering entrepreneurship and tech careers when I visited in 2018. Carolyn Long, the campus president, is on a mission to bring new economic opportunity to a region devastated by the decline of coal. She touts the hundreds of graduates, many from coal mining families, who now work in innovative sectors such as financial services, information technology, automotive design, and advanced manufacturing.

The campus has tailored innovation to the local strengths of the region, recognizing that their needs are different from those of Silicon Valley, Boston, or New York. It launched a degree for Adventure Recreation Management, allowing students to specialize in businesses focused on outdoor activities, as well as a degree in construction management, recognizing the region's need for infrastructure projects. The school also takes great pride in its diversity. I was amazed to see that one of the most respected professors was a Pakistani woman with a thick accent teaching computer science. When I asked the school administrators for a success story, I expected to hear about some student who came from a family that had generations of coal miners. Instead, they said if they were to "select one student who embodies the sense of invigorating and innovation our school has taken on in the last five years, it would be Nima Sahab Shahmir." Nima lived in Iran until he was sixteen. He majored in computer science and had already established a promising start-up creating biodegradable plastic from mushroom roots.

Imagine if we also had many such campuses across the U.S. It would boost economic growth in hard-hit regions and foster the type of multiculturalism that accompanies innovation. China builds a new technology-focused university almost every week. If we are to compete in the twenty-first century, we must establish digital capability, training, and research at many of our regional universities.

NATIONAL DIGITAL CORPS

America has an unrivaled tech base with star power that captures the world's imagination. This base should be mobilized to shrink the digital gap. We should create a national digital corps where the brightest minds in technology spend three to six months partnering with universities, community colleges, and local businesses to build effective credentialing and apprenticeship programs and mentor newly trained workers in left-behind communities. Similar to the Peace Corps, participants would receive a stipend for living expenses and would enhance their own résumés by taking a service role as well as develop a better understanding for the preferences of their rural user base and new opportunities in rural markets. David Simas, the Obama Foundation CEO, has funded tech professionals seeking to make this kind of a social impact. As he has learned, the key to success is that they recognize that any initiative "has to be done by local communities, not to them" and that local leaders oversee projects.

The University of Idaho partnered with an initiative called Innovation Collective to tap into Silicon Valley digital expertise. Even though the program is severely resource-constrained, they convinced Apple and Facebook employees to train hundreds of Idahoans in app development and data science. This program helped strengthen the economy of Coeur d'Alene, a mining and manufacturing town that now has more than a hundred new businesses, many focused on robotics and AI.

A national digital corps could help scale such training and entrepreneurship across our nation. And it could also help local retailers and local governments adapt to the digital age. The average retail store does not have proprietary products or large enough margins to sell on Amazon. However, these stores can craft plans for how to build brand loyalty online and use technology to better manage their operations. They also can promote online sales on their social media platforms, partner with third parties that sell on e-commerce sites, or collaborate with local retailers to create a digital mall that provides an alternative to Amazon by combining the online and in-person shopping experience. Finally, small businesses can learn to geotarget online, which is more effective and far cheaper than traditional sources of advertising such as television or radio. As far as local governments go, a digital corps can help them train and employ residents to build what scholar Ethan Zuckerman calls "digital public infrastructure," including digital libraries, online forums where local residents can "talk, share, and relate" about local events, and interactive government websites for services.

COMPUTER SCIENCE FOR ALL

Every K–12 student in America should have computer science as part of their curriculum, alongside math, reading, and science. According to Code.org, there are more than 400,000 open computing positions in the U.S. However, only 47 percent of high schools teach computer science, and only ten states provide classes for all grades. This leaves tens of millions of students without access to the education needed to prepare them for some of the best-paying jobs in the country.

The call for universal computer science education is not some conformist vision to make everyone a coder in an economy where people have different talents and interests. Rather, computer science is valuable even for the vast majority who have no desire to pursue a tech career. Many would benefit from understanding the basics about apps, coding, and the internet. In the same way that math classes teach logic, shop classes teach us about making things, and humanities classes teach us about critical thinking and empathy, computer science classes teach problem solving and give us confidence about using technology. In today's workplace, people cannot be afraid to use computers or operate machines.

It is no wonder that even the Trump White House chose to feature Apple CEO Tim Cook and IBM chair Ginni Rometty to launch their "Find Something New" campaign touting twenty-first-century jobs not requiring college degrees. This initiative, kicked off at the height of the Covid-19 crash, was too cavalier about finding new work, but it speaks to the bipartisan recognition that technical know-how is essential. Almost all of the new jobs that the campaign advertises, including numerous blue-collar ones, require technical training where some proficiency in computer science is helpful.

Computer science consistently ranks as one of the most popular subjects among students, and 90 percent of parents want their children to study computer science. According to a Microsoft survey, 88 percent of teachers believe computer science is essential to preparing students for the workplace. But currently there is an acute shortage of computer science teachers. To achieve universal computer science education, we must invest in training and certifying more teachers, with a target of at least twenty thousand new computer science teachers in the next five years. Ali Partovi, the founder of Code.org, estimates that a $1 billion investment in teacher training and computer science education can help achieve that goal.

FEDERAL SOFTWARE HIRING INCENTIVES FOR RURAL AREAS

The federal government should give favorable consideration to contract bids from companies that have 10 percent of a project's professional workforce in rural communities. Federal software contracts can be worth billions of dollars. We recently saw intense competition between Microsoft, Amazon, Oracle, and IBM to win the Department of Defense's $10 billion cloud computing contract, which supported thousands of jobs.

Imagine if the competing companies received favorable consideration for hiring people for tech jobs from left-out regions. Government IT projects, moreover, currently specify the exact degrees and credentials of each employee at a contracting company; but if this were switched to outcome-based criteria it would widen the aperture of the candidates companies can hire.

An incentive for a more dispersed workforce would be effective in a post-Covid world where companies encourage remote work. Big tech or Fortune 500 companies would not necessarily have to hire locally to qualify but could encourage existing employees to move to rural areas, particularly back to their home states. Companies with offshore locations typically send a couple high-skilled employees from their headquarters to launch and manage them. There is no reason that they cannot do that *within* the U.S. The few employees who move can oversee projects and help seed a successful tech culture in new locations. Companies could also retain tech contractors from rural areas, which could make up a percentage of the 10 percent requirement.

As an additional incentive, we should have a federal tax credit of up to $10,000 per tech employee hired in a rural community. This type of tax incentive was successful in Quebec, which introduced hiring incentives for older workers. Such a credit may not have moved the needle pre-Covid, but it will now accelerate the trend of working from locations outside expensive, superstar cities. Tulsa, for example, found great success with this approach, attracting more than 250 professionals to their community to work remotely with a $10,000 cash grant. Similarly, West Virginia has begun to offer $12,000 plus free recreational activities and coworking space for anyone who will move to the state and work remotely. There are examples in the private sector as well. Stripe, a financial technology company, offers its employees a $20,000 incentive to move away from expensive cities like San Francisco and accept a 10 percent pay cut. In fact, polling done on Blind, an online community of 3.6 million, shows two thirds of professionals in Silicon Valley, Seattle, and New York are willing to relocate to cheaper places.

REVITALIZING MAIN STREET

Incentivizing the dispersion of tech jobs is only part of the battle, however. Anyone who lives or works in rural communities will tell you it's insufficient to focus just on job creation. Young people want a vibrant downtown that will be an engaging place to live and raise a family. Zachary Mannheimer, a high school classmate of mine from Council Rock, focuses on rural development in Iowa. He argues that as second- and third-tier cities get saturated, Americans will have an incentive to move to rural areas. He is passionate about reversing the trend that David Autor documented of college graduates moving to cities and settling down there.

Mannheimer shared with me that the key is "the work of creative place making." If rural communities want to attract tech employees to live there, or convince college graduates to stay, they need to invest in new restaurants, affordable housing, public transportation, theaters, music venues, and sports facilities.

Federal programs aimed at rural job creation and retaining a young workforce must include public funds for reimagining downtowns. This can mitigate the "chicken and egg problem" that Abhijit Banerjee and Esther Duflo pinpoint, where towns cannot invest in vibrant shopping and dining districts before they have enough young people to frequent them. We need to subsidize communities taking this leap of faith, especially considering the possibilities for remote work and local entrepreneurship that the post-pandemic world has opened. Left-behind communities should have the opportunity to pursue new dreams, and, ultimately, attracting young professionals may be as important as attracting the jobs themselves.

THE NEXT GREATEST THING: INTERNET IN YOUR HOUSE

According to House Majority Whip James E. Clyburn, in the 1940s a farmer speaking to a gathering in a small rural Tennessee church said: "Brothers and sisters: I want to tell you this. The greatest thing on Earth is to have the love of God in your heart. And the next greatest thing is to have electricity in your house." FDR understood that "electricity is a modern necessity of life and ought to be found in every village, every home and on every farm in every part of the United States." Today, the next greatest thing and the next modern necessity is internet access.

The story of Peter and Elizabeth Leo, both thirty-six, who settled just outside Storm Lake, Iowa, earlier this year highlights how much work we have remaining. Peter teaches middle school social studies and Elizabeth is the city clerk for nearby Aurelia. They both complain of slow and spotty internet service. "It's a huge hassle," Peter says. He has to drive thirty miles from his home to buy an AT&T SIM card for his modem, and less-reliable Internet also means Peter has problems on Zoom calls, which makes it challenging to teach during the pandemic. As for Elizabeth, she will often make a forty-minute round-trip drive to City Hall to release an urgent public notice over the internet.

Currently, about 21 million Americans lack affordable internet access, including more than 25 percent of people in rural areas. A staggering 15 percent of households with children at home still lack a high-speed internet connection. If our country can afford more than $3 trillion of relief spending during Covid-19, over $6 trillion on wars since 9/11, and a Pentagon budget of nearly $740 billion annually, we can make the $80 billion investment necessary to provide affordable high-speed internet to every American.

Whip Clyburn has a proposal to do this, helping both red and blue counties, both white areas and communities of color. It gives federal grants to municipalities, co-ops, or private companies to provide affordable internet services to places without access. The bill prioritizes fiber to rural, rejecting the conventional wisdom that only big cities need fast internet service. This provision is opposed by many telecom lobbyists. They fear that a fiber public sector option, subsidized by taxpayers, will put pressure on companies that use copper cable and telephone wires which are much slower and inferior, to upgrade. What is sad is that the opposition of the telecom industry has stood in the way of rural

Americans accessing the best tech opportunities. That is why a significant share of the funding in the Clyburn bill goes to municipalities or co-ops that pay prevailing wages and have strong labor protections. They would own the infrastructure they build so that big companies could not sweep in later and undercut them. Doing so would finally invite the 21 million Americans who still lack connectivity into the digital economy.

DEMOCRATIZING CAPITAL

Communities need access to capital. As economist Stephan Weiler and his coauthors have demonstrated, the lack of lending and capital investment is one of the biggest impediments for new business creation in rural communities.

AOL founder Steve Case preaches that talent in America is everywhere, but nearly 80 percent of the venture capital funding goes to only three states: California, New York, and Massachusetts. While California had nearly 4,000 VC deals and New York 1,400 in 2019, the state of West Virginia had only one. A state like Iowa, where the digital computer was invented, had only about 30 deals. Case is trying to solve this problem. His pioneering fund, Rise of the Rest, is allocating $300 million to invest in talented entrepreneurs outside the superstar cities.

There is only so much, however, a committed entrepreneur like Case can do without government assistance to scale. We should establish at least twenty regional venture capital funds of $500 million each to supplement private money and invest in start-ups with high growth potential. As Brad Feld, a leading entrepreneur and thinker about venture capital, shared with me, these funds should be public-private partnerships led by local entrepreneurs without conflicts of interest, including next-generation leaders. They should bet on promising entrepreneurs from a locally developed tech workforce who may revitalize regional economies. Some of the fund recipients may turn out to be the next Brian Armstrong, a former midlevel software engineer who started Coinbase, or Jack Dorsey, founder of Twitter, who attended the University of

Missouri–Rolla. The venture model is admittedly limited to less-capital-intensive businesses, with a focus on early-stage innovation and software start-ups as public policy expert Dan Breznitz fairly points out, which is why we also need federal grants, loans, and purchase agreements to support private industry that is engaged in production.

As important, we need financing options for businesses that are not aiming for astronomical returns. Small businesses, including start-ups, in many towns depend on community banks. Many of these businesses may not have the connections to get loans from big banks, which make bureaucratic assumptions about credit risk without knowing the character of a particular entrepreneur. According to Weiler's research, counties with strong community banks have higher job growth and greater resilience to economic shocks like the Great Recession. Former Iowa governor Terry Branstad used to say that a vibrant Iowa town usually had two things: locally owned community banks and a good local newspaper.

We need strategies to infuse community banks with more capital and prevent their decline. Approximately half of the country's nearly five thousand community banks are in rural counties of populations under fifty thousand. But they have only 15 percent of financial assets—a combined total of about $3 trillion compared to the big banks, which have more than $15 trillion. Economist Jason Furman floated an intriguing idea: Congress could authorize the Federal Reserve's regional banks to provide nonrecourse loans to community banks to cover a significant percentage of their small business loans, particularly for higher-growth businesses. For example, if a community bank lends a business $50,000, the Fed could lend the community bank most of that capital ($47,500), charging a small haircut so that the bank still has some skin in the game. The bank would be obligated to pay the Fed back as long as the business does not go under. This would reduce the risk of lending for community banks and limit their losses if a business does fail.

Although lending to large, legacy companies has less risk than to any particular small business, the Fed regional banks could dilute the risk by empowering many community banks to lend to a broad range of small businesses and also help distribute economic development in our nation to left-behind communities. This is consistent with the Fed's original charter of promoting regional economic development, and Congress could explicitly authorize them to do so. Furman's proposal is an invitation for other creative solutions. For instance, an alternative is having the Fed lend to a third-party institution like the Small Business Administration, which could partner with community banks to support local business activity.

AMERICAN CENTERS OF TECHNOLOGY

Vannevar Bush, the director of the Office of Scientific Research and Development during World War II, and Senator Harley Kilgore of West Virginia debated back in the 1940s whether peacetime federal investment in science should be distributed geographically. According to Daniel Kevles, a historian of science, Bush advocated for an approach of prioritizing elite institutions such as MIT, which he believed would do the "best science." Kilgore wanted scientific funding to be "in the best interests of meeting the nation's social and economic needs" and favored money going to every state to create jobs. Bush won the argument.

Today, the trade-off between the best science and geographical distribution is in fact not as stark. Even though tech jobs have been concentrated, our nation's leadership in innovation across all sectors does not stem from just a few top universities. It is far more broad-based. The U.S. claims eighteen of the top twenty spots for academic institutions with the most patents in the world, including schools in Indiana, Michigan, and Wisconsin. The breadth of our top research institutions fuels competition and allows for unique schools of thinking to emerge and specialization to take place. We have more than 60 percent of the world's top one hundred research universities, and many could anchor tech hubs.

We should create American Centers of Technology near research universities in every state in this country by the end of this decade. Jonathan Gruber and Simon Johnson show in *Jump-Starting America* that there are 102 cities that have the ingredients to become successful innovation centers. Their conclusion is similar to the Brookings report entitled "The Case for Growth Centers: How to Spread Tech Innovation Across America," which finds thirty-five promising cities, many overlapping with Gruber and Johnson's list.

A policy of creating new tech hubs should begin with the most promising locations and then gradually expand. A place that already has a tech-savvy research university or national laboratory and a few startup successes under its belt will likely have an angel network that can increase the odds of success. The mission of these hubs is to promote breakthrough science, commercialization, and industrialization, leading to new businesses and high-paying jobs. The program would be administered by the Commerce Department with a board of independent PhD scientists and successful business leaders to evaluate proposals. According to Johnson and Gruber, the cost would be at least $3 billion over ten years to set up each hub of one million people. This funding would establish faculty endowments, data infrastructure, land acquisition, technical facilities, STEM education, and career training—investments that have positive externalities for a region and that companies focused on quarterly earnings reports would not underwrite on their own. Each hub would specialize in a few technologies based on their regional assets and expertise. The cutting-edge fields would include quantum computing, data science, clean energy, cybersecurity, robotics, electronics manufacturing, and synthetic biology. Gruber tells me that public investment in research and development has, over the long run, a 50 percent annualized rate of return, compared to only 20 percent of private sector R&D.

The idea for technology hubs has already gained bipartisan traction in Congress because it provides significant opportunities for noncoastal cities in the Midwest and South and also is pro-growth. With Senate Majority Leader Chuck Schumer and two Republicans, Senator Todd Young and Representative Mike Gallagher, I introduced the Endless Frontier Act in 2020, named after Vannevar Bush's 1945 report calling for more science investment. The bill, which is expected to pass, proposes the creation of, at least, ten hubs and provides more than $50 billion in new money for the Department of Commerce, Department of Energy, and the National Science Foundation. Our largest hurdle was frankly overcoming the risk aversion, territorialism, and institutional stagnancy of many House Science Committee staffers who, though knowledgeable about science and technology, opposed the legislation at almost every turn and simply wanted to default to how they did things. In certain cases, longtime Hill staffers, captured by decades of status quo interests and thinking, are the unseen barriers to bold policy and change.

Our bill is rooted in principles that made America an economic powerhouse in the first place, such as the "Wisconsin idea." As Gallagher often notes, the Wisconsin idea is the philosophy that fundamental university research can be applied to make huge leaps in improving people's lives and thereby create vital industry and economic growth. Advances in applied science in turn lead to advances in theoretical science. The process is dynamic and interdependent. Our legislation empowers cities to partner with the private sector and decide what technologies to prioritize. While some cities will choose to go all in for fast-growing green jobs, a city like Pittsburgh may diversify its investments in biotechnology, additive printing, and robotics in addition to its solar industry. Cities can also focus on advances in the manufacturing processes in critical industries to make existing products "better, more reliable, and cheap enough"—what Dan Breznitz calls "continuous innovation"—instead of only betting on research to launch entirely "novel products."

The reaction to our legislation has not all been positive. When Fox News did a piece on my proposal to bring tech jobs across the country, which was a precursor to Endless Frontier, some readers commented, "If you come to middle America leave your liberalism in California." And "Look at Ro, Omar. Rashida—is that what you want your Congress to look like." The racism stung. Although the burden should never be on marginalized groups to earn acceptance from the "group in power," I was nonetheless hopeful that my bipartisan work might reduce stereotypes about Asian Americans by highlighting that we are job creators, not outsiders or offshorers. For many years, I have been sensitive to the perception of India as a tech outsource hub and the suspicion that an Indian American as the face of Silicon Valley may engender. The comments on the Fox article invoked for me the memory of a young campaign volunteer of mine, visibly shaken, as he recounted how a man spit on him and refused to accept a campaign pamphlet because of an assumption that I was exporting jobs. I told him we should continue to show up in that neighborhood. Since I have been in Congress, I have been showing up. Good policy will not win over everyone, but I have seen how concrete initiatives to create innovative jobs, particularly for the next generation, can break through.

CHALLENGING *NIMBYISM*

Regan Forge, an Iowa native, told me with great enthusiasm how she met Mark Zuckerberg during her 2019 college internship with the Chan Zuckerberg Biohub in San Francisco. There she spent ten weeks working on image processing and AI to analyze different stages of the malaria infection in red blood cells. But she could not afford to move there long-term. Restrictive land use policies have prevented the construction of affordable housing, to the point where most would-be residents have no idea how they could afford an apartment, let alone a house in the Bay Area. An attitude of NIMBYism, meaning "not in my backyard," is currently blocking new housing and quashing the aspirations of many young people like Regan who want to work in the Valley. In fact, Enrico Moretti and his colleague Chang-Tai Hsieh estimate that the lack of sufficient affordable housing in places like Silicon Valley reduces our GDP by nearly $1.4 trillion.

We need a federal program that incentivizes cities to build affordable housing near public transportation with grants for education, transportation, and infrastructure. These grants could propel a race to the top for rational zoning policy that addresses all the equities. Solving housing and traffic problems is critical for Silicon Valley's own growth and dynamism. To keep and attract new entrepreneurs, California also needs to expedite the permitting process without sacrificing environmental concerns, insist on reinstatement of the federal SAALT deduction for local and state taxes, and limit new taxes that impact start-ups. In the absence of reform, California risks losing talent. Last year, we saw headlines about Oracle moving their headquarters to Austin, Hewlett Packard Enterprise to Houston, and Tesla building its new 4-million-square-foot facility in Austin. Start-ups and techies are likewise leaving for other booming cities such as Seattle, Denver, and Chicago.

Reports of the demise of Silicon Valley are, however, greatly exaggerated. Migration in and out of Silicon Valley always ebbs and flows. People rush in when there is a boom, it gets crowded, and then people leave to go somewhere with a lower cost of living or lower taxes once they've made their money. The Valley's base is exceptionally strong with our anchor companies like Apple and Google, risk-taking and immigrant culture, global leadership in AI and quantum computing, great weather, and the world's premier research universities. We also have nearly 50 percent of the nation's venture capital and are flooded with new wealth in the Bay Area with recent IPOs like Airbnb, valued at more than $100 billion. My friends at Y Combinator, one of the top start-up accelerators, shared that even during the pandemic up-and-coming techies traveled to the Bay Area to set up shop, inspired by the Valley's culture, history, and folklore.

Silicon Valley today is exclusive in a double sense. It has concentrated digital jobs and wealth and also set up a moat in the form of high housing prices to deter many from getting in. Placed-based policies would both spread out the jobs, including to small towns that are not already thriving hubs, and build drawbridges to welcome more inside the high-tech capital.

REIMAGINING WHAT IS POSSIBLE: SILICON VALLEY MEETS JEFFERSON, IOWA

On a Saturday night in September of 2019, more than five hundred Iowans packed into the Greene County Community Center to learn about tech training and jobs that were coming to Jefferson, Iowa. Jefferson is a town of about four thousand people. I was there with the Republican governor, Kim Reynolds, who'd had the ambition to complete her college degree as a grandmother in her late fifties, when she was lieutenant governor. Something about our presence onstage together—a progressive Indian American from the Bay Area with an Ivy League degree, joined by a conservative governor from the heartland who was a nontraditional student—conveyed that we could look past our bubbles to discover the value of building a digital future in smaller towns across America.

The Jefferson project is the brainchild of Linc Kroeger and Chris Deal, who believe that rural America has the talent to contribute to the digital economy but has lacked the opportunity. They want Jefferson to become a rural hub for a tech workforce, and to start it on this path they leveraged a $600,000 loan at 0 percent interest from the United States Department of Agriculture, as well as grants and loans from the local city and county, plus Chris's own financial commitment. They began by renovating a vacant building into a tech training facility and collaborated with Pillar Technology, which was acquired by Accenture, to jump-start the project by providing an advanced four-month training in software design at the facility. They also had the foresight to partner with educational institutions, so that Jefferson would not be dependent on a single tech employer. Des Moines Area Community College (DMACC) became an active partner by offering a nine-course, high-technology certificate that would prepare students either for the four-month training or for other tech job opportunities. Rob Denson, the college's president, and Joel Lundstrom, the provost, personally follow each student in the nine-course program and are invested in their career success.

The community was also inspired to vote for a multimillion-dollar bond to build a new high school and career academy that allows students to take college-level technology courses as juniors and seniors. Iowa Central Community College is running the career academy, which provides practical training not just in software development but also in ag tech, advancement manufacturing, and construction with computer-aided design. The bond for the career academy would not have passed without the excitement and buzz about the prospect of software develop-ment jobs. The pursuit of tech jobs can inspire a community's broader economic revitalization initiatives.

A year before the launch, Kroeger and MD Isley, the dean of Business, Management and Information Technology at DMACC, visited my dis-trict to form partnerships with Silicon Valley, and Valley leaders stepped up. Kevin Scott, the CTO of Microsoft, wrote a check for scholarships to be used at DMACC or Iowa Central. Ron and Jane Olson, a philanthropic California couple with Iowa roots, covered tuition for promising Latino students. Greg Sands, a prominent venture capitalist, funded a local en-trepreneur. The Tech Interactive, a venerable Silicon Valley institution, agreed to train participating high schools in curriculum design. Ripple, a cryptocurrency company, helped fund a tech center on Iowa Central's campus, and other companies pledged either internships or money. But the real contribution these Silicon Valley leaders provided was challeng-ing coastal insularity. For too long, tech companies and policymakers neglected potential talent in places like Jefferson. But these leaders broke the mold and made an unconventional business bet on expanding the sources of the future workforce.

The message was not lost on Nikki McCloud, twenty-eight, who grew up in Halbur, Iowa, a town of about 250 people. She participated in the Jefferson program to show her three-year-old daughter that "if you really want something you will do what you can to achieve it." Nikki went to college briefly but had to quit to support her parents. For years, she worked three part-time jobs as a medical manager at a nursing home, an optician, and a pharmacy technician to make a combined annual sal-ary of $24,000. She then found a job making nearly $56,000 a year as a contract relations manager at an appliance repair company. But she is a techie at heart and wanted to pursue a tech career. For her, Covid-19 highlighted how much "we are at the mercy of technology." Nikki aspired to be a builder, not just a consumer, of technology. She was committed to doing that in Iowa, so her parents and extended family could be part of her daughter's life.

The Jefferson project provided her with exactly that opportunity. Nikki finished the nine-course, high-tech certificate at DMACC as an evening student while working her day job and juggling her duties as a mother. She was initially concerned about how she would do the four-month training with Accenture in the winter of 2021 without any salary. But Accenture delivered. The company not only gave her a stipend of $19 an hour during her four-month training as a "knowledge transfer analyst" but structured the program to allow her to keep her other job. Nikki had a "great experience" saying that the "amount of education and courses" Accenture made available to her was "overwhelmingly impressive." Because of her experience, she was able to return to her previous employer with a major promotion as a data analyst and an increase in salary by over 25 percent.

Imagine how many Nikki McClouds we are overlooking who have the grit and ambition to pursue technology jobs but lack pathways. If Jefferson could set up a comprehensive tech training program and a career academy, why has the federal government not made similar investments? Would we not improve our competitiveness if technology companies were incentivized to have 10 percent of their workforce composed of employees like Nikki? And wouldn't communities across the nation benefit?

The Jefferson project is now facing the hurdle of attracting a pipeline of students signing up. As Nikki put it to me, you are "either in the skilled trades or do factory work or work at a bank or a restaurant." It will take time to convince families that their child should forgo other options, or that a software career is possible without leaving home. But no one understands this better than Chris Deal, one of the founders of the project. He told me most of his classmates left Jefferson after graduating and never returned. As he put it, "the mindset was that success wasn't something that was possible in small rural communities like Jefferson. If you were going to be successful, you had to go elsewhere." Deal came back to Jefferson determined to expand the horizon of possibilities for the next generation. He is not concerned about overdevelopment or gentrification because tech salaries in Jefferson reflect the cost of living and scaling up will be a gradual process over years. The reality is that housing values are depressed in Jefferson, as in many rural communities, and they are losing young people, so they would "gladly take the problems of increasing housing prices and rapid population growth."

Accenture's commitment to provide internships to some of the early DMACC and Iowa Central students, like Nikki McCloud, was also key to getting the Jefferson project off the ground as it diversifies its employer base. Robert Hoffman, the company's former director of government affairs, Robin Boggs, the U.S. corporate citizenship lead, were evangelists for the program with their bosses, insisting that the multinational corporation could not abandon it when the economy took a nosedive because of the pandemic. Given Covid-19, they had to transition from on-site training to a remote training model for their inaugural 2021 class. One lesson is that tech-to-rural development initiatives must have many stakeholders to be flexible and resilient in overcoming unanticipated challenges. Accenture also had to reevaluate their goal of providing apprenticeships to successful interns at the Jefferson facility itself, clarifying that apprentices would likely have to move to major offices like Chicago to pursue additional opportunities with the company. Even with remote work, it is naive to underestimate the challenges of bringing high-paying, global jobs to rural communities, especially absent strong government incentives. As Chris Deal told me, "If it were easy, someone would have done it" already.

When all is said and done, the country, not just Jefferson, is better off because of the determination of local leaders to see the project through choppy waters. Employees like Nikki McCloud, who had the opportunity to work for one of the world's premier tech consulting shops, are ambassadors for the new economy in their hometown. They generate new income, ideas, and networks for their local community, linking it to our broader nation.

3

RACIAL AND GENDER EQUITY

As Ifeoma Ozoma watched the iPhone recording of George Floyd's lynching, she reflected on the lynching of Emmett Till and the chilling photographs of the open casket that had helped spark the civil rights movement. Those images had exposed the brutality of American racism nearly sixty-five years prior. Now, a smartphone recording of the helpless cries of a dying Black man launched a modern movement, as social media users ensured the footage went viral. Having worked at Google, Facebook, and Pinterest, Ozoma was part of the new tech world that helped make this movement possible. But she felt helpless and angry as she saw tech companies profess solidarity with Black Lives Matter.

Ozoma had experienced a very different side of these Silicon Valley powerhouses, and the hypocrisy gnawed at her. It was easy to oppose racism when the perpetrator is the "other," a cop in Minneapolis far removed from Valley offices. But where had their outrage been at the inequality happening closer to home, under their own roofs? Where was their stand against the issues these companies could easily control: the unjust Silicon Valley hiring practices, promotion decisions, pay scales, retention efforts, and management structures that, on a daily basis, devalue Black lives? Ozoma knew the indignity all too well. She had been chased out.

Ozoma's journey to Silicon Valley was improbable. She is the daughter of Nigerian immigrants, spent her early childhood in Anchorage, and then was raised by a single mother in North Carolina. Her voice broke when she spoke to me about losing her mother to cancer during her sophomore year at Yale. Her mother was a beloved chemistry teacher who instilled in her children a passion for education, and Ozoma excelled. She studied political science and wrote a thesis on privacy and the Fourth Amendment. It took a Yale degree, a tour-de-force thesis, and two Google internships for her to be hired as a Black woman in Silicon Valley. From the day she started working, she was aware Black women needed to be twice as good, and insanely credentialed, to find a seat at the tech table.

She did well at Google and soon landed a job at Facebook to lead counterspeech efforts and a program assisting small businesses across the nation. The program was Sheryl Sandberg's brainchild. At both Google and Facebook, Ozoma felt the burden of being the only Black woman in many meetings and social gatherings but did not face overt discrimination. After Charlottesville, she mustered the courage to ask Facebook CEO Zuckerberg to share his thoughts about the traumatic event with the employee community. She and other Blacks found his answer vague and lacking in any depth of understanding about the pain and legacy of historical racism. But she soldiered on and did her work. In time, Pinterest became aware of her stellar reputation and made a full-court press to recruit her. Ozoma heard Pinterest was a place that valued diverse perspectives, and she took a position there hoping to put her education to use in designing an inclusive public forum.

But what happened at Pinterest was so hurtful that Ozoma left Silicon Valley and moved to New Mexico. Ozoma launched efforts to align Pinterest's promotion with its values, including an effort to block the promotion of content about slave plantation weddings and to block anti-vaccine content. Soon after, however, her manager gave her negative performance reviews because she did not discuss both sides of these issues. The review impacted her pay. A white coworker, moreover, targeted her and released her personal information, including her cell phone number, street address, and email, to a conservative group. While Pinterest fired the employee responsible for the information leak, they had no system in place to help her lobby other tech companies to remove the information from cyberspace. She had to beg friends at Facebook and Google to help remove the information while Pinterest stalled in taking any action.

When Ozoma shared her experience on social media, a significant number of former Black employees at Pinterest came forward to *Business Insider* with their own accounts of a racist work environment. Kara Swisher soon after detailed in *The New York Times* how female executives at the company, even in very senior positions, were marginalized and disrespected while an insular group of men made the key decisions. As Swisher memorably put it, Pinterest, like many companies in the industry, is more of a *"mirror-tocracy"* when it comes to leadership roles than a meritocracy, "reflecting only those who look just like themselves."

It was not just her experience at Pinterest, however, that made Ozoma want to leave the Valley. She told me she never wants to go back to a place where people act as if race and gender are immaterial. Her ideas were not taken seriously, she was ignored in the hallways, and she always felt she had to prove she belonged—all while her coworkers and managers never seemed to pause to consider what it might be like to be the rare Black woman in tech. Ozoma became fed up with the Valley explanations for not hiring other Black and Latino women. It cannot be dismissed as merely a pipeline issue, she explained, as a significant percentage of employees at these companies are in marketing, finance, legal, advertising, communication, and nontechnical fields. What explains the lack of hiring and retention of Black accountants and lawyers when there are many Black graduates to choose from in these fields?

The irony—as Karla Monterroso, the CEO of Code2040, observes—is that Ozoma is exactly the type of person the Valley needs to appeal to a growing black and brown customer base. Yet the reality is that "unfair behavior and treatment," which includes stereotyping and condescension, is the top reason employees leave tech jobs. Layllen Sawyerr was one of fifteen Black employees who either left or was fired from the hot cryptocurrency start-up Coinbase. She said, "It was the first time I realized what racism felt like in the modern world . . . I felt like I was being bullied every day at work." Black employees at Coinbase were "treated differently." They were prominently featured in photo shoots to display the company's "diversity," but they were "talked down to and ignored" in meetings after the cameras left.

Monterroso finds it incomprehensible that the Valley is not putting in the resources to retain employees like Ozoma. Valerie Jarrett, President Barack Obama's former senior advisor, similarly told me: "Diversity is actually a strength for these tech companies. They would be stronger if they hired more Black people and women, who then will bring new ideas to make the company more diverse and more successful." Indeed, numerous studies show that companies with greater gender and racial diversity in their leadership attain more profitability, productivity, and shareholder value.

It's also an issue of American competitiveness. If even top graduates from Yale leave the Valley without financial equity, it will only continue to exacerbate the racial wealth gap that has grown over the last three decades. Economists estimate that the racial wealth gap will reduce our *overall GDP by nearly 5 percent* over the next decade because a significant percentage of the population will continue to face discrimination that constrains their earning potential, productivity, and consumer spending. For those not inclined to prioritize issues of racial inequality, this statistic alone should be a wake-up call for change.

The exclusion of women and Black and Brown talent also means the marginalization of their issues. Lisa Jackson, a vice president at Apple, told me that "if you bring in a bunch of Black developers and say write me an app, it is almost always about a social issue." Similarly, women often bring ethical and community issues to light that otherwise go unnoticed. Shouldn't the toolmakers of all platforms that shape contemporary discourse and culture be diverse?

Tech should aspire to mitigate, not exacerbate, our segregation. Studies show that 75 percent of white Americans have "entirely white social networks." Tech has the potential to break that paradigm and create more integrated networks, centered on joint work. The industry can begin by cultivating more women and Black and Brown leaders, who, in turn, can hire from communities of color, which is now possibly easier to scale through telework. The modern workplace may be one of the few spaces where Americans can escape from our own social bubbles and interact with those who have different backgrounds and perspectives. Ultimately, empowering brilliant young leaders like Ozoma to succeed in technology work environments is pro-dignity, pro-growth, and pro-democracy.

However, we still lack intentionality and urgency in addressing racial and gender equity in tech. The most driven Silicon Valley founders and investors often have tunnel vision—so focused on scale, on market size, on valuations, on moving fast, and on exit strategies that they barely pause to consider the ramifications of their actions on the deep racial and gender divides in our society. Since the beginning of tech's rise, leaders like Reverend Jesse L. Jackson have called on companies to diversify their boards, executives, and recruits. This effort pushed big tech to report their numbers annually, but those numbers have not significantly improved. What frustrates Valerie Jarrett, as she shared with me, is that it takes a crisis like Covid-19 and George Floyd's murder "to wake people up to the fact that many Black people don't have access to the internet: no Wi-Fi, laptops, or ability to work from home," and they are underrepresented in tech jobs. Mignon Clyburn, a former FCC commissioner, told me that after Covid and Floyd, "things are forever changed. No company or business can ever go back to how they did things prior." Aware that Majority Whip Clyburn, her father, spent time in jail during the civil rights movement, Mignon Clyburn argues for bold action on the digital divide to live up to our moment in history.

There is overlap between an agenda to provide digital opportunity to Black and Brown communities and to white Americans in places left behind. While the causes and depth of exclusion and marginalization from our economy are very different, there are some commonalities in both the effects of this exclusion and in the solutions needed. Anne Case and Angus Deaton have written powerfully about the "despair" of middle-aged white Americans due to a lack of good-paying jobs. They see parallels in William Julius Wilson's work documenting the social harms caused by the flight of manufacturing jobs in many Black communities in the 1960s and 1970s. In fact, Deaton and Case's description of "despair" is echoed by philosopher Cornel West, who observed, "when you economically abandon a people" such as the Black community, they are "going to respond with very sad forms of despair." He goes on to say, "that's true for everybody. I don't care what color you are. It's true with Appalachia, it's true with indigenous people, it's true around the world."

A modern jobs platform can have a broad coalition of support. A number of proposals from the previous chapter can be tailored to empower communities of color. Contrary to common perception, it is worth remembering that people of color make up nearly 20 percent of rural America. Many Black and Latino communities in both rural and urban areas desperately need high-speed broadband, computer science education, and funds for community revitalization. The national digital corps should be explicit in seeking partners in Black and Brown communities, and we should locate a high percentage of tech hubs in cities with significant populations of color.

As Ifeoma Ozoma's story highlights, however, an agenda that does not specifically speak to race and gender inequities—and the ways in which those inequities often intersect—is blind and inadequate. It is impossible to achieve equity without addressing the unique needs of communities with an awareness of the overlapping historical exclusions of those communities' identities, which is what Kimberlé Crenshaw means by intersectionality. This applies to the disability, faith, LGBTQ+

communities, and other marginalized groups as well. The task calls for far more than just affinity groups at companies.

This chapter highlights the additional interventions needed to promote racial and gender inclusion where the Valley is most visibly lacking. It is by no means comprehensive, but my hope is to invite further proposals by offering specific recommendations for structural change within tech companies as well as policies to invest in new credentialing, jobs, and entrepreneurs in communities of color. As the late Representative John Lewis said, "in many ways, technology rights are the new civil rights." Economic empowerment in a modern economy is a key component of social justice.

RESTRUCTURING TECH COMPANIES

Tech needs more than chief diversity and inclusion officers. Although well intentioned and committed, these diversity officers are often siloed and lack meaningful authority about hiring, promotions, and doing business deals. Catherine Bracey, founder of TechEquity, says the creation of diversity officers is just a way for senior white, male executives to "offload responsibility usually to a person of color." She finds it offensive that the burden to carry the ball forward for equity falls on members of underrepresented groups, an arrangement that only furthers the retention problem. Instead, tech CEOs and senior executives must take ownership of diversity goals with their compensation tied to metrics, just as they own sales or revenue numbers.

Another common tactic for shirking responsibility for diversity in Silicon Valley is to blame the pipeline problem. Yes, women represent less than 20 percent of computer science graduates, and the Black and Latino populations are underrepresented in computer science programs; and in turn, we do need more opportunities for women and people of color to acquire employable digital credentials. But the problem runs much deeper than that.

The exclusionary culture of tech drives many away from pursuing the career in the first place. It is not a lack of capability or interest: women, after all, constituted "most of the computing workforce" in the 1960s. But Emily Chang shows in *Brotopia* that the introduction and marketing of the personal computer created a young, male ethos around coding that was often sexist. And over time, that ethos became the dominant culture. In recent years, nearly half of women reported discrimination in the hiring process, and 41 percent of women leave tech midcareer compared to only 17 percent of men. Similarly, in a Code2040 study, nearly 70 percent of Black tech workers report feeling excluded because of their race. Karla Monterroso shared with me that less than one third of Black and Latino computer science graduates end up in tech careers despite nearly 700,000 open tech jobs. The systemic bias in tech will not be solved simply with more training sessions, reports, or conferences. What is needed are concrete, comprehensive policies that incentivize inclusion.

For starters, we should adopt a national law that requires a certain percentage of women, Black, and Latino leaders on the boards of public companies. Consider that nearly 70 percent of Fortune 500 companies do not have a single Latino member on their board, and 37 percent do not have a Black member. California successfully passed a law requiring companies to have at least one woman on the board by 2020 and up to three by 2022. The law has had an impact already, as 90 percent of California companies now have a woman on the board compared to 75 percent before the law was passed. More important, it triggered a conversation at almost every Silicon Valley company, including startups, about the need for gender equity. According to the Deloitte Global "Women in the Boardroom" report, more women on boards predictably leads to more women on the executive team, which in turn leads to a more diverse workforce. In addition to being morally right, it's also good business practice. McKinsey's "Delivering Through Diversity" report found that companies with more gender and ethnically diverse boards are significantly more likely to experience higher profits. More recently, California passed a law requiring companies to have two to three directors from underrepresented Black and Brown groups by 2022, though the impact remains to be seen. A law requiring a threshold percentage is better than a fixed number, so that companies cannot dilute diverse representation by expanding their board.

Diverse board members are better able to address inequities in a corporate culture than current chief diversity officers. They are better equipped to call for internal investigations upon hearing complaints that executives promote their own friends at the expense of high-performing people of color and to press CEOs on improving retention numbers. They are far more likely to recommend Black- and Brown-led vendors who they know to be exceptional from their own networks. They can push for cultural change so corporate leaders give deals to overlooked Black and Brown financial, legal, and technology service firms instead of simply holding minority business fairs or offering coaching that can frankly come off as patronizing. And they can apply more diverse perspectives and rolodexes for recruiting talent, filling senior roles, and developing business strategy.

At the same time, Joan Williams, author of *White Working Class*, observes that many working-class women "would never get near the C-suite" which has offices for high-level executives. So it would be a mistake to assume that diversifying the top echelons speaks directly to bread-and-butter economic issues. But it still matters. As one of the first Indian Americans to make it to Congress, I can tell you that it was a matter of pride not just for the professionals at the top, but for the larger community who trusted me to understand their unique experience and wanted their kids to have role models in public service. In today's America, serving in senior corporate roles can similarly uplift the aspirations of underrepresented groups. More practically, people in these positions are determining the salaries and careers of hundreds of thousands of Americans, including blue-collar contractors.

Beyond corporate boards and executive teams, smart policies can facilitate diversifying the broader workforce. Similar to policies suggested in the previous chapter, our government should provide favorable consideration for software contracts to companies with diverse executive teams and at least 10 percent Black or Latino workforce on a project, with that benchmark indexed to increase as the overall tech workforce diversifies. We should also have a tax credit of up to $10,000 per employee for companies that hire tech workers in heavily Black and Latino areas. This may lead to reform in recruiting practices, such as eliminating whiteboard interviews that put candidates on the spot to write out code, deemphasizing pedigree, anonymizing applicants, or rejecting consensus hiring, which makes it more difficult to onboard those who are different from the existing members.

TECH PARTNERSHIPS WITH INSTITUTIONS THAT SERVE COMMUNITIES OF COLOR

Growing up, Princess Sampson never took her MacBook for granted. "It takes a lot of privilege to get into tech," she explained. Now a junior at Spelman College, she is struck by how many of her peers shared a computer at home with family members. Unlike her, they never had their own laptop nor the opportunity to experiment with its capabilities. Some were still not comfortable typing.

For Princess, it's not just about access to laptops. She observed, "A lot of folks do not understand what tech is, what it means, or what it takes to get there." At an early age, Princess started a blog on *Star Wars* and learned to customize it with layouts and graphics. Her father persuaded her to attend a rigorous three-month coding boot camp as a high school senior where she learned developer culture and how to think like a programmer. If anything, she found the training there more helpful in securing an Amazon internship than her education at Spelman.

The boot camp taught Princess how to build software and use commercial tools that academic computer science courses don't cover. She saw her classmates who took rigorous computer science classes in college struggle in interviews because of their lack of familiarity with commercial software products.

Rodney Sampson, Princess's proud father and the cofounder of

Opportunity Hub, wants to expand the resources that Princess was able to tap into. He has a vision to bring a technology credentialing program to every HBCU (historically Black college and university) in the nation. Sampson believes we need to credential at least one million Black and Latino Americans for high-skilled tech careers in coding, developing, and cybersecurity. He estimates this would cost $15,000 per person for an intensive, full-time three-month program at a total cost of $15 billion. The Divine Nine, an umbrella of the nine historically Black fraternities and sororities, has already endorsed this vision as essential for wealth creation in the community.

The heart of Sampson's proposal is an effort to overcome the existing racial credentialing gap and address the challenge that automation poses for communities of color. He can cite from memory a McKinsey report showing that Black workers have jobs that are at a higher risk of automation and warning that 4.5 million Black jobs could be eliminated over the next decade. Latino workers are even more at risk because they are disproportionately in food service roles, jobs which McKinsey estimates will have the highest displacement rate per share of jobs. There are a number of efforts in place to help train at-risk workers for new fields—including McKinsey's Generation program, Per Scholas, Year Up, and Goodwill—but Sampson is concerned with how such programs rarely slot Black and Brown people into digital roles. He applauds these programs but believes they are insufficient for opening avenues to higher-paying jobs. He wants Black and Brown Americans designing the next iPhone and its apps, not just staffing Apple stores.

Sampson has a track record of success with Opportunity Hub. In more than three hundred coding boot camps, his graduating students have a 90 percent placement rate, with an average starting salary of $50,000. The program should be a model for setting up federally funded tech training programs at one hundred HBCUs. The key is for HBCUs to partner with boot camps such as Thinkful, Flatiron, and App Academy that provide a job guarantee at the end of their training with leading tech companies. Such boot camps provide industry-specific credentialing and placement that can help Black students overcome the networking gap, as well as the doubts they face from prospective employers.

I witnessed firsthand the challenges of establishing partnerships between Silicon Valley employers and HBCUs at Claflin University in South Carolina. In 2018, Majority Whip Clyburn invited me, Representative Tim Ryan, and prominent venture capitalists to his district to meet Claflin's students. Clyburn started his civil rights activism on the Claflin campus, and on our bus ride there from D.C., he shared that the university is a regional leader in innovation. I was impressed by the entrepreneurial ambition of the students and how much they wanted a career in technology. It validated for me the 2016 Google report I read in *Wired* which showed that "Black and Hispanic students were 1.5 and 1.7 times more likely to have an interest in learning CS," computer science, compared to white students. I was so moved by the students' determination that I pledged to Claflin's administration that I would work to facilitate internships with a Valley company. I figured this would be an easy lift, but the reality became a bit embarrassing for me. Dr. Ramaier Sriram, chair of Computer Science at Claflin, would send his best 4.0 students for interviews for internships, and the Valley companies rejected them one after another, claiming that the whiteboard interviews revealed a lack of proficiency in commercial software use and development.

Dr. Sriram, of Sri Lankan origin, was a good sport about it. We bonded over the recognition that HBCUs provided jobs for so many South Asians who came to the U.S. after the passage of the 1965 Immigration and Nationality Act, when few other universities were willing to hire these brilliant immigrants because of their accents, long names, or nontraditional pedigrees. This history is, alas, lost on the Valley, which now has many South Asians in leadership positions. Many continue to be simply unaware of both the history and the present talent of Black institutions. Dr. Sriram did not mind sending résumé after résumé to Valley companies seeking internships for his students. But one day, he politely explained to me that the rejections hurt his students' self-esteem. He was open to learning about how Claflin could improve its curriculum, but he also wanted to protect his best students from disappointment.

Fortunately, Zoom stepped up, winning the admiration of both Dr. Sriram and Dr. Dwaun Warmack, Claflin's president. Zoom made a commitment of $1.2 million to Claflin, including guaranteed paid internships, which can lead to full-time jobs; merit and need-based scholarships; and workshops and curriculum help, so students can acquire industry skills. Zoom's chief operating officer, Aparna Bawa, also agreed to join the board of trustees for Claflin, making a generous personal financial and time commitment. What makes the Zoom-Claflin model work is its true partnership with deliverables beyond just a promise to review résumés or provide scholarship money. Zoom empowered their chief diversity officer, Damien Hooper-Campbell, who has an economics degree from Morehouse College and a Harvard MBA, to get the job done, giving him far more authority than his peers have at other companies. He did not approach the project as something to check off a corporate responsibility checklist. Rather, he saw it in Zoom's strategic advantage to access a new pool of talent and expand their market.

The benefit to Claflin extends beyond the money or jobs. Zoom affirms their brand as a tech-savvy institution for their students, faculty, and other prospective employers. There is already buzz in the South Carolina community that Claflin is the place to go for a tech career. There is no reason why other leading tech companies cannot partner with HBCUs to prepare the Black workforce of the future. Apple, under Lisa Jackson's leadership, made a recent commitment of $100 million to support the Propel Center at Clark Atlanta University for tech training and start-up incubation programs and to establish a Developer Academy in Detroit, Michigan, focused on Black youth. Netflix CEO Reed Hastings, who made a $120 million donation to Morehouse, Spelman, and the United Negro College Fund, also demonstrated leadership that his peers can emulate.

Tech partnerships should extend to other institutions that serve Black and Brown students, including the thirty-five tribal colleges and universities (TCUs) and Hispanic Serving Institutions (HSIs), which are colleges or universities that have at least a 25 percent Hispanic population. Federally supported TCU-tech partnerships would provide a unique opportunity for the U.S. to recast its historical relationship with tribal nations by ensuring that Native American communities are helping to shape the new economy. The Southwestern Indian Polytechnic Institute (SIPI) in Albuquerque, New Mexico, neighbors the Santa Ana Pueblo (Tamaya) tribal lands, and already hosts students from many tribal nations that have flocked to SIPI's state-of-the-art Science and Technology Center. Native American leader Dr. Richard Luarkie pointed out to me that the Tamayan traditions are "steeped in multidimensional connections between humans and the environment," which can be leveraged to advance climate resilience, biosciences, and other new tech frontiers.

HBCUs, TCUs, and HSIs all have different structures for serving communities of color. Karla Monterroso of Code2040 cautions that "HSI's are not run the same way HBCUs are. There is not a Latino teaching core heading them up. There aren't similar traditions or even plays to get the community to come. So HSI strategy is important but needs more awareness and nuance." She believes Latino employees need to run the HSI boot camps with cultural content that will interest Latino students. Targeted Latino outreach cannot be confined, moreover, to HSIs but must take place at institutions of higher education more broadly. Monterroso has come to see the fate of Black and Latino students in tech as interlinked, as there is often a correlation between Black and Brown representation at tech companies. "When you fix systems for the participation of Black people, it can end up also helping Latino candidates," she says. Ultimately, opening doors for one underrepresented group paves the way for others.

STARTING EARLY

The best way to overcome the cumulative effect of systemic racism is to intervene as early as possible. Princess can attest to the value of having your own laptop as a child, and it is well worth supporting programs that give students early access to their own computers. A gadget is not a substitute for the education offered by teachers and parents, and research shows that laptops do not improve reading or math scores. But they do help give students skills in operating a computer and navigating technology, and these skills are foundational in a digital age.

The federal government should establish a $5 billion fund over the next five years that school districts can access to provide Chromebooks, MacBooks, or Windows laptops for the 11 million students who lack their own. Schools should receive at least $500 on average per laptop and have flexibility to obtain a more advanced model for students who show an interest in coding. Preschool and kindergarten students can use the program to acquire tablets to develop basic digital skills and intuition. School districts would also receive funding to provide parents with training on keeping children safe online and limit their screen time appropriately.

The Covid-19 pandemic shone a light on many inequities, and it found glaring holes in our education system. As schools closed and learning went remote, low-income students were placed at an even greater disadvantage. Not only were many of their parents essential workers who had to leave their children at home during the day, many lacked the proper resources to keep up with their wealthier peers. Upper-income parents were more likely to work remotely and could at least supervise some of their students' work online if not hire tutors to augment their children's learning. Representative Alexandria Ocasio-Cortez put forward an innovative way to help low-income students continue learning online. She created the Homework Helpers program, which used the internet to recruit people to virtually help low-income students with their homework. The program was so popular at the outset, garnering thirteen thousand volunteers, that they had to close the sign-up list because it was not ready to scale that fast. The program shows the power of the internet in bringing people together to make a dent in societal inequalities. These are the types of initiatives that the government should help fund at a larger scale.

Access to laptops and instruction is a start, but it must also be supplemented by exposure to tech classes and careers. This is where Reshma Saujani, my former law school classmate, is changing the game with Girls Who Code. Her organization provided more than 300,000 girls, over half Black and Latino, with either a two-week immersion in digital learning or an after-school coding club. The goal is to pique their interest in tech with a curriculum that speaks to girls' desire to be change makers, to expose them to extraordinary female role models, and to do so while preventing the type of microaggressions that often discourage girls from speaking up. Saujani shared with me her belief that our educational institutions "have not caught up" with the techniques for cultivating a passion for tech in girls by appealing to their aspirations. Her goal is to set a higher standard, and the organization has already had success. She told me that nearly 60 percent of the eighty-thousand college-aged alumni of Girls Who Code end up pursuing a computer-science-related major. Saujani says, moreover, that female enrollment for computer science majors in the top universities has increased to more than 20 percent today. While this is progress, we are still not at our 1980s levels, when the percentage of female computer science graduates was 37.1 percent.

When I asked Saujani why she focused her talent on building a tech organization, her answer was simple. She wants more women—who are increasingly becoming primary breadwinners—to have jobs "where you can make $120,000 a year." She knows that tech is where many of the high-paying jobs will continue to be concentrated this coming decade, and she is frustrated that so many tech companies are founded and funded by men but have a large female customer base. Young girls, she knows, aspire to be more than consumers of technology. For Saujani, building wealth for underrepresented communities is tied to their access to these jobs.

While Girls Who Code provides immersive tech education for older girls, Saujani emphasizes that exposure to tech must begin at a very early age. She touts Black Girls Code as a leader in this field. The organization teaches Black girls as young as six about app development, game design, artificial intelligence, and programming. Every year, they provide weekend and after-school workshops as well as summer camps to thousands of students.

At Saujani's suggestion, I reached out to Black Girls Code's founder, Kimberly Bryant. Bryant saw the transformative impact that a game design course had on her daughter. After taking that course, her daughter became fascinated with a career in tech, and Kimberly wants other Black girls to have the chance that her daughter did. She is saddened that so few Black women have leadership roles in Silicon Valley and hopes her organization can make a dent in changing the face of technology.

In addition to cultivating future careers, the program's early tech exposure gives teenagers the immediate possibility of a modest source of income from app development, posting videos, taking surveys, providing reviews, or doing online jobs. These are opportunities that many born to middle-class families, even with no interest in a STEM profession, readily have as a source of extra money to help pay for education or accumulate savings. Black Girls Code is now in fifteen cities and has support from companies like Microsoft. What is now needed is for the federal government to invest resources with leading tech companies to enable programs like Black Girls Code and Girls Who Code to scale as widely as possible.

ACCESS TO CAPITAL

Black, Latino, and women entrepreneurs receive less than a few percent of the more than $130 billion venture capital funding given every year. A big problem is the lack of diversity of investors. Only 11 percent of venture capital partners are women, and less than one percent are Black or Latino. As Theresia Gouw, a leading venture capitalist, explained to me: the best way to increase the diversity of funded entrepreneurs is to increase the diversity of those writing the checks. Organizations like BLCK VC, LatinX VC, and All Raise are pushing to change the face of venture capital, and there is also a movement to better finance Black- and Brown-run firms, which can serve as alternative sources of funding to the marquee names. But there is still bias against women and venture capitalists of color. A Stanford study concluded that institutional investors discriminate against high-performing venture funds with Black leadership. Here is what I know: relying on the goodwill of venture capitalists or senior tech leaders to fix these problems is simply not going to cut it. In order to make a dent, it will require not just voluntary leadership, but better policy.

One way to democratize access to capital is by providing institutions such as Stanford, CalPERS, Blackstone, or BlackRock a capital gains tax credit to invest in nontraditional, Black- and Brown-run firms or those led by women. These firms often are small and lack the capacity to land $100 million plus investments. But with proper tax incentives, big investors will themselves seek out funds that, in turn, invest in Black- and Brown-led VCs. To the extent investors are putting money in traditional funds, moreover, there should be tax benefits for picking those with diverse partnerships. There would be tremendous pressure on Sand Hill Road to promote more people of color if their fund-raising depended on it. Finally, we should provide commercial banks with Community Reinvestment Act (CRA) credits if they invest in Black- and Brown-led VCs. Brian Trelstad, who teaches social entrepreneurship at Harvard, believes that would open potentially $100 billion as a revenue source and would be "a game changer for racial equity in the venture capital industry."

Rodney Sampson, cofounder of Opportunity Hub, also helps operate a VC fund, 100 Black Angels & Allies, that manages about $5 million. He estimates that Black-led VC funds, such as Lightship, Base10 Partners, and Harlem Capital, have collectively raised only a few hundred million dollars—much less than one percent of the $130 billion deployed every year. According to a Harlem Capital report, as of 2019, there are only two hundred start-ups led by Black or Brown founders that received more than $1 million in funding, and the total investment in these Black- or Brown-led start-ups is just $6 billion over nearly a decade. The racial wealth gap is not just based on legacy assets but on a current, ongoing racial *wealth generation* gap.

Sampson believes we need Black- and Latino-led VCs to have a few billion in funds (a 10x increase) so that at least one thousand Black and Latino start-ups receive VC funding out of the nearly eleven thousand start-ups that close VC deals each year. As Sampson sees it, if capital gains tax incentives are not sufficient to drive more equity, the federal government should set up a matching fund to partner with Black and Latino VCs. The federal government lacks the network or expertise to identify promising Black and Brown entrepreneurs, but a joint initiative with Black VCs would allow the federal government to do just that through the creation of regional venture capital funds. This also ties into the last chapter's methods for expanding funding for rural entrepreneurship. On issues of tech and financial capital exclusion, there is an opportunity to build a broad, bipartisan coalition in Congress.

The challenge for entrepreneurs of color is not just securing venture capital but the early funding needed to get a business off the ground. Ricardo Garcia-Amaya, a leader of Top 50 Latino Tech Leaders, shared with me that he sees the biggest hurdle for Latino founders as being acquiring their first $100,000 to $500,000, which needs to be in the bank before they can even seek venture capital. He laments that the Latino community does not have "several generations of angel investors," and "tech investing is simply not a thing." He started Top 50 Latino Tech Leaders to give budding entrepreneurs a network of Latino leaders who control nearly $120 billion of assets and could be angel investors. The six-year-old group helps launch high-growth businesses, providing the type of funding that comes with the greatest risk. Garcia-Amaya has seen an explosion of opportunities for Latino entrepreneurs as they've leveraged the network to pursue their start-up dreams. Good policy can help Garcia-Amaya's initiative scale; for instance, just as it can support diverse VC investment, the federal government should provide capital gains tax incentives to promote angel investing in Black and Brown start-ups in high-growth fields.

Still, even before getting to the angel stage, entrepreneurs of color face a stark financial deficit. In fact, a 2016 Stanford study concluded that Black start-ups have far less early-stage capital than white start-ups because they have difficulty receiving loans from banks or attracting early investment from their networks. The reality of the racial wealth gap is that people of color often have limited parental support or inheritance. Unlike many white founders, they can't afford to quit their job while they risk the financial loss of founding a start-up. Latino entrepreneurs, according to a Kauffman Foundation report, face similar financial barriers.

Currently, there is not a single federal agency that targets direct grants toward Black and Brown entrepreneurs. Congress should allocate a multibillion-dollar fund to the Small Business Administration (SBA) to provide grants or forgivable loans to Black and Brown businesses over this coming decade. There should also be some allocation for early-stage, high-growth start-ups. This should be coupled with a commitment to spend a significant share of the nearly $100 billion federal information technology budget on Black- and Brown-owned tech service companies, who can in turn hire men and women credentialed in the digital training programs that Rodney Sampson envisions.

We also need an infusion of funds into Community Development Financial Institutions (CDFI) and Minority Depository Institutions (MDI) to extend loans to Black- and Latino-owned start-ups. Although most people in Silicon Valley have never heard of these banks, the model dates back to the end of the Civil War, when Congress established the Freedman's Bank to provide wealth-building opportunities for formerly enslaved Black people whose savings were often stolen by traditional banks. CDFIs have less than one percent of banking assets, and MDIs have about 2 percent of assets. MDIs traditionally have been a source for home mortgages or commercial real estate loans. But they can be tasked along with CDFIs to also focus on start-up loans, which the Fed could cover with a partial guarantee. Most important, these institutions need more direct funding from Congress. Tech companies have a role to play. We should incentivize fintech firms to help MDIs and CDFIs compete with big banks by ensuring they can offer mobile banking, which is even more important post-Covid.

BLACK TECH STREET

Investing in entrepreneurs of color is pro-growth. Many business opportunities that specifically address the needs of people of color are overlooked by traditional investors. Tristan Walker proved the profitability of considering their preferences by founding Walker & Company, which makes "health and beauty simple for people of color." He started the company in Palo Alto, but moved it to Atlanta to be in a more diverse environment. He shared with me that his four-year-old son traveled back and forth a few times and observed, "Dada, Atlanta is where all the Black people are, and Palo Alto is where the white people are." This insight is borne out by data. According to a McKinsey study cited in *The Wall Street Journal*, only 9 percent of the Black population is in the West while 60 percent is in the South.

When he was in Palo Alto, Tristan was bewildered as to why Silicon Valley did not realize how many business opportunities they lost because of the lack of Black representation. He put it bluntly, "Black folks make Twitter, Twitter. They are the most early adopting consumer group on the planet." Whether in food, music, movies, or the earliest social media trends, as Tristan says, the Black community's early and active engagement is often what makes products and topics popular. The new Andreessen Horowitz–backed start-up Clubhouse recently raised $100 million and is Silicon Valley's new billion-dollar unicorn that allows for people to chat in various online groups using only audio. Much of its success can be attributed to its Black users. While Black users are driving creative growth on the platform, they are not adequately represented on the founding and executive team, board, or early investment firms to reap the astronomical financial rewards from this success. Clubhouse today may not be rife with sexism and racism with zero content moderation and exclusive groups that face no accountability if the team who built it were more diverse. Silicon Valley would only benefit by having more Black-led start-ups, executives, coders, and VCs, as greater diversity would lead to greater understanding of diverse market opportunities and more equitable design. The previous policies all provide routes for developing a home for Black founders in Silicon Valley, but we should also explore opportunities to create hubs elsewhere.

Perhaps Tyrance Billingsley II offers the boldest vision for building a start-up ecosystem of Black entrepreneurs. He has sought to create Black Tech Street in Tulsa, Oklahoma, which was once the home of Black Wall Street. Tulsa thrived in the early 1900s as a place where Black Americans owned many successful businesses and held significant financial capital. Driven by racism and jealousy of Black success, white mobs destroyed the community during the Tulsa Race Massacre of 1921. Decades later, when the Black community rebuilt their business ecosystem, Tulsa city planners destroyed it again by intentionally building an overpass through the community. Tyrance, whose relatives fled during the massacre, seeks to contribute toward making amends for that historic injustice by turning Tulsa into a Black tech metropolis. He believes the anchor can be Lightship Capital, one of the few Black-led venture funds, which raised $50 million to invest in entrepreneurs of color in Tulsa and the broader Midwest.

Tyrance is clear-eyed about the difficulty of creating a tech hub. He pitches tech leaders on establishing a presence in Tulsa, by allowing remote work from the city, creating a second office there, investing in promising start-ups, or partnering with local community colleges and universities on credentialing programs. A vibrant Black Tech Street, connected to a larger ecosystem in Silicon Valley and across the nation, would be far harder to sabotage than Black Wall Street. The digital age makes it easier for distinctive communities like Black Tech Street to emerge because the internet facilitates remote work and investment. It will not be a replica of Silicon Valley, of course, and needs to find its own unique customer base and areas for specialization. But Black leaders have positioned it as one launch pad for Black entrepreneurs building the next generation of companies. Hubs such as this would fit into a broader policy push to provide new tech jobs and funding beyond the handful of reigning superstar cities.

TECH AS A TOOL FOR REHABILITATION

Tech pathways can even help in our challenge with incarceration and lowering recidivism rates. The U.S. accounts for 25 percent of the world's prison population yet holds 5 percent of the global population and has a recidivism rate of more than 50 percent. Mass incarceration disproportionately impacts the Black and Latino community, which comprises a staggering 56 percent of those incarcerated. Chris Redlitz, a prominent tech venture capitalist, and Beverly Parenti, his wife and a successful entrepreneur, use technology to provide second chances for those incarcerated. Chris is particularly motivated to help people of color who are incarcerated, recognizing a stint in jail can destroy an entire family's life. As Chris and Beverly have grasped, technical training can be completed from a jail cell with a computer, internet connection, and workstation. Their organization, The Last Mile, teaches software development over two six-month courses to people who are incarcerated, and then attempts to place them in jobs upon their release. This program, which began in San Quentin State Prison in California, is now in four states and expanding. Over seven hundred have completed the program, and about a hundred subsequently found successful tech jobs making up to six figures. Not a single graduate has returned to jail. Adnan Khan, who spent time in San Quentin, shared with me that there are still many barriers for people who receive the training when they enter the job market because they are not "as skilled as those who have learned to code from a young age" and must overcome the stigma of their record. For the program to scale, he believes there needs to be a more concrete link between training and available jobs.

The Last Mile shows how technology can uniquely help people who are incarcerated, enabling them to acquire new, employable skills. The program speaks to participants' creative energy and ambition while helping give them a sense of purpose when reentering society. Of course, it is foolish to suggest that technology in and of itself can solve the racist legacy and structural causes of mass incarceration. We need numerous policy reforms to end this societal crisis, including but not limited to reforming mandatory minimum sentencing, ending cash bail, curtailing draconian drug laws, and expanding reintegration programs. Most urgently, we must root out racial injustice in the criminal justice system. But what Chris and Beverly understand is that, when channeled through a prism of dignity, technology can open up new opportunities even in the most challenging conditions. Our government should partner with The Last Mile or similar programs to scale up to prisons in all fifty states, providing more people across the country with a path to success after prison.

TECH AND SEGREGATION

Chapter 2 discussed how tech's multiplier effect was greater than that of traditional manufacturing, but the reality is that tech's multiplier effect does not lift all boats. There are many neighborhoods within superstar cities that do not benefit from the tech boom. As economist Raj Chetty discovered, Los Angeles, Austin, Boston, and New York—all cities with solid tech hubs—also have neighborhoods with terrible social mobility. These areas are also usually made up disproportionately of people of color. Workers in these neighborhoods have difficulty commuting to provide services to the professional class, and they also face racial and zip code discrimination when seeking work.

Alana Semuels writes powerfully about how young Black men in many of Chicago's poorer neighborhoods such as Englewood are not benefiting from the city's innovation economy, which has seen tech grow from 3 percent to almost 14 percent of the past decade. Semuels cites research from Great Cities Institute showing that, despite this growth, around "40 percent of Black 20-to-24-year-olds in Chicago are out of work and out of school today, compared with 7 percent of white 20-to-24-year-olds in Chicago." The innovation economy siloes wealth into select neighborhoods, far more than the manufacturing economy that featured factories scattered across a city.

In fact, tech growth exacerbates economic segregation. In a trailblazing paper, economists Enrico Berkes and Ruben Gaetani showed that the tech economy often leads to high-wage professionals congregating in certain neighborhoods and then seeking amenities, such as "elite schools or fitness centers" and upscale places to eat and shop. This leads to inflated property values, making it harder for blue-collar workers to buy a house or afford rent in those neighborhoods. They are then pushed out of their hometown neighborhoods and replaced by a gentrifying crowd that flocks to the new Sweetgreen or SoulCycle. Richard Florida, an urban theorist, writes extensively about how the tech-led economy forces workers out, particularly in the service sector, because their wages fail to keep up with soaring housing costs. He believes that "finding ways to mitigate innovation-spurred economic segregation is a crucial project of our times," to prevent an "anti-innovation," "anti-immigrant" or "anti-tech industry backlash."

But what are some concrete steps we can take to course correct tech's track record of excluding and pushing out communities of color? For starters, expanding access to the innovation economy must be supplemented with robust investment in infrastructure and public sector jobs, especially in neighborhoods of color. We need affordable housing in places where tech thrives, so that service workers, who are often disproportionately people of color, are not displaced. Tech progressives often talk a big game about Black Lives Matter but, as Ezra Klein, a *New York Times* columnist, has provocatively highlighted, this has not translated into antiracist zoning policies. I discuss housing policy as well as a host of other equity issues for service workers in tech metropolises in the next chapter.

The most important lesson of Chetty, Berkes, and Gaetani's scholarship is that conversations about spreading innovation must be granular enough to address geographical inequities within tech hubs at the neighborhood level. Leaders like Murali Vullaganti with PeopleShores and Kagan Coughlin with Base Camp are doing just that. They are training and employing Black workers without college degrees to do complex technical work in communities that saw manufacturing move offshore. They set up successful tech centers in Clarksdale and Water Valley, Mississippi, in counties that have the worst social mobility in the U.S. Far less capital intensive than factories, these centers create well-paying jobs within depressed neighborhoods instead of expecting people to move away for better opportunities. PeopleShores, in particular, offers an explicit and inspiring vision for using technology to take steps toward racial healing and transformation.

THE EMMETT TILL TECH CENTER

Marquisha Lester, a single mother to a four-year-old, worked nights at Walmart, sorting clothing from boxes and putting items on the shelves from 11:00 p.m. to 7:00 a.m. Around Christmas of 2018, she lost her $11.50-an-hour job. She was stressed about finding something new and regretted never finishing her college degree at Ole Miss. At the time, she found it impossible to juggle five days of school with a newborn. The employment prospects for a laid-off, young, Black, single mom without a college degree were bleak in Jonestown, ten minutes outside of Clarksdale, Mississippi.

One month later, Marquisha's entire life trajectory changed. The state's unemployment agency told her to apply to be part of the inaugural class for software development jobs at PeopleShores. She never expected to be selected. She had worked as a waitress, as a cashier, and as a sorter—but had never worked with computers. Little did she anticipate that a year later she would be building bots and training others in robotics process automation. She is now a public face for PeopleShores, which excels at training individuals to manage sophisticated, analytical projects. These are not IT call center jobs but are the jobs of the future.

When I spoke with Marquisha, she kept mentioning that she had been to PeopleShores's executive chairman's home. As Jon Livingston, the economic director who helped bring PeopleShores to Clarksdale, explained, that was not a trivial thing. The civil rights movement was not that long ago. Black people in Clarksdale are still "discounted and looked down upon." Murali regularly invited Black employees to his home to have a meal, not as a rich owner, but as a colleague. He shared his dream of having two hundred software developers in Clarksdale and a tech center in every state, and he asked for everyone's help to make that a reality. He treated his employees like extended family. Marquisha mentioned that Murali knew the names of her family members and cared about the well-being of her child. She was moved that Murali treated her and her coworkers with a kindness and dignity that they were not used to. The success of Murali's approach surprised the local establishment. They thought, as Jon put it, that Indian Americans "run cheap motels and convenience stores." Now, they started to think, "maybe the Indian guy is on to something."

Murali ended up in Clarksdale by happenstance. "The world conspires in a positive way to help you if you are doing something good," he says earnestly. He established PeopleShores' first center in San Jose, California, in 2018. A year later, he was searching for a location in a disadvantaged community of color to set up a second center, seeking to prove his thesis that tech jobs could bring prosperity to almost any region. Jon persuaded Murali to choose Clarksdale and helped secure about $500,000 in state grants for building the new center plus an additional six figure grant to set up the program. PeopleShores partnered with Automation Anywhere, one of Silicon Valley's start-ups most responsible for driving automation by designing bots to perform repetitive business tasks. PeopleShores has had stunning success in training young men and women in Clarksdale on how to customize and use these bots. Yes, Murali has turned the leading automation technology into a job creator in a working-class, Black community. The company pays every employee hourly for three months of initial training, which is both a demonstration of the value the company sees in its employees, and a way of making the program viable for individuals who would otherwise not be able to afford the time investment.

During Covid, the company was retained by a state agency to help expedite the processing of unemployment checks. As a result, it grew to seventy-five employees, with an average age of twenty-five, preparing a new generation for promising careers. Consider Spencer George's story. He grew up in Clarksdale and finished his associate degree in automotive technology in his early twenties. But he could not find a job in his field, so he worked days and many nights as a cook at Church's Chicken fast food restaurant for $7.25 an hour. He received one 25-cent raise during his two years there. He applied to PeopleShores after seeing a newspaper ad and is now on his way to making $15 an hour as a software developer. When I asked how he liked the work, he was straightforward: "It's better to have a tech job. I can sit down. Don't got to be tired. It's better. One hundred percent better. Nothing bad to say about PeopleShores." His siblings who work at Walmart and on a factory floor are proud of him, when they're not teasing him for wearing collared shirts.

Despite these success stories, PeopleShores is still in start-up mode and barely profitable. Murali has a clear vision for continuing to grow and hopes to do work for Google, Accenture, Microsoft, and other marquee tech brands. He is convinced he can offer far cheaper rates than other digital service firms and prove that his employees can compete in the robotics industry. But he needed government subsidies to get started to pay up front for months of employee training. On the flip side, it would have been nearly impossible for the government to train people in Clarksdale without the involvement of an entrepreneur like Murali. PeopleShores' success points to the type of public-private partnership that can create high-paying jobs in left-behind regions. It also highlights the need to incentivize companies like Google or Microsoft to hire and retain workers in these communities. Murali has been banging at the door of both tech giants to solicit work from his Clarksdale center; his company is outside their traditional network, but Murali is confident that his team is well trained for the work required.

PeopleShores's Clarksdale center is named after Emmett Till because Murali hopes that it can uplift the talent, stories, and experiences of those who have been written off and bring them to the attention of

Silicon Valley and the nation. He was haunted by a line in an Emmett Till documentary that "a Black man's life is not worth a whistle." Murali's awareness about the historical debt he owes to the Black community and the civil rights struggle drove his decision to go to the Deep South, to a region with the deepest racial scars, and put tech in the service of social justice. The promise of tech is that it can go to even the most depressed areas and offer hope for a better future. The irony is that tech has not ventured far beyond homogeneous spaces. Murali is on a mission to change that. He wants Sundar Pichai and Satya Nadella to know about Marquisha Lester and Spencer George. Never before has it been so cost effective, so logistically easy, or so time efficient, to have the worlds of prosperous businesses collide with talent in the most remote or hardest-hit parts of our nation. We have more tools at our disposal to connect these worlds than any previous generation. What holds us back is only our moral and political imagination.

4

EMPOWERING WORKERS

During the pandemic, Amazon packages arrived frequently at our doorstep. Whether we needed groceries, household essentials, books, or toys, Amazon was often the most convenient and cheapest option. It was the same for many of my friends. They did not want to risk catching the virus by going to a grocery store or mall, so they ordered what they needed online. People I knew in rural communities marveled at the access that they now had to almost any product in the world, so affordably and so quickly. But online retail has a hidden, darker cost. When we opened these packages, we rarely stopped to think about the working conditions of the warehouse employees who shipped our items. We did not consider the functions that Amazon outsourced, and the ethical implications around that. Many drivers, who wore the Amazon uniform while delivering our goods, were considered contractors and did not have health care benefits during the pandemic. While we marveled at our convenience and access, the working class paid the price.

Over the last few decades, this has been a major problem of the digital revolution. The gains from tech's wins are not just unequally distributed geographically and across racial and gender lines, they've also failed to benefit the working class. Instead, many workers have seen their livelihoods or neighborhoods upended and their roles shifted out of sight and out of mind.

Courtney Brown was invisible to the customers she served. She worked alongside her sister as a dockworker at an Amazon fulfillment center in New Jersey. Her job was to load trucks that carried products to customers around the country. She was less than an arm's length away from other workers, and as the pandemic took hold she worked in constant fear that she would contract Covid. In the early months of the pandemic, Amazon's warehouses did not have masks for everyone or even basic cleaning supplies. It did not take long before numerous cases of Covid-19 were reported at the fulfillment center. But Courtney, her sister, and many of their colleagues, like so many other essential workers, had little choice but to physically go into work. They needed the paycheck.

Even though Amazon told employees they would receive paid sick leave during the crisis, Courtney said that almost all such requests were denied. They even had limits on *unpaid* leave and faced penalties for not showing up to work. Amazon was so consumed with delivering for its customers during the pandemic—becoming their lifeline even—that they expected machinelike monotony from employees like Courtney. She worked long days with few breaks. And while Amazon gave a $2 raise to frontline workers at the beginning of the crisis, that was quickly rescinded in June of 2020 despite the pandemic raging well into 2021.

Courtney and her coworkers were packed like sardines during the greatest public health crisis our nation had seen in a hundred years. Customers were first but workers came last, and Courtney understood the absurdity of it all too clearly. As she put it amid the pandemic's first wave:

> We're being told every day that we're heroes, and we're essential, and we're everything, but at the moment, we don't even feel like heroes.

We're not heroes. To be honest, Amazon workers, none of us are heroes right now. We're just scapegoats or we're no better than the masks and the gloves that some of us have that we throw away. He [Jeff Bezos] uses [us] and he throws us away. So, that's literally what we are right now. We're just a money-making machine for him, and we need better everything. We need help. And it's not getting any better.

Courtney's story has echoes of *The Jungle* or *The Grapes of Wrath*. But what makes it so jarring is that such labor exploitation persists in a time of unprecedented wealth and innovation. The business leaders I talk with regularly often acknowledge that there was a time at the turn of the twentieth century when the country needed laws against child labor, overtime, and unsafe conditions. But they like to think of these as the needs of a bygone era, believing that modern-day capitalism has evolved and has internalized Dr. King's lesson that "all labor has dignity." But this self-image is blatantly contradicted by the experience of workers like Courtney.

The unfair treatment of workers is not a problem confined to Amazon. For the last four decades, workers have not received their fair share even as their productivity skyrocketed. As Josh Bivens and Lawrence Mishel at the Economic Policy Institute have detailed, worker productivity over that period increased by nearly 70 percent, but pay only increased by just over 11 percent, defying the traditional principles of market economics. A belief shared by Americans of almost all ideologies is that, as employees become more productive and generate more profit for their company, their pay should increase and their quality of life should improve. But since the 1980s, this simply has not happened.

Carter C. Price and Kathryn Edwards of RAND Corporation have tracked the divergence in worker pay and corporate profits over time. They show that for two decades following World War II, Americans' income growth across the "full income distribution" correlated with GDP growth. But after 1975, the gains started going largely to the one percent. Price and Edwards estimate that "had income growth remained as equitable as it was in the first two post-War decades," the bottom 90 percent of Americans would have had nearly $50 trillion of additional income in their pockets. Now, some of the wealth creation was a result of the genius of entrepreneurs like Steve Jobs, Bill Gates, and Elon Musk, but that cannot explain why our market failed to compensate workers, who are more educated and productive than ever before, for the value they created.

The disparity between the hardships of workers like Courtney and the gains of tech companies became particularly staggering during the pandemic. Apple, located in my district, reached an unprecedented $2 trillion market cap. Amazon, Microsoft, Google, Facebook, and Netflix all posted huge numbers for their shareholders during the pandemic. Tech benefited enormously as the quarantine made Americans more dependent on laptops and apps, and the success of big tech largely explains why the market was so resilient during the pandemic. In fact, in the last five years, big tech stocks accounted for virtually all growth of the S&P 500.

But as the gap widened, the Covid-19 pandemic also gave us a chance, as a society, to reassess the value of blue-collar work and create policies over the coming years that firmly reject the notion that any workers should be invisible. During the crisis, few people spoke about the urgent need for lawyers, investment bankers, consultants, or programmers. Rather, they expressed appreciation for the workers who drove trucks carrying produce, prepared food, cut hair, and delivered mail. Even in a digital age, we are dependent on physical labor.

This book places a lot of hope on the possibility of telework to connect communities and distribute economic opportunity. But telework alone cannot drive our economy or meet our daily needs. A University of Chicago study found that nearly two thirds of jobs in the United States cannot be done from home online. A core democratic challenge is to ensure that these workers are fairly compensated, respected for the value they are adding both to our biggest tech companies and to our broader economy, and empowered to use the tools of technology to make their jobs safer, more efficient, and more rewarding.

The question, of course, is whether our newfound appreciation for physical work will result in a change of policy. Steve Kelley, a custodian at the Four Gateway Center in Pittsburgh, Pennsylvania, is skeptical that will happen. Like Courtney Brown, he too joined Senator Elizabeth Warren and me for a Zoom panel about worker's rights where he shared that some of his colleagues make $8 an hour: "What is that?" he said. "This is what, 2020? And we're living on 1970s wages?" He fears that post-Covid, life for workers, even those suddenly hailed as essential, will just go back to normal. But Kelley does not want normal. "Normal means you put me back in the shadows, and devalue my work," he says. "Will you treat us like we are as important as you are treating us now?"

We must answer Kelley's question in the affirmative. That's why Senator Warren and I introduced the Essential Workers Bill of Rights during the height of the Covid-19 crisis. The Essential Workers Bill of Rights is a new framework built to ensure that no worker is invisible in the modern economy, either during a pandemic or ever again. It is founded upon four broad principles—a family-supporting wage, worker voice, high-quality child care, and affordable housing—which are the main subjects of this chapter.

The moral case for prioritizing workers is that they've been denied the gains they've helped create, and the dignity that they've deserved, for multiple decades now. But the dollars-and-cents economic rationale is straightforward as well. While paying workers more may not maximize short-term shareholder value, in the way that stock buybacks or dividend payments do, it will lead to more consumer spending. Any initial and temporary adjustment in stock market value because of higher business costs and fewer payouts to shareholders can be offset by increased business revenue. For example, if we pay workers like Courtney Brown and Steve Kelley more, then they will buy more products, including from companies like Amazon and Apple. This is in contrast to the relatively affluent stockholders, who will likely invest their gains in more stocks and assets of global companies. Workers will also buy more from businesses in their community and support local jobs. It comes down to a basic question: do you believe that the resilience and growth of the American economy is driven principally by broad-based consumer spending, or do you believe it is more dependent on a handful of sophisticated investors who know best how to allocate capital? Putting more money in the hands of workers is putting faith in distributed job creation and democratic capitalism. It also helps workers determine the shapes of their own lives, rather than just scraping by or relying on government beneficence.

As the prosperity from digital gains continues to grow, it's essential for us to ensure that workers can take their rightful part in that growth. In keeping with four of the main principles of the Essential Workers Bill of Rights, the following sections explore how to achieve dignity and fairness for workers in the twenty-first century.

A FAMILY-SUPPORTING WAGE

During the worst months of the pandemic, spanning from March to April of 2021, America's 719 billionaires saw their wealth increase by $1.62 trillion, more than 50 percent. According to Inequality.org, while many businesses shuttered, Jeff Bezos's wealth increased almost 75 percent to nearly $200 billion, Elon Musk's wealth went up almost 600 percent to more than $150 billion, and Mark Zuckerberg's wealth doubled in thirteen months to more than $100 billion.

Working-class Americans were perplexed at how billionaires reached record wealth while they struggled to pay the bills. They were befuddled that Bezos could make more than $50 billion in months, while Amazon, with surging revenue and a huge cash balance, could not find the money to give Courtney Brown and her fulfillment center colleagues hazard pay for working through the pandemic while risking their own health.

A nation that can create staggering wealth for billionaires should also have the resources to ensure that working Americans earn a family-supporting wage. By this, I mean a wage that allows a person to rent a modest place and buy food, clothing, and other basic life necessities for themselves and their children. To get there, we can combine several important policies.

$15 MINIMUM WAGE

The simple starting point for giving American workers a raise is increasing the minimum wage to $15. This would not simply help the workers at the bottom of the totem pole but would push the pay scale up for many blue-collar jobs. In fact, economist Dean Baker has observed that from 1938 to 1968, the federal minimum wage "rose in step with productivity." If that trend continued, the minimum wage would be $24 today. This is assuming, as Ryan Bourne at the Cato Institute astutely points out, that there has not been a sharp divergence in the relative productivity of high-wage and low-wage workers. And, given the extent to which low-wage essential workers have kept the country functioning over the course of the Covid pandemic, you would be hard-pressed to argue for a vast divergence in productivity.

The constant argument against raising the minimum wage is that it will end up costing workers jobs. That fear is overblown. In their famous paper, economists David Card and Alan Krueger showed that increasing the minimum wage does not automatically result in automation or job loss. They argue that when workers are paid more, their increased spending can in turn create new jobs. At the same time, better-paying jobs are easier to fill. This is consistent with leading labor economist Arindrajit Dube's recent survey that concluded "the employment effects are small"—that is, there's little change in net jobs—if the United States were to shift to a minimum wage up to 59 percent and as high as 81 percent of the median income, which is currently about $19 an hour.

A couple of recent studies caution that a substantial increase in the minimum wage can result in the automation of low-wage work. But even if that is true, the legislation we passed in the House of Representatives that called for an increase to a $15 minimum wage by 2024 mitigates that effect. According to the Economic Policy Institute, phasing in an increase provides time for "employers to adjust to the new standard" and can reduce the automation impact and or job loss.

Interestingly, some of the most recent studies suggest that when there is a high minimum wage, employers do not reduce jobs but instead require a high school degree as a prerequisite. This suggests that increasing the wage to $15 likely means a more educated and productive workforce. Nearly 90 percent of Americans over eighteen have a high school diploma. In short, a significant increase in the minimum wage can help workers earn more *without* taking away adult job opportunities, especially if it is coupled with an investment in basic training and credentialing for workers. Studies show that towns with relatively fewer employers may actually *gain* jobs from a minimum wage increase. When employers have market power, they under-hire because they are not willing to pay the competitive wage and prefer a smaller workforce at depressed wages. Forcing them to raise the wage instead leads to more recruitment and job growth.

Unfortunately, this type of nuanced discussion was completely missing from the withering critique Senator Bernie Sanders and I received when we introduced the Stop BEZOS Act in the fall of 2018. The legislation would require any billion-dollar public company to pay the public benefits of their employees if they were not paying a $15 wage. It was intended to expose the unfairness of taxpayers subsidizing the employees of wealthy multinational corporations, and it worked. Within a month of introducing the legislation, Amazon raised their minimum wage to $15 an hour. In a tweet, Bezos thanked Senator Sanders and encouraged other companies to follow Amazon's lead. But the idea for this legislation did not come from the far left. It was actually the brainchild of Bill Galston, a senior advisor in Bill Clinton's administration. Galston, echoing Adam Smith, made the case to me that no person shipping or bagging groceries should be unable to buy groceries. In other words, employers should pay their workers enough that they don't need food stamps. Billion-dollar companies, by underpaying their employees, leave American taxpayers to foot the bill for government services like Medicaid and housing assistance.

It seemed to us like common sense, but the Beltway erupted in objections to our legislation. The most common fear was that it would lead to mass automation and hurt Amazon's profitability. These concerns proved to be fanciful, of course. Even before the pandemic, the number of Amazon's employees grew by nearly 25 percent, to almost 800,000 in 2019, which was the first full year after they moved to a $15 wage. Most of these 150,000 new jobs were in warehouses, so the $15 wage did not result in automation as the doomsday and fearmongering pundits prophesized. During the pandemic, Amazon hired thousands of new warehouse and delivery workers. By 2020, they were already at 876,000 regular full- and part-time employees, not including temporary and seasonal employees (which, if included, bring the total to more than 1.2 million). They simply did not replace their workers with robots, even with the higher wage. Amazon does have more than 200,000 robots that help move packages across the warehouse, but the skill of picking and placing different packages on shelves is still beyond the scope of robotics. Although Amazon is "chasing the Holy Grail" of having robots do everything that "the human hand can do," that is years away. The company will make that transformational investment regardless of whether they are paying current workers $12, $15, or even $20.

What about Amazon's stock? Did the increased wages hurt its profitability? Absolutely not. In fact, Amazon's stock was about $2,000 at the time of our legislation and was trading at over $3,000 by the time of the pandemic. It should be no surprise that Amazon's profitability and value were barely affected by the higher wages considering the company's staggering $55 billion in cash on their balance sheets and profits of more than $21 billion in 2020.

Finally, thoughtful critics raised concerns that companies like Amazon would refuse to hire candidates who were likely to need public benefits if the company would be on the hook for the cost. But that is why we have antidiscrimination laws. Gary Becker, the late Nobel Laureate in economics, showed that if you make the penalty severe enough, you can deter illegal conduct that is hard to monitor such as statistical discrimination against candidates who may be single mothers or have underlying health conditions. Even if the chances of getting caught are low, executives at billion-dollar companies are unlikely to take such risk if the penalties could be career-ending or publicly embarrassing. What most companies would do is pay their workers $15, or whatever wage floor Congress sets, so they have a safe harbor and are not responsible for paying the public benefits.

Although the increase in minimum wage did nothing to stunt job growth or the stock price of Amazon, we should be clear-eyed about their actions. While they increased their minimum wage to $15 an hour, they did cut stock options and monthly production bonuses for these workers. Some also believe the company's subsequent push to lobby Congress for a $15 minimum wage was a strategic business move to hurt competitors like Walmart. Whatever their motives, research by Berkeley economist Ellora Derenoncourt and collaborators has shown that Amazon's wage hike had positive spillover effects, as other firms in the same commuting zone increased wages by about 5 percent on average in the months after Amazon's announcement. Many of these firms emulated Amazon's wage policy, significantly increasing the share of hourly jobs paying a $15 wage. For instance, Target recently raised its own wage to $15 to compete for employees, and Walmart now faces pressure to do the same. As Dube shared with me, the fact that these national retailers chose a single national minimum as opposed to adopting regional variance suggests the efficiency and simplicity of taking that approach, especially when $15 is now a reasonable floor even in low-wage states. It is imperative that when we raise the wage, we offer generous tax credits for small businesses to compete with national chains.

My biggest disappointment about the presidency of Joe Biden so far has been our inability to get the $15 wage passed despite the president's strong support for the policy. The obstacles have been the restaurant industry, which does not want to see a $15 wage for tipped workers, and powerful corporate lobbyists. We have no chance of passing this through the Senate with sixty votes. Even Republican proposals by more moderate senators like Mitt Romney for raising the wage to $10 contain anti-immigrant provisions placing additional burdens on undocumented immigrants. The irony is these proposals will not lead to many more deportations but will result in less bargaining power for immigrant workers and further depress wages. Recognizing that we will not have Republican votes for a $15 wage, I led a letter with twenty-two House colleagues to the White House arguing that Vice President Kamala Harris should overturn the Senate parliamentarian so we can pass an increase through the reconciliation process, which requires 51 votes. I still believe that is the best way to get this done and an urgent need.

EXPANDING THE EARNED INCOME TAX CREDIT

The route to a true family-supporting wage will be best achieved if we complement an increased minimum wage with a strategic expansion of the earned income tax credit. The EITC is a tax break offered by the federal government that's best understood as offering supplemental income to households who work but fall below a certain income threshold. The tax credit rewards hard work, puts money in Americans' pockets, and incentivizes businesses to hire. Jesse Rothstein, a labor economist, finds that roughly 70 percent of the government benefit goes to the worker directly, and 30 percent of the subsidy goes to the employer.

In 2017, Senator Sherrod Brown and I proposed a bill to expand the EITC and raise incomes for 47 million American households. For families with children, they'll see their EITC roughly doubled. We believe that full-time caregiving must count as work. Workers without children will see their EITC increase by almost six times. Tens of millions of working-class households, namely those without college degrees, would get a substantial raise to make up for wage stagnation over the past four decades. President Clinton once told me something I'll never forget: Beyond the economic jargon, what stagnation means is that people wake up every day of their lives, year after year, with little hope that things will get better. They slowly give up on their plans of buying a decent house and live with constant regret of not being able to do more for their kids. It is a life of diminished aspiration.

A broad, fifty-six-member coalition representing diverse congressional constituencies backed Senator Brown and my EITC expansion legislation because it would benefit a wide swath of Americans. More than half of the recipients of the EITC would have been white and nearly 40 percent Black or Latino. Studies show that most families would use this money to provide better education for their children and invest in nutrition and medical care, which lead to better health outcomes. This would also help families provide for their teenage children, which may be a greater responsibility if many minimum wage jobs begin to require a high school diploma. The total cost of our proposal is about $1.4 trillion over ten years, which is less than the price of the tax cut Trump passed in his first year. President Biden deserves credit for incorporating a substantial increase in the EITC for workers without children for 2021 in the American Rescue Plan . Our work is now to build on that progress.

The irony of the Trump tax cuts is they helped tech companies on the coast much more than they helped forgotten Americans. Apple, in my district, received a tax cut of nearly $43 billion. Much of this money went into stock buybacks and higher dividend payments. What is even more shocking is that Amazon was able to claim a tax rebate of $129 million in 2018 despite U.S. revenue of $11 billion because of tax credits for stock options, depreciation, and capital loss. Perhaps the tax cuts incentivized companies like Apple and Amazon to expand their domestic hiring and spending with domestic manufacturers, but the trickle-down impact on working families was marginal. Real average hourly wages stalled in the wake of the tax cut, and real average hourly earnings slightly decreased for some. An expansion of the EITC would have done far more to improve the lives of the working class.

America's tax policy under recent Republican presidents has been to give tax breaks to affluent Americans and corporations hoping that it will fuel hiring and that this might, in turn, put upward pressure on wages. But a more direct approach is to put that money directly in working people's pockets. Their spending would fuel broad-based and local hiring. Put even more bluntly, if you want to help the working class, just target the tax relief to the working class. Do not concoct some elaborate economy theory that hasn't delivered since its advent in the days of Ronald Reagan.

EMPLOYEE BARGAINING RIGHTS

Marcie Silva, a bus driver for a tech company in the Valley, shared with me that she sleeps in her car and showers at the gym. The company that retains her services does not provide any facilities for her to get ready for work in the mornings. She has very little control over her schedule and is summoned at odd hours. Many times she has had to cancel family commitments or doctor's appointments to show up to work. The indignity is that she's considered an independent contractor, not an employee. She is unable to negotiate any of her terms or conditions directly with the company she services.

Marcie's story is, unfortunately, common in Silicon Valley. Tech firms outsource bus drivers, security guards, food service workers, janitors, and building services to contractors. As Deaton and Case have shown, the economic incentives are compelling to outsource these jobs. If family health care premiums can cost upward of $20,000 for a lower-wage employee making between $40,000 and $50,000, then companies have little incentive to put them on their payroll. The Affordable Care Act, commonly referred to as Obamacare, requires that companies not discriminate against their employees when it comes to providing health care benefits. So instead of providing lower-wage workers with the same health care as software programmers, tech companies hire contracting companies for that work. The contracting companies then offer high-deductible and high-copay plans with lower premiums that cost less per worker. The bottom line is that contract workers like Marcie receive worse health care, have less wage-negotiating leverage, and are blocked from the mailroom-to-boardroom upward mobility that previously embodied the American dream.

The truth is that a family-supporting wage is not going to be a realistic possibility for many working Americans if their jobs are relegated to contract work where they have no bargaining rights and threadbare benefits.

Tech executives will tell you that they are only outsourcing jobs to contractors that are not part of the core functions of their business; this is just good management practice. They argue that Apple's focus should be on designing the best iPhone, Google's on optimizing search, and Amazon's on managing the flow of e-commerce. They do not want the headache of managing thousands of employees and developing best practices in fields where they do not have expertise. But even if tech companies do not want to undertake extensive management obligations, they should still be held responsible for negotiating the pay and benefits of these contract workers by being classified as joint employers.

Prior to 1984, the law would have found that Marcie was an employee not just of the bus contracting company but also the tech employer she serviced. The standard was set forth by a 1965 National Labor Relations Board case, *The Greyhound Corp.*, which held that a company is considered a joint employer if it exercises even indirect control over employment by setting the conditions of the workplace. In other words, a tech company that sets and schedules bus routes as well as the conditions for who can ride them would be seen as a joint employer of the bus driver. This standard was changed in 1984 as the Reagan NLRB predictably limited the scope of the joint-employer standard. In *TLI, Inc.* and *Laerco Transportation*, the Reagan NLRB ruled that an employer had to exert active control over an employee to be deemed a joint employer. As long as a company can show that it is not actively managing an employee's payroll or hiring or firing them, they can avoid the responsibility of being employers.

Many tech companies take advantage of this Reagan-era framework to avoid providing their service workers with the wages and benefits they deserve, but not everyone is a bad actor. In response to the activism of Silicon Valley Rising, an organizing campaign of low-wage workers, some employers like Google and Facebook took constructive steps to pay their contractors well and adopt model standards for how contractors should be treated. They encourage contractors to unionize with their vendor companies, and nearly half of service workers are now unionized in the Valley. At the beginning of this year, hundreds of Alphabet contractors and employees took matters into their own hands and formed the Alphabet Workers Union. The union, affiliated with the well-known Communications Workers of America, will include all types of workers, from AI engineers to contract workers. Although it is a minority union lacking the support of the majority of workers and therefore cannot negotiate for higher wages, it gives employees a structure to voice their concerns and can act as a model for other tech employees.

In 2019, the House of Representatives passed the Protecting the Right to Organize (PRO) Act to reinstitute the broader, pre-Reagan joint employer standard. If this bill becomes law, it would be a game changer for many tech service workers, who will get the same health care and retirement benefits as software developers, regardless of who signs their paychecks. They could force employers to recognize their union if a majority sign cards for it without allowing for anti-union campaigns, flooded with millions of dollars, to manipulate election outcomes. For Marcie, this would translate into a higher wage, a better health care plan, and a better retirement plan. She could negotiate for more predictability in her schedule and better facilities during rest breaks. It should be noted that her tech employer would have no obligation to provide her with the same generous leave policies as they provide their software developers, but as a practical matter it is hard to imagine them discriminating against service workers who are classified as employees. Even so, Congress can require employers to allow workers to tend to their own health and emergency needs by passing permanent paid sick and family leave, as we temporarily did for some workers in our Covid-19 relief bill, and as we did for all federal employees in 2019. Only then would Marcie have, at least, a minimum amount of leave guaranteed.

The most egregious misclassification of employees as contractors concerns Uber and Lyft drivers. For the purposes of illustration, I will focus on Uber because the company had the audacity to argue in court that it is a technology company designing a mobile app and that it is not in the business of transportation. It considers only tech workers to be its employees and views all of its drivers as peripheral to its core mission. Imagine thinking, when you sit in an Uber, that a software developer is servicing you more than your driver! The proposition is absurd, and it failed to impress the court, which found Uber's misclassification illegal under California law. The company then, in coalition with Lyft, Door-Dash, Instacart, and other ride-sharing and delivery apps, spent a staggering $188 million on a ballot initiative to overturn California law in the 2020 election and succeeded. Now, Uber and Lyft have returned to their practice of misclassifying drivers as contractors. The real problem is the arrogance of these ride-sharing companies. They see techies as driving real value and everyone else as dispensable—subject to replacement or eventual automation. How can we expect the working class to embrace the tech industry when the young tech elite often view working-class jobs as accessories to the main pillars of the new economy?

The status of Uber drivers is not just about legal rights. It is also about recognizing and respecting how much value drivers bring to the customer experience. No one would deny the genius of an app that makes it easy to flag down a ride anywhere in the city. The problem is that the Uber drivers working long hours are not fairly benefiting from the gains of that innovation. Uber sits on more than $5 billion of cash. It can afford the additional $500 million a year that properly classifying its employees entails. Even if this adds significantly to its current operating loss, Uber can explore increasing prices for its services or raising more capital at a lower valuation to make it work. Underpaying drivers to cut costs for ride hailers is not innovation, it's regression.

Drivers, moreover, can continue to work part-time as employees. When I taught economics at Stanford, I had a very flexible schedule and taught part-time but was considered an employee. The rules should not be different for blue-collar workers, who want flexibility in their jobs but also the security and benefits of being employees. Classifying gig workers as employees would not be an unreasonable burden on Uber's financials, contrary to the company's apprehensions. Our law already provides businesses with flexibility in how they can treat part-time workers or those with multiple employers. For example, under current law, Uber is not required to provide health care insurance to part-time workers who log less than thirty hours a week. It is simply a red herring to claim, then, that the traditional employee model would sink ride-sharing companies that have many part-time drivers.

The bottom line is simple: workers deserve fair compensation for their work and the basic labor protections that have been established over this country's history. When these are stripped away by legalistic interpretations that leave the most precarious workers with even less control over their lives, then the growing working-class resentment against the tech sector is both foreseeable and justified. We need to close misclassification loopholes and recognize that the digital age cannot become a convenient excuse to deprive working-class Americans of hard-earned bargaining rights.

RETIREMENT INCOME

Matt, a Google security guard and member of the Service Employees International Union, shared with me his anxiety about aging in Silicon Valley and the state of his wages: "I am fifty-eight years old. I don't want to work until I drop dead!" Retirement is a scary prospect for many workers in my district. They have lived through both the 2008 Great Recession and the 2020 pandemic, both of which depleted their meager savings. Their situation is similar to that of the average American worker. Studies show that 45 percent of American workers have no retirement account, and those nearing the end of their careers have only about $15,000 in retirement savings.

Techies and the working class have different attitudes about retirement planning. I have almost never met a young techie who is worried about their future finances. They assume that life will work out fine.

Their charmed existence can make them blind to workers who are often twice their age, putting in long hours, and desperately want financial peace of mind. Workers like Matt never received generous stock options in their thirties or forties. They just want to know they will not lose their house or their modest standard of living once they retire. This means that a realistic family-supporting wage for working Americans needs to take the prospect of retirement into serious consideration.

A community as affluent as Silicon Valley should not leave anybody insecure about their retirement. Workers may put up with techies bossing them around, driving ostentatious cars, or ignoring them in hallways, as long as they know that they are on a path toward financial stability. They can take pride in a job, despite daily slights, that allows them economic self-sufficiency. As Joan Williams, who has written extensively about class, puts it, "For most, the dignity work affords is from what it allows you to buy and whom it allows you to support, not from the job itself." But it is too much indignity to work in the midst of excessive wealth and have nothing to show for it at the end of a long career.

One solution is to ask high earners, including techies, to pay a Social Security tax on earnings above $250,000 that are currently exempt for such tax, so that retiring workers can have more generous Social Security benefits. By doing so, we could provide workers like Matt with a few thousand dollars of additional retirement income every year. Senator Warren has a detailed plan along these lines that would increase the average yearly Social Security benefit from $16,248 to nearly $19,000. Most software developers I spoke to at Google, Apple, or Facebook would not mind paying a payroll tax on their incomes above $250,000 if it means workers who service them can have a decent retirement. They also are open to paying a few percent Social Security tax on their investment income, recognizing that they had the opportunity to build their fortune through stock appreciation that is inaccessible to most workers.

At a time of economic disruption and increased automation, our political class should debate how to expand Social Security versus cutting it. It's surprising that this commonsense observation even has to be made.

If people are more at risk of losing their traditional jobs in their fifties or early sixties because of automation or globalization, then why would anyone push to *raise* the age of Social Security? Because of economic insecurity, 60 percent of workers claim benefits before they reach the current retirement age of sixty-six. It makes no sense to make them wait even longer to qualify for full benefits. Moreover, if the data shows that workers have not received their fair share of economic gains compared to investors and executives over the last forty years, then shouldn't we increase the income workers receive in retirement to account for the disparity?

The argument that somehow a small, additional tax on the wealthy will hurt economic growth has little support in economic literature. Does anyone believe that companies like Apple, Amazon, and Facebook would be less successful if their highest-earning employees and shareholders had to pay a little bit more federal tax? Employees would not suddenly lose their ambition to climb up the corporate ladder if they had to pay Social Security tax on income more than $250,000. They already pay it on every dollar below $142,800; the current cap makes little sense.

Berkeley economist Danny Yagan shows, moreover, that corporate investment would not be impacted by a small tax on investment. It is unlikely that it would have any impact on venture capital and angel investment either. Most investors in these sectors, knowing that most of their bets will fail, are looking for, at least, a 1,000 percent return on a successful start-up. The prospect of paying a few percent investment tax will not deter investment in the next Facebook or Google. Investors are more concerned with assessing the quality of a business plan and the risk of failure than about whether they will make a 950 percent or 1,000 percent return on their initial investment.

In addition to expanding Social Security, we should have retirement savings plans for all. This is the brainchild of Gene Sperling, an economic advisor to Presidents Clinton, Obama, and Biden. President Clinton pushed this idea in 1999 for workers making under $80,000 but faced Republican opposition. Given that income inequality has only become worse since then, the time has come to try again. Currently, every federal employee receives a government match for contributions that we make into a retirement fund. For congressional staff, the federal government matches up to 5 percent of an employee's income based on what they choose to save. Our government should simply do this for every American worker making under $100,000, in both the private and public sector. As Sperling argues, the match amount should be higher for moderate- and low-income workers.

Under this proposal, Matt would receive a federal match for any money he puts away for retirement. A progressive match will incentivize employers to offer automatic enrollment and to increase their contributions to maximize federal money employees receive. This program is an example of promoting mutual responsibility between government and tech to benefit workers. It would also give workers the sense of long-term income security they need to make a wage that can truly support a family through the present and the future.

WORKER VOICE

Work is about far more than compensation. It provides meaning, structure, and solidarity. As the writer and social activist Wendell Berry observes, work binds us with others in society:

> Good work finds the way between pride and despair.
> It graces with health. It heals with grace.
> It preserves the given so that it remains a gift.
> By it, we lose loneliness:
> we clasp the hands of those who go before us, and the hands of those
>   who come after us;
> we enter the little circle of each other's arms,
> and the larger circle of lovers whose hands are joined in a dance,
> and the larger circle of all creatures, passing in and out of life, who move
>   also in a dance, to a music so subtle and vast that no ear hears it
>   except in fragments.

Professionals in the tech industry, including software developers, venture capitalists, and executives, see their work as mission-driven in the way Berry poetically captures. They speak with satisfaction about participating in different teams and working long hours. A sense of accomplishment, though perhaps on a different vector, also extends to many blue-collar workers in tech. Even when facing unfair work environments, they are grateful earning an honest living and doing important tasks that contribute to the company's goals. Whether or not their identity is tied to their specific job title, they are aware of the skill they bring to their work and what that means for colleagues and family members who depend on them.

We need to spend more time as a society asking what a good job means for blue-collar workers in a digital age. Thinking that robotics and artificial intelligence will render such work obsolete is dismissive of the complexity of manual labor. Such prognostications usually come from highly educated professionals who would struggle to assemble a storage box and lack sufficient competence or appreciation for blue-collar work. Silicon Valley techies or philosophers who envision a transformed working class as fungible machine operators are out of touch with everyday reality. What they may see as mundane and easily automatable tasks actually are skilled ones, requiring dexterity, balance, judgment, practice, patience, precision, mapping, and a specific attention to detail. Annie Lowrey, a journalist for *The Atlantic*, writes about how the term *low-skill workers* is offensive and many of them are "physically and emotionally taxing" and require a "great deal of skill." This is not to deny that aspects of blue-collar jobs will be automated and probably to a larger degree than aspects of professional jobs, nor does it discount that there will be job loss because of automation for the working class, particularly in highly repetitive tasks. But Paul Krugman is right to note that worker productivity has "been growing much more slowly than in the past" suggesting that workers are not being "replaced by machines" at some unprecedented scale. The relevant question is what voice will blue-collar workers have in incorporating new technologies and in writing their updated job descriptions?

The question of worker voice is central to dignity. Most of us spend the majority of our days at work. Joshua Cohen, philosopher and Apple faculty member, explains that firms should not be able to exercise "arbitrary authority" over workers and boss them around without taking into account their perspective of the nature of their job. At a minimum, this means that workers should be able to bargain for their compensation and terms of employment. They should have a strong say in what they are signing up to do and their salary. But Cohen goes beyond a call for collective bargaining or unionization that would safeguard worker interests. He is not simply asking that workers be respected as equals when engaging in initial negotiations over their employment contract. He calls for ongoing worker input and engagement in shaping the nature of their jobs. Presumably, this demand for a voice is not something that can be bargained away. Much like our government would not let someone bargain away the eight-hour workday, overtime pay, or safe working conditions, Cohen suggests that the right to meaningful participation in one's workplace ought to be guaranteed as an affirmation of equal democratic citizenship.

What would this look like in practice? At the most basic level, it means respecting the expertise of workers concerning their own safety. Senator Warren and I called for workers and their representatives to be at the table in developing protocols for dealing with Covid-19. Workers like Courtney Brown and Steve Kelley knew what personal protective equipment (PPE) their colleagues needed during the pandemic and what social distancing practices were required. Their employers made dangerous and unnecessary mistakes by not consulting them or their representatives. Another example is Stanford's mishandling of Covid vaccine prioritization based on their reliance on a "a very complex algorithm." They failed to prioritize medical residents who were regularly seeing patients and provided the vaccine instead to more senior administrators and doctors working remotely. If Stanford had asked the people who actually care for patients day to day who had most frontline contact and how to prioritize vaccines, they would have done much better than relying on algorithms.

Beyond safety concerns, workers deserve a voice in selecting their own training programs, building strategies to use technology creatively, and structuring their roles. Joel Rogers, a law professor at Universtiy of Wisconsin, famously laid out the "high road" strategy, arguing that firms that foster worker participation and develop worker talent will generate more wealth compared to firms that use a top-down, command model to get the most out of their workers at the cheapest wage. Rogers argued that "shared prosperity," "environmental sustainability," and workplace democracy were "necessary complements, not tragic tradeoffs," in maximizing revenue growth.

California has had success with the High Road Training Partnerships (HRTP). Private industry and union leaders collaborate to run this program to create high-value blue-collar jobs. Most famously, the program produces green janitors. These are janitors who are trained and credentialed in meeting local and state climate standards, and they have significantly decreased energy and water usage in the buildings they service. They also help promulgate green practices with other employees at their places of work and neighbors in their local communities. In addition to green janitors, HRTP created apprenticeship programs for bus drivers, which teach incoming drivers about customer service, tackling mental health issues, public safety, and conflict resolution. The results have been phenomenal. Rider complaints have fallen, employee absenteeism is down, and drivers are seen as counselors to their regular riders. By involving workers in designing training curriculums that interest them and expand their skill set, these workers see clear benefits and so does society.

How can the high road strategy be applied specifically to the digital economy? As a starting point, employees should have representation on the corporate boards and substantive committees of tech companies. This applies to both software programmers who may not be driven by the same monetary pressures as executives as well as blue-collar workers. Economists have found that when employees have a seat at the table, it leads to more productivity. It also facilitates less knee-jerk and reactive decision-making about laying people off. Most important, it builds social cohesion. If those doing physical work are represented on the board and on various committees, they will have an opportunity to mix and make plans with employees who spend their time on laptops and in Zoom meetings. This interconnection is needed in an increasingly virtual workplace, which, left to develop in its current form, risks furthering the separation between white-collar and blue-collar workers.

Employee perspectives are particularly valuable when it comes to distinguishing between technology that will be productivity-enhancing and "excessive automation" strategies focused obsessively on reducing labor hours and costs. According to MIT economist Daron Acemoglu, "many automation technologies, such as self-checkout kiosks or automated customer service, are not generating much total factor productivity growth." One reason for this market failure is that our government taxes labor at a much higher rate than investments in equipment or software investment. Acemoglu points out that labor is taxed at almost 25 percent, but investments in new machines or software are taxed at close to zero with depreciation, thereby incentivizing technological displacement even when workers are better. Fixing this distortion in our tax code should be a high priority in any tax reform agenda.

Beyond the distorted tax incentives, corporate executives may also fail to appreciate the human dimensions to blue-collar jobs. For example, studies have found that customers are far more likely to shoplift when using self-checkout machines. Additionally, customers often ask to speak to a live agent or store clerk even when they have automated options. How often have you checked out at CVS or Walgreens and either deliberately chosen to check out with the human because it's easier, or tried the automated checkout only to end up needing the worker to come over to assist with the purchase? More promising approaches to automating checkout are emerging—for instance, Amazon Go, an app that scans groceries as you shop, may crack the code—and there is a place for automation to provide consumers with more convenience in their shopping experience. But in assessing how much is needed in any particular context and what type of human interaction will remain helpful, businesses should consult employees actually doing the job.

Worker input can also mitigate the negative consequences of remote work on blue-collar services. When employees worked from home during the pandemic, thousands of janitors, cafeteria workers, and bus drivers lost their jobs. To the extent that teleworking becomes the new normal in the tech sector, the tech demand for blue-collar services may decline. Companies will still need a core group to take care of their office buildings and serve employees food. But they may not need as many service workers as they did when their offices were fully occupied every day. Tech companies can begin strategizing with worker representatives about how the service workforce can provide housecleaning, transportation, and culinary services to at-home employees, and still be part of the company's team culture.

As a final thought experiment, consider the difference providing workers with a voice would make at the Amazon fulfillment center in Kenosha, Wisconsin. The Amazon facility on the west side of town has nearly three thousand workers. The city, after years of deindustrialization, needs these jobs. But they pay less than the manufacturing jobs that left, offer less upward mobility, and require physically exhausting labor. John Nichols, a writer for *The Nation* who spoke to workers in Kenosha, told me that the Amazon workers are treated as "accessories to the robots." Many would leave in a heartbeat if they could get any other job at a similar salary. So is it any wonder that people in Kenosha have an ambivalent view about tech? It is not unreasonable for them to expect more than subsistence jobs. The quality of jobs in these towns matter as much as the quantity.

It would be a game changer if Kenosha workers were to have a voice in corporate committees about their workday. They would be able to speak out against being controlled, tasked, and bossed by electronic gadgets or abusive supervisors. Tech tools must never become instruments for a power grab by the managerial class. Workers could also insist on human interaction with colleagues instead of dealing with electronic gadgets all day long, which becomes monotonous and lonely. Of course, not every Amazon practice is bad. Amazon's A2Tech (associate to technician) program shows some promise in providing upward mobility for thousands of warehouse workers to transition to tech roles. But even this program would benefit from worker participation in designing it and ensuring that it is more widely available locally. Beyond representation, Kenosha service workers need federal workplace standards as well as strong unions to stand up for their interests.

Now imagine if federal policies incentivized Amazon to locate some software jobs in Kenosha—as a commitment to the next generation in the city. These remote workers may still face the risk of being marginalized or exploited by managers sitting in headquarters, but they would bring income and economic vitality to the region. The key is for our federal government to develop a list of specific rights for remote workers, recognizing that a decentralized workplace makes them more vulnerable and less able to organize. These rights should include protections for their physical and mental well-being, which can be strained with long, consecutive days of virtual meetings and desk work.

We need a comprehensive vision for the digital economy where tech does not simply extract value from places like Kenosha but partners with the community to create an ecosystem of good jobs and local prosperity. Cities like Kenosha deserve some share of the trillions of dollars of wealth that big tech is generating; and the workers who help create that wealth deserve to be more than cogs in our sprawling digital infrastructure.

HIGH-QUALITY CHILD CARE

There is a stark divide between tech professionals and the working class concerning access to child care. This became obvious during Covid. Most parents struggled during the pandemic, balancing distance learning at home and their children's emotional needs with their jobs' demands. Tech professionals, at least, had support from their employers. Google, Microsoft, and Facebook offered more than a month's worth of generous paid leave for employees to care for their kids. They offered backup child care for up to ten days, flexible schedules, and encouraged full-time remote work from home. One of my friends at a big tech firm had a manager who allowed him to block out four hours every morning to spend with his kids.

Blue-collar workers did not have these options. Google and Facebook were explicit that the child care benefits they provided were only for their employees and not for their hundreds of thousands of contractors. Those providing child care had to raise their employer's family during the day and their own kids at night. To cope, many blue-collar workers split the seven-day week with their spouses and juggled their jobs and kids to the point of fatigue, leaving almost no time for families to be all together. Some left their kids with grandparents, aunts and uncles, cousins, or older teenagers in the neighborhood, putting at some risk their nutrition, development, or even safety.

The tragedy is that most working families cannot afford child care. The financial cost of child care to American families is astronomical, constituting over a third of a couple's household income. This is higher than in any EU country and more than two times what people in Germany, France, or the Scandinavian nations pay. As a result, it is hard for young parents to move away from their extended family, even for good job opportunities, because they need familial support systems to raise their kids. Many working-class parents will complain about their child care challenges more than even their salary or workplace conditions. Ultimately, all of these factors conspire to increase inequality between tech professionals and the workers who service them.

This is why Senator Warren and I called for child care in our Essential Workers Bill of Rights. We focused on workers like Courtney Brown and Steve Kelley who kept our society functioning during the Covid-19 crisis. How could anyone argue they did not deserve, at the very least, high-quality child care while they took care of our needs? Moreover, why should it take a pandemic for us to understand the basic needs faced by every working parent?

Senator Warren offers a targeted plan to make this happen. She describes child care as "part of the basic infrastructure of this nation," like the roads and bridges that are necessary for parents to get to work. The Warren plan directs federal investment in state-of-the-art child care centers and in-home care programs in every community. She envisions these services being free for any family making less than 200 percent of the poverty line and capped at no more than 7 percent of any family's income. To his credit, President Biden adopted Senator Warren's commitment to affordable child care. Biden's proposal calls for giving families tax credits of up to half of their child care costs, with a ceiling of $8,000. While his plan leaves in place a financial burden on working parents, the proposed subsidy brings child care costs down to be more in line with their cost in other nations. A hybrid approach with direct investment in high-quality child care centers for those struggling to make ends meet, coupled with tax credits for those who would prefer other child care options (through their employers, faith institutions, or nonprofits), is a promising way forward and part of the president's bold infrastructure package that is likely to pass. A refundable caregiver tax credit also should be available to families who choose to have a stay-at-home parent.

Even in a digital age, robots will not raise our kids. So we must consider how parenthood factors into any conversation about the future of work and recognize that a healthy, well-educated child will contribute to a stronger economic future.

AFFORDABLE HOUSING

The final pillar of a worker's bill of rights is affordable housing. To put it lightly, working-class families do not live in the same neighborhoods as tech professionals in Silicon Valley. Their children do not go to the same schools, play in the same leagues, eat at the same restaurants, or hang out in the same shopping malls. My district is a reminder that the class divide within communities can be as pernicious as our divides across race, gender, and geography. Consider that the average rent in my district is more than $2,000 a month, and the median home price is more than $1 million, well out of reach for most working families. For families in my community who make under $50,000 a year, a staggering 57 percent are "extremely rent-burdened," with over half of their income going towards rent. The story of Silicon Valley is as much about these rent-burdened workers who live in low-income housing in San Jose as it is about the tech millionaires and billionaires who build their own mansions in Woodside, Atherton, Palo Alto, Los Altos Hills, or Fremont. Some were forced to leave the Bay Area altogether, and third-generation working families living in the area suffer the indignity of hearing twenty-something techies who just moved in ask aloud: "If they can't afford to live here, why can't they just move?"

The Valley was not always so economically segregated. Back in the 1970s and even 1980s, a software engineer may have had a mechanic or electrician as a neighbor. The engineer's children would go to school and engage in activities with the children of those who worked in blue-collar jobs. But the advent of the internet completely transformed the region. The rise of Apple and Google, both now trillion-dollar companies, along with other tech giants like Facebook and Netflix and thousands of new tech entrepreneurs and venture capitalists, drove property values through the roof. Engineers and computer scientists displaced doctors and lawyers as the new aristocrats, with an unfathomable magnitude of wealth. Restrictive zoning laws in places like Cupertino and Mountain View added fuel to the problem. Residents already wary of how tech companies were contributing to added traffic, a lack of parking or space for local retail stores, and overcrowding of local schools did not want to approve even more development that would bring more people to these cities. The working class—particularly Black, Latino, and other marginalized communities—paid the heaviest price.

The extreme concentration of tech's wealth hurts not only communities that have been left behind across our nation, but also the working class within Silicon Valley. Put differently, tech's unbalanced growth is not good for our country and has negative implications for the Valley itself. People often ask me how I can advocate creating jobs outside my district—what congressman can get elected on such a platform? My initial answer is that more balance in the distribution of tech's prosperity is in the interest of *many* who live in my district and do not want their small cities to become crowded metropolises or their cost of living to continue skyrocketing. The full story is, of course, more complicated. Big tech creates jobs for thousands of blue-collar service workers. That has undoubtedly been a boon for the region in keeping unemployment low, and reflexive opposition to tech expansion in our region would limit opportunities for workers as well as hurt our tax base that funds many social services. But the wages these service jobs pay have historically never kept up with dramatic rent increases, and the overdevelopment of tech without sustainable policy leads to displacement, draining commutes, and even homelessness.

Tech innovation should enhance and diversify a local community, not completely overrun it. A future where everyone in a neighborhood works for Google or Facebook and talks about tech deals and IPOs is boring, myopic, and impoverished. It fosters political thinking that can be elitist and insular, in a way that is unappreciative of the contributions of working Americans, unaware of their struggles and aspirations, and awkward in treating them as equal members of society.

Aside from spreading tech to other parts of the country, what else can be done? We need to increase the supply of affordable housing. Again, Senator Warren has one of the best proposals. She and then Representative Cedric Richmond introduced the American Housing and Economic Mobility Act (AHEMA), which calls for $445 billion over ten years to build 3.2 million new affordable housing units for low-income and middle-class families. The legislation encourages the idea of social housing, meaning that the subsidized units would be integrated in the same building as units for higher-wage residents who pay full market value. This is a better model than traditional public housing, which too often isolates and concentrates low-income families with harmful results. AHEMA also provides funding for the maintenance and rehabilitation of the housing units to prevent community blight.

Warren and Richmond strategically call for $10 billion in education and transportation grants for localities that adopt inclusive zoning policy. This will incentivize more affluent cities in places like Silicon Valley to increase their stock of affordable housing in downtowns and near transit stations. The grants are unlikely to move the needle for Cupertino, which has a vocal constituency opposed to new development and would likely be willing to forgo additional federal revenue. They could, however, have a positive impact on cities like San Jose or Milpitas that already require developers to set aside 15–20 percent of units in new buildings for lower-income residents. Both San Jose and Milpitas also have adopted measures to limit rent increases and evictions. These cities may accelerate their efforts to build more housing and rental units for working families as well as more schools if they receive federal support. Federal incentives can drive local zoning reform while still giving communities the flexibility to have certain less dense, residential neighborhoods.

There is no denying that the technology revolution exacerbated the class divide in the Bay Area. Far from facilitating interconnected communities that this book envisions, tech alienated many working families. The working class does not have a sense of solidarity with techies who keep to their own social circles and often have more in common with friends in New York or Berlin than residents in East San Jose. Many blue-collar workers resent the fancy buses that transport Googlers to their offices, the recent college graduates gentrifying their neighborhoods, and the brash millionaires oblivious to their hardships.

The tragedy is that much of the local backlash to tech was preventable with a concrete vision for including workers in tech's incredible prosperity and in city planning. It is not too late to implement policies that give workers a greater stake in the success of innovation and integrate them in the neighborhoods where tech professionals live. Their experiences, values, preferences, and ambitions must no longer be marginalized from the culture of technopolises, and their voices must be given equal standing in shaping our future. Indeed, it's crucial for our country to find effective ways to close the chasm that has grown between those at the top and our service workers over recent decades. To that end we have a dual mandate: we must build healthy and balanced communities within tech hubs and also imagine how to connect them to communities hundreds of miles away. Progress toward one helps the other—and each will strengthen our democracy in the digital age.

5

PROGRESSIVE CAPITALISM

Even in his late eighties, Charan Das Khanna, my paternal grandfather, took an hour-long walk at 7:00 every morning. Throughout my childhood, whenever he visited us in Bucks County, I set my alarm extra early so I could join him. On these walks he shared his perspective on life, and his ideas have stayed with me through all these years. It was my grandfather who told me that the two most important things in life are good health and education, that it's these which give us the freedom to pursue our dreams.

I'm grateful to have been blessed with both. The greatest privilege in my life was a good education: I have memories of a nursery school teacher at Bensalem Christian Day School telling me it was silly to be afraid of fingerpaint, of my father reciting the times tables, and my mother flipping vocabulary flash cards. There was the high school teacher who dressed as Theodore Roosevelt, a professor who offhandedly remarked that the quietest student is often the most thoughtful, and constitutional scholars who to this day are the sources for my best legislative ideas. These experiences prepared me to seize opportunities that I could hardly have imagined as a child.

Along the way, I have also been fortunate to have had quality doctors to treat my allergies and asthma, ophthalmologists and dentists for regular exams, and emergency care whenever I needed it. The truth is, I often take the health care services I use for granted, much like the water we drink or the air we breathe.

After law school, I headed to Silicon Valley for the same reason many venture there—a vague sense that it was a place where big things happen. It was not an easy decision, however. I worked the summer of my second year at law school at a firm in Philadelphia, expecting to settle down close to my parents and brother. My parents, who were already far from their family in India, were disappointed that their oldest son was moving to the opposite coast, with a flying time similar to that of London. Even so, the call of the Valley was something I needed to listen to, with the hope of being part of one of the most creative places in world history.

At the time, unlike many who wish to make a similar move today, I could at least afford to go to Silicon Valley. Even in the early 2000s, right after the dot-com bust, rent was expensive, and I also had large student loans. I was able to convince an acquaintance to let me pay for a room in his two-bedroom San Francisco apartment. But even at a rate of $1,000 a month for the room, coupled with my monthly student loan payments, I was only able to afford to stay because of the overly generous compensation for even junior law firm associates.

Silicon Valley is where I developed a true appreciation for entrepreneurs. When many think of the Valley, they think of big tech or brash billionaires, but there is more to the Valley than money and fame. There are three attributes that make it a magical place for start-ups and founders—which incidentally are in direct contrast to how Washington, D.C., works. First, people are willing to take risks and are not penalized for failure. This pertains not just to those who give up salary to start a company, but also to the angel investors and venture capitalists who are willing to fund them based on nothing more than a strong business plan and a qualified team. Wealthy individuals in the Valley are willing to make more aggressive bets, including on previously failed entrepreneurs, than their peers in other parts of the country. Second, people think big. There is little interest in solving small problems, but instead a desire to fundamentally change society and to pursue products or services with a gigantic market. Valley entrepreneurs aim not to just improve something, from "one to n"— a techie expression for incremental progress—but to build new products, going from "zero to one." This is not to denigrate product improvement, but to recognize that daring ambition is necessary to drive technology breakthroughs. Finally, those who are unconventional are not shunned. Like anywhere, the Valley has groupthink, but entrepreneurs who differentiate themselves from the crowd still have many avenues to secure funding for compelling ideas. Contrast this to Washington, D.C. Here, risk is avoided because of the potential political fallout of a failed program, legislation tends to be narrow as opposed to aspirational, and most politicians are afraid to buck their party leaders. If Congress were to serve as the board of directors for a company, there is no chance it would approach the creativity or innovation that you see from most successful American tech companies or start-ups.

My belief in free enterprise, then, stems from an awareness of the difference between how Washington operates, with its special interests and stagnancy, and how Silicon Valley works, with the opportunities it creates for scrappy individuals with fresh ideas. Of course, the ways in which these opportunities are distributed needs to be improved; the previous three chapters have shown how tech markets are exclusionary along geographical, gender, and racial lines, and how certain workers often get a raw deal. We need new rules and incentives to ensure fair markets. But this doesn't change the fact that there is great value in giving individuals freedom to create businesses and follow their career aspirations without micromanagement from the government. Although the market imposes its own discipline, it affords people more discretion to pursue novel approaches and bold projects that contribute to human progress than an economic system wholly subject to the whims of a political majority, rich patrons, or a governing class.

As I developed an appreciation for the start-up culture in Silicon Valley, I also noticed something critical: most who succeeded had good health and a good education. My grandfather may have been from a different era, but his insights stand the test of time. Entrepreneurs I met spoke about their favorite teachers—or a parent, neighbor, or tutor—who encouraged them to develop their talents and passion for computers. Mark Zuckerberg's parents hired a computer science tutor who came to their house weekly and his dad taught him Atari BASIC computer programming. His parents also sent him to an elite private boarding school, Phillips Exeter Academy. Bill Gates attended a private school in Seattle that provided him and Paul Allen, a cofounder of Microsoft, with access to some of the world's first computers. Reflecting on the school's impact, he said, "If there had been no Lakeside, there would have been no Microsoft."

It takes not just a visionary idea to launch a life-changing venture, but an environment that can foster and support it. My experiences in the Valley over the last two decades have driven this understanding home and underscored the importance of progressive capitalism for the twenty-first century. We should celebrate a free enterprise system that makes room for and invests in new entrants and bold thinkers, but we also need to ensure markets are inclusive, the rewards fairly distributed, and people develop their capabilities to become active participants in the modern economy. As Joseph Stiglitz, a progressive capitalism champion, puts it, "the true source of the wealth of a nation is the creativity and innovation of its people." The previous three chapters have offered a path toward a more progressive system of capitalism, ensuring that opportunity is more justly distributed. But to create a full vision of progressive capitalism—where everyone has real freedom to develop their goals and excel—we will need to create an ecosystem that ensures health care, education, and a basic support system for all.

EXPANDING OUR FREEDOM

The grand promise of the digital age is the possibility of aligning the aims of political justice with economic growth. Our nation has created unprecedented wealth in recent decades, and now can invest in the development of "substantive freedoms" for every American to foster even greater prosperity over the long term. Amartya Sen coined this phrase, *substantive freedom*, to mean our capability to lead a life we "have reason to value." Different people will have different life missions and will value things differently. Sen's philosophy acknowledges that, and his key point is that each of us should have the freedom to pursue the life we envision. To that end, even if we may have different conceptions of the good life, Sen argues there are some basic capabilities that everyone needs to develop to be able to pursue their ends. Ensuring that someone can develop those basic capabilities is to ensure that they have "substantive freedoms."

Sen's thinking echoes Franklin Roosevelt's famous expansion of the American conception of freedom. As FDR put it, "true individual freedom cannot exist without economic security and independence." FDR's Economic Bill of Rights called for the right to medical care, education, adequate food, and a job, and it is a vision for the type of social development necessary to increase the freedom of ordinary Americans.

The frame of enhancing freedom is important. It is mind-boggling to me that progressives have allowed conservatives to appropriate "freedom" as their constant theme. Conservatives claim to stand up for the freedoms of Americans, but their vision is, by their own admission, limited to restricting state action. It's freedom from excessive government regulations and interference—but it is silent about the most pressing economic and social constraints that Americans face every day. And these too are questions of freedom. Think of the contract worker whose schedule is nonnegotiable and changed at a whim, who has no bargaining power, no health care, no paid time off. Is this freedom?

Progressives have the opportunity to reclaim a more developed concept of freedom, one that reflects the full texture of American life in the digital age. We are for freedom, not just from state overreach, but also freedom to live up to one's potential.

At present, we often defend our policies by appealing to fairness. While a fundamental principle, it needs to be married to the rallying cry of freedom. We often rail against billionaires becoming exponentially richer while the working class falls behind. Some start to believe we are for redistribution for redistribution's sake. But that is not true.

The animating spirit behind many progressive policies is the aim of nurturing the freedom of every American to succeed. We want people to have health care so they can be free to pursue their dreams. We want them to have a quality education so they can be free to explore interesting jobs. We want them to be well nourished so they can be free to study and work hard. Grounding our policies as supporting, instead of curtailing, American freedom is not just true to our goals and beliefs, it will help us win over skeptics to our cause.

Our policies are also pro-growth. They will lead to an increase in national economic output. Amartya Sen, who rejects GDP as our north star, observes that public investments in health care and education create a more productive workforce and lead to long-term prosperity. Similarly, Gary Becker, a champion of free markets, observes that in the technology era, a nation's economic success depends on "how extensively and effectively people invest in themselves." He said that the fuel for modern economic growth are investments in "schooling, on-the-job training, health, information, and research and development." In fact, Becker argued that human capital, which is the "knowledge, information, ideas, skills, and health of individuals," is "over 70 percent of the total capital in the United States."

Sometimes, people wonder how I graduated with an economics degree from the University of Chicago and taught economics at Stanford, yet advocate for bold, progressive policies. They don't mean it as a compliment. If I'm looking for a jab, I provoke them further by pointing out that Bernie Sanders is a product of the University of Chicago! But my substantive answer to critics is that they have not carefully studied the work of economists and scholars like Gary Becker, one of the pioneers of Chicago's school of economics. This is not to imply that Becker, whom I interacted with as an undergraduate, would endorse any of my proposals. But he would certainly recognize nations that cultivate "more educated and healthier populations" grow faster in the digital age.

This book, thus far, has focused on extending high-technology ecosystems with good jobs to communities left behind to foster dignity and economic growth. I devoted outsized attention to the jobs problem because it is one of the most visible causes of contemporary alienation and despair. Sen himself holds that the lack of a good job is an infringement on a person's substantive freedom. He argues that jobless people face "social exclusion" and do not have choices about how to make a contribution to their family or community. Unemployment, moreover, hurts economic growth "because of a wastage of productive power, since a part of the national output is not realized." Sen's focus on employment is echoed by philosopher Martha Nussbaum, who sees "being able to work as a human being" as necessary for a meaningful life.

It would be a mistake, however, to think that good jobs policy is sufficient to overcome the stark barriers to opportunity in our society. Even if we make jobs programs available in places like Jefferson, Iowa, and Clarksdale, Mississippi, we still need an educated and healthy population to take advantage of those opportunities. Sen suggests that every society should deliberate through the democratic process to craft a list of capabilities—what is needed to achieve our life goals. Nussbaum argues that societies can debate the amount of resources to provide for cultivating each capability, but they should guarantee, as essential to promoting dignity, health care, education, nourishment, and a means of generating income.

Influenced by Sen's and Nussbaum's work, my argument is that advancing substantive freedoms requires foundational investments. The central aspiration of progressive capitalism is to cultivate the potential of every American. One part of that entails a widely distributed, well-paying job market that allows them to make use of their talents. An equally important part entails developing the capabilities that will allow Americans to do those jobs and pursue their larger life goals. All Americans should have the opportunity to flourish through their participation in our economy, if they seek that, instead of being confined to look for fulfillment outside of it. This chapter fleshes out how we can prepare Americans for the opportunity to thrive in a modern economy.

MEDICARE FOR ALL

If you believe every person has dignity, the absurdity of tying health care to a job quickly becomes self-evident. Most Americans appreciate that a successful career may lead to a larger bank account, a better car, a nicer house, gourmet meals, and luxurious vacations. But what faith tradition or ethical doctrine justifies denying someone care for cancer, diabetes, asthma, or their sick child, simply because of their economic status. Covid-19 exposed the brokenness of our system, as millions of Americans who lost their job at the start of the pandemic had to navigate the worst public health crisis in their lifetime without insurance.

Of course, the shortcomings in our health care system existed prior to the crisis, even in the wealthiest parts of our country. A constituent of mine from San Jose, Sarah Fay Broughton, died of a sinus infection at the age of twenty because she could not afford health care. Her death haunts me. Her job working with special needs children gave her coverage, but her application for Medi-Cal was stalled in the bureaucracy. Sarah knew that seeing a doctor meant expensive medical bills and calls from debt collectors, so she ignored the symptoms until the pain became unbearable. At that point, she went to the emergency room. But like many uninsured patients, she was given painkillers without proper treatment. The infection eventually spread to her brain, at which point it was too late. Sarah would still be alive if she had health care coverage without exorbitant co-pays and premiums.

We have a moral urgency in this country for Medicare for All. Simply put, it would prevent any other American from having a similar fate to

Sarah, and make health care possible and easier to manage for everyone. The political right caricatures this vision as "socialized medicine," but it's not as if such a system would be a radical experience. Numerous other developed countries have universal coverage, and Sen notes how unusual it is to have ideological opposition to such an arrangement. Typically, the barrier to universal health care in developing nations is that they cannot afford it. But the U.S. "can certainly afford to provide healthcare at quite a high level for all Americans."

So, what is the problem? Detractors purposefly conflate national *insurance* with national *health care service* to scare people. The truth is that under Medicare for All, most hospitals, doctors, nurses, and clinics will remain *private*, and we will need more of them. Currently the U.S. will need more than one million new nurses in the next few years and 120,000 new doctors in the next decade—many in the private sector. A single payer system will help fill these new jobs, by having clear staffing standards and by redirecting the money currently going to insurance and hospital executives to pay medical personnel. As long as we have adequate reimbursement rates, private sector health care organizations and professionals will thrive. Furthermore, national insurance will also increase choice for patients. Every doctor would be considered in-network. This means patients will not have unexpected co-pays or high deductibles when selecting a medical provider. They can keep their current doctor without ever having to worry about co-pays again, or select someone new without worrying about a bureaucrat denying their claim. They will also have shorter wait times. Studies suggest that a single payer system, like that used in Taiwan, has shorter wait times than in the U.S. because of streamlined administration, less paperwork, and ready access to any doctor.

There are other macroeconomic benefits as well. Universal health care will mean a healthier population, which will increase national economic output. As Sen observes, there is "a strong relationship between health and economic performance . . . given the centrality of health for better lives and enhancing human capabilities." Fewer medical liabilities or bankruptcies will also potentially increase consumer spending. Sen points to Japan, South Korea, Taiwan, and Singapore as real-world examples of nations where adopting universal health care facilitated economic growth. There is no doubt that there would be job loss in the insurance industry during any transition. But these employees could work for an expanded Medicare or in other insurance sectors. While Medicare will be administered by civil servants, the program will continue to rely on private sector consultants and partners to bring efficiency and deliver results.

Likewise, when you focus in on the more granular level, a single payer system has positive microeconomic impacts. Firms will not need to pay exorbitant health care premiums and can use that money for wage increases. In fact, Deaton and Case, authors of *Deaths of Despair and the Future of Capitalism*, have shown that rising health insurance premiums are one of the biggest causes of wage stagnation for blue-collar workers, as expensive premiums eat up labor costs. Employers will also face less pressure to outsource or automate low-wage jobs if they do not have to hand what amounts to a high employment tax over to private insurers. Increased labor mobility is yet another advantage of universal health care. Under the current system, many employees are locked into their jobs because they do not want to lose their health care. In a widely read study, the economist Brigitte Madrian estimated that before the Affordable Care Act, the fear of losing health care made employees 25 percent less mobile in pursuing better opportunities. National health insurance would increase our freedom to pursue the jobs we want and would create, overall, freer labor markets.

Medicare for All is pro-business. Aspiring entrepreneurs will no longer face the pressure of clinging to their day jobs to provide health care for their families. Their start-ups will also not be saddled with burdensome premiums, which can doom early businesses before they generate revenue. Midsize businesses, particularly manufacturers, also will be better off. They will be more competitive with Chinese manufacturers without the albatross of escalating health care costs for their workers. Even CEOs of Fortune 500 companies such as AT&T privately say that up to 30 percent of their payroll goes to health insurance. While they are reluctant to wade into a contentious political debate, they would welcome the government taking care of insurance, so they can focus on their core business.

The digital age only heightens the need for universal health care. My father had the same job for nearly thirty years after finishing graduate school, with good benefits and a steady track for promotion. Employer-sponsored health care worked for him. But today is different. There is seldom a culture of corporate loyalty. At the same time, the lack of national health insurance disincentivizes people from taking jobs the market needs, hampering economic growth. It also leaves many without insurance at crucial transitional periods in their life or burdens them with the administrative hassle and uncertainty of changing plans. In an economy where more people are working as independent contractors and where there will likely be increasing pressure over the next decade to transition into new roles, it makes no sense to cling to an old model of employer-based health care.

What about the nearly 150 million Americans who currently have employer-sponsored private health care plans? Their health care will also improve. According to a Kaiser Family Foundation poll, 53 percent of Americans who *have* health insurance are worried about bills they may receive when visiting a doctor or hospital and often "cut back on healthcare." The handful of times people have asked to borrow money from me, it has always been for medical bills. These were families that were already going through the trauma of caring for a child with cancer or the uncertainty of arranging long-term care for an elderly parent; it's enraging that our nation imposes such acute financial stress on families when they're already at their most vulnerable.

Misinformation campaigns often suggest that Medicare for All would do away with or reduce one's choice in private plans, but this is not the case. If someone does not trust that government insurance will be as good as their existing plan, they can purchase supplemental private insurance. Nothing bars them from having private insurance to cover nonduplicative procedures, and many Medicare beneficiaries currently have such policies. For example, if a rich person wants to buy insurance to cover concierge medicine with home visits, a private hospital suite, or foreign travel, they can pay for that. Sen observes that "European examples richly illustrate [that providing universal health care coverage] is compatible with allowing the purchase of extra services for the especially affluent (or those with extra health insurance)." Simply put, under Medicare for All, everyone in our country would have the same opportunity for health care as our seniors.

Of course, even if I am correct that a national health insurance model is preferable for the new economy, skeptics will still ask whether we can afford it. The federal cost will increase as more people enroll in Medicare. Enrollees also will use more medical services because they will not have co-pays or deductibles. Economists express concern about Medicare for All because the utilization rates will go up. Ultimately, it's a good thing if people receive health care, especially preventive care. It is cheaper to prescribe blood pressure medicine now than treat an emergency stroke or heart attack later. Furthermore, while utilization rates may go up, they won't increase beyond what people think is necessary. Most people don't look forward to visiting their doctor or dentist, and this won't change significantly; this isn't like frequenting your favorite restaurant. Taiwan's experience supports this point, as their utilization did not go up substantially when they transitioned to a single payer system.

Contrary to critics' fears about rising costs, MIT professor Simon Johnson and President Obama's former director of Medicare and Medicaid Don Berwick believe our overall health care costs would decrease in a single payer system, because the government could bargain with hospitals and drug companies for lower prices. Studies further show that Medicare for All could lower administrative costs by nearly $250 billion a year. In the end, Johnson and Berwick argue that the federal government can provide universal coverage without raising taxes on the middle class. This is well within the realm of possibility, and I discuss potential sources of additional tax revenue and spending cuts in the federal budget later in the chapter. Medicare for All isn't the pipe dream that critics make it out to be; instead, it's a realistic and sound proposal to enhance the freedoms of Americans and the dynamism of the modern economy.

UNIVERSAL HIGHER EDUCATION

Ivanka Trump's Find Something New campaign aimed to help millions of Americans find work at a time when "jobs are changing." She engaged tech leaders like Tim Cook to deliver the message, and nearly 500,000 people visited the campaign's website in the first two months. The campaign highlighted jobs that do not require a traditional four-year degree, making the pitch that many jobs now require just an associate's degree, online credential, or customized training program.

The problem is that when a laid-off worker or job seeker visits the website and looks into receiving relevant training, they learn these programs require tuition and in some cases have tricky prerequisites of their own. Even if job seekers do qualify, the programs often have hefty fees, leaving workers who are already in a precarious financial position with the added burden of incurring more debt for an uncertain outcome. Columnist Michelle Singletary diligently researched the cost of each credential and discovered that one job required an Apple "App Development with Swift 4.2" certificate for $3,750 and another to become an accountant required a "$10,548 for tuition" at Gateway Technical College in Wisconsin. Who is going to pay for that?

We cannot lecture people about finding new jobs without supporting them in acquiring the credentials they need. The reality is that a high school diploma is now insufficient for most blue-collar work, which increasingly involves some level of technical know-how. Despite that shift, our nation has not made a commitment to extending K–12 education to account for modern times. Nor have we made serious efforts to make free college and vocational education a reality. But we need to do just that. By lengthening the years of public education, we prepare our young people to compete in a globally digitized economy.

Bernie Sanders carried my Silicon Valley district in the 2020 presidential primary because his message that free public college and vocational education gives people the freedom to pursue their dreams resonated. His appeal to young people was not complicated—he promised to free them of their health care costs and student loans, offering a concrete and dramatic improvement in their lives. Beltway critics purposely misrepresented Sanders's policy as free college only for elites. That is untrue. Sanders's proposal also has free vocational training for the trades and free credentialing. If someone wants to learn Apple's Swift programming or the basics of electricity and electric codes, they could take courses for free at a public college or university and receive a certificate. The private sector would have an incentive to partner with the public colleges to offer their courses and internships as part of their campus recruiting strategy. Sanders's proposal would not lead to tuition inflation because public institutions are required to cap increases to qualify for federal funds. Additionally, the plan would ensure that low- and middle-income students have access to grants and low-interest loans to cover the cost of living while in school. This would be coupled with oversight that prevents schools from price gouging with exorbitant student costs.

Some worry that free college would mean that students don't have "skin in the game." But schools could, of course, impose a requirement for students to maintain attendance and basic performance to stay enrolled. For that matter, University of California president Michael Drake cleverly dismissed the "skin in the game" argument by pointing to the current norm among affluent students: Drake paid for all his children's education and they did just fine. Affluent students rarely have to pay their way through school, yet no one questions their motivation.

Others have raised concerns about the unfairness of making public higher education free for the wealthy. But this is political propaganda without much substance. Mike Konczal, a fellow at the Roosevelt Institute, shows only 1.4 percent of the benefits of free college and vocational education would go to the top one percent. Most of their kids go to private universities or to out-of-state public colleges anyway. We do not complain when rich families send their children to public elementary, junior high, or high school—why is higher education different? If anything, it may be good for society if the children of the privileged also attended Ohio State, Michigan, or an HBCU instead of clustering in the Ivies. This is not in any way to knock an elite education, which I benefited from immensely. For a middle-class kid and son of immigrants like me, the chance to study with some of the world's leading scholars is one of the many reasons I am profoundly grateful to our nation. But we could use more diversity at Ivy League institutions, and having a greater economic mix at public colleges may help mitigate the "old boys" network that exacerbates our class divide.

The cost savings of excluding the rich from free higher education, for that matter, is not high enough to justify the administrative complexity of means testing. If you only provided free college to those making under $100,000 and reduced tuition for those under $150,000, it would cost $500 billion over ten years compared to $600 billion for everyone. For perspective, $10 billion annual savings is less than one percent of our annual federal budget. This price is worth paying to support integration and interaction among different social classes in our colleges. As Paul Krugman further observes, "means-testing college tuition relief doesn't save much money" considering that almost all Americans need an education, in comparison to poverty assistance or guaranteed income. He argues that universality makes sense because "it makes the program simpler and the base of support stronger."

If you still have grave concerns about the cost, perhaps it is worth considering this counterfactual to put the cost issue in perspective: we could have provided a free college education or vocational training to every single American over the last decade instead of the $731 billion we have spent in continuing the war in Afghanistan since 2010. Which would have better served us? Which would have done more to promote freedom?

EARLY CHILDHOOD EDUCATION

Nobel Laureate James Heckman has shown that the period from birth until the age of five may be the most critical for the cognitive *and* emotional development of a child, shaping their quality of life for years to come, including their income, intelligence, physical health, and even mental well-being. His work is an amplification of Adam Smith's call for investment in human development but a correction in understanding just how early it must start.

Heckman's revealing scholarship shows that even in a digital age, the highest return of investment is from early childhood education programs rather than high school classes or vocational job training. His research is evidence that quality and comprehensive early childhood development programs dramatically improve long-term life outcomes. An immersive program for children from birth to age three can have a 13 percent annual rate of return for each dollar spent, higher even than the 7–10 percent return for an investment in preschool. The highest return, in fact, is for programs at the prenatal stage, emphasizing maternal health and parental education.

As important as it may be to teach a high schooler to code, it may well be more impactful for their economic outcomes to ensure that we nurture their imagination, ambition, curiosity, emotions, interpersonal skills, and health when they are young. It expands their freedom to pursue many different career options. This is especially valuable in an era when we cannot predict what changes machines or software will bring to the nature of work. Although it should be studied, I would venture to bet that the success of Silicon Valley leaders is more correlated to positive experiences in their early years than a computer science class they happened to take later on.

No agenda for preparing the workforce for the twenty-first-century economy will be complete without a robust commitment to early childhood education. Young children need nutrition, access to doctors and nurses, emotional support, engaged parents who set good examples, challenging activities, and interaction with trained educators who can cultivate both intellectual and practical life skills. We have many siloed federal programs for each of these essential needs, but James Heckman urges us to "coordinate these early childhood resources into a scaffolding of developmental support for disadvantaged children and provide access to all in need."

In my district, Santa Clara County's Head Start requires a bachelor's degree for those providing care and instruction, and it provides a robust nutrition program, conducts home visits to coach parents, remains open five days a week, and facilitates access to medical professionals and dentists. Although not perfect, the program has most of the features Heckman recommends. The problem is that the cutoff income for a family of four is about $26,000. The program can increase to 130 percent of the poverty line, which means they can accept households of four with an income up to about $34,000. But this still leaves out most working-class families in my area. Even more shocking is only 2 percent of children eligible in Santa Clara for early Head Start and only 27 percent of children eligible for Head Start preschool can secure a place.

The explanation for these abysmal statistics is our nation's cruel underinvestment in early childhood education. We spend a total of $10 billion on Early Head Start and Head Start combined: less than 1 percent of the Pentagon budget. Congress has failed to act on Heckman's findings so far, though Senator Warren's child care plan, described in the previous chapter, would make major progress. It is, in essence, a call for expanded and improved Head Start. Her plan would build high-quality centers with wraparound services not just for the poor, but also for the working class and those in the middle class barely scraping by. It calls for a sevenfold increase over our current Head Start spending and provides wide-ranging development resources for every child in America whose parents face economic stress. Those who dismiss her proposal as "far left" should study Heckman's work more carefully. When I talked to Heckman, he did caution that these programs cannot be stretched too thin and must offer highly specialized attention on each child to be helpful complements to the role of the family. The state grants in President Biden's infrastructure plan for universal preschool should be targeted to scale programs with comprehensive approaches such as Head Start and with high-quality standards.

In addition to federal programs, tech companies can help create public-private partnerships for high-quality child development centers. Lively debates ensue whenever big tech moves into town. We saw this with Amazon's HQ2 announcement in New York, or with Google's proposed office park for twenty thousand employees in San Jose. In the case of the latter, San Jose officials wanted the new revenue and jobs, on the one hand. But a vocal group of longtime residents opposed the move, fearing an increase in cost of living, rents, traffic, and further gentrification. They preferred that the land be used primarily for affordable housing. The San Jose Council eventually approved the arrangement by making a compromise with Google, stipulating that the company commit to a community benefit fund for housing and education. What could go a long way is if Google, through this fund, makes a significant investment in expanding early childhood education. Such a model is already in place at Educare California in Silicon Valley, a 34,000-square-foot facility with sixteen high-tech classrooms and a public-private partnership for early learning and teacher training. When technology companies use their wealth to invest in disadvantaged children in their own community, we see concrete applications of what progressive capitalism can look like in action at a local level.

PUBLIC EXPENSE FOR K–12

Despite my focus on early childhood and post-secondary education, it would be a mistake to ignore the importance of K–12 education. This book cannot do justice to such a large topic, so my main purpose is to highlight just how *limited* our federal investment in education is. Currently, we spend about 5 percent of our entire discretionary federal budget on education compared to over 50 percent on defense. More than

90 percent of K–12 education is still funded by state and local governments, even when we know that the development of human capital is the most critical factor for our nation's long-term competitiveness.

To that end, there are a few areas where increasing federal investment in K–12 education will yield significant returns. A place to start is for our federal government to fund special needs education. Many school superintendents and school board members tell me that they cannot afford new technology or new training because of the resources required for special needs students. When Congress passed the Individuals with Disabilities Education Act (IDEA), they committed to funding 40 percent, leaving the rest to state and local governments. Today, federal funding covers about 15 percent of these costs. According to Senator Warren's estimates, fulfilling our promise costs approximately an additional $20 billion a year. Not only will it ensure all students, no matter what their talents are, receive the instruction they need, but it will also allow school districts to invest in art, music, sports, and computer classes.

Second, we should guarantee all teachers make at least $60,000, a reasonable wage for people who often have a graduate degree and are on the front lines of the knowledge economy. The current average salary for teachers is only $39,000—which is below the median national income. If the federal government commits to matching $10,000 of salary for every school district that raises teacher salaries to a $60,000 floor, then we can achieve that level for our 3.2 million teachers by investing less than $30 billion.

Finally, we must invest in school infrastructure and staff. The pandemic taught us how much we still need physical schools for our children to thrive. I have honestly yet to meet a parent who believes that remote learning was a success for their children. What we came to appreciate is that many schools need more resources not only to upgrade their classrooms, hire key personnel, and implement training programs, but also for basic technology needed to prepare students for the digital world. While running for president, Biden called for tripling Title I funds to $45 billion and spending $100 billion on modernizing America's schools.

He delivered. The American Rescue Plan includes $123 billion for K–12 schools, which is "the largest-ever one-time federal investment in K–12 education" in our history.

ADEQUATE NUTRITION

Some days I spend less than 45 seconds on DoorDash or Caviar to order meals. No visit to a grocery store, no effort to rinse or peel produce, no need to cook. I do not even have to drive to pick up takeout. I simply scroll for a spicy dish and a favorite dessert, and with a few clicks it's on my doorstep within a half hour. Think of all the human innovation that went into making it so effortless to provide for one of our most basic needs. Yet it is bewildering that a society that can deploy technology to meet my any dietary whim, suffers from a hunger problem where 42 million Americans, including 13 million children, may go hungry. Those of us who are delivery app regulars seldom think about the young children who go to school hungry or make sure to grab an extra apple to take home for their siblings. I once visited an elementary classroom in the heart of Silicon Valley where a young boy's classmates would fill up his backpack at the end of each day with healthy snacks. I was struck by how aware children are of basic human needs and by how indifferent we are that we lack their capacity for empathetic action.

Social entrepreneurs are using technology to make empathy a more significant part of our digital identity. ShareTheMeal is a United Nations World Food Program app that allows you to buy a meal for a disadvantaged child around the world in a matter of seconds. It is as seamless as DoorDash and accepts Apple Pay. Although the app focuses on developing nations, there is no reason someone cannot develop a U.S. equivalent. Existing platforms like Uber and Lyft are experimenting with this in the U.S. Lyft allows you to round up each ride and donate that to charity. Uber has options to donate to a fund for Uber drivers paying for school or to support the International Rescue Committee. While such programs are limited right now, technology companies can take the lead in building platforms that encourage us to take a few seconds out of our busy lives to donate, volunteer, or advocate for causes that help the least well off in our own communities or the larger nation and world.

Of course, we cannot rely on charity to ensure that all Americans have adequate nutrition. The buck stops with our government to make sure families, particularly children, have access to healthy food. An expanded government role to do so expands the freedom of millions to lead healthy and productive lives. We know that children lacking food have difficulty in school, exhibit behavioral problems, face anxiety and depression, and develop lifelong health impediments—all significant costs to society. Studies, moreover, show that poor nutrition in adults hurts worker productivity.

Fortunately, there is consensus around the policies needed to reduce hunger in America. First, we should put more money in the pockets of families that struggle to afford food. We can do this by expanding the EITC and increasing the refundable child tax credit for families with kids. We should also provide universal school meals, so that every child has food at school, and no one feels stigmatized for eating what their school subsidizes. Senator Bernie Sanders and Representative Ilhan Omar proposed legislation to do that at the cost of an aircraft carrier. Finally, we should increase the Supplemental Nutrition Assistance Program (SNAP) allowance for families, which currently is about $250 a month for groceries. President Biden's American Rescue Plan increased the benefit by 15 percent until September of 2021. We should make that increase permanent; it would cost a little over $10 billion more per year and give millions of families more food security and opportunities to buy healthy food.

There is nothing inconsistent about cheering for start-ups to succeed, celebrating hard work, and valuing innovation while also believing our government has a responsibility to ensure no one goes hungry. The favorite buzzword these days for right-wing pundits seeking to delegitimize any public expenditure (except the Pentagon budget) is to call it "socialism." But preventing hunger is a far cry from socialism; in fact, it is more consistent with Adam Smith's vision of capitalism, on whose work Sen builds, which calls on the government to provide basic necessities to support freedom and promote social cohesion.

TRANSITIONAL INCOME

Every person needs an income for a dignified life. It is not just tone deaf to talk about tech training and opportunities for those who can't afford basic needs, it leaps past the interventions that are needed for their success.

Think back to Ivanka Trump's Find Something New campaign. It ignores the biggest obstacle that stands in the way of people acquiring new skills or looking for or starting new jobs. Not everyone looking to start a new job will have the good fortune of being lent millions of dollars by their father, as was the case for Donald Trump. Most people have families to feed, or rent to pay, or student loans. Many have no choice but to drive Uber, deliver Amazon packages, or work at Starbucks, just to get by. They cannot go months without income, preparing for a new career.

If we truly want working- and middle-class Americans to have the freedom to "find something new," at a minimum, our nation should make funds available to support that transition. Currently, as Gene Sperling has observed, the only federal program providing income to those who lose their job is Trade Adjustment Assistance (TAA), which continues support after a person's unemployment benefits expire. But according to his calculations, this serves less than 5 percent of those typically out of work given its focus on trade dislocation.

Sperling calls for a more accessible "UBI to Rise," which is a basic income for a finite period for Americans pursuing a new career. This would help middle-aged workers who are laid off, as well as young people in their twenties who take a chance by enrolling in an apprenticeship program or coding boot camp. We can have guardrails on this program to limit it based on net worth and household income, while also preventing abusive, repeat uses within a short time frame. This type of program would appeal to working-class Americans who often fear that government subsidies only go to the corporate elite or to the poor and overlook them. It would provide everyone with the safety net to take some risk. You may ask why "UBI to Rise" should be means-tested but not college for all. The honest answer is a truly *universal* basic income would cost a fortune, whereas providing college for all will not break the bank given the low number of wealthy students attending in-state public colleges. As Banerjee and Duflo show, a universal income of $1,000 a month would cost nearly $4 trillion in the U.S.—almost the size of our current federal budget! Well-off Americans are also more likely to be able to ride out a transitional period of no income to make an investment in their future.

Many of us who succeeded in our careers conveniently forget about our own safety nets. I remember when I quit my law firm job to work at the Democratic National Committee for a $1,000-per-month salary in 2004. That opportunity ended up being my break into politics as my work caught the attention of Nancy Pelosi. I knew in the back of my mind that I could borrow some money from my parents to pay the rent if I absolutely needed their help. I also had credentials to fall back on, so I would be able to pay off accumulating credit card debt. We cannot replicate the same privileges for everyone, but we can give people a threshold level of support at critical junctures in their lives, so they can seize promising opportunities instead of letting them pass by.

This is all the more important in a digital age. Tech companies serious about helping create new career pathways for those left behind should pay for training. We saw with the Interapt story in Paintsville, Kentucky, and the Accenture example in Jefferson, Iowa, that successful programs provide a stipend during an apprenticeship. For decades, Americans have witnessed too many job-training programs that do not lead to employment or coding boot camps that charge exorbitant fees but do not significantly improve job prospects. Tech can go a long way to build trust with communities skeptical of the changing economy if they deliver even a limited number of actual jobs, and help deliver the training needed to fill them, instead of lecturing from afar about the need to acquire new skills.

THE LEAST WELL OFF

Not everything is about preparing people for the jobs of the future. In an age when a lucky few can earn unprecedented wealth on the technology revolution, while others are pushed to the street by soaring rents, we have a moral responsibility to support the most vulnerable. We can afford to do more for the disabled, those with mental health conditions, and the elderly poor. Currently, those who are temporarily unable to work receive about $1,200 a month in Social Security Disability Insurance (SSDI), which is almost impossible to survive on anywhere in the country. This starvation wage can lead to depression and stress and make it harder to find any opportunities in the workforce. We should bump that by 50 percent to $1,800, at a cost of an extra $5 billion. We also need an increase in the Supplemental Security Income (SSI) for those who are unable to work on a permanent basis. Recipients receive about $783 a month, but this is again not enough to help many of them meet their needs. At the very least, we should bring the support up to $1,063 a month—the federal poverty line for a single adult.

One of our biggest challenges to break the cycle of poverty is helping children in low-wealth families. Many antipoverty advocates call for a child allowance that would be directly deposited each month. President Biden championed on the campaign trail $300 a month for children five and under and $250 for each child between six and seventeen. This is nearly a $100 billion annual investment to ensure disadvantaged children have food, clothing, and school supplies to have a shot at life. One of the historic achievements of this Congress, under President Biden's leadership, was passing this child allowance as part of the 2021 American Rescue Plan. We now need to make it permanent.

The sad truth is our nation struggles to build political support for government programs that provide benefits to those in need. Many

Americans simply do not like the idea of giving away things for free. Arlie Hochschild's scholarship has shown that working-class Americans often feel that our government cares about the rich, and it cares about the poor, but it forgets the working class. Most are not looking for a government check, they just want better opportunities; and they resent that their hard-earned tax dollars go to those not working while their own wages stagnate.

Still, nearly half of Americans support increasing government assistance to the needy. Perhaps if we put forth a robust agenda to create good jobs, skeptics may be more supportive of universal programs for health care, education, and nutrition that are needed to prepare for them. Even then, it will remain a challenge to build the overwhelming public support necessary to focus programs on low-income Americans.

The most promising approach might be an appeal to faith traditions, as Reverend William Barber's Poor People's Campaign is heroically doing. By organizing around the Christian Scriptures, he reminds Americans that "Jesus said that nations would be judged for how we treat the poor, the sick, the stranger, the immigrants and the least of these." If we take seriously the aspiration of ordinary Americans for stability and pride in the modern economy, and embrace faith-based and community organizing, we stand the best chance of implementing social policies consistent with the principles of distributive justice.

A final observation is that Americans historically have been most supportive of providing financial assistance during times of national crisis. One of my most popular proposals was, along with Ohio representative Tim Ryan, for $2,000 monthly stimulus checks for couples making under about $260,000 or individuals under $130,000 during the Covid-19 crisis. In the case of Covid, government agencies shuttered small businesses and prevented employees from working to stop the spread of the disease. Low- and middle-income families, therefore, had a reasonable expectation that the government should provide some source of income. And our government came through with checks. One hopes that the personal experiences of economic hardship that millions of Americans have had to face during this pandemic may make our nation more empathetic to help those Americans who have grappled with constant financial crisis in their everyday lives, even since well before the pandemic.

PAYING FOR IT

By this point, I imagine some readers have taken out their calculator to tally up the total costs of all of the programs I recommend. It's a fair question to ask how we will afford these investments without risking large structural deficits that could eventually lead to inflation and higher interest rates. But we should begin by examining what we are choosing to spend money on right now. We would go a long way in affording many of these new or expanded programs if we reversed most of the $1.6 trillion Trump tax cut that went to the wealthy and to large corporations. We could also save over $100 billion a year from our defense budget if we simply cut the overseas war contingency fund as well as the funds to modernize ICBM missiles. Even with these cuts, the defense budget would still be left significantly higher than it was when President Obama left office. More broadly, we can commit to stopping our endless wars overseas, recognizing that the Iraq and Afghanistan wars combined have cost us over $5 trillion since 2001. If that money could instead have been spent on jobs, health care, and education for the American people, we would have changed the very culture of opportunity in this country.

We can also do more to increase tax revenue from the wealthy to fund broad-based programs. The U.S. is a low-tax nation compared to our peer Western democracies. MIT economist Jon Gruber shared with me that, at around 24 percent of GDP, our tax burden is lower than any European country other than Ireland, which is an outlier given that it acts as a corporate tax haven for multinational corporations. Even if we raised our tax burden by a few percent of GDP (about $600 billion more of revenue a year), we still would be at the bottom of OECD (Organisation for Economic Co-operation and Development) countries.

The low-hanging fruit is to go after tax cheaters. I worked with

Dr. Natasha Sarin and former treasury secretary Larry Summers on a bill that would staff up enforcement professionals and IT systems at the IRS to audit the wealthiest Americans and corporations. What is unjustifiable is that the IRS is currently auditing lower-income, working Americans more aggressively than the most affluent. Sarin and Summers estimate that the wealthiest 1 percent and richest corporations are responsible for 70 percent of the gap between taxes owed and taxes paid. They believe that we could raise a staggering $1.15 trillion over the next decade if we stopped their cheating.

We can, moreover, increase taxes on corporations and the wealthy who most days wake up richer simply through their passive investments in the stock market. It is outrageous that many of the richest corporations, led by tech companies like Amazon, take so many deductions that they avoid paying anything close to even the reduced 21 percent corporate tax that Trump established. These special tax breaks need to be eliminated by instituting a minimum tax on corporate profits as President Biden has proposed. In addition, most corporations would prefer to pay a reasonable health care tax to fund national health insurance rather than paying escalating premiums to private insurance companies. Eliminating preferential tax policy for real estate and private equity, while taxing financial transactions on stock trades, would also raise significant revenue. As far as wealthy investors are concerned, those with portfolios that make more than a $1 million a year should pay ordinary income rates so they are not paying a lower rate than nurses, police officers, factory workers, and teachers. President Biden supports such tax reform, which better recognizes the dignity of work, as does Warren Buffett, who is one of the proudest and most successful capitalists of our time. Similarly, we should eliminate the step-up in basis, which allows heirs to not pay capital gains tax on the accumulated appreciation of an estate that they inherit. We can do all this while capping the aggregate federal, state, and local tax on entrepreneurs so we still incentivize job creation and innovation.

All of these measures amount to one all-important truth: there is no need to raise taxes on the already burdened middle class or working class. We are all in this together. That means we need the affluent to pay more considering the economic sacrifices that students, blue-collar workers, and even ordinary professionals have already made. We can fund the programs I've mentioned thus far—we can afford a progressive capitalist agenda—without adding to the strain of those treading water to realize the American Dream. Instead, we can find the funding we need by cutting back on our overseas military forays, raising taxes on corporations and the ultrarich who have reaped the lion's share of the rewards of digitization and globalization, and then actually making sure we collect them.

OPPORTUNITY FOR ALL

The Social Progress Index ranks nations across various metrics of well-being to look at criteria beyond GDP growth. It's an approach that is consistent with Sen and Nussbaum's capabilities theory and offers an important perspective on where our country stands and where it can go. Nicholas Kristof, a *New York Times* columnist, recently observed that the U.S. ranks 97th when it comes to access to quality health care and 91st for access to quality education. He also cites research showing that the U.S. has less economic mobility than Canada or Europe. These are eye-opening metrics.

A vision for progressive capitalism aspires to do better. We can celebrate the unique flexibility of labor markets in the U.S. and our boldness in taking risks and starting new companies, while catching up to the rest of the developed world in making sure all of our citizens have a fair chance to succeed.

There is, of course, an important role for the family and for civic, charitable, private sector, and religious institutions to support this goal. Our government should have humility about its limitations in shaping our lives. In an important paper looking at policies in Denmark, economists James Heckman and Rasmus Landersø show that even with generous welfare benefits and significant redistribution, the most important determinant of a child's success remains his parents' education, wealth, and direct engagement. Government can never truly equalize opportunity to make up for the luck of birth. But what it can do is provide families, including nontraditional ones, with guaranteed health care, parenting classes, high-quality education options, nutritious food, and access to jobs—empowering them to act on their love and dreams for their children. For those who do not have supportive families, the buck stops with the government to provide what is needed for basic opportunity in modern society.

When I think of my father-in-law's remarkable success, I am struck by how much his parents, grandparents, and entire extended family believed in him and supported him before he ever stepped foot in America. He was the center of his family's attention and aspirations from the day he was born. Monte Ahuja arrived at the Ohio State University with just $8 in his pocket after a long trip from India. During his first job, he took MBA night classes at Cleveland State University. As one of the few Indian Americans in Ohio in the 1970s, he started an auto transmission business that succeeded beyond his wildest dreams. He and his wife made enough money to provide for his family for generations to come, and to give back to his community by donating to hospitals, schools, and universities throughout Cleveland. They have made a significant contribution to the city they love and to our nation. I admire their journey.

I also believe that those who have achieved extraordinary success, like my in-laws, should pay higher taxes to expand the circle of Americans who can have the chance they did to make a mark. Doing so will not cripple capitalism or stunt American growth. My in-laws have led great American lives, but they are the products of incredibly supportive families and received an excellent education at institutions supported by our tax dollars. While we cannot replicate their advantages simply through governmental policy, we can make it easier for other Americans to obtain some of the basic ingredients that paved the way for their rise. I want their story to be possible in places our country has written off and for people we have abandoned for too long.

PART 2

TWENTY-FIRST-CENTURY CITIZENSHIP

6

INTERNET BILL OF RIGHTS

"Congressman, iPhone is made by a different company," said Sundar Pichai, Alphabet's CEO, with mild amusement. He was at a congressional hearing in 2018, and a lawmaker regulating his industry could not distinguish an Apple product from a Google one. When another congressman pressed him as to whether Google could track his location on an iPhone, Pichai replied, "not by default." But the congressman then failed to follow up with Pichai on the central issues: what *are* the default settings that Google uses, does it always require opt-in consent for every service on every device whenever data is collected, and does it use cookies to track user information? Instead, he changed the subject and incorrectly accused Pichai of making "$100 million a year." The hearings with Mark Zuckerberg earlier that same year were not much better. When asked how Facebook makes money if their product is free, Zuckerberg explained: "Senator, we run ads." The technological illiteracy of Congress is one notable reason why we still lack a comprehensive federal data privacy law or well-crafted antitrust regulations. Lawmakers have not done enough homework to hold tech companies accountable and engender public confidence that they should be trusted to write the rules for a digital age. The dirty secret in Silicon Valley is that Congress will hold a hearing every few months, yell at a CEO or accuse them of theft to launch a viral clip, maybe even publish a blistering report—but then nothing changes and nothing happens.

The book so far has focused on expanding economic opportunity for people and places left out in a digital age. If we seek to spread the footprint of the digital economy to support communities and facilitate interconnections, then protecting our rights on digital platforms becomes even more important. Otherwise, we risk further commodifying Americans and increasing big tech's power. The goal of the second half of this book is to understand how we can protect our autonomy and encourage deliberation online, thereby tackling the vitriol, abuse, and sensationalism dominant in cyberspace and seeking to affirm our dignity as citizens.

The recent "techlash" should not come as a surprise to any student of history. A rush of enthusiasm for a new innovation is often followed by sharp criticism. Most famously, Erasmus, after initially championing the printing press and using it to write many popular books, turned into a major critic. He became concerned printers only cared about profits and filled "the world with pamphlets and books that are foolish, ignorant, malignant, libelous, mad, impious and subversive; and such is the flood that even things that might have done some good lose all their goodness." Today, few would seriously argue the world would be better off without the printing press. But it is not a linear story. It is one of humanity's greatest accomplishments that over the course of decades we successfully built liberal democracies to prevent violence resulting from reactions to written works. We know now there is no turning back from a digital world. Instead, we must put in the work to make it ethical and equitable.

There is a fundamental difference between digital technology and previous advances in human communication like the printing press, radio, or television. Digital technology does not simply proliferate speech but also *extracts* data from the speaker and listener. This difference explains why we need formalized protection of our rights in cyberspace.

Every time we participate in an online platform, we share detailed information about ourselves that is used by others to influence our thoughts and behavior. In the physical world, we of course share personal information with neighbors, colleagues, or even businesses. Sharing basic information is necessary for most human interactions, but no one who steps into a store to buy a coffee is asked to share thousands of data points about every aspect of their life. The problem is that the internet enables a different magnitude of data gathering, which facilitates the construction of full user profiles that follow us wherever we go. In addition to the data we enter directly on their platforms, Facebook, Twitter, and Google use cookies to "track users across the internet" and "collect data about what web pages people visited and what they have done there." Businesses and politicians, in turn, benefit from this data when they target their message on these platforms based on sophisticated modeling of consumer or political preferences. But there are huge potential costs and dangers to such powerful tools. At its most extreme, China has used tech surveillance to imprison Uighurs just for using WhatsApp and is relying on biodata to harvest their organs. As Apple CEO Tim Cook put it in his Stanford commencement address:

> If we accept as normal and unavoidable that everything in our lives can be aggregated, sold, or even leaked in the event of a hack, then we lose so much more than data. We lose the freedom to be human. Think about what's at stake. Everything you write, everything you say, every topic of curiosity, every stray thought, every impulsive purchase, every moment of frustration or weakness, every gripe or complaint, every secret shared in confidence.

Drawing on Cook's profound words, Professor Evelyn Aswad shows in her piece "Losing the Freedom to Be Human" why the collection and use of data for targeted advertising or recommending content poses a threat to our dignity. She explains that users of these digital platforms may not act with true autonomy. The platforms deliberately push content that manipulates users into taking actions to maximize their time online. We live in the attention economy, where more "eyeballs" and time spent online means more advertising revenue. Aswad cites internal discussions within Facebook that revealed "64% of all extremist group joins are due to our recommendation tools . . . Our recommendation systems grow the problem." The QAnon conspiracy theory, which maintains that Trump fought against a cabal of Hollywood and liberal elites overseeing child sex trafficking, initially gained traction largely through Facebook from 2017 until the site banned it in 2020. During those three years, QAnon groups developed millions of followers as Facebook's algorithm encouraged people to join them based on their profiles. Twitter also recommended QAnon tweets, which regularly appeared in their trending news section; and QAnon also thrived on YouTube, where it was actively recommended until 2019 when it was demoted.

Roger McNamee, an original investor in Facebook turned critic, shares Aswad's concern that social media's recommendation engines spread conspiracy theories, misinformation, and extremism online. He refers to the problem as algorithmic amplification: social media companies extract data from users and then feed them advertisements, organic posts, and recommendations that trigger intense reactions and keep them active on the platform. It is as if a nutritionist were recommending ice cream to a diabetic, knowing their weakness for sugar, just to keep the client coming back. Because of the advocacy from people like Aswad and McNamee, Facebook decided to temporarily stop recommending political groups to U.S. users in the lead-up to the 2020 election. It took the January 6 Capitol attack for the company to make this a permanent policy, and soon after it applied the policy globally. But the larger problem remains—Facebook and the other large internet platforms still push sensational and divisive content to susceptible users based on their profiles. Every one of us who uses these apps is subject to subtle manipulation in the content we see, and our data, moreover, can be used to further ends that are contrary to our own ideals.

THE INTERNET BILL OF RIGHTS

Concerned about the dangers tech poses for democracy, Speaker Nancy Pelosi asked me to draft an Internet Bill of Rights to safeguard the privacy and autonomy of the American people online. I reached out to Sir Tim Berners-Lee, the founder of the World Wide Web, to collaborate on the project. In consultation with experts, Tim and I proposed ten principles we hope will be the basis of federal privacy legislation. These principles would apply to both government agencies and private sector corporations, but as UCLA professor Ramesh Srinivasan shared with me, we could provide a safe harbor for start-ups so they are not overburdened at existential stages with regulatory compliance.

Each of the ten principles of the Internet Bill of Rights is described in the sections that follow. When all ten come together, they'll establish a baseline of online protections for Americans consistent with our democratic values. These principles don't seek to put tech companies out of business. The most invasive parts of their business models must change, but our framework is consistent with their own mission statements of encouraging the free exchange of ideas among a community of equals.

1. OPT-IN CONSENT

If there is one law that would improve the online experience, it is to require that users affirmatively consent before their data can be *collected, transferred,* or *used.* This would reduce the unwanted targeting of individuals and the improper use of their data to pry into their personal lives. Most people have no idea how to opt out of data collection. As of December 2020, you could go to the privacy and security settings on your Google Chrome browser to rejigger the settings, but let's be real, almost no one knows where all of these complex functions are. In early 2021, Facebook sent a notification to its users asking if they want data that is collected by third parties to be used to personalize ads they see. This notification, however, does not require consent for the use of data that users directly input into Facebook. Twitter allows for broader restrictions on what the company can do with your data; for instance, users can disable all data gathering after reading a warning that it may make the tweets they see less relevant. But, again, the process is hard to navigate, even for someone like myself who represents Silicon Valley in Congress.

We need to reverse the default setting. Users should not be burdened with protecting their data; rather platforms should obtain consent before collecting, transferring or using it. This does not mean bombarding users with pop-up screens counting on them to summarily consent to avoid the nuisance. Instead, every tech platform should have a data policy section in plain and simple language on their home page. The section should outline the different categories of data and different potential uses, so that users can decide up front what is appropriate for them. A user could make it clear, for example, that they do not want any of the data they enter to be used for advertising, political recommendation functions, or as part of a site's algorithm or sold to data brokers.

Regulations should also restrict the possibility of making access to products and services *conditional* on opting in, as law professor Daniel Solove warns may happen. And they should limit the number of items a consumer can consent to in one click while requiring a clear explanation to consumers about the choices they can make about key areas of data use with different options. All of this should also be accompanied with a comprehensive national digital literacy education campaign for users, which I discuss in the next chapter. Users must know exactly what they consent to.

Many of us would consent to certain uses of our data. Someone might consent to allow their credit card information to be shared with a third-party merchant, their email address or name to be used for notifications, or their location to be used for mapping services. Many may even welcome a limited number of targeted ads, preferring to see ads for television shows that they are interested in as opposed to children's toys. It should be more than a binary choice though. For example, users may be fine with targeted ads for pizza joints or dry cleaners based on their geography while restricting the use of dietary or professional group affiliations in targeted advertising. When it comes to the use of race, gender, religion, or proxy affiliations, those should be strictly prohibited by law. On the other hand, geotargeted ads have been a lifeline for many local businesses that cannot afford television or radio rates and seek to reach consumers online; and they're a useful method of online advertising that can work just as well without requiring a mountain of other connected data points.

Users under an opt-in policy deserve more choice over the type of algorithm a company uses to organize their data. If users want, they should be given some ability to either customize algorithms or choose from a number of options. As an example, they could choose whether they only want stories that match their ideological perspective or whether they want alternative perspectives. In the next chapter, I discuss how platforms can offer choices that improve public discourse. Empowering users also may mean that someone suffering from an eating disorder can decide to block images and advertisements that are not body positive. The decentralization of social media algorithms is already a work in progress at Twitter. Jack Dorsey wants users to have more options over what and how they see content by providing them an "app-store-like view of ranking algorithms" where they can select which ones they interact with. This can potentially increase users' trust in social media and online discourse.

As business models adapt, there is a real risk that low-income users would feel pressured to submit to broad uses of their data given their inability to afford fees. In fact, many Americans may conclude that they are perfectly fine giving up their privacy if they do not have to pay for online services. A solution is to regulate social media platforms so they cannot charge users to participate in a digital forum, requiring any potential service fee be passed on to institutional content generators, such as businesses and political campaigns. Sites could, furthermore, still make money through nontargeted and limited-targeted advertising. More broadly, companies should be barred from discriminating against users who choose not to provide data.

One final consideration is that social media companies can construct profiles about us based on data from millions of similar users even without our personal data. In a brilliant paper, economists Dirk Bergemann, Alessandro Bonatti, and Tan Gan concluded that internet companies are able to infer our preferences and behaviors by collecting data from other people who share "similar characteristics or behaviors." This is what they call a "data externality" that an opt-in consent framework cannot solve. Essentially, the ability of tech companies to construct predictive models means that individual consent cannot eliminate societal privacy issues. At a minimum, therefore, consent should be required not just for the use of our own data, but also for *any* targeted advertising that is directed at us.

The European Union experience with their General Data Protection Regulation (GDPR), which requires consent, provides important lessons for American policymakers as we finally tackle the issue of data collection. First of all, enforcement matters. Many of the member states in Europe, such as Ireland, where most big tech companies have their European headquarters, have been reluctant to go after companies whose brands remain popular with their consumers for noncompliance. They sometimes impose modest fines that are hardly a nuisance for companies with trillion-dollar market caps. In fact, tech companies like Google have increased their market share in Europe post-GDPR, as they have more compliance resources than smaller competitors. Most concerning, the big tech companies were successful in implementing designs to nudge users into clicking a box to give their consent. Regulators must be aware of these dark pattern techniques and require third parties to design consent forms which have neutral default options. Enforcement agencies need the counsel of those who have been immersed in the tech industry to understand trade-offs and counter sophisticated manipulation online. Otherwise, tech companies will simply run circles around them. If anything, the FTC and FCC should recruit techies who are willing to serve, even for a few years, into new technology divisions dedicated to safeguarding digital rights. The motto in Brussels is that "America leads in innovation. We will lead in regulation." But that does not work when successful regulation requires cutting-edge, technical expertise that the EU has candidly been lacking. That is why America, home to the software engineers who are designing these platforms, must lead in creating policies for enforceable guardrails in a digital world we largely created.

In the absence of a U.S. legislative framework, both Apple and Google have made progress on their own. Both banned the use of X-Mode, a tracking software that allowed apps to use their platform, cannot collect and sell users' location data. Apple took additional, constructive steps to build privacy safeguards into its latest iOS 14 operating system on the iPhone. They require any app to get user permission before tracking their data on third-party websites. The Apple privacy guidelines, however, were delayed until 2021 because of implementation challenges, and this shift is just another small example of the root problem. Our privacy should not hinge on the design choice and timeline of software developers or company executives.

2. KNOWLEDGE OF DATA USE

Most consumers do not know what internet platforms do with their data. This was the central problem at the heart of the Cambridge Analytica scandal. The scandal was not complicated. Millions of Facebook users who were friends of those using the Cambridge Analytica third-party app had no idea their data was collected. They were further unaware that Cambridge Analytica then used their data to build models to help the Donald Trump and Ted Cruz campaigns and to advance the Leave.EU campaign supporting Brexit.

Facebook knew that Cambridge Analytica exploited user data well before November of 2016, but never revealed this. Instead, it confronted Cambridge Analytica privately and was falsely assured the data was deleted. If users had the right to inquire about their own data, the scandal could have been prevented or, at least, mitigated. Many different journalists and nonprofits would have submitted information requests, and the magnitude of Cambridge Analytica's data acquisition would likely have become public before the 2016 election. Citizens would have been aware of potential manipulation before casting their votes.

The right to know what is happening with our data is not only fundamental to preempting such shadowy campaigns, but also would lead to more transparency regarding algorithms. As Professor Aswad told me, we should have a right to know what a company's algorithms are "optimizing for," what the variables are in that process, and how they evolve. This does not mean a company needs to disclose every new iteration of their algorithm, which is updated almost daily. Digital platforms also would not have to reveal proprietary information. The point is simply that consumers deserve to have a basic understanding of how content is sorted and filtered for them. This includes understanding why certain content is downranked and why other content appears on the top of feeds.

Why should we impose this disclosure burden on digital platforms when we do not ask *The New York Times* to explain their decision to "accept or reject a letter to the editor," asks Stanford professor Daphne Keller, or about their placement of a story? One answer is that newspaper readers can easily look up who sits on the editorial boards of newspapers and can even direct letters to them, while social media users have no idea who creates the algorithms determining what will be at the top of their newsfeed. More fundamentally, they deserve to know because it is users' own data that is being funneled into these algorithms.

3. DELETING PERSONAL DATA AND ABUSIVE CONTENT

Every person should have the right to delete their personal data from digital platforms and businesses' databases. California's recent privacy law gives consumers the right to delete photographs, email and physical addresses, phone numbers, interests, and preferences. Consumers can ask companies to delete any personal information they provided. There are limited exceptions, for instance, if a business needs the data to complete a transaction or comply with a legal order.

The EU in the GDPR goes much further than a right to delete personal information and gives its residents a right to be forgotten. In other words, Europe allows residents to petition search engines like Google to remove information that *others* may have posted, if it is about their past and not in the public interest. For example, if someone committed a crime in their youth, they may petition a search engine not to link to articles about that incident, arguing that the embarrassing incident is no longer relevant to who they are today. The problem is that individuals' motives for removing past information may not always be innocent. Perpetrators of crimes, including those who violate human rights, may have a perverse interest in forgetting the past to escape accountability.

In the American context, a right to be forgotten likely runs afoul of our First Amendment. This would be particularly relevant, for instance, if politicians or celebrities were to hire reputation management firms to cull the web of anything unfavorable from their past. Their efforts would run up against those websites' First Amendment rights to post such information, especially when relevant for public figures.

There are limited circumstances, however, where abusive content should be deleted. When it comes to cyber-harassment and cyberstalking, individuals need a remedy. Professor Danielle Citron's work in this area has helped bring needed reform to an unregulated internet. Her scholarship in *Hate Crimes in Cyberspace* shows the devastating impact that online abuse has on its victims. The rampant racism and misogyny online include fake accounts pretending to be Black women who put out content to perpetuate the ugliest stereotypes. Citron argues that we need stronger criminal laws to protect women and vulnerable populations online. We also need tech companies to delete abusive content expeditiously. Today, thanks in part to Citron's influence on the public debate, Google Search allows users to request the deletion of nonconsensual nude images, "doxxing content" that exposes personal contact information posted with "an intent to harm," and content that creates a risk of theft, fraud, or violence. Twitter and Facebook both have policies to delete fake accounts and accounts that engage in targeted bullying or harassment. These are all steps in the right direction to address the unprecedented scale of harassment now made possible by the internet and social media. But much work remains to be done so that victims neither have their lives ruined, nor are bullied off our digital forums. America can reject a broader right to be forgotten, due to its potential chilling impact on speech, while still expecting tech companies to remove abusive content and accounts that violate our fundamental belief in respecting every person's right to participate in discourse.

4. SECURITY AND NOTIFICATION

People have the right to expect that companies will take reasonable measures to protect their data online and notify them in a timely manner if there is a breach. But time and again, we see companies fail to do that. Most famously, in the Equifax scandal, nearly 147 million people had their personal information compromised, including their address, Social Security number, date of birth, and credit card information. According to *Wired*, Equifax knew for months its software was vulnerable to attack but took no action to fix it. Even more problematically, it took Equifax over six weeks to notify consumers that their data was compromised, meaning consumers were unable to act quickly to mitigate harm.

There is a need for clear federal standards for protecting data and timely disclosure of breached data, and a new data protection agency should be tasked with enforcing them. Currently, according to Hayley Tsukayama of *The Washington Post*, we have forty-eight different state notification laws for data breaches, all with different time requirements. This creates confusion for consumers and compliance headaches for businesses. Any federal standards need to be carefully constructed, and like any internet regulation, the details matter. There may be legitimate reasons for a delay in notification, as in cases where public disclosure would invite more hacking. A business may need time to build an adequate defense before it acknowledges its vulnerability.

We also need a strong, bipartisan commitment to encryption to secure our data. Trump's attorney general William Barr advocated for tech companies to construct back doors to encryption, to assist with law enforcement investigations. But it makes no sense to empower Apple or Google to go into every American's phone and read our emails, phone logs, browsing history, and texts. No one in government or at a corporation should have the key to unlock every American's data. This could open the floodgates to the kind of digital overreach and surveillance that exists in China with their absolute control over internet companies. Furthermore, the possibility that such a master key could be hacked by a bad foreign actor is reason enough that it should not exist. The same back door used by law enforcement would be vulnerable to hackers, making all of our data even more vulnerable.

None of this is to say law enforcement can't develop their own effective tools to investigate criminals and terrorists. In many cases, they can find information on social media to prevent a crime or imminent attack. They can, moreover, work with certain security companies to break encryption codes as was the case in the San Bernardino and Pensacola shooters' iPhones. The solution consistent with American constitutional values is to oppose the creation of any master key that would be subject to widespread abuse and hacking; instead, we should authorize law enforcement to develop their own capabilities to break codes, and to only use them on a case-by-case basis contingent on a court order.

5. PORTABILITY AND INTEROPERABILITY

The network effects for social media are extraordinary. People want to be on the platform that everyone else uses, which leads to a few big platforms controlling most of the online conversation. Today's online world is reminiscent of the historical era in television when we had three major broadcast networks. As a result, there is a very select group of individuals—mostly techies in their thirties and forties who live in the Bay Area such as Jack Dorsey and Mark Zuckerberg—who have final say over what we see and how it is presented to us.

One way to encourage alternative platforms to emerge is to allow users to move their data to different sites. This would give users more freedom of choice to migrate to a new and exciting platform. Under this framework, Facebook would not only have to allow users to take their friends, network, and profile to a competitor's site (portability), but also would design its platform so core features were in a common language compatible with many competitor's sites (interoperability). A key is to have easy-to-implement standards so users, in practice, can navigate effortlessly between different digital platforms.

If consumers have more options among different digital platforms, there may be more competition for developing robust privacy tools and a range of community standards. Increased competition has bipartisan support, and it would reduce the power of the biggest platforms to dictate terms of use to users.

One important tension within this proposal is that portability can very easily conflict with privacy concerns. As Zuckerberg has argued, the move to data portability is partly what facilitated the Cambridge Analytica scandal. The easier a platform makes it for users to transfer data to third parties, the more risk there is that the user's data or their contacts' data could be compromised. As a result, any portability legislation must be linked to comprehensive privacy legislation so data transfers require the consent not simply of account holders, but also other contacts in their social graph whose personal data may be implicated.

6. NET NEUTRALITY

The internet should be equally open and accessible to every person. That is the principle of net neutrality. Internet service providers (ISPs) should not be allowed to charge higher prices for faster access, block content they disagree with, or slow down service as a result of increased data usage. This is not a technical issue but one that impacts everyday life.

We saw the consequences of the Trump administration FCC's repeal of net neutrality in my district. Verizon slowed down data service for Santa Clara County Firefighters while they were in the middle of fighting the Mendocino wildfire. In fact, Fire Chief Anthony Bowden stated in a declaration that "the data rates had been reduced to 1/200, or less, than the previous speeds." Verizon claimed the firefighters exceeded the data usage allowed in their plan and had to upgrade.

Although we have not seen the most egregious possible abuses within a few years of net neutrality's repeal, ISPs have taken instrumental steps to prioritize the quality of their own streaming services, charge consumers more for faster speeds, and slow down data from their competitors. The risk is eventually these corporations will charge different prices for different internet services and slow down poorer customers while providing the fastest lanes to the highest bidders. This may be a gradual process so consumers become acclimated to the new normal. There also remains a real danger that a broadband provider, if ever it chose to, could throttle ideological perspectives it considers hostile.

Congress must pass a law to give the FCC the power to regulate ISPs as common carriers. Common carriers, such as airplanes or trains, must provide services to everyone at a fair price. The hope is that the digital age—with its staggering and unprecedented potential to connect every person at high speeds—will, if anything, be more democratic than airplanes or trains, and not offer a first-class tier or fast lanes. While money will still be able to amplify a person's online voice, it should not buy them special or faster access.

7. DATA MINIMIZATION FOR INTERNET ACCESS

The principle of data minimization is that companies should not collect more data than they absolutely need to provide a service. Many ISPs such as AT&T, Verizon, and Comcast have figured out that the big money is in data. They look with jealousy at providers like Google, Facebook, and Amazon and want in on the action. So they often attempt to collect data that has nothing to do with providing a phone service or access to the internet, such as information about a person's interests, favorite sports teams, special occasions, or hobbies.

We need regulation to prohibit data requests that are unrelated to the service that companies, including ISPs, are providing. Most such data requests should be limited to the basics, such as a person's name, physical and email address, phone number, and payment information. The concept of data minimization is an important corollary to the need for informed consent, and each benefits the next. Consumers may not know what data is necessary for a service, so they may consent to most requests. Data minimization would ensure that companies could only make appropriate requests, while informed consent would keep users in control of what they agree to.

8. MULTIPLE PROVIDERS AND PLATFORMS

We should have access to a number of affordable ISPs and multiple, open platforms online. The importance of affordability cannot be overstated. The political conversation often focuses on providing people with high-speed broadband so they can connect to the internet. That is important, but there is also a cost problem. Americans pay almost twice as much as Europeans for internet access because we have fewer ISPs. Most Americans either have no choice in their ISP provider or must choose between just two. We need the FCC to require more competition and choice of broadband service for consumers in every market, and we need to support the development of local broadband service, both public and private, as a competitive alternative to incumbent providers such as Comcast, Verizon, and AT&T.

But even if we have multiple ISPs, the dominance of a few digital platforms will still be a significant concern. Bigness in itself is not the primary issue of concern. Large platforms have beneficial network effects and economies of scale. Tech is driving some of the most exciting innovations in our nation, providing an alternative to Baidu, Alibaba, and Tencent in China, and is envied around the world. The industry remains popular in the U.S. as well. Amazon has a favorable rating of 73 percent compared to 21 percent unfavorable, Google has 69 percent favorable compared to 22 percent unfavorable, and Apple has 60 percent favorable compared to 25 percent unfavorable. Those are stratospheric numbers compared to any politician, or frankly, any other American institution with the exception of the military. Even Facebook, the outcast in terms of approval, is at 39 percent favorable and 53 percent unfavorable, making it more well liked than Congress, which hasn't broken 30 percent in over a decade.

But with such outsize popularity and presence in our lives, these companies must not be allowed to abuse their power. Barry Lynn and Matt Stoller at Open Markets Institute and legal scholar Zephyr Teachout have appropriately warned that, as these platforms become essential to daily life, they must not construct artificial barriers to shut out sellers or competitors. How to accomplish such antitrust measures in the digital age is a pivotal question, and it is the primary focus of a later section in this chapter, where I offer a framework for an effective antitrust doctrine for digital platforms.

9. PREVENTING UNFAIR DATA DISCRIMINATION

Artificial intelligence makes it possible to detect patterns in large quantities of data and make recommendations based on that analysis. However, these capabilities run up against rights and protections that are central to this country's ideals. There is a real danger, for instance, that a person's race, gender, class, or religion may be among the variables an algorithm considers, and that these data points lead to forms of discrimination both large and small. Even if an algorithm does not explicitly consider these highly sensitive categories, it could use correlated data that ends up having a negative impact on a particular group. For example, a hiring software program that sorts out candidates based on their level of debt may have a negative racial impact given the racial wealth gap. It would be illegal for any human hiring manager to enact such a policy, and it should be illegal when an algorithm does the same thing. Ultimately, there must be clear rules that impose liability on institutions that use personal data in discriminatory ways or that rely on algorithms that further disparities based on race, gender, or other demographic considerations. I offer a more comprehensive ethical framework for addressing AI in Chapter 8.

10. FIDUCIARY DUTY

Financial institutions have a legal obligation to manage money with the best interests of their account holders in mind—not the institutions' own bottom lines. Similarly, the institutions that hold and manage our data should have a responsibility to act in our best interest when it comes to protecting our privacy, even after we consent to share data with them. Yale Law professor Jack Balkin developed this idea of "information fiduciaries." He argues that people who hold data in today's world have similar professional responsibilities to accountants, lawyers, and doctors—all of whom have firm obligations to the people they serve.

Balkin's point is that a person should be able to hold Facebook or Twitter liable if their data is compromised on these platforms, and if they can show that the platforms did not take reasonable measures to safeguard their data. This standard would incentivize companies to adopt business practices that put the interests of data owners front and center. Apple is a good example of a company that has a culture predicated on protecting consumer privacy, explicitly rejecting the idea of monetizing the consumer as a product. On this issue, they provide a model worthy of study. As the first $2 trillion company, they've clearly shown it's possible to be a profitable tech company without selling a trove of monetizable customer data. Of course, there are still going to be some companies that rely on advertising for their revenue—but if they are in the business of personal data, they need to be in the business of protecting personal data. Under a new fiduciary standard, they will have to do more than convince users to click a box that absolves the company from responsibility. Data exploitation and abuse will only become more daunting potential problems as the digital age advances. To protect citizens, privacy needs to become both a corporate priority and a major policy priority.

THE POTENTIAL: APPLE AND GOOGLE'S COVID-19 APP

Apple and Google design the basic architecture for over 99 percent of the global smartphone operating system market, including China, thanks to the prevalence of iOS and Android. This gave them more power than sovereign nations in constructing an effective Covid-19 contact tracing app. Apple and Google had the authority to decide the trade-offs between privacy and security in this critical piece of technology. Although governments could require these companies to meet certain privacy standards, they had no ability to demand the installation of their own intrusive apps that would transmit individual data to a centralized public health database. In the U.S., moreover, the absence of federal privacy laws gave Apple and Google wide latitude in the design that they selected. Even so, the companies prioritized privacy when designing the app, recognizing that Americans would be reluctant to participate otherwise.

The ultimate design of Apple and Google's Covid app is consistent with many of my Internet Bill of Rights principles, and it is an example of technology designed to meet these standards. The app requires a user to consent before any data is collected, and it offers an easy-to-understand explanation of how the data will be used. There is no centralized database, negating the macro risk of data theft in a breach or the need for deletion. If someone is Covid-positive, then they receive a digital code from their local health department to enter into their phone, which sends an anonymous exposure alert to every user in contact with them while they are infectious. Apple and Google both prioritized the need for interoperability, so the app can work across platforms on any smartphone in the world. They made a concerted effort to minimize the data collected and committed not to have access to the data.

Adoption was the Covid-19 app's main limitation in the U.S. As of mid-October in 2020—almost eight months into the pandemic—only twelve states rolled out the app or a pilot. A number of the state apps could not interact with each other because of a lack of political coordination, even though the design allowed for interoperability. Another reason adoption was slow is that few national leaders or media personalities touted the need to download and use the app. There was no television or social media campaign. Washington, D.C., sent a push notification analogous to an amber alert to all its residents, but it was an outlier in employing that strategy. Many Americans simply did not know of the app's existence. On top of the awareness problem, people had a lurking fear that their data could be compromised.

However, the app succeeded in other countries. In Ireland, nearly 30 percent of the country downloaded the app within the first two days, and in Germany 15 percent of the population did within the first week and more than 20 percent by September. The U.S. adoption rates were dramatically lower, as low as 4–5 percent in many states. Despite the missed potential, the program showed the promise of Internet Bill of Rights principles, especially in high-stakes situations. The information involved was some of individuals' highest risk health data, and despite fears, it remained secure in large part because of the privacy-focused approach that Apple and Google adopted.

ANTITRUST PRINCIPLES FOR HIGH TECH

Although Google and Apple successfully protected user data with the Covid app, their enormous power has appropriately drawn bipartisan scrutiny and calls for strengthening antitrust law. In fact, in October 2020, just as states rolled out the Covid app, the Trump administration, along with eleven state attorneys general, brought a lawsuit against Google because of its search engine deal with Apple. Google pays Apple between $8–12 billion a year, which includes sharing a percentage of advertising revenue they make as the default search engine for Safari on the iPhone. The allegation is that this perpetuates Google's dominance in the search market, where it already has around 90 percent control, and excludes Bing, Yahoo, or new entrants from search on mobile. The alleged victims are not simply Bing or other search engines, but many small businesses and independent media outlets who face a dominant supplier when they buy search ads.

More broadly, there is concern that both Google and Apple exclude key apps and sellers from their platform, preventing new businesses around the country to emerge and reducing consumer choice. The House Antitrust Subcommittee issued a scathing report concerning the anticompetitive and exploitive practices of Google, Apple, Facebook, and Amazon. These concerns about the dominance and competition-stifling effects of big tech are very real. They're essential to consider in an environment where companies can achieve remarkable reach quickly and can hold back the very project of democratizing the digital economy.

The critical question is how we promote innovation while preventing a few tech giants from having the power to reap the rewards and control the internet. Tech giants are anything but complacent as they compete intensely against each other and invest heavily in R&D, acutely aware of the history of AOL, Yahoo, and Netscape. They recognize that tech moves fast, that venture capital spending in new cloud ventures dwarfs their own investments, and that the existential threat to their companies is any discontinuous innovation which they fail to anticipate. Nonetheless, their concentration of resources limits design and creative possibilities to what fits within their own institutional culture and gives them too much power to box out competitors. The sections that follow seek to weigh the main considerations and map out an effective antitrust philosophy for the digital age. We need a balanced approach that holds tech accountable and promotes competition without enacting legislation that is overbroad or destroys services that consumers want. Any congressional action must be grounded in detailed knowledge about how tech platforms work and consider the perspectives of all stakeholders.

ABUSE OF DOMINANCE STANDARD

The EU has an abuse of dominance standard that prohibits any corporation with a "dominant position" from exploiting it and treating sellers or other businesses unfairly. But the EU can only regulate companies to the extent they operate in Europe. Their enforcement capability is limited, and their remedies are typically fines, as opposed to structural change. American leadership is required in order to rein in the largest corporations in history. The Congress should clarify that the abuse of dominance standard should inform the interpretation of the Sherman Act, our country's primary antitrust legislation. The purpose of the Act is to prevent large corporations from wielding their power to engage in exploitive practices that are undemocratic. An abuse of dominance standard would prevent big tech from leveraging their market power to charge premiums, unfairly restrict competitors, or privilege their own products.

Under this standard, Google and Apple's search agreement would likely violate the law. Google should not be allowed to use the revenue it generates from its dominance in search to pay Apple for a default setting that allows it to entrench that dominance. Google maintains in its defense that "people don't use Google because they have to, they use it because they choose to." The company claims that a user can change a default setting "in a matter of seconds." But if Google is so confident in the quality of its own product, there is no need to pay an exorbitant fee to be the default option, given that users will simply choose Google when given the option.

It also is unfair for Apple, which has dominant share in the mobile space, to demand such a premium. Apple should not burden users to go into settings and actively choose Bing, Yahoo, or DuckDuckGo in Safari if they seek an alternative to Google. Instead, the company should prompt users to pick their preferred search engine when first using the phone. For the sake of consumer convenience and simplicity of use, perhaps Apple should be allowed to have some preferred partners who pay a reasonable price to be on that list. The key is for Apple to offer enough options so that one or two search engines are not dominant.

Google makes a serious argument that its deal with Apple is similar to a cereal brand paying for a premier shelf. But this objection does not consider its or Apple's dominance. Paying for premier shelf space is not as innocent as it sounds when you are dealing with companies that have dominant market share in a service that almost every small business in the nation needs. That is why tech giants should not be allowed to enter promotional agreements that give them a significant leg up on widely used digital platforms. The outlawing of such arrangements might lead Apple to create its own search engine, an event that Google fears. But more competition and multiple search engines will benefit the consumer and small businesses looking to advertise.

Microsoft's antitrust settlement from 2001 is instructive as it prohibited the company from entering into agreements with third parties that would exclude rivals, thereby opening space for new competitors like Google to emerge. The irony is that the original push for antitrust enforcement against a tech giant came from companies like Sun Microsystems, Novell, and Netscape based in Silicon Valley! Think about it this way: in a world where Microsoft's anticompetitive practices were never curbed, today we might find ourselves searching with Bing and using Internet Explorer with no other options. When companies must compete on fair grounds, users win. Ultimately, despite hand-wringing about the new regulations it faced, Microsoft continued to thrive. The company grew from a market cap of about $260 billion in 2002 to nearly $2 trillion by April of 2021, which makes it one of the most prosperous ever.

An abuse of dominance standard would also curb some of Amazon's most egregious practices. Amazon controls more than 50 percent of online retail sales and leverages its market power to impose terms on small businesses. For example, Lina Khan, the current FTC chair, has observed that Amazon manipulates who has access to their "Buy Box," requiring them to purchase Amazon's delivery services. The Buy Box is what allows consumers to add a product directly to their shopping cart with a click and is responsible for 82 percent of sales on the platform. Amazon's bullying of sellers to use fulfillment centers in order to access the Buy Box is not only potentially an illegal tying arrangement, but also an abuse of dominance. Khan, moreover, argues that Amazon's practice of charging merchants ancillary fees for advertising, in hopes of securing a prominent ranking, is taking advantage of its platform power. What may be most problematic is Amazon's manipulation of its algorithm to privilege its own products in search via its website. Under an abuse of dominance standard, Amazon would be prohibited from favoring its own products over competitors who are offering better prices. And it would be forced to change many of the practices it uses to bully third parties and other retailers.

DUTY TO DEAL FAIRLY

United States case law gives tech companies too much latitude in controlling their digital platforms. The presumption in the case law is that a company is allowed to control who can design apps, interface, and sell on its platforms. In *Sambreel Holdings LLC v. Facebook, Inc.* (S.D. Cal. 2012), a California federal district court held that Facebook was within its right to kick off a third-party app developer competing for advertising dollars on its platform. The court said, "Facebook has a right to control its product, and to establish the terms with which its users, application developers, and advertisers must comply in order to utilize this product."

The problem with giving tech companies autonomy over their platforms is that too many people and businesses have come to depend on them. Many small business owners will attest that Facebook and Google ads are critical for their survival and growth. Retailers would say the same about access to Amazon's site, and app developers about accessing Apple's App Store.

We should categorize these digital platforms as "essential facilities" because sellers and consumers would be severely harmed without access to them. Although the essential facilities doctrine originated in the

United States, Europe developed it more fully. Under European law, if a tech company has a dominant position and a platform that is for other businesses to compete, then they have a duty to deal fairly with third-party sellers. The presumption is that they must allow other companies to design for their platform or sell on it, unless it is obvious that doing so would harm consumers. The U.S. Congress should make explicit that a duty to deal fairly is required by our Sherman Act and should, more generally, lessen the pleading requirements on government and plaintiffs for antitrust cases so courts do not continue to dismiss them as a matter of routine.

It's worth noting that deeming digital platforms "essential facilities" is very different from making them public utilities, which would prescribe their rate of return and involve the government dictating many aspects of how they can run their business. Digital platforms should be free to innovate and design their own business models, but not to arbitrarily or unfairly disadvantage other merchants.

The line between innovation and exploitation is not easy to draw. This tension is most apparent when deciding whether tech companies should be allowed to add new features to their existing product. We want companies to improve on their product design, including integrating new functions, provided they are not hurting competition in clearly distinct product markets. The semiconductor chip is a classic example of an integrated product with many components that clearly serves the consumer interest. The judgment about whether a new feature constitutes a product improvement or a separate product has always been difficult to strike in antitrust jurisprudence and is highly fact intensive. It requires careful deliberation by judges and juries about what benefits the consumer experience versus what is exclusionary conduct that leverages market power—not general political sound bites.

The key is to insist on a balancing test when applying the duty to deal fairly standard. Consider the Facebook example. While the company could continue to add new features to its site, it would no longer have the presumption of denying access to third-party apps that seek to build on its platform. If Facebook has concerns about the quality or data security of a third-party app, the company could make a case for refusing to deal with that vendor. But Facebook would have to show that consumers or the public benefit from any denial.

Under a duty to deal fairly standard, Facebook would likely need to make their site interoperable with other platforms and enable data portability consistent with the principles of the Internet Bill of Rights. According to the United Kingdom's Competition & Markets Authority July 2020 report, Facebook's "limited interoperability" with other social media companies is a source of its market power. Currently, Facebook has a "Download Your Information" feature that only allows downloads of data into a zipped file or PDF which is hard to transfer and make useful. The company would need to go further, designing their site so a person can either export their FB friends easily or communicate with them through a different social media site, provided the contacts consent to any of their personal data being transferred.

Apple would also have to open their platforms to more vendors at a reasonable price. Apple maintains strict control over its App Store, citing privacy and quality concerns. Under the new doctrine, Apple would still be able to maintain control of its operating system, but it would be required to allow competitors to sell their products directly to iPhone users provided they comply with its standards. These competitors would have to pay fair value for the use and upkeep of Apple's platform but not its current excessive 30 percent commission. If Apple has genuine reason to believe an app violates privacy and cybersecurity standards or their terms of service, it would have to show that, as it did when it expelled Parler from the Apple Store. If Parler was merely an app for conservative discourse and banned because of ideological concerns such exclusion would be unjustified. But Parler became a forum for organizing mob violence and assassination plots, and its repeated refusal to take down violent content was enough justification for Apple to refuse to do business with Parler. Notably, Apple has already voluntarily taken a positive step to open its platform by reducing the commission to 15 percent for entrepreneurs with under $1 million in revenue. They should lower it further to expand access to the digital economy for app developers across our nation, but this move should not shield them from appropriate antitrust scrutiny with the larger players.

Similarly, Google Search would have to allow users who type in a location to choose from multiple map services unless it could show that would be a bad user experience by making the interface too busy and unnecessarily complicated. The company would face a presumption of not privileging its own distinct services or products on its platform which it could overcome by demonstrating consumer or public benefit. Finally, Amazon would be prohibited from arbitrarily kicking merchants off its platform, deprioritizing their rankings, or preventing them from using the Buy Box.

Big tech will undoubtedly push back on regulating business decisions they make about their own platforms, arguing that it will sacrifice quality, encourage freeloading off their work, and disincentivize or slow down investments in innovation. On balance, however, it stops short of reflexively breaking them up or making them public utilities and will give millions of Americans and small businesses more opportunity to thrive in the digital economy.

RIGHT TO REPAIR

When you break your smartphone or laptop, you're stuck with sending it back to the companies to fix it. Why? Most big tech companies will place many restrictions on sharing the parts and tools needed to fix their products. They do not want you to take your smartphone down to your local repair shop, or tinker with it yourself. They prefer you send it back to them or purchase their newest model. This is why we should pass right to repair legislation. Not only will it cut down on the environmental impact of our consumer economy, especially given tech products' significant toll on our planet, but it will also empower the do-it-yourself culture across the country in small towns and rural America. It will allow tinkerers across the country to participate in the tech economy by fixing their iPhone, without having to always take direction from the engineers in Cupertino.

LIMITING MERGERS

According to the American Antitrust Institute, over the last three decades big tech conducted over seven hundred mergers and acquisitions. The report finds Google did 234 such deals, Microsoft did 221, Apple did 108, Amazon 83, and Facebook 77. Shockingly, federal agencies challenged only one of these deals—"the Google–ITA Software, Inc. matter"—in federal court. Since Robert Bork made his famous argument in the 1970s that mergers often improve efficiency and consumer welfare, agencies have been too deferential to businesses that seek to acquire other companies to improve their own product and bring the price of goods down. Since then, numerous industries, tech included, have come to be dominated by a handful of powerful players, and mergers and acquisitions have shown no sign of slowing down in recent years.

There is no doubt that many of these acquisitions are pro-competition. As a practical matter, many entrepreneurs in Silicon Valley hope to be acquired as part of their exit strategy. If we were to severely restrict big tech from engaging in acquisitions, then a lot of the funding would dry up for tech start-ups. The innovation that happens outside these companies may move in-house, depriving entrepreneurs of equity and limiting out-of-the-box approaches and thinking. There is little reason to oppose many midsize acquisitions, particularly in the range of $50 million to $100 million, that improve consumer experience on a digital platform, are not with potential competitors, and create wealth for founders who are independent of big tech.

The problem is that tech giants also engage in mergers to prevent rivals from emerging and to lock in their network advantage. Facebook's $1 billion acquisition of Instagram and $19 billion acquisition of WhatsApp reduced competition. Those who follow Silicon Valley deals knew at the time that these were preemptive moves by the incumbents to prevent losing market share. Although Facebook accelerated Instagram's and WhatsApp's growth, both of those platforms were already growing and attracting unique demographics. That is precisely why Facebook paid billions to acquire them.

Those acquisitions should not have been approved. Last year, almost every state and the Federal Trade Commission agreed, and they took it a step further. They filed lawsuits to unwind WhatsApp and Instagram from Facebook. The lawsuits, which stem from an eighteen-month investigation into the companies' behavior, allege that Facebook partook in anticompetitive behavior, squashed rivals, and stifled innovation with these mergers. Although a federal district court dismissed the initial complaint, the FTC can revise the deficiencies with more specific allegations of Facebook's monopoly power, and they can appeal as well. The legal proceedings against Facebook should be fact-based and consider all factors. The intermingling of platforms, data, employees, and product features will make unwinding code and teams complicated. But if there is a clear showing that splitting up the companies will lead to more competition and innovation, then the benefits will likely outweigh these costs. There is precedent for separation, as well. When the government broke AT&T into a long-distance company and seven different regional ones, Americans benefited from lower prices and increased competition.

But instead of just breaking up companies after the fact, we need a stricter standard *before* companies acquire potential rivals. Currently, the Department of Justice and FTC must make a detailed showing of how acquiring a potential rival hurts competition and harms the consumer before they can block the action. We should change the burden of proof and require dominant tech companies to show why an acquisition will not lessen competition before they can get approval. Of course, it is very difficult to get this analysis right, given acquisitions of potential competitors in their early stages may still evade regulatory review. The pendulum, though, should swing from the default celebratory attitude we've had to mergers and acquisitions since the 1980s to one of greater scrutiny. Senator Amy Klobuchar has introduced a bill to change the burden of proof for deals above $5 billion, which Wall Street defines as megadeals; this would scrutinize the most anticompetitive mergers while continuing to allow acquisition of start-ups in cutting-edge technologies that need corporate management, customers, and resources to scale. According to Scott Sher, one of the nation's leading antitrust attorneys, less than 3 percent of deals are more than $5 billion annually, and mega deals already raise the most flags with the DOJ and FTC. So the Klobuchar proposal is narrowly tailored and is a starting point to enact the reform on mergers we need without hurting smaller, growing businesses.

ANTIDEMOCRATIC IMPACT: LOCAL JOURNALISM, ARTISTS, AND RETAIL SHOPS

The economic power of Facebook, Google, Amazon, and Apple has created issues beyond impacting competitors or consumers. Some of the most serious effects of the tech boom are in areas of the economy and society for which even antitrust enforcement is an insufficient tool. Three key examples concern the effects that big tech has had on local journalism, artists, and retail shops.

The digital age is not easy for newspapers, especially rural and regional ones. These papers conduct important oversight as watchdogs, help build an informed citizenry, and provide an important sense of community by reporting on civic leaders, sports teams, family milestones, service organizations, student initiatives, and current events. I remember reading the *Bucks County Courier Times* multiple times a week growing up. The paper gave me a chance to develop my voice by submitting letters to the editor. But it also made me aware of the larger issues facing our county, state, and nation, and provided a common framework to discuss matters with classmates and neighbors. So many conversations in town began with a reference to a story in the *Courier Times*. Opinions differed, of course, but most operated on a shared understanding of basic facts.

Today, we have far easier access to far more information than when

I grew up. Almost anyone can write a blog, post on Facebook, compose a tweet, or create a video that goes viral. The internet also provided us with a more global perspective. It is easy to access online articles about a cricket match in Australia or a local election in South Korea, neither of which would have been covered in a local paper. But the explosion of online information came at a cost, resulting in the closures of newspapers all across the country. Not all content is "fit to print." Not all information is credible. And when newspapers fold, we lose critical thinkers who are pillars of their community and dedicate their careers to a search for truth.

Look at what happened to Stockton mayor Michael Tubbs, who was subject to a smear campaign about alleged corruption on a Facebook page with more than 100,000 followers. The city's local paper, which suffered budget cuts, was unable to serve as an independent source of facts because it had a declining readership and had reduced its coverage of local politics. Instead of having respected local sources dig up and vet the truth, locals were left with a swirl of rumors. As a result, Tubbs lost his race. More generally, studies show local newspaper closures lead to higher government salaries, tax hikes, less federal funding, larger deficits, and riskier municipal bonds. When no one is there to unearth the most important local stories, an important check on regional power is lost.

Why have local newspapers taken such a hit? The internet has made information free and moved many ads, particularly classified ones, online. Some staunch defenders of the digital economy argue that advertising has just become more efficient and that citizens would still pay for local papers if they provide unique value. This underestimates the structural barriers local papers face, such as the scale needed to have a successful digital subscription campaign. The *New York Times* or *Wall Street Journal* may have enough digital subscriptions to pay for their staff, but local papers have a hard time surviving without classified and print ads. Many readers, moreover, skim the headline and summary on a Google search link instead of reading the local paper, "depriving the content creators of digital ad revenue." Finally, the market is not the final arbiter of social value. Even if people are unwilling to pay market price for local journalism, that does not take away from the benefit a local community derives from a strong paper.

One solution is to impose a small tax on the astronomical advertising revenue that Google and Facebook generate and put it into an independent fund to support local newspapers. This is a better alternative than banning targeted advertising altogether, given that many small businesses and even newspapers today rely on digital ads. PEN America, a community of writers, advocates for a digital tax to support local newspapers. They propose a 2 percent tax on all digital revenue, which would raise about $2 billion annually. This can be put into a "National Endowment for Journalism," as Yale Law professors Bruce Ackerman and Ian Ayres have advocated. From my perspective, the endowment should be distributed to the states to set up independent commissions to make grants to local newspapers, prioritizing papers with long, positive track records while also offering some seed money to promising upstarts. PEN recognizes that there would need to be a strict separation between a newspaper's finance department applying for a grant and their news and editorial departments. The state commissions making grants should be filled with retired journalists and academics, and it should be as separate from donor and political influence as possible. This will admittedly be hard to pull off in the current political climate and will require a lot of vigilance from nonprofits and current investigative journalists. But the benefits for communities around the country will be enormous.

In addition to setting up an endowment for local papers, the federal government should provide tax credits to newspaper subscribers, small businesses who advertise in local papers, and community papers for hiring journalists. Most important, we need to give local newspapers the chance to "band together" and seek novel arrangements for compensation for content creation while balancing the fair use of their articles and the need to make information broadly accessible to the public.

Just as local newspapers have been routed in recent decades, so have many local artists. A public endowment funded by a tax on digital ads can also support them. It can provide artists not only with loans, grants, and prizes but also with venture funding, technology, and media resources. The endowment can incentivize cities to adopt favorable zoning laws for local art dealerships or music stores. This could help create a local art or music scene as a buffer to the impact of gentrification on a city's culture. It could also free artists from having to be discovered by agents of big corporations.

Legal reform is also critical to protect creator rights. Technology writer Kevin Roose has suggested that blockchain technology might provide opportunity for artists to sell their work directly to consumers without a middle person and to guard against piracy. More immediately, we need to explore thoughtful reforms to the current Digital Millennium Copyright Act to protect artists' rights to their work while also allowing for fair use and guarding against overly restrictive limitations on speech. Neil Turkewitz, an activist for artists' rights, argues that artists believe "the internet has the potential to expand choice" and are not opposed to participating in a digital economy, but they should be compensated fairly for their work instead of being subject to abuse by large business platforms with broad, safe harbors for dissemination. The digital age does not have to lead to the displacement, marginalization, or commodification of artists if we adopt policies that empower them to develop an independent voice.

Perhaps retail shops, which like newspapers and artists define a place's character, have taken the biggest hit. Since 2010, the rise of e-commerce has led to a retail apocalypse where thousands of stores shutter annually. In 2020, more than fifteen thousand stores closed when the pandemic brought in-person shopping to a halt. The impact of these closures on small towns and rural America cannot be underestimated. When they die, it becomes harder for Main Streets to thrive and for towns to retain their population and tax base. Laid-off middle-aged and older retail workers find themselves with few options for comparable jobs. Even if the tech economy brings new business to a town and new opportunities, the résumés of older, laid-off workers are often ignored.

One of the biggest factors for Amazon's rise is its exemption for years from paying any sales tax. Amazon had an unfair advantage against every local retailer because many consumers decided to shop online with them to save on tax. Amazon used this subsidy to gain market share in many different sectors. Now Amazon is a trillion-dollar company, and tens of thousands of retail stores no longer exist. Yet local brick-and-mortar stores are still essential to the structure and community of many towns. They need federal assistance as much as local newspapers and artists.

One approach is for the federal government to cover 50 percent of the sales tax that consumers pay when shopping at small retailers worth less than $1 million. This would be poetic justice for all the years that companies like Amazon avoided sales tax. It would allow small retailers to offer cheaper prices to consumers and compete with dominant companies like Amazon and Walmart. Businesses would still pay the full tax immediately so that state and local governments would not lose any revenue to fund education and essential services, but they could then claim a refundable tax credit worth 50 percent of that tax on their returns.

In addition to a tax credit, the federal government should provide forgivable loans to many of these retailers who retain middle-aged employees. Congress provided such loans in the Paycheck Protection Program for small businesses as part of the $2.3 trillion CARES Act that was our main response to the pandemic, but we can do even more. We should pass a ten-year extension of that program for small retailers and give Main Streets around the country a fighting chance.

There is no denying that tech companies have contributed in unprecedented ways to improving our convenience, connectivity, and access to information. That is why these brands retain high popularity numbers and poll much higher than pharmaceutical companies or Wall Street. But we need guardrails. For too long, policymakers have been afraid to question tech's practices, particularly in the halls of Congress. No one wants to be labeled a Luddite. The mood in the Beltway, however, is changing with recent scandals involving tech companies and bipartisan fears of their growing power. The very vibrancy of our culture depends on safeguarding our freedoms online. It depends on creating space for new business entrants in different regions as well as for local newspapers, artists, and retail shops. A check on the power and influence of big tech is ultimately about valuing a diversity of voices to craft the digital age.

7

DELIBERATION ONLINE

The heyday for tech optimism came in 2011, at the beginning of the Arab Spring. Across the Middle East, citizens were using social media to ignite protests for democratic reform, beginning with the ouster of Tunisian dictator Zine Ben Ali and culminating in the overthrow of Hosni Mubarak's regime in Egypt. It may seem hard to remember, but at the time tech companies were seen by many as beacons of freedom, and their leaders as respected global statesmen. But the Arab Spring had mixed success at best. State repression of unarmed protests led in some cases to the outbreak of bloody civil wars; in others, uprisings only solidified authoritarian leaders. Even so, throughout the early 2010s, there was a widespread belief in Silicon Valley that the internet was a reliable force for good. As technology spread, it would unleash prosperity in the remotest corners of the world, douse ignorance with the dissemination of knowledge, empower everyone to have an equal voice, and usher in peace through increased connectivity.

This was the context in which Eric Schmidt, then the chairman of Google, and Jared Cohen, an executive at Google, wrote *The New Digital Age* in 2013. They offered an optimistic prognosis for cyberspace. They made several accurate predictions. For instance, they foresaw that activists would use digital platforms to "organize" and "mobilize" in "constructive" ways for various causes over the coming decades. The #MeToo movement is a recent example that embodies what Schmidt and Cohen envisioned—an online community of support, discussion, and amplification. Many victims courageously shared their experience of sexual abuse and harassment on Twitter, while tagging threads made by figures such as Tarana Burke, Alyssa Milano, or Ashley Judd. They instantaneously became part of a community who believed, retweeted, and supported one another. Many found it easier to tell their story online than in person, and Twitter became an outlet where service workers, junior staffers, and high school students could be heard by tens of thousands, or even millions. Black Lives Matter and the Sunrise Movement are also prime examples of decentralized movements that have mobilized change through the power of social media.

However, Schmidt and Cohen's vision also had blind spots, which even they would acknowledge. While they pointed to the dangers of surveillance and loss of privacy, they discounted the problem of political echo chambers and polarization, believing that users would have a wide selection of information at their fingertips to defeat, rather than spread, conspiracy theories. They predicted that people of different backgrounds and cultures would be able to resolve disputes through direct dialogue, because "everyone . . . will have access to the same source material" online. Thus far, that has not proven to be true.

Fast-forward to January 6, 2021, and it becomes clear that something has gone very wrong. January 6 will live in infamy in the history of the digital age. I watched firsthand from my window in the Cannon House Office Building as a mob of rioters rushed the Capitol, spurred by online conspiracy theories pushed by President Trump and Republican lawmakers. Even amidst the bedlam, as I waited it out locked in my office, I was thinking about how social media had precipitated the day's violence. It was not just that the rioters had developed a distorted view of the outcome of the presidential election through online conspiracies. They literally plotted their assault using the app Parler, telling other march participants, "Storm the Capitol" and "No change without Bloodshed," while organizing through #fightback, #firingsqaud, and #civilwar.

The insurrection of January 6 was the shocking culmination of years of online radicalization. But it is just one of many acts of violence fueled by social media over the last decade, both in the United States and abroad. In a seminal report titled *Complicit*, Muslim Advocates, a Washington-based civil rights organization, detailed how the Buddhist military in Myanmar used Facebook and its subsidiary, WhatsApp, to plan the mass murder of Muslim Rohingyas. According to the report, more than 25,000 Rohingya Muslims died and over 700,000 were driven out of Myanmar. The U.N. found that Facebook played a "determining role" in this human rights catastrophe.

Closer to home, social media platforms have been implicated as organizing grounds for white nationalist and extremist groups. In 2017, amid protests surrounding the Unite the Right rally of white supremacists and neo-Nazis in Charlottesville, Virginia, Heather Heyer was murdered by a man belonging to Vanguard America, a white nationalist group that had a significant presence on Facebook. Three years later, in the summer of 2020, Facebook hosted a Kenosha Guard Facebook group with three thousand members that called to "take up arms" to defend Kenosha, Wisconsin, from racial justice protesters after Rusten Sheskey, a white police officer, shot Jacob Blake, a twenty-nine-year-old Black man, paralyzing him from the waist down. This led to a white teenager traveling to Kenosha with an AR-15-style rifle and killing two protesters.

Mark Zuckerberg likely never imagined that a site that began as a platform to rate the attractiveness of classmates would two decades later be used to organize racial violence and human rights abuses. But that is the reality we're all now grappling with. January 6, 2021, gave the United States an unforgettable vision of how online rancor can build into organized violence, as millions watched live as a crowd of self-described "digital soldiers" attacked the oldest institution of democracy.

In less than a decade, tech has gone from democracy's great hope to poster child for the crisis of modern democracy. But it does not have to be this way. We have seen that creating opportunities to work together online can facilitate meaningful bonds and affirmative democratic movements. This was the case for Alex Hughes, who was hired in by Interapt in Paintsville, Kentucky, and Marquisha Lester, who works for PeopleShores in Clarksdale, Mississippi, as well as for #MeToo and Black Lives Matter. The dramatic rise of social media has revolutionized how many of us stay informed and speak out, and this in turn has increased participation in our democracy. So how do we maintain the many benefits of digital media while avoiding its most destructive extremes?

This chapter offers a new vision for the structure of social media and online forums. Democratic values, not data or attention maximization, must define the digital age. There are actions that both the government and tech companies can take to this end, in ways that are consistent with both our constitutional principles and our fundamental values as Americans. My analysis falls into three basic categories over the course of the chapter: first, the topic of free speech in the digital age; second, the conundrum of disinformation and digital deception; and, finally, the importance of digital literacy and opportunities for participating in digital institutions that influence governance.

FREE SPEECH IN A DIGITAL AGE

The events of January 6, 2021, reflect a failure of both government and tech policy. Within days of the attack, Apple and Google removed the Parler app from their stores, and Amazon Web Services (AWS) suspended its services, taking the site temporarily offline. But this only came after seven-plus weeks of explicit calls for "civil war" and assassinations on Parler, in violation of its customer agreement with AWS and the First Amendment. Conservatives online cried foul at the tech companies' decision, claiming the ban was an attack on free speech. Yet tech had allowed the forum to exist for years and only stepped in to take down Parler after the speech hosted on the platform turned into calls for violent attacks and assassinations, which in turn led to real-world violence, at which point Parler had still failed to act in a comprehensive way. Even after the fact, in an interview with Kara Swisher, John Matze, the Parler CEO at the time, lacked any introspection. When asked about the Capitol attack, he said, "I don't feel responsible for any of this and neither should the platform, considering we're a neutral town square that just adheres to the law."

Facebook and Twitter also share blame for the rise of well-organized extremist groups and the attack on the Capitol. Although Facebook, unlike Parler, devoted substantial resources to hiring staff to take down violent content with calls for violence, the "Stop the Steal" and "Red-State Secession" Facebook groups and Twitter threads still contained numerous posts that crossed the line from advocacy and organizing to the encouragement of violent action against the government. In *An Ugly Truth*, Sheera Frenkel and Cecilia Kang document that Facebook's own security team was concerned that posts on their pages could trigger violence on January 6.

The day after the attack, Facebook and Twitter suspended Trump's account. Trump engaged in classic incitement by urging a mob of his supporters—some armed with guns, IEDs, and zip ties—to go to the Capitol and fight. His tweeted video calling on the rioters to go home while telling them "we love you" and praising them as "patriots" and "special" was reminiscent of Marc Antony's manipulative funeral oration of Julius Caesar that incited the crowd, *minus* Shakespeare's rhetorical genius.

Both Twitter and Facebook eventually announced a permanent ban of Trump's account after the companies saw plans for future riots proliferating on the platform. This was a much harder decision considering the high bar for deplatforming and the risk of setting a precedent of banning controversial political viewpoints. Twitter appropriately prioritizes the ability for the public to hear from national and world leaders directly. In reaching its decision, Twitter emphasized that, even after the temporary suspension, Trump continued to violate its rules. Twitter's challenge is to apply its policy consistently, banning the account of any leader, regardless of ideology. Facebook decided to maintain the ban for two years while acknowledging the need for clearer standards about the severity of penalties for violations of their terms of service. The drastic action against Trump's account marked an implicit recognition by tech of their own culpability in the storming of the Capitol.

But the question of how to ensure that these lessons are applied effectively—so that they can curtail future eruptions of extremist violence, while protecting the essential tenets of free expression—remains complicated. It will take continued action from both the federal government and tech companies themselves to strike the right balance. Let me offer some principles that can guide debate about what the rules for online discourse should look like.

GOVERNMENT RESPONSE

On the subject of free speech, it is important to distinguish between the role of the state and private actors such as Facebook and Twitter. As far as what federal regulations are appropriate, the governing standard remains *Brandenburg v. Ohio* (1969), a unanimous Supreme Court decision that is arguably one of the finest in the history of the law. The Court held that the state can only prohibit speech if it is "directed to inciting or producing imminent lawless action and is likely to incite or produce such action." This means a speaker must intend to cause specific violence within the "very near future" and that violence must be likely to occur.

Following exceptional acts of violence, there is inevitably a temptation to pass laws banning any speech that *may* lead to violence. However, this urge is overbroad and potentially in violation of the First Amendment. Acting to tighten free speech laws beyond *Brandenburg* could silence social justice champions, censor religious texts, and ban renowned novels such as Salman Rushdie's *Satanic Verses* or J. D. Salinger's *Catcher in the Rye*, which inspired John Lennon's assassin. Professors Eugene

Volokh, Evelyn Aswad, and Nadine Strossen, all legal luminaries, helped me understand the consequences of overly restrictive laws. To begin with, Professor Aswad shared that the state has often been most aggressive in censoring the speech of reformers such as Dr. Martin Luther King and other civil rights leaders, labeling them threats to law and order. Eugene Volokh expands on this point, telling me that "most political movements—antislavery, antiwar, civil rights, labor, pro-life, pro-socialism, anti-federal-government, environmentalist, anti-police-brutality—and many religious movements have a large base of law-abiding supporters and a small group of supporters who are willing to use violence." An effort to eradicate any possibility of violence will likely be overbroad and have a chilling impact on many movements.

To avoid going down a road of government censorship of constructive dissent, Nadine Strossen writes that an effective counter to racist speech is promoting counterspeech that refutes prejudice directly and stronger laws against actual discriminatory conduct and violence. We will speak to the subject of counterspeech later in the chapter, but when it comes to government response, the right question to ask is: How, under the *Brandenburg* standard, can we deal with the proliferation of violence on social media?

Congress should pass a law requiring social media platforms to take down any speech where there is a court order that a particular post is inciting imminent violence or a direct threat or solicitation of violence and is illegal under the *Brandenberg* standard. Currently, platforms have no obligation to do so, and plaintiffs, therefore, do not have an incentive to pursue legal action. For instance, as we've already seen, Parler's CEO had no desire and no incentive to remove posts that were actively inciting violence. And while other tech companies ended up removing both the Parler app and some posts inciting violence on their own platforms, these actions were taken of their own volition, which puts a major onus on tech companies to determine which posts meet a standard for removal. A report from CounterAction about calls for violence on Facebook underscores the scale of this challenge. Over a two-month period, they found more than 2,715,842 comments on public Facebook posts, including 59,853 against public officials, with "an intention to inflict pain, injury towards an individual or group."

Daphne Keller, one of the nation's leading experts on platform regulation at Stanford, shared with me that a "court order exception" for violent or abusive speech to Section 230, which gives broad immunity to digital platforms from being sued for content on their site, is a "promising way forward." That is, tech companies would be liable for failing to remove content on their websites when a court finds that it incites violence or abuse (whereas, at present, they are not liable for such content). If courts are given the authority to order the removal of posts calling for riots or assassinations, it may only impact a small subset of the comments that CounterAction cites (since the *Brandenburg* standard requires specific violence in the "very near future"). But it will facilitate the development of jurisprudence around these complex issues that can guide social media companies in making determinations of what to remove on their own. Civil rights organizations such as the NAACP and the Southern Poverty Law Center would monitor digital platforms and seek temporary restraining orders when appropriate. If such a standard were in place, there is little doubt that Facebook's security team would have felt more empowered and obligated to remove incendiary posts that they worried were going to cause the January 6 insurrection and to coordinate with law enforcement ahead of the tragic events.

Furthermore, the Alien Tort Claims Act (ATCA) should be amended to provide foreign nationals access to U.S. courts to seek the removal of content inciting violence that triggers significant human rights abuses. The bar to bring such cases would be very high. For example, a plaintiff from Myanmar could seek relief in the U.S. for posts on Facebook that call for the killing of Rohingya Muslims at a specific time. Currently, victims abroad have little recourse but to petition social media companies, which, by their own admission, are too slow to act. Providing them access to the U.S. courts for removing online speech that causes widespread human rights violations—speech that may constitute a conspiracy to commit violence—would make it possible to mitigate the harm that social media platforms are causing around the world.

TECH RESPONSE

Social media companies do and should go beyond court orders and the strict *Brandenburg* framework when it comes to voluntarily restricting speech that glorifies violence on their platforms. They are private actors who must make determinations about what speech to include on their sites and what resources to put into content moderation. Although we should be wary of multibillion-dollar corporations defining the boundaries of acceptable speech, we should not settle for digital forums with no standards. These standards should consider international human rights law as well as engaging the voices of the civil rights community and other faith and civic leaders. Imagine if the *New York Times*, *New York Post*, or *Wall Street Journal* published an op-ed by a QAnon rioter or a member of the Ku Klux Klan. They would have the First Amendment right to do so but would face public excoriation for legitimizing such content and voices. Social media companies are not simply telephone providers or internet service providers. If they were, they would not have community standards in the first place. They are creating a speech community, and they should be ethically accountable for the standards they establish.

There are, of course, important differences between traditional publishers and social media. As Nadine Strossen helped me understand, the former affirmatively selects content for inclusion, whereas digital platforms, not limited by similar resource constraints, default to publishing everything unless they decide to expressly exclude an item. The bar for exclusion on a platform with millions of other posts, or worse for deplatforming a user, is certainly higher than the one for deciding not to publish an op-ed. Nonetheless, it is important for digital platforms to continue to refine and transparently *enforce* ethical guidelines to govern their own sites.

Some argue that if Facebook or Twitter go beyond the strict

incitement test in *Brandenburg* and further restrict speech glorifying violence or racial hatred then it would just migrate to other sites such as Parler, Gab, or 4chan. This does not, however, absolve tech companies from making tough decisions. It is better to have such speech contained in niche zones on the internet rather than reaching a mainstream audience. Speech filled with racist slurs or calls for violence—even if short of incitement—does not deserve amplification or the imprimatur of legitimacy, whether that be in a prominent publication or on a prominent social media site. Although isolating such speech limits our ability to challenge it and admittedly may allow it to grow virulent among like-minded participants away from society's reach, that is preferable to spreading it. Marginalizing that speech has often proven a more promising strategy than allowing it to spread widely. For instance, while hate groups existed well before the internet, social media gave them a place to expand beyond the isolated fringes of society. In most towns, white supremacists are shunned as outcasts, condemned by educators, civic and faith leaders, journalists, Little League coaches, and local businesses. This makes it difficult for them to grow and organize. But if they're able to amplify hateful ideas openly online, they can find larger platforms and spend their time interacting with those who share their perverse ideology. The central problem is people on social media can escape social repercussions or social obligations in a way that they cannot in physical communities. So denying radicalized online groups an opportunity to grow unchecked on mainstream digital forums is necessary.

There is a fine line between enforcing ethical standards and censoring controversial content that deserves to be heard. Tech companies should take the least restrictive approach that will still be effective and also should be transparent, consistent, and nonpartisan in their decision making. As global platforms, they should look to international human rights norms that call for developing tools for "de-amplification, de-monetization, education, counterspeech, reporting and training" as often preferable to the outright "banning of accounts and the removal of content." These norms are surprisingly consistent with our own American cultural tradition of placing a premium on free speech. All in all, the best check on big tech having too much power over speech is not resignation to an internet where everything is permissible everywhere, but policies that foster more competition to provide many outlets, including niche ones, for expression.

Facebook's recent move to create an Oversight Board of constitutional scholars, Nobel laureates, cyberlaw experts, and world leaders is a positive step to create and enforce guidelines for quality discourse that go beyond what the state is permitted to do. The OB can help Facebook develop high-level principles for what violent content to not amplify or, in extreme cases, remove while protecting free expression and making space for vigorous dissent. However, the OB will not have the bandwidth to address all complaints on the platform. That is why Facebook should make an investment in building an internal adjudication system consisting of many teams that can then apply principles quickly, fairly, and transparently to the most viral and egregious cases. There should be an appeals process where the OB or its designees are the final arbiter, not Mark Zuckerberg. Every major social media company should have an independent oversight board to rebuild public trust across our nation. While Americans may understandably be wary of private tribunals placing restrictions on their online speech on private platforms, this is preferable to an internet with minimal ethical standards or one which is subject to the whims of billionaire founders. Finally, these boards should be responsible for enforcing policies mentioned in the previous section to ensure that content moderation teams are expeditiously removing the most inciteful speech which violates the *Brandenburg* standard.

CORPORATE CENSORSHIP

There always is the danger that digital platforms go too far in removing speech. Although they have a First Amendment right to do so, corporate censorship undermines public confidence in having a fair chance to participate in public debate. After social media came under scrutiny for its role during the previous presidential election, this issue surfaced repeatedly in the 2020 presidential election. For example, Twitter blocked the account of the *New York Post* as well as the personal account of Kayleigh McEnany, President Trump's press secretary, for posting an article about hacked Hunter Biden emails. The article itself couldn't be shared either. Facebook stunted the article's promotion and reduced the number of people who saw it until they could verify its validity. Although I am convinced there was no truth to the salacious allegations, Hunter Biden's emails themselves referencing his father were of public interest.

Twitter's rationale stemmed from its policy barring the dissemination of any hacked material. But their decision went too far. I reached out to Jack Dorsey at the time and made the case that under Twitter's policy, the Pentagon Papers and Iraq War Logs would be banned on their platform. Hacking Hunter Biden's laptop was likely a crime that should be prosecuted. The private pictures and messages should never have been broadcast. But publishing information concerning a major party nominee for president should be part of our expansive public domain.

Twitter later recognized they made a mistake, both in the initial decision and in their lack of transparency over why the decision was made. But despite the prominence of right-wing news sites and similar content on social media, the incident eroded many conservatives' confidence that social media companies are committed to an unbiased forum. There is also growing anger about social media platform censorship among factions further toward the left. A coalition of seventy civil rights organizations accused Facebook of "racially biased censorship," arguing that "content from Movement for Black Lives, Palestinian and Native American activist users on Facebook has been removed without evidence of any violation, while obviously racist and hateful content has been allowed to remain."

Oversight boards can help tech companies make decisions more consistent with allowing a rich diversity of nonviolent political speech, particularly about public figures, into the public domain. They should not discriminate against speech based on ideology. Providing space for a diversity of speech rests on a belief that the American public, more than big tech, should sort through the noise of a messy democracy. In the case of Hunter Biden, the American public did. Most American voters heard of the story despite the ham-handed efforts by social media companies to muzzle it. If anything, the censorship only heightened interest in the story. What helped Joe Biden win is the discerning ability of the public to sift through what matters to their lives, not the paternalistic efforts of billion-dollar companies to restrict what viewpoints they see months before an election.

DISINFORMATION AND DIGITAL DECEPTION

One of social media's most destructive effects on American public life is the substitution of news with gossip, and at worst, conspiracy theories. To be sure, talk radio and cable news have offered a one-sided worldview to many Americans for decades. Partisan podcasts have also proliferated, and conservative groups have spread their message by building visible organizations in small towns and strategically winning over local newspapers. But in my experience, pushing back against the lies people see on Facebook because of algorithms that target them is often the most challenging. I have had long conversations with listeners of the late Rush Limbaugh or watchers of Tucker Carlson. We can sometimes find common ground on the corruption in Washington, power of big corporations, ending endless wars, or the need for a jobs and wages agenda. But conspiracy theories are conversation stoppers. According to an MIT study, a falsehood on social media spreads six times faster than a true statement and is 70 percent more likely to be shared. As David Brooks, a *New York Times* columnist, astutely observes, a person's susceptibility to falsity might depend more on "economic, cultural, or spiritual" anxiety more than online engagement. Nonetheless, digital platforms make it easier than ever for demagogues and attention seekers to identify and exploit these weaknesses with provocative content that repeatedly and casually circulates in their social circles and overwhelms, allowing falsehoods not simply to inform a person's worldview but also to become defining attributes of their identity.

Social media has no demarcation between ordinary conversation and news. False information comes not from an on-air anchor, but with the personal endorsement of a trusted family member or friend. Life online can quickly become an unexamined life, filled with memes of misogyny, stereotypes, misleading statistics, and xenophobia that are shared effortlessly. It allows people to judge, dismiss, condemn, and even cancel others with one click while exuding moral condescension.

I experienced Facebook's right-wing echo chamber on Facebook firsthand when Ben Shapiro's *Daily Wire* took a clip of mine about the minimum wage out of context and circulated it online suggesting, falsely, that I did not want small businesses to thrive. It was amplified by *Breitbart*, the Republican National Committee, *TheBlaze*, and within hours a few conservative friends of mine were texting me asking whether I had said that I do not care about small business. The coordinated and rapid spread of cleverly edited clips made an impression on millions of Americans that was hard to overcome. This constituted asymmetrical speech, where neither I nor my allies could respond or correct the record, although Shapiro, to his credit, offered me the opportunity to come on his podcast later. This kind of experience is common on digital platforms, and many Americans are siloed into impenetrable social realities. They see the false sound bite, but not the correction.

Although recent academic literature has suggested that online users may be exposed to more diverse views and news sources than the filter bubble theory originally posited, echo chambers can still emerge because the engagement with information—including what to discount or amplify—is based on discussion in segregated social groups. Evidence suggests that echo chambers are particularly pronounced on the right, leading to "insular" and "extreme" views.

The federal government is limited in what it can do about this problem. In *United States v. Alvarez* (2012), the Supreme Court held that it was illegal to punish blatant falsities, including making false statements about earning military medals. The Court reasoned that the harm to the freedom of thought that can result from the state making decisions about matters of truth outweighs any benefit of stopping false statements or from spreading. However, there are steps we can take to create more space for reasonable dialogue on these platforms so that their chief function is not to whip up and inflame polarization. The sections that follow outline concrete measures consistent with our constitutional values that would help us combat disinformation and allow us all to get the best out of social platforms.

PUBLIC REPORTING

Although the federal government is constitutionally prohibited from banning falsity online, it can and should require public reporting of content moderation policies. Much like public companies need to file their financials with the SEC, large social media companies should be required to file an FCC report on how they control and amplify speech without having to reveal proprietary information. Such a disclosure requirement goes beyond the second principle of the Internet Bill of Rights, which as you may recall gives individuals a right to know what is happening to their data, by giving the broader public access to information about content moderation decisions a company makes. Facebook already puts out a high-level Community Standards Enforcement Report on a quarterly basis, but at present it does not contain sufficient detail about what speech it prioritizes, bans, or removes. A formal disclosure requirement would also provide insight about how much time users spend with different pages, groups, and accounts, and the relative insularity of various social networks on their platforms.

If Facebook and Twitter submitted quarterly reports, civil rights groups would be able to assess the companies' commitment to removing hateful content and curtailing the rise of extremist groups that violate their terms of service. Activists across the right–left spectrum, in turn, would better understand whether they are the victims of bias when it comes to removal. UCLA professor Ramesh Srinivasan has persuasively made the case for "third-party accountability" and stakeholder inclusion when it comes to the design of platforms.

A NEW PARADIGM FOR SOCIAL MEDIA

Public accountability may lead to design reform, particularly in a well-regulated market that protects our online rights and promotes competition. Currently, social media platforms are built to maximize user engagement, and elevate attention-grabbing and addictive content. Incendiary posts in online groups garner many shares and likes, contributing to radicalization and polarization. This is inconsistent with Dorsey's vision of "building towards a common understanding, and a more peaceful existence on earth," or Zuckerberg's goal of promoting "supportive," "safe," "informed," and "inclusive" communities. These networks put their thumb on the scale for speech that is popular with particular subgroups, which may be good for revenue; but it does not forward the company's stated objectives.

If tech companies are serious about promoting constructive dialogue, they should work with behavioral scientists, political theorists, psychologists, and mental health professionals to experiment with new designs. Software engineers should not only optimize for attention with like and share buttons, but to also optimize for engagement with a wide range of perspectives. They could construct platforms, for instance, that incentivize users to participate in diverse online communities. Pushing opposing material to users can motivate them to become even stronger proponents of their ideologies. But a platform that provides attractive options for users to *choose* more diversity, including when they customize algorithms, may help challenge parochialism. One way of doing this is inviting people to engage with alternative viewpoints that their acquaintances or friends like, so that their own network can help point them outward instead of simply reinforcing their worldview.

The key is to foster open communication, not simply self-affirmation.

The call is for these private digital platforms to have spaces that are not wholly transactional in maximizing ad revenue through attention maximization. These spaces could, as one of the world's most important philosophers, Jürgen Habermas, might put it, have a "commercial basis" without being fully "commercialized." We need a recentering of Silicon Valley values so that companies embrace their dual responsibility, not simply to shareholders, but also as key stewards of the modern public sphere. This would have practical impact. For instance, social media sites could allow users to accumulate points for posts that others believe respond to disagreement thoughtfully. With enough points perhaps the user could earn that coveted blue checkmark or a favorable score on their account. This type of point system can encourage threads with genuine back-and-forth, while still allowing for responses of anger and outrage to injustices. Just as guests and hosts receive poor reviews for behavior on Airbnb, social media users could receive reviews for how they engage with others so they have incentives beyond just maximizing likes and shares. Interesting exchanges on key issues, moreover, could be promoted in ways that draw users in and motivate others to engage similarly.

Procedural regulations of these private platforms are needed to prevent a race to the bottom on digital platforms and bring about a change in the Valley's culture. A world that has regulations to protect consumers, as would be fostered by an Internet Bill of Rights, would help incentivize platforms to develop more constructive communities. Opt-in consent will lessen the value of extractive data collection, transparency about standards will increase civic pressure on tech companies, and antitrust laws will allow competitors to emerge. The rewards for the current model that preys on vulnerabilities to maximize attention will be reduced in an opt-in framework where platforms will have access to less granular data. Sites must still, of course, aspire to capture users' interest and time. But they may be less able to do that simply by targeted sensationalism, appeals to impulse, or pushing the online equivalent of junk food—especially with the increased public attention that disclosure laws will bring. Tech companies will have to pay more attention to the quality of the user experience. They may discover that there is a market and a branding advantage for speech communities that foster an authentic human connection online.

Any diversified market of digital platforms should also include public social media options, funded by tax dollars and free of data collection, where people can debate ideas without fear of manipulation. The public social media option could include the design priorities described above, challenging for-profit platforms to innovate in order to compete. If a public platform does not engage in viewpoint discrimination, it can adopt reasonable restrictions to promote civility and decorum. Government could fund a national platform—think of it as an online PBS—as well as local ones sponsored by cities and local libraries with designs similar to Nextdoor where residents engage about the latest community events. We would need strict privacy safeguards as a prerequisite, as the last thing we want is for the government to collect data about our preferences that it could use for surveillance.

These platforms could have video forums, audio conversations, or textual exchanges, recognizing that each medium may offer different advantages and disadvantages in promoting thoughtful dialogue. Video and oral communication allow us to assess another speaker's authenticity, facilitate lengthy conversations, and temper our willingness to launch ad hominem attacks. On the other hand, textual communication mitigates social biases based on appearance, is often linked to articles which can help us dive deeply into a topic, and may zero in on the central issues and disagreements at hand. There is a reason that Socratic conversations in a classroom are not based solely on spontaneous expressions or improvisation but centered around books that awaken our minds and that assignments require written papers to sharpen our thinking. The question of whether a medium is effective depends on the participants and topics involved and on the specific design of a platform.

The best we may be able to hope for in an imperfect democracy is a plurality of online forums for political conversation that (a) demonstrate a threshold respect for our agency as participants by not engaging in data extraction, (b) are transparent in terms of both their speech standards and the priorities of their algorithms, and (c) comply with legitimate restrictions on unlawful speech consistent with our First Amendment jurisprudence. Although there is a risk that this causes the further fragmentation of our public discourse, only a few sites at any given moment are likely to attain national reach, as people are not inclined to spend time on dozens of social media sites. Realistically, it is also hard to imagine that any public sites would replace Facebook, Twitter, or other emerging apps as places that drive the national conversation. Even if well regulated, private digital platforms will attract prominent social influencers, be open to the provocative language of social movements, provide space for protest and activism, and have sophisticated bells and whistles to capture people's interest. They are likely to be staples of our messy and wide-ranging discursive ecosystem for many years. But increased competition, along with the regulations discussed, can facilitate consumer choice and public scrutiny that improves the quality of discourse on the most popular sites. Over time what I hope emerges is a rich body of social media ethics, rooted in our values, as platforms face both market and democratic accountability that they have thus far largely escaped.

FAKE NEWS

One promising design reform big tech should pursue is to introduce the option of vetted content based on crowdsourcing in users' newsfeeds. Tech companies have been by turns unwilling and ineffective at deciding what constitutes legitimate news. They are often caught between a rock and a hard place. When they take down information downplaying the threat of Covid-19 or calling into question the effectiveness of vaccines, they are accused of censorship. When they let evidence-free statements about the pandemic or climate change circulate on their sites, they risk corrupting the public discourse and face allegations of "killing people." They have too much power and frankly never imagined that in the pursuit of obscene profits they would be burdened with so much social responsibility.

Crowdsourcing the news might offer one way to untie the Gordian knot. It turns out that, despite our partisan divide, Americans are capable of agreeing about what news sites are most credible. According to a fascinating study by Gordon Pennycook and David G. Rand, Republicans and Democrats converged in trusting about twenty mainstream news sites more than partisan or fake news sites. While they had differences in which mainstream sites they believed most, "both Democrats and Republicans gave mainstream media sources substantially higher trust scores than either hyperpartisan sites or fake news sites." The fake news sites like conservativedailypost.com and notallowedto.com ranked at the bottom, well below even partisan sites such as commondreams.org, dailykos.com, and breitbart.com. Republicans and Democrats had the most trust in mainstream sources such as ABC, Fox News, *The New York Times*, and *The Wall Street Journal*. This suggests that social media could construct a stream of news based on sources that have high trust scores from *both* Democratic and Republican users. The stream could even include a couple of hyperpartisan sites with relatively strong trust scores to ensure ideological diversity.

Users could choose to receive this stream in their newsfeed and adjust the amount of news they consume. Some may even choose to have all news-related posts in their feeds prioritized based on a crowdsourcing algorithm. In short, crowdsourcing on social media sites has the potential to establish a baseline of common material that can be the foundation for deliberative democracy online. It can help vindicate Schmidt's and Cohen's hope expressed nearly a decade ago that citizens will have some common starting point in a digital age. While newsfeeds and online groups will still include biased or misleading stories, users at least will be exposed to what their fellow citizens collectively believe is the range of information that is credible. This mix is certainly better than the status quo.

The elegance of the crowdsourcing approach is that, to return to Nadine Strossen's point, it relies on counterspeech. That is, it counters misinformation with *more* speech and does not give social media companies the power to restrict access to nontraditional and provocative world-views. There still will be a need for blunter tools. When users post blatant misrepresentations about public health that may cause physical harm, social media companies should remove those posts expeditiously and refuse to amplify them. The stakes, moreover, are too high for such decisions to be left only in the hands of tech companies. Consistent with our First Amendment jurisprudence, courts should have the authority to order the removal of posts that are an imminent threat to public health and public safety.

Labeling posts as potentially false is another tool to combat misinformation. Platforms tagged, for example, any post that called the 2020 election results into question as "disputed." While this was a well-intentioned effort, the problem with labeling is that it often just draws more attention to the post itself. Facebook's internal data shows that labeling Trump's posts as false barely decreased the amount that they were shared.

It seems that the best chance of overcoming disputed realities in the political context is widening users' organic exposure to a diverse range of sources that does not trigger their defenses instead of having platforms conspicuously confront them about a misinformed viewpoint. Although removal and negative labeling can provide some guardrails against the most extreme propaganda campaigns, the functioning of democracy depends on discourse to defeat disinformation when educated citizens can draw from common source materials. I turn to digital literacy later in this chapter.

FAKE ACCOUNTS AND BOTS

Fake accounts and bots only add to the divisiveness and sensationalism on social media. At least 5 percent of active Facebook users at any given period of time are fake accounts or bots, and a staggering 45 percent of tweets concerning Covid-19 were bot-generated. During the time of President Trump's announcement to withdraw from the Paris Climate Accords, Twitter accounts "suspected of being bots comprised roughly a quarter of all tweets about climate change," dramatically increasing climate disinformation on the platform. An Indiana University study that analyzed millions of tweets during the 2016 presidential election concluded that bots are a large contributor to the spread of misinformation and conspiracies. They share fabricated stories, make salacious content trend, and overwhelm investigatory teams with volume that makes it hard to find the offending posts. Most shockingly, the presence of fake accounts helps explain why "over 86% of shares and 75% of comments on German political Facebook from October 2018 to May 2019 were Alternative für Deutschland content" even though the far-right party never "exceeded 15% of public support in polls during this time period."

The easiest way to reduce disinformation from bots is with strong, front-end verification. Currently, Facebook and Twitter understandably want to make the process of signing up as frictionless as possible. A person can sign up for a Facebook or Twitter account by authenticating their email or phone number. Instead, at minimum, social media companies should require *both* email and phone verification. They should also give users periodic Captcha tests, which require them to identify numbers or images that verify the users are not bots. We walk through a metal detector before boarding a plane and take a driving test before driving; it will not be the end of the world if it takes a little bit more time and effort to open a social media account. The benefit of more honest conversation is well worth the cost of some inconvenience.

Removing malicious bots will undoubtedly improve online discourse, but not all bots are bad. As Carnegie Mellon Computer Science professor Kathleen Carley emphasizes, we should welcome bots that are transparent about their identity and serve a legitimate purpose, whether to warn of a natural disaster, market a business, or disseminate quotations or excerpts from literature.

Verification, for that matter, is not fully sufficient to prevent bots from spreading misinformation. Bad actors can instruct human beings to verify an account before handing it over to a machine to churn out propaganda, and there will inevitably be ways to circumvent Captcha or two-step authentication. We need both federal dollars and more private investment to develop the tools for removing bots that have managed to integrate into an online community but are spewing toxicity. When John Stuart Mill was extolling the marketplace of ideas, he likely never imagined that automated responses drafted by narrow interests would occupy a prominent space in the public sphere. At scale, these have the chance to undermine democratic debate, and it is important not to let the problem of bots reach a truly alarming level before we enact real solutions.

FAKE VIDEOS

Social media companies should also be aggressive in removing fake videos that pose a high risk of sowing confusion or chaos. I'm referring to videos that use digital technology in order to fabricate statements by public figures or private individuals. This contrasts with video that might make a false claim or factually inaccurate statement. There is for example a qualitative difference between a video claiming falsely that President Biden is a socialist and a fabricated video where President Biden himself says he will be ushering in socialism. The former is part of the messiness of public debate, whereas the latter could radically distort democratic conversation itself and lead to market turmoil and civil unrest.

Consider, for instance, the doctored video of Speaker Nancy Pelosi that showed her slurring her speech. This video wasn't an advanced deep-fake but instead used simple video-editing software to slow down an actual video of Pelosi. Even *Fox & Friends*, the popular Fox News show, made a point of telling its audience: "Not a real video. It's doctored." The Fox shows did not air the distorted video, and none of the other major broadcast or cable networks amplified it. Yet Facebook and Twitter refused to remove the video. They labeled it fake and deprioritized its distribution but kept it on their platforms. This allowed President Trump and Rudy Giuliani, former New York mayor and personal lawyer for Mr. Trump, to share the video, receiving millions of views and thousands of shares. Facebook defended their decision as standing up for free expression, claiming that manipulated videos could be satire, art, or a form of political expression. There has to be a line, however, between satire and blatant misrepresentation with an intent to deceive. While it is likely a step too far for such distorted content to be outlawed by the government, digital platforms should recognize their aim and impact.

Social media sites should still make space for comedians and artists by allowing appropriately labeled fake videos online, as long as the content does not cause mass confusion in the public sphere. But their oversight boards should systematically make difficult, contextual decisions of recommending the removal of videos that are highly misleading such as the manipulated Pelosi clip. Ultimately, digital platforms are engaged in fostering political conversation, and they have a responsibility to not allow such damaging, deceptive videos that severely restrict the possibility of rational exchange.

DIGITAL LITERACY AND DIGITAL INSTITUTIONS

The history of pamphleteering in our founding era offers parallels into our contemporary challenges online. The most famous American pamphlet was Thomas Paine's *Common Sense*, which called for independence from Great Britain. But most pamphlets were unsigned and filled with "barbs and fiery accusations." Numerous pamphlets incited violence, with some leading to duels. The maturation of American democracy saw the development of independent journalism, academic institutions, and eventually think tanks to provide third-party verification of facts. Public schools emerged that emphasized critical thinking skills, and citizens created many public forums and grassroots organizations, such as the League of Women Voters, to encourage civil debate. Millions of Americans worked hard to build a sophisticated democracy that did not just devolve to the most sensational or loudest voices. Substance mattered. As the Canadian essayist Stephen Marche puts it:

Making the comparison between the Internet and the printing press has always indulged in this laziness. "Hey, look, that was good in the end. Things worked themselves out for the best there." No. They didn't work themselves out. People worked them out. People of great intelligence and good will, able to think beyond their narrow interests, worked them out, and they only worked them out partially, incompletely.

The burden of improving our public discourse online does not fall simply on regulators or tech companies. As Tim Berners-Lee, founder of the web, recognizes in his Contract for the Web blueprint, citizens have the most important role to play in "adopting the best practices for civil discourse" and "educating the next generation on these matters."

What then can a new generation of Americans do to improve discourse on social media? It begins with digital literacy, and the first place to start is in school. We must teach students from elementary school onward that social media posts are filled with as much gossip as news. There is something about seeing information in writing online with a link to a blog or article that makes us think it has more credibility than a casual conversation. Our challenge is to train young people to consume information from digital platforms with the same skepticism they apply to the spoken word. A friend's midnight stream-of-consciousness musings on Facebook are different from sourced and vetted stories in *The New York Times* or *The Wall Street Journal*.

While it may seem difficult to put these ideas into a classroom setting, Finland provides a model for teaching students about misinformation and fake news. Beginning in elementary school, students take a class that teaches them to identify distortions and manipulation online, to recognize the need for multiple sources, and to think critically. Remarkably, it has worked. Finland is a constant victim of Russian disinformation and anti-immigrant propaganda, but the country ranks first out of thirty-five European countries in resilience against disinformation campaigns. We should study the Finnish curriculum concerning online media and require a similar class in every grade, while looking at how we can incorporate these lessons into public awareness campaigns that reach both children and adults. Such classes could be offered, for example, in libraries across America, according to Nina Jankowicz, an expert on tech policy. Digital literacy classes and awareness campaigns should also go beyond "fake news" identification to educating the public about safeguarding digital privacy. Comprehensive digital literacy is key to ensuring that users are not merely checking the boxes of digital "security theater," which are features that may give us the appearance of protection without having much impact, but that they have all the information they need to be agents of their digital life.

As adults, we should continue digital literacy efforts and adapt them to the basic needs of citizenship in a digital age. For instance, one approach could be to reach out to people in different regions and with different ideologies for a Zoom version of a living room dialogue. For decades, Americans of different persuasions have gathered in neighbors' living rooms or front porches to hear each other out on issues impacting their community and nation. There is no reason we cannot apply this approach to the twenty-first century and create online groups that transcend geography. Living Room Conversations is a nonprofit founded in 2010 committed to fostering exactly these kinds of conversations among participants from across the country, gathering groups of fifteen people at a time. In this context, companies like Facebook could potentially be a force for good if they use their data, obtained after consent, to help participants construct diverse groups that still have a threshold level of commonality to make initial conversations easier. This is just one way in which social media design could be tweaked to foster both diversity in addition to shared interests.

One crucial step that we all can take toward improving online discourse is to speak up for civility on social media platforms. The potential for incendiary rhetoric to alienate, silence, offend, or spark violence is higher in a multiracial and religiously pluralistic democracy than a homogenous one. Marginalized communities face the most vitriol online, and they are often the first to withdraw from a hostile environment.

Although nothing on the left is close to as vile as Trump's feed, we are not innocent actors either. Many of us on Senator Sanders's presidential campaign publicly spoke out when supporters posted snake emojis on Senator Elizabeth Warren's Twitter replies. I also spoke up when Twitter started trending with messages of vengeance about those who served in the Trump administration, including calls to deny them any future employment. That said, an examination of my social media accounts will certainly reveal moments I fell short of calling out bad behavior.

Our social challenge is to engage schools, politicians, employers, and civic and faith-based institutions to build an online culture where the norm is to stand up for victims of insults and harassment much like we would if we witnessed such abuse in public places.

PROTECTING CHILDREN FROM ONLINE ADDICTION

The health of our democracy depends on our ability to raise children who can cultivate their own independent and imaginative thinking. As a parent of very young children, I can attest to the challenge of keeping addictive apps and videos away from them. My wife is ahead of the curve, insisting I leave my phone addiction at work and not use phones at meals or when interacting with the kids. When it comes to limiting screen time, Common Sense Media and the Center for Humane Technology both have useful recommendations for parents.

Even so, it would be helpful to develop commonsense legal reforms to help parents on this front. Colleagues of mine who know I represent Silicon Valley often seek me out to share that their biggest concern raising kids is social media manipulation. We are not helpless. We can begin by enforcing the Children's Online Privacy Protection Act (COPPA), which prohibits collecting data or targeting young users. A study found that a staggering 78 percent of children under thirteen use YouTube daily, 45 percent use Facebook daily, and 40 percent use Instagram. The

FCC, armed with a new technology division, must hold these companies strictly liable for any violations of the COPPA.

A strict liability standard will incentivize tech companies to develop better techniques for keeping minors off their platforms. Apple is an industry leader in doing this by asking questions only adults can answer, but this technique only deters young children. Drawing from the Apple example, the FTC should seek to partner with leading technologists to understand what innovative solutions are possible for accurate identification of teenagers who may lie about their age. This may include the use of simple artificial intelligence to assess whether an account has public content primarily related to the junior high school experience.

We also need regulations on social influencers who create videos to sell products to young children. Ryan Kaji is a ten-year-old whose site has 25 million subscribers and earns over $20 million a year for hawking toys in videos where he unboxes and plays with them. Although some lower-income families in my district tell me this allows their children to virtually appreciate toys they cannot afford, it also can be manipulative and hook children to the screen for hours. In 1990, Congress passed the Children's Television Act, which restricts commercial advertising to children, including product promotion, and requires a significant percentage of children's programming on any network to have an educational component. These protections should be extended to online videos.

Beyond regulating videos, we need rules for any online content geared toward children. The Supreme Court recognizes that minors do not have the same First Amendment rights as adults and allows limiting materials "harmful to minors" or "educationally unsuitable." The FTC should be tasked with promulgating and enforcing design standards that consider issues of addiction, bullying, self-esteem, interaction with strangers, and mental health when it comes to children. As a threshold matter, the agency should bar any social media company like Facebook that serves an adult audience with addictive content from creating a social media app for kids. The last thing we should permit is for Facebook to proceed with their plan to create an Instagram for kids and get young people hooked for life on their products.

DELIBERATIVE FORUMS

The hardest challenge facing modern democracy is not simply to regulate private actors, but to build civic and public institutions for deliberation that are inclusive and facilitate constructive discussion. We need to provide those currently spending hours on social media sites with better opportunities for shaping public opinion and influencing governance.

To this end, Audrey Tang, Taiwan's digital minister, provides a model that the U.S. government can emulate. She helped institute two government-led initiatives, vTaiwan and Join, which are designed to find consensus on difficult policy. Millions of Taiwanese citizens participate in these discussion forums. They do not allow for robust back-and-forth exchange, but they do allow individuals to submit comments and weigh in on others' submissions. The forums then use artificial intelligence to determine the most popular comments from participants based on voting, and they identify areas of agreement and disagreement between the leading alternatives. Policymakers in Taiwan have relied on proposals with wide participant support to craft laws regulating Uber or online alcohol sales.

Imagine if Congress had the benefit of such a tool. Americans could have helped forge consensus through upvoting the key provisions of, say, the 2020 Covid relief bills. Certain apps, like Countable and Brigade, have tried this without official government involvement and without widespread success. But the Taiwan experience suggests that having the government as an active partner and promoter is key. Admittedly, it would have been a challenge to ensure the participants on these digital platforms were representative of the nation and included the elderly, those from rural communities, and people of color while excluding bots. But systems to conduct outreach, verify identities, and cross-section participants could help in this regard.

At a bare minimum, Congress should put working drafts of legislation online, updating it every forty-eight hours, for members and the public to see and comment. It is an outrage that the language of a five-thousand-plus-page Covid-19 relief bill was made available to rank-and-file members and the public only hours before the vote, just a few days before Christmas. That leaves little time to strike problematic language, leaving members with the highly constrained choice of an up-or-down vote. Powerful committee staff spends weeks drafting bills like these, with input from lobbyists, think tanks, and leadership staff. They should use modern digital tools that are commonplace in any private sector workplace to make the process far more transparent and open to comment.

The internet can also facilitate more robust deliberation by hosting virtual forums on social media that are modeled on America in One Room. This program, which was the brainchild of Stanford political scientists James Fishkin and Larry Diamond, convened 526 diverse Americans of both parties in a conference center near Dallas in September of 2019. The participants received common source material from experts of differing ideologies on hot-button issues. After a few days of discussion, the group was able to garner more than 70 percent support for a few innovative proposals addressing these themes. In addition to publicly backed deliberative forums, Facebook, Twitter, and Zoom should partner with Fishkin and Diamond to create them online across the nation. Each forum could have hundreds of participants from different geographies and racial backgrounds and would engage with a diverse range of experts. Think of them as national town halls for the twenty-first century.

In a similar vein, Connecting to Congress, the brainchild of political scientist Michael Neblo, is organizing online town halls with representatives and a sample of their constituents to discuss a single important topic in depth. Surprisingly, an award-winning political science study found that the working class, younger voters, and women of color are more willing to participate in these forums than voters who are affluent, older, or white men. The convenience of participating online seems to outweigh inequities in digital access or familiarity. The glib assumption that the working class is not online is false. When it comes to Facebook, for example, studies show the working class is almost proportionally represented. They are, at least, as present as they are in more traditional public forums. While they may not be as active in expressing their opinion, they are tuning in. Twitter is a different story. David Lazer, a leading computational social scientist, led a groundbreaking study about the composition of Twitter followers of members of Congress. They concluded that, in almost every district, Twitter followers had a significantly higher median income than nonfollowers and a higher propensity to follow political accounts. What the various studies underscore is the need to be intentional about inviting a wide range of citizens to participate as equals in online discussions. Our federal and state governments should partner with tech companies to make the tools for organizing inclusive, online town halls available to elected officials, candidates, and activists.

Although I appreciate that the regular town halls I've held on Facebook Live have allowed many of my constituents to participate who wouldn't normally be able to join in person, we should be mindful of the limits of digital platforms. Participants are not as aware of each other's body language or emotion, and it is hard for them to gauge when to interject or to have lengthy, spontaneous exchanges. There also needs to be extensive outreach and support to get people comfortable with online forums, and we must be conscious that older Americans as well as those who do not have sufficient technology exposure or affordable internet may be excluded. Technology always comes with trade-offs, and we need to make certain that we are also creating opportunities for participation that don't require technological know-how.

That said, the federal government can make major strides by improving its digital design to invite more citizen engagement and to ease the use of its online systems. Design is about function. The better the design, the more it serves citizen needs. Anyone in Silicon Valley will tell you elegant design is at the heart of how Apple, Facebook, and Airbnb succeeded. The situation is very different with our federal government. For example, if you look up Social Security Supplemental Income, the government website supposedly to help people understand it is a complex maze we're asking society's most vulnerable to try to navigate: https://www.ssa.gov/ssi/text-understanding-ssi.htm.

Two of my signature bills that passed into law during the Trump administration—the Information Technology Modernization Centers for Excellence Program Act (CoE) and the 21st Century Integrated Digital Experience Act (IDEA)—call for modernizing federal technology and making digital services more useful for Americans. They require agencies to build cloud and data management capability and to be digitally modernized and mobile friendly, including e-signatures, digital forms, and easy-to-navigate and attractive websites.

What is also needed is the creation of a chief design officer with adequate funding to attract top tech talent and the authority to make changes. This person could work in coordination with chief information officers to implement standard guidelines and interoperability across agencies. If the federal government can attract a core group of outstanding tech professionals, they will be able to better engage the private sector to build out government platforms that prioritize the needs of citizens. Just as importantly, we need to cultivate in software developers an interest in public service akin to what inspires lawyers to give up seven-figure salaries at big law firms to work either on Capitol Hill or as judges. Emphasizing public service in any computer science curriculum, however, is not enough. To attract software developers, government agencies must empower them to drive innovation.

Affirming dignity in the digital age requires centering the citizen's voice and citizen's experience in an online world. We must design platforms, public and private, that do not promote lies or divisiveness but facts and constructive discussion, as Tim Berners-Lee had originally hoped. In the wide sea of the internet, we must find ways to uplift even the quiet citizen who still yearns to make a contribution to our democracy through reason, dialogue, and imagination. We should aspire to build a digital public sphere, with a plurality of speech communities, where the "noncoercive coercion of a better argument" can over time carry the day instead of entrenching inequality and mediocrity by requiring that participants be skilled at perpetual self-promotion and branding to be heard. At stake is whether we can succeed in building broad consensus for a shared conception of justice and the common good in our democracy.

8

SCIENCE IN DEMOCRACY

For the past fifteen years, Matt Russell, a fifth-generation Iowa farmer, and his husband, Pat Standley, have managed their 110-acre Coyote Run Farm with a commitment to sustainable farming. They have built a customer base that buys food directly from their farm, including grass-fed beef (where cows are not injected with hormones), heirloom tomatoes, poultry (which are not fed any antibiotics), and eggs. Pat and Russell, who spent eleven years in training for the Catholic Diocese of Des Moines, share the belief that farmers must help find solutions to the world's biggest problem: climate change. For example, the two adopted a rotational grazing system for their livestock to minimize greenhouse gas emissions. When cows overfeed on grass, the soil's ability to store carbon is destroyed. Rotational grazing allows cows to feed on the grass while enabling the soil to keep carbon in the ground and serve as a carbon sink. This simple technique makes Coyote Run Farm a model for responsible "stewardship of the land."

During the 2020 presidential campaign, Matt was eager to share his story with any politician who passed through Iowa. The media published headline visits to Coyote Farm by then candidates Joe Biden, Kamala Harris, and Beto O'Rourke. But Matt was not interested in the media spotlight as much as pioneering a new way of talking about science policy in our democracy. Over a beer in Knoxville, Matt shared with me his frustration about how politicians and scientists lecture farmers about climate change with no acknowledgment or understanding of their love of the land or their need to make a living. Farmers who express hesitation about changing how their family has farmed for generations due to practical concerns about costs run the risk of being labeled anti-science, anti-climate, and anti-innovation. At a time when family farms struggle to survive, many farmers have come to resent a scientific establishment that judges them.

In today's democracy, an understanding and acceptance of science and technology plays a pivotal role in many individuals' lives and career prospects; it is also necessary in an age of climate change, artificial intelligence, and ongoing digital transformation. Yet when it comes to science-based policies, resistance is usually not due to a lack of citizen aptitude; it generally comes down to a sense of marginalization, where citizens feel like they are left out of the very conversations that will impact their lives, instead of being invited to participate. This chapter tackles head-on the challenge of engaging Americans on the scientific and technical issues that will shape the communities in which they live as well as our nation and world.

Matt Russell understands that you cannot lecture people about abstract science without engaging them about what it means for their way of life. So he convened small groups of farmers in church basements, meeting over a meal for a couple hours to discuss climate action. He showed them respect by acknowledging their love for the land and allowed them to steer the conversation. Farmers, who previously had never been asked for their perspective, were enthusiastic about having this dialogue. They agreed on the value of rotational grazing, cover crops, no-till farming, crop rotation, and generating renewable energy. But the central theme that came up in almost every discussion group was the need to pay farmers for this new way of operating. The changes required up-front costs that many couldn't afford, so the way to convince farmers to adopt new techniques that would keep carbon in the ground was to help them pay for adoption. By compensating farmers for being environmental entrepreneurs, the participants reasoned, family farming could remain profitable and also help save the planet. Matt understood intuitively that when farmers begin to think of climate change as an economic opportunity, there is much more openness to understanding the science and changing traditional practices.

Although Matt never studied deliberative democracy theorists, his project is consistent with their aspirations. Mark Brown, a leading science policy theorist, writes that "constructive public engagement" with scientific information is critical before citizens embrace, let alone act on, the principles. Citing the philosopher Jürgen Habermas, he advocates for "public deliberation" to direct administrative agencies. In the context of Matt's gatherings, this would mean that the United States Department of Agriculture should invite farmers to recommend and discuss policies, rather than simply dictating terms to them. As Brown sees it, what often seems like a disagreement about science is really a disagreement about policy. If people know they are empowered to make policy choices, then it mitigates the prospect of politicizing science because an acceptance of a certain scientific fact or principle will not surrender a person's political agency to a nameless bureaucracy. Brown points to the concept of "ecological reflexivity," as one potential way forward on climate policy. In *The Politics of the Anthropocene*, John Dryzek and Jonathan Pickering develop this idea, which essentially calls for giving ordinary people a voice in developing "principles for collective action." Matt Russell embodies this approach, bringing together the voices of people who've been excluded from political decision-making to develop imaginative approaches to issues that have lingered unchanged for decades.

Matt's work offers a glimpse of hope that our nation can build a broad consensus around new policies to tackle the climate crisis and technologies to lead the twenty-first century. Elizabeth Anderson, a leading philosopher, has observed that people often discount science when they fear the outcomes or do not identify with the experts. When they feel alienated from elite institutions and excluded from the prosperity that could result from scientific proposals, they are likely to be skeptical. This suggests a didactic or argumentative approach is in and of itself unlikely to persuade. Instead of villainizing, shaming, or hectoring ordinary Americans making a living in traditional industries, we should see farmers and oil and gas workers as essential partners in developing new solutions to the climate crisis with workable incentives.

Chris Buskirk, the conservative publisher of the journal *American Greatness* and staunch supporter of former president Donald Trump, shared with me that he is optimistic about the potential for "broad agreement" on environmental policy if the language is not "overblown" or unaware of "unintended adverse consequences." Shockingly, almost no progressives or Democrats have ever reached out to him to discuss crafting an environmental agenda. We have little hope of passing bold policies if we are making no effort to understand the values and aspirations of the nearly 74 million voters who supported President Trump. It turns out that Buskirk strongly supports sustainable agriculture and believes that many conservatives would as well because they think nature "is an essential predicate to everything else in human life." As Buskirk sees it, many evangelical Christians who believe in protecting God's creation and being stewards of the planet are open to taking action to prevent climate change.

Buskirk has a vision that is quite similar to the farmers Matt convenes. He outlines a framework that can cut through congressional gridlock, has a global impact, is easy to understand, and can be the basis for bipartisan legislation. It involves "replacing industrial agriculture with sustainable agriculture, combined with a program of soil revitalization. Soil revitalization of the kind seen in the Loess Plateau in China is not only beautiful and productive but also acts as a massive, *natural carbon sink* [emphasis added]."

Beyond recognizing and respecting that many conservatives view nature and the land as worth conserving, our communications challenge, Matthew Nisbet argues, is to present climate change as an opportunity to "grow the economy" and for "economic development." At its best, the Green New Deal, originally coined by Thomas Friedman, a *New York Times* columnist and best-selling author, is a vision for engaging local communities to create new renewable energy industries and spark economic growth. The Green New Deal legislation is a vehicle for conservation and for twenty-first-century job creation. Republicans attacking the plan have alleged that it costs $93 trillion, but the reality is nowhere near that; this figure is a completely made-up number that includes the potential cost of providing health care without any of the savings and a guaranteed job to everyone. Rather, as I see it, the Green New Deal is an aspirational framework for concrete investment in new technology development, and policies to move that technology into the market, so that we can become the world leader in new energy and achieve the climate goal of a future with net zero carbon emissions. So, let's dig into what the broad contours of an effective, democratic, and pro-growth climate plan would look like.

BUILDING A GREEN FUTURE

There is no issue that inspires young people more than tackling climate change. I have seen students hold sit-ins, sleep outside the Democratic National Committee building, chase down senators and members of Congress, hold protests, attend rallies, and organize social media tweet storms all demanding action. When I ask young people why they are phone banking, registering people to vote, knocking on doors, or giving money online, they almost always respond by expressing their frustration with congressional inaction on the biggest crisis facing their generation. They know that they and their children will be the ones that will feel the costs of our inaction on the climate, not the current leadership. If you want to mobilize the younger generation that is the future of the Democratic Party, you have to speak to their passion for the environmental movement.

The language of climate activism is about ecological justice, environmental racism, preventing mass extinction, equity, and divestment. But how do we build a bridge between this language and language that can speak to older generations and small towns? What can stay true to the goals of the environmental movement but also resonate with the farmers who meet in Matt's church basements or drillers in Butler County, Pennsylvania? This is the project that John Kerry, who is now special presidential envoy for climate, and I took up in our op-ed for *The New York Times* titled "Don't Let China Win the Green Race." We make the case that for America to win in this new century, we must lead in clean technology. The themes in our piece are similar to what eight mayors from the Ohio River Valley call for in their *Washington Post* op-ed titled "We Need a Marshall Plan for Middle America." They argue that the Ohio Valley "stands to lose 100,000 jobs as the fossil-fuel economy continues to decline in the face of superior, cost-competitive renewable energy development." The mayors make it clear that market pressures and automation are causing job loss, not regulation. A government program promoting clean technology could bring good jobs to the region. They want to position the government as the helper, not the villain to blame for transitioning jobs away.

An effective and ambitious green agenda can be founded on proposals that appeal to both sides of the aisle. Below are five proposals that frame important climate policy goals in terms of jobs, market incentives, and economic growth and have the potential to attract broad-based support across our nation if we engage local communities.

MASSIVE INVESTMENT IN SOLAR AND WIND

If we want to substantially decarbonize the economy by 2035 and prevent the temperature from rising by more than 2 degrees Celsius, the world needs massive investment in solar and wind energy. The good news is that, despite critics' concerns, solar and wind actually generate *more* jobs than the fossil fuel industry does. In a groundbreaking report appropriately subtitled "Jobs, Jobs, Jobs, and More Jobs," Saul Griffith and Sam Calisch estimate that renewable energy jobs could create about 3.6 million jobs by 2035 compared to approximately 1.2 million that are currently needed in the traditional energy industry. Although "it takes more labor and maintenance to access" renewable fuels, Griffith and Calisch argue that the price of renewables is ultimately lower because "fossil fuels cost money," whereas the sun's rays or wind are free. It is possible to create renewable jobs and meet our green energy goals with an investment of nearly $3 trillion over the ten years, which is about 1.5 percent of our GDP annually. This investment would also help us become the world leader in solar and wind production.

Why is there so much political opposition to solar and wind if it will lead to many more jobs for an affordable investment? Communities heavily reliant on fossil fuel industries are understandably skeptical about whether those new jobs will be in their regions or whether they will provide a comparable tax and philanthropic base. Before my trip to Beckley, West Virginia, I remember speaking with Senator Joe Manchin, who told me how the 2009 stimulus package did not allocate enough funds for job creation in the left-behind communities in his state. Manchin's point is a good one. If we want states that are currently dependent on a fossil fuel economy to support green energy development, they deserve *prioritization* in federal funding to create new jobs. We should provide larger federal grants for renewable energy production to communities with a significant percentage of fossil fuel jobs. This way, residents will view a clean tech jobs program as additive to their community as opposed to merely substituting or even subtracting jobs. Griffith and Calisch show that solar and wind jobs can be "highly distributed geographically and difficult to offshore." These should be "located in every zip code," and they should be good, union jobs that provide better pay and benefits than what fossil fuel workers currently earn. We will only win the argument for massive investment in renewable energy if we engage communities that fear displacement and show them that we will bring good new jobs to them first.

CLEAN TECH INNOVATION

Although solar and wind can make up a large share of renewable energy, we also need innovation for new energy sources, storage and transmission, and the removal of carbon from the atmosphere. According to the Center on Global Energy Policy at Columbia University, our current spending for this type of innovation is inadequate, at $8 billion per year. They call for more than tripling the funds to $25 billion by 2025 and for channeling research to ten focus areas: carbon dioxide removal, carbon capture and sequestration, the smart grid, clean agriculture systems, clean buildings, clean fuels, advanced transportation systems, clean energy generation and storage, foundational science and platform technologies, and industrial decarbonization. To achieve this, Bill Gates has called for creating a single organization for clean energy research called the National Institutes of Energy Innovation akin to the National Institutes of Health. It could finance, for instance, promising research projects on fusion—the elusive dream—which would allow us to create energy like the sun does.

Advocates for investment in clean tech innovation can learn from the political effectiveness of the defense industry. When I joined the House Armed Services Committee in 2017, I began to realize why the defense budget was more than 50 percent of our discretionary federal budget. The defense industry has literally spread out jobs to cover almost every congressional district. There's a reason why Lockheed Martin builds the F-35 using suppliers in forty-five different states and touts its creation of more than 250,000 jobs. The lesson to be learned is that clean tech innovation, like defense, should take place in communities across our nation, as opposed to in the Beltway. Quite simply, the distribution of clean tech innovation outside Washington agencies will help build broader support for public investment.

Another promising approach is BlueGreen Alliance's call to invest in green American manufacturing. BGA is a coalition of labor and environmental organizations committed to finding climate change solutions that create thousands of new jobs. Nearly 22 percent of greenhouse gas emissions come from the industrial sector, but this issue does not receive much media attention. There is an opportunity to build broad consensus supporting tax credits for clean tech manufacturing, as well as grant and loan programs to help American manufacturers dramatically reduce their emissions. These policies are necessary for American manufacturers to be competitive in a world where the EU is moving toward implementing an import tax based on carbon emissions. The policies will help create union jobs installing and operating next-generation machinery on the factory floor. Many of these new jobs will be in traditional, industrial towns and will help position green policies as consistent with ambitious plans to rebuild and revitalize these areas.

The much harder lift will involve policies that regulate the supply of fossil fuel production. Even if clean tech innovation succeeds in reducing the amount of fossil fuels that businesses and consumers use, there is still the difficult issue of exports. Annie Leonard, executive director of Greenpeace USA, estimates that if we continue to produce and export fossil fuels, even potentially expanding our capacity to supply other nations, we could cancel out up to 50 percent of the emission reductions that would be achieved by transitioning to domestic consumption of renewables. We simply cannot ignore the question of the fossil fuel production and exportation. That is why in California, which already has many diversified sectors, Annie and I called to stop building new fossil fuel projects and to institute a 2,500-foot buffer between oil drilling and residential neighborhoods. This should not apply to more fossil-fuel-dependent states, and the politics were candidly hard even in California. Although a large coalition of environmental groups, led in many cases by passionate young activists, supported these policies as part of the Last Chance campaign, both Governors Jerry Brown and Gavin Newsom did not act. Representative Barbara Lee and I were the only California members of Congress who supported the campaign. Much work remains to be done, and to make progress we need to consult with fossil fuel workers in California about how to ensure that their futures are secure even as we invest in future generations.

ELECTRIC VEHICLE REFUNDABLE TAX CREDIT AND FEDERAL FINANCING BANK

We are losing to China in the race to produce electric vehicles. China produces about 60 percent of the electric vehicles for the world market while we produce about 25 percent. China provides its citizens subsidies to buy electric vehicles and heavily subsidizes auto manufacturers to set up plants for producing electric vehicles. We currently offer an electric vehicle income tax credit for up to $7,500 for as many as 200,000 cars per manufacturer. This is inadequate and benefits those who can afford to wait for the end of the year when they file. Instead, we should offer a refundable tax credit available at the time of purchase for all electric vehicles until they make up over 75 percent of annual new car sales.

Even that proposal, however, cannot be the end of the conversation. Many autoworkers have shared with me that moving to electric vehicles means fewer jobs for them. As the United Auto Workers union has noted, companies need fewer workers to make electric power trains compared to internal combustion engines, "transmissions, exhaust systems, and fuel systems." In fact, when General Motors closed their plants in Lordstown, Ohio, and Warren, Michigan, its reasoning was that it needed to restructure them to focus on electric cars. We cannot glibly proclaim an electric vehicle future without considering the interests and aspirations of the workers in these communities.

A possible solution is to structure the refundable tax credit to incentivize the purchase of vehicles from reopened plants and to require domestic manufacturing and a percentage of American component parts. Imagine if the tax credit would be twice as large for any electric vehicle manufactured in a plant that was previously shut down such as the ones in Lordstown or Warren. This could be for any plant shut down before 2020, so there is not a perverse incentive to close plants. With the availability of a large tax credit, GM and other auto companies would think hard about putting new electric vehicle manufacturing, particularly for sport utility vehicles which have higher demand, in towns that suffered plant closures. At the very least, the credit should be restricted to vehicles manufactured in the United States, and a threshold percent of component parts must be American made. This would spark new union jobs in towns that faced deindustrialization. We can also tie the tax credit to a requirement that companies must invest significantly in worker training and apprenticeships to prepare workers for new technologies. Finally, we should consider a larger tax credit to first-time electric car buyers so we are not spending a lot of money on consumers who are already committed to buying these cars.

A more direct approach would be to use the Federal Financing Bank at Treasury, which currently lends to other federal agencies, to encourage investment in advanced manufacturing plants in left-behind regions. For instance, it could be authorized to make purchase guarantees or lend to companies committed to building new plants in these regions. And it could apply not just to electric vehicles but also to new solar plants, battery plants, and decarbonized steel production with hydrogen gas. These are the type of industrial projects that neither traditional banks or venture capitalists are funding and where we need a new financial lender. If the United States Development Finance Corporation can undertake such financing arrangements to help American companies develop overseas, there is no reason we should not have an agency facilitate such investment within our borders.

Too many policymakers have tunnel vision when advocating for an all-electric fleet. They add an abstract paragraph about a "just transition" to their plans, thinking that will satisfy the concerns of those who may be displaced. But such boilerplate language has not and will not. We will not reach broad consensus on climate policy unless we involve the workers that will be most impacted. The point is not to sell a plan to them, but to listen to their needs and ideas. New, high-paying green jobs cannot simply be scattered on the coasts or in urban centers, but also need to be in auto towns. At the same time, we should be open to the possibility that hydrogen vehicles may be an attractive, environmentally sustainable alternative. Policymakers should not be wedded to a particular technology solution, but ensure that any framework is flexible to support the technology that best advances climate change goals while prioritizing the needs of autoworkers.

PAYING FARMERS FOR REGENERATIVE AGRICULTURE

The United States Department of Agriculture should implement Matt Russell's vision of paying farmers for being environmental entrepreneurs. I worked with Matt to introduce a congressional resolution that lays out specific principles for how such payments should work. First, the payments should be outcome-based, as opposed to compensating farmers for implementing specific practices. In other words, we should pay farmers to be innovators and for general improvement in air, water, or soil quality. An outcome-based approach would complement current underfunded initiatives at the USDA, such as the Conservation Reserve and Stewardship programs that already pay farmers, for instance, to "remove environmentally sensitive land from agricultural production."

Second, when funding agriculture programs, we should provide grants to projects where farmers and researchers work together. I helped Iowa State researchers secure funding from Silicon Valley for a program where they collaborate with farmers to assess the effectiveness of inserting prairie strips in corn and soybean fields for improving soil quality and carbon removal. What made the Iowa State program attractive to the Valley's social impact investors is they're able to collaborate with farmers as active participants in their research.

Finally, farmers should serve as advisors to the Department of Agriculture to help structure the programs that would pay them for ecological services. We need to think of the expertise as residing not just in the academy but in the work of farmers who know their land and could help craft more effective policy. If we center farmers in the conversation about regenerative agriculture and pay them for their skills, we can earn the trust of many traditional agriculture towns in supporting climate change policy.

A 50 PERCENT RENEWABLE GOAL THROUGH THE DEPARTMENT OF DEFENSE

While in office, President Barack Obama highlighted how, "Obviously, the situation in the Middle East implicates our energy security." He said that, in order to reduce our energy dependency on the region, we need to be "reducing our overall dependence on oil with cleaner alternative fuels and greater efficiency." The world's reliance on oil impacts almost every notable foreign policy issue, and the United States' reliance on fossil fuels is not just an environmental issue but a national security concern. Our extensive military footprint around the world requires the massive use of fossil fuels, to the extent that former secretary of defense Jim Mattis even cited strategic vulnerabilities because our military is so dependent on fossil fuels. He patiently explained to members of Congress on the House Armed Services Committee in public appearances that oil convoys in war zones are susceptible to attack. It would in fact be much safer to use solar-powered vehicles and equipment for overseas operations. Mattis also recognized that the geographical instability caused by climate change could hurt U.S. military missions and operational plans and could lead to more global conflicts due to increased competition for natural resources. Such conflicts, of course, only cause more destruction, of human lives, of communities, and of the environment on a massive scale. It's within the interests of our defense establishment and the country as a whole to protect the climate and transition to green energy sources while we still have the chance.

The Department of Defense currently has a goal of using 25 percent renewable energy for the Army, Navy, Air Force, and Marines by 2025. This requirement passed in the 2007 National Defense Authorization Act under President George W. Bush. The Navy already has exceeded this target. I have worked with members on the Armed Services Committee to increase the goal by 2025 to 50 percent renewable energy. Framing renewable energy as being in our national security interest is another way to cut through the partisan divide on climate change. As

Mark Brown told me, "There tends to be more bipartisan agreement on policy than on science because people on different sides of an issue often support a shared policy for different reasons. Democrats might support investment in renewable energy for environmental reasons, while Republicans might support it for national security."

Our military can become a model for how private industry can reduce their carbon footprint. For that matter, if the military can do it, when its investments are matters of life and death, the Coca-Colas and Nikes of the world would be hard-pressed not to follow suit.

ETHICAL FRAMEWORK FOR ARTIFICIAL INTELLIGENCE

One of the most pressing sectors for responsible scientific engagement and policymaking over the coming decade is the field of artificial intelligence. Much like the Covid-19 pandemic or climate change, issues related to AI will end up affecting everyone in the United States and around the world—and it will be a hot-button issue that cannot simply be regulated by scientists or technologists behind closed doors. While we allowed the internet to emerge without a strong ethical or legal framework in place, we should not make the same mistake when it comes to the emergence of artificial intelligence. After witnessing massive privacy breaches and the toxicity of social media, we hopefully have learned our lesson about the need for strict guardrails as new technology develops.

At a high level, artificial intelligence is the capability of computers to detect patterns in source material, draw conclusions, and recommend or take actions based on that analysis. PricewaterhouseCoopers has an outstanding report which concludes that, by 2030, AI will add over $15 trillion, larger than China's entire GDP, to global GDP through productivity gains and also improvements in the personalization, cost, and utility of products. This new technology will bring new business opportunities and be a boon for many consumers, offering them more convenience and better quality at lower prices. As a member of the House Artificial

Intelligence Caucus, I'm excited about the potential of this new technology to improve our lives.

We risk, however, aggravating the inequality and discontent already caused by globalization and the digital revolution if we do not have democratic accountability for the use and development of AI. Thinkers at both the Consortium of Science, Policy & Outcomes at Arizona State University and Stanford Institute for Human-Centered Artificial Intelligence are engaging with many stakeholders to ensure that artificial intelligence platforms are accountable to the values and needs of a diverse public. As the Consortium eloquently argues in its mission statement, the "advance of science and technology," including AI, needs to be explicitly linked to "the achievement of desired societal outcomes."

As we usher in new artificial intelligence developments, there are five principles that can help guide our nation. First, we need to require government audits and certification of "high-risk" AI systems. This was the conclusion of a multidisciplinary group of experts in tech policy at Stanford. Before a car manufacturer sells a vehicle, a builder a home, or a pharmaceutical company a drug, they need certification about the safety and quality of the product. Why should it be any different for AI technologies? Without compromising proprietary information, regulators at the Federal Trade Commission should inspect whether a particular AI system or data set compromises privacy or creates other types of serious harm. If an AI system is automating decision-making about an activity that will have a significant impact on people's lives, such as software that makes recommendations about candidate hiring or about financial transactions, then it should face appropriate scrutiny before it is rolled out.

Second, we need disclosure of algorithmic bias. There is a real danger that AI systems can disparately impact people of color by denying them employment opportunities, loans, admission to college, housing opportunities, or subjecting them to racial profiling by law enforcement agencies. We know facial recognition programs, moreover, are less accurate for people with darker skin because of the unrepresentative data sets that they have to work with. This fact was most strikingly demonstrated when Amazon's facial "Rekognition" software incorrectly identified twenty-eight of my colleagues in Congress as criminals who had been arrested. At the time, 20 percent of members of Congress were people of color, but 39 percent of the misidentified members were people of color. This led to a hearing in the House Oversight Committee—which I sit on—where we heard from the ACLU, who called for an indefinite federal moratorium on the use of facial recognition technology until companies fix the data discrimination.

A groundbreaking Brookings report recommends AI companies that make decisions about people be required to issue Bias Impact Statements. Such statements should include potential limitations about data sets and blind spots in any recommended outcomes. The Algorithmic Accountability Act, introduced by Senators Cory Booker and Ron Wyden and Representative Yvette Clark and championed by civil rights groups, would also be a foundational step. If passed, it would require companies to ensure a threshold level of fairness in automatic decision-making systems and conduct detailed assessments about meeting that standard. The FTC in turn can mandate that developers include and prioritize certain ethical constraints or parameters within the very design of algorithms.

Third, we need bold federal investments to prepare for the job loss and displacement that AI will cause, ensuring that people in every geographical region are positioned to take advantage of the new opportunities it will create. The McKinsey Global Institute's pioneering report on AI concluded that nearly a third of workers in the United States may need to find new jobs and develop new skills by 2030. They likely will have to learn how to operate machines or work with software that will do the most repetitive parts of their work, without eliminating their jobs completely. It will create many new high-paying jobs in technology-oriented fields and also will facilitate business efficiency and growth that will lead to new job openings. But as the report puts it, the most difficult challenge "will be to retrain mid-career workers." It goes on to note that,

"There are few precedents in which societies have successfully retrained such large numbers of people."

Many of the recommendations from Part I of this book will help the country adapt to these concerns. But to address this challenge, we need a major commitment from our federal government. Currently, the federal government spends a paltry .03 percent of our GDP on worker training and placement programs, which is sixfold *less* than Germany. It would be a colossal mistake for our national government to stay a passive bystander, content to let techies, nestled far away from the corridors of power, drive AI's rise and make giant fortunes at the expense of the rest of the country in the process. At some point, our governing institutions must intervene, help people understand what lies ahead, and partner with the private sector to provide them with modern tools for success.

We also need federal regulations to ensure that the hundreds of thousands of workers that label, record, or input data for AI machines to process are paid fairly and have opportunities for upward mobility. These are jobs that are very difficult to automate. Saiph Savage, director of the Civic A.I. Lab at Northeastern University, has shown that many of these workers, who have a significant presence in rural and urban communities, end up making less than $2 an hour for the tasks they perform on digital platforms. Corporations such as Amazon, Facebook, and Microsoft don't take into account how long these projects take that power their AI systems. Savage notes that those doing AI-related tasks often "call themselves tech workers." But the question of whether AI can support a broad range of middle-class jobs depends on the policy choices we make.

Fourth, when it comes to the use of AI by military, border control, or police departments, we need to ensure that meaningful human control is maintained in the use of all weapon systems. Intrinsically human qualities like empathy are invaluable to any complex ethical decisions. Meaningful human control as a standard also ensures that there is a pathway toward holding people accountable, and that no one can ever simply evade responsibility by blaming a machine for an unjust arrest, injury, or even loss of life.

Trump's secretary of defense Mark Esper released principles for the Defense Department's AI use calling for its development to be "responsible," "equitable," "traceable," "reliable," and "governable." There was no mention of protecting human life. The Defense Department must adopt additional principles explicitly clarifying that any use of AI in military strikes must be used to minimize civilian loss of life and be ultimately controlled by humans tasked with meeting that objective. This would ensure that there is human empathy and responsibility involved in the decisions that are augmented by AI-driven intelligence. We should also negotiate a common set of AI rules with other countries to ensure that an AI arms race does not unfold.

Finally, we should commit to a strategy for maintaining our lead in AI development, since it will be a critical technology for the future of our country. John Mearsheimer, one of the leading scholars for international relations, put it to me bluntly:

> The United States simply cannot allow China to win this technological arms race. If that were to happen, it would have disastrous consequences for America's prosperity as well as its security. After all, being on the cutting edge in developing a wide array of new technologies helps fuel economic growth and also helps maintain a first-class military that can protect the national interest. China is no ordinary challenger. Indeed, it has the potential to zoom past the United States and replace it as the go-to country for cutting-edge technologies. America's future success, in other words, is bound up with Silicon Valley's future success.

The AI race implicates more than our strategic interests. It is also about values. We do not want China's AI systems or development approach to become a leading model for the world. China's model has little regard for privacy, human rights, or individual liberty, as the country has no qualms about building a trove of unlimited data and using it to surveil its own people. The voluminous data which it can obtain given its population, especially without consent, is an advantage for China, as data is the lifeblood of AI. But according to MIT president Rafael Reif, researchers at places like MIT are working on new algorithms inspired by our understanding of the brains of toddlers that make it possible to train computers with much less data. As he memorably put it to me, "a little child does not need to see a billion pictures of cats to recognize a cat." MIT professor Josh Tenenbaum is a world leader in helping model how the human brain works. His team is "engineering Kant" so that machines can identify objectives based on time, space, and other categories such as cause and effect. If we achieve this kind of breakthrough, then we would go a long way in overcoming China's data advantage.

Creating new approaches to AI such as Tenenbaum's is the kind of innovative, scientific project that calls for federal investment. Unfortunately, a bipartisan report authored in 2020 in consultation with former representative Will Hurd and Representative Robin Kelly concluded that China is slightly ahead of the United States in government spending on AI. Our private spending on AI, however, dwarfs China's, with companies such as IBM, Alphabet, Facebook, Microsoft, and Amazon spending nearly $80 billion compared to the $9 billion spent by China's AI leaders such as Alibaba, Baidu, and Tencent. The problem is that private investment may not support cutting-edge research that is being done in leading universities, which tends to be less focused on short- or even medium-term market advantage. Big tech also does not have as much of an incentive to pursue new modes of AI thinking that lie outside their revenue models based on heavy data collection. That is why the report recommends increasing the AI budget to $25 billion a year, or about 1.5 percent of the total federal budget. We should couple that increased appropriation with the establishment of a consortium of private industry leaders, government officials, and academic computer scientists charged with developing and implementing a strategic plan to ensure American leadership in AI. By drawing on every facet of our tech leadership, we can develop AI systems that both foster growth and reflect our democratic principles.

THE INFRASTRUCTURE OF TECHNOLOGY

One final challenge for America's science leadership is to lay the technology infrastructure across the country. China is doing this every day in their country. We should "build back better" not only by fixing our roads, bridges, and airports with as many "shovel-ready" projects as possible, but also by constructing the architecture, or hardware, of a digital economy. That would be a grand achievement on par with President Dwight Eisenhower's creation of the interstate highways.

We need the type of commitment we had in the Apollo era of the space race with the Soviets. As President Biden often emphasizes, back then we spent nearly 2 percent of our GDP on science and technology development, but today we spend only .7 percent. Our past federal investments have fueled revolutionary advances in more than space. Silicon Valley leaders understand that Defense Advanced Research Projects Agency (DARPA) funding led to the creation of the TCP/IP protocol to transmit data in the 1970s that made the internet possible.

At a time when we face climate change, pandemics, rapid AI advances, and a constantly digitalizing economy, MIT economists Jon Gruber and Simon Johnson call for increasing it to a little over 1 percent of GDP with a focus on applied science in cutting-edge fields. China is, at least, at 1.3 percent of GDP. Guber and Johnson estimate that additional federal funding of $100 billion annually will get us in the same ballpark at 1.2 percent of GDP and lead to 4 million new jobs. These would not just be PhDs or engineers, but also construction and manufacturing workers engaged in the project of modernizing America. The Endless Frontier legislation discussed in Chapter 2 is a first step toward achieving this ambitious goal.

Gruber and Johnson propose a list of technologies of the future to capture the public imagination and attract support across the political spectrum because they have the potential to generate distributed jobs and widespread prosperity. The following sections examine several highlights of their list, including the possibilities of 5G, semiconductor manufacturing, and synthetic biology.

DEVELOPING AND DEPLOYING 5G

At a Munich security conference I attended in 2019, Trump administration officials were unified behind the message that other nations must not use Huawei's 5G technology. A former president of Estonia asked Defense Secretary Esper a pointed question that struck me: "I understand you do not want us to do business with Huawei. But what is the alternative that you are offering?" The answer was nothing. The U.S. had fallen behind on 5G, and we find ourselves at a geostrategic disadvantage vis-à-vis China. If Americans or Europeans rely on Huawei for their internet, there's nothing stopping the Chinese from stealing our data. Devices from pacemakers to cars, in the near future, will all run on 5G internet, and the question of who controls that infrastructure poses serious national security risks.

So when I arrived back home, one of my first calls was to MIT president Reif, a Venezuelan American engineer. Reif had his team of experts at MIT, led by David Goldston, the former lead staffer of the House Science Committee, put together a short framework for me outlining a potential U.S. strategy on 5G. President Biden would be well served to have leaders like Reif and Goldston working to restore the public's confidence in the federal government's ability to undertake moonshot projects.

The issue is that China has a much higher number of 5G smartphone users than the United States and many more 5G base stations and boxes, all produced by Huawei. Because we missed the boat, the U.S. has no domestic 5G manufacturer and relies on Finland's Nokia, Sweden's Ericsson, and South Korea's Samsung for our equipment. The most straightforward aspect of federal policy should focus on the widespread deployment of 5G boxes, which need to be thirty feet aboveground on towers. An investment in installing boxes and building towers would create thousands of well-paying blue-collar jobs in every region and help all Americans access high-speed 5G wireless service.

Our government should also assist American companies that have an interest in collaborating with Nokia, Ericsson, or Samsung on 5G manufacturing, providing generous credits or loans for any production of 5G equipment in the United States. Huawei spends more than $20 billion on research and development annually, with subsidies from the Chinese government. Competitors are at a significant disadvantage if they do not have some assistance from the United States to develop cost-effective alternatives. The most controversial policy aspect is whether we need a single, nationally run 5G spectrum, as senior officials in the Trump administration advocated, or whether we should allocate the spectrum to different American companies. This is a debate that should not be held behind closed doors. What we need is to hold roundtables across the country to explain the trade-offs of having the government build a secure 5G network versus allowing multiple competitors in the free market to drive innovation.

The American public can engage on these issues if we have thinkers such as Reif to make science policy accessible. Part of the blame lies with our academic institutions themselves, where scientists are too often content to talk to other scientists in prestigious journals with insufficient consideration for communicating with the public. Our elite science and technology universities must incentivize faculty to communicate with a general audience and reward those scientists who show great skill in doing so. Public funding for their research obligates leading researchers to consider how to engage respectfully with citizens on policy debates. America can still right the ship on 5G if we invest broadly in its deployment and production, while engaging the American people in decision-making. Our failure thus far is less a result of technological limitation, but one of uninspiring leadership.

SEMICONDUCTOR MANUFACTURING

The United States continues to lead the world in semiconductors, accounting for nearly 50 percent of the global market compared to only 5 percent for Chinese companies. Intel, the world leader in sales, is headquartered in the heart of my district, as is Nvidia. Both Micron and Qualcomm also have a significant presence in the Valley. Although consumer-facing companies like Apple, Google, and Facebook get all the media attention, the semiconductor industry, which produces the chips that power all these companies' technologies, is the crown jewel of Silicon Valley. There is a reason the Valley takes its moniker after the silicon chip. The challenge for our nation is that currently about 12 percent of chips are manufactured in America and nearly 80 percent in Asia. In 2019, none of the six major fabrication plants (fabs) that opened were in the United States, and four of them were built in China. There is bipartisan concern in Congress about the need to expand our semiconductor manufacturing capacity. This will create high-paying jobs and ensure that our technology infrastructure is not vulnerable to the decisions of foreign actors like China.

The good news is this is the rare area in which Congress is surprisingly competent and forward-looking. In 2020, Representatives Michael McCaul and Doris Matsui led the CHIPS for America Act, bipartisan legislation passed by both the House and Senate that provides massive investment and tax incentives for semiconductor manufacturing. I was proud to cosponsor this bill, which directs the secretary of commerce to create a $10 billion matching fund to help support new fabs in the United States for both prototype and high-volume commercial manufacturing. These fabs will create a wide range of local jobs including workers on the factory floor, lab technicians, and research scientists and engineers. The bill also provides a generous 40 percent tax credit for the purchase of any equipment for semiconductor manufacturing or any investment to build a fab. It sets up $20 billion in programs for advanced semiconductor research and workforce development. This is not a corporate handout, but necessary to compete with other Asian nations that are rolling out the red carpet to attract semiconductor companies to their shores.

What enabled CHIPS to succeed? The key was McFaul and Matsui's decision to include their bill as part of the FY2021 National Defense Authorization Act. They successfully made the argument that building semiconductor fabs in the United States is a national security imperative.

CHIPS also enjoyed broad support from my colleagues on the House Armed Services Committee, because they were convinced that new semiconductor manufacturing jobs would be spread out in many congressional districts. It provides a model for how, even in polarized times, it is still possible to get things done to improve American competitiveness and create twenty-first-century jobs.

SYNTHETIC BIOLOGY

The scientific process of using biological material to produce food, energy, consumer products, and medicine is potentially transformational for our economy and can even help us tackle climate change. We now can understand the component parts of organisms in detail and synthesize those parts into new products. With synthetic biology, now a $4 trillion market, we can lower emissions by reducing the need for plastics that are made of oil and gas. In addition to the environmental benefits, the new industry has the potential to create hundreds of thousands of new manufacturing jobs, including in rural America.

John Cumbers, the CEO of SynBioBeta, a consortium of leading synthetic biology entrepreneurs and investors, proposed a "Bio-Belt" through middle America. He believes that wherever there is "abundant land," biomass can be made into valuable products. Cumbers wants the United States, not China, to lead in this new industry. The truth is the U.S. was the first to develop this technology and invested more than $800 million from 2008 to 2014, thanks to funding from the National Science Foundation and the Defense Advanced Research Projects Agency. Since then, other nations have been catching up. According to experts Cumbers regularly consults, China has built more than a hundred life science parks with biotech incubators and large fermentation plants. It has a goal of growing the sector 15 percent every year, while investing billions in research and development and the necessary infrastructure. In such an important field, we need to increase our investment in biotechnology laboratories, factories with fermentation technology to turn microbes into products, and workforce development. We also should offer tax credits for investments in research and development and provide incentives to those who purchase from American suppliers.

The task of building support in Congress for these policies depends on linking the work being done by PhDs at Stanford and MIT with new job opportunities in left-behind communities. As with other rapidly advancing fields, calls for increased investment in science are likely to fall on deaf ears if the prosperity is concentrated in districts like mine. As elementary an observation as this is in a nation where 435 members of Congress shape federal policy, it is often lost on the most brilliant minds who come seeking support on Capitol Hill. Regardless of their sophisticated PowerPoint decks showing the rate of return or job multiplier impact of their research, they are not exempt from the messiness and accountability of democracy.

For that matter, we should also consider the ethical implications of synthetic biology. Despite all of its promise, there are a range of concerns, from dangers surrounding the weaponization of the tools of synthetic biology, to the ethical quandaries that accompany the ever-increasing ease in altering DNA, to the displacement effect that the industry's advances could have on other areas of the economy, disrupting livestock farmers, chemical manufacturers, and others. These concerns don't necessarily overshadow the promise that advances in synthetic biology have to offer, but they do underscore the importance of tying our scientific pursuits to the principles of democracy.

The search for knowledge and control over our environment are noble endeavors. Those who dedicate their lives to these pursuits deserve our respect and admiration. But in a world where so much is in flux, where change itself can be threatening, scientists and technologists must be participants in our democracy and work with humility to influence our culture. Science, at its best, should endeavor to challenge and enrich public opinion without harboring the false and counterproductive expectation of dictating its course.

9

DECENTRALIZING FOREIGN POLICY

One of my proudest moments of political advocacy happened when the *Bucks County Courier Times* ran my essay titled, "Read This 14-Year-Old's Lips, George." Mrs. Raab, my ninth-grade teacher, challenged us to submit our papers to the local paper's op-ed section. My piece argued that the first Gulf War was not worth fighting to secure oil or for "balance of power" politics, but only to vindicate international norms of sovereignty. I remember being convinced that the president or his senior advisors would read my essay once it got into the local paper. Now, even as a member of Congress, I understand how hard it is to get the attention of the White House; it takes more than a well-timed op-ed, even in the *Washington Post* or *New York Times*. But the memory of my ninth-grade op-ed lingers, kindling a flickering belief that anyone in this country can have a say, even on the weightiest decisions of war and peace.

Today's fourteen-year-olds are doing far more than writing opinion pieces in their local papers. They are creating viral posts demanding bold action on climate change, speaking out about human rights abuses in Yemen, and reminding leaders about our obligations to refugees, the global poor, and immigrants. They are organizing walkouts during the school day, starting online petitions, coordinating virtual advocacy days, and creating memes that capture the attention of celebrities, journalists, politicians, and other social media influencers.

The internet has empowered more than students. Millions of ordinary Americans now have an opportunity to participate in conversations traditionally reserved for a rarefied and seemingly impenetrable foreign policy community. This final chapter considers the impact of the digital revolution on how we treat people outside the United States and new ways they may respond to us. We have looked thus far at how to respect dignity in a digital age domestically by focusing on distributing jobs, empowering workers, cultivating our freedoms, protecting online rights, creating deliberative forums, and including a multiplicity of voices in science policy. In this chapter, we'll consider issues of global justice. The argument is that we may be able to advance the dignity of people around the world as a wider spectrum of American citizens weigh in on issues of national security, war and peace, and the need to build transnational public spheres.

EXPANDING THE NATIONAL SECURITY CONVERSATION

In 2020, my most viral tweet posed the question: "What would make you feel safer right now: more aircraft carriers or $2000/month in your pocket?" At the end of 2020, Congress overrode President Trump's veto on the $740 billion dollar Pentagon budget, but only passed a Covid-19 relief bill with $600 checks. Republicans in Congress said we couldn't afford $2,000 for Americans making less than $75,000, even though we could continue to spend hundreds of billions on our military. This was an example of the Beltway being out of touch. Friends and family in the Bay Area, Pennsylvania, and Ohio were more concerned about the threats from microbes at the time than threats from missiles or attacks from Russia, China, or Iran. They wondered how it was possible that our Navy could detect the smallest mines in vast oceans, our Air Force could detect any movement into our airspace, our Army could detect weapons caches in tunnels in the most remote mountainous areas of Afghanistan, yet we lacked the infrastructure to detect a lethal virus infecting millions of people right here at home.

It is not science fiction to imagine how we could have had the infrastructure in place to prevent Covid's rapid spread—and we can still build that infrastructure to keep Americans safe from the next pandemic if we treat these diseases as the national security threats they are. In fact, the National Institute of Allergy and Infectious Diseases (NIAID), where Dr. Anthony Fauci has served as director since 1984, has a program to develop a portable diagnostic needle that clinicians could use to detect almost *any* virus, including the one that causes Covid-19, within two hours. In the best case, this could lead also to the development of at-home tests that could be deployed at scale quickly. They also have a program to develop a few broad-spectrum antiviral therapeutics to help defeat any new virus as soon as it is discovered. One would think that a nation that spends $740 billion annually on defense would invest a sizable amount in these two programs. We do not. We have only been spending about $100 million annually in each program—less than a quarter of what the Pentagon spends on its musical bands each year.

Imagine if we increased the funding tenfold to $1 billion each. It still would be a fraction of our annual defense budget and the $16 trillion that the pandemic is expected to cost the U.S. When we talk about expanding the definition of national security, programs like these to keep people safe in their day-to-day lives should have the same priority as building new ships or aircraft carriers. Our nation's incredible mobilization in developing vaccines for Covid-19 in less than a year demonstrates that our government can collaborate with the private sector to produce breakthroughs. In this case, Congress appropriated funds for procurement contracts which helped pharmaceuticals with early manufacturing, and

National Institutes of Health (NIH) scientists made key underlying discoveries for some of the vaccines. This success has increased public confidence and support for critical scientific endeavors. President Biden's success in getting the vaccine into the arm of every American who wants it has also helped increase people's faith in the competence of the government to tackle large projects.

Our interconnected world has meant American scientists have worked with other countries to tackle the pandemic. As fraught as the U.S. relationship is with China, it was a Chinese scientist who shared the original sequence with the rest of the world. According to *Time* magazine, Professor Zhang Yongzhen did so without notifying the Chinese government, any international governing body, or the U.S. He collaborated with Professor Edward Holmes, a colleague in Australia, who posted the research online on January 11, 2020, on virological.org. Many scientists at NIH admit that it was a game changer to have access to that sequencing so early. Yongzhen and Holmes's research formed the basis of our early testing and also jump-started our vaccine research. That said, Zhang's contribution should not obscure the fact that China may have developed the virus in the first place. Any collaboration with Chinese scientists must be grounded on principles of complete openness and transparency.

Today, nonstate actors are also involved when it comes to the distribution of the vaccine to the global poor. The Gates Foundation committed $100 million to COVAX, the World Health Organization's initiative to ensure global equity in vaccine distribution. Development officials from the foundation have been more engaged in that effort than our own government.

The decentralization of foreign policy is not just about giving American citizens more of a say in our foreign policy decisions. It also is about empowering them to collaborate with people across the globe to solve global problems and step in when national governments and their diplomats have been paralyzed. An expanded vision of national security includes an expanded role for citizens on the world stage.

BLOATED DEFENSE SPENDING

Defense, which has consistently been more than $700 billion in the past few years, is more than 50 percent of our discretionary federal budget. It is significantly higher than it was during the height of the Cold War even with President Reagan's defense buildup, when it reached a peak of $610 billion in 1985 adjusted for inflation. We currently have about eight hundred military base sites in about eighty countries. Meanwhile, the entire NIH budget of $40 billion is less than 3 percent of our discretionary budget and the entire Centers for Disease Control (CDC) budget of $8 billion, less than 1 percent.

There are specific areas where cuts can reduce waste, such as the Overseas Contingency Operations fund (OCO). What started out as a pot of money for our wars in Afghanistan and Iraq, OCO has become a Pentagon slush fund, as even President Trump's former acting chief of staff called it. We've spent almost $2 trillion since 2001 in OCO and it has ballooned in recent years because it's not constrained by discretionary spending limitations from the 2011 Budget Control Act. OCO is almost $70 billion, meaning if it were its own federal agency, it would be the fourth largest, only behind the Department of Defense itself, Health and Human Services, and the Veterans Administration. The Biden Administration relabeled OCO funding as "enduring requirements" for war and as part of the base budget, but they did not make any meaningful cuts. We should reduce these reserve funds for fighting endless wars to save tens of billions a year.

Another area to cut back is on the cost of building new nuclear weapons. The U.S. plans to spend more than a trillion dollars just to modernize our nuclear arsenal over the next thirty years. There are ways to save tens of billions of dollars that won't impact our nuclear deterrence posture. I've championed one that focuses on our ground-based nuclear weapons, better known as ICBMs (intercontinental ballistic missiles). According to the Department of Defense's public statements, we currently have four hundred ICBMs, named the Minuteman III, which were first deployed in 1970. The Air Force plans to do away with the Minuteman III missiles and replace them with new ones, the Ground Based Strategic Deterrent (GBSD), that could cost more than $100 billion. Instead of making new ICBMs, we should just extend the life span of the Minuteman III, which would still deter potential attacks while saving us almost $40 billion over the next twenty years. Plus, ICBMs are less secure than nuclear weapons when on U.S. submarines because their location is known and they can be destroyed more easily. It is not strategic for the U.S. to invest in building new missiles with the same vulnerability. When I offered a provision in the annual National Defense Authorization Act markup to freeze funding for the GBSD and transfer it to Covid-19 response, despite the support of Chairman Adam Smith and former secretary of defense William Perry, only twelve of the fifty-six members of the House Armed Services Committee supported it, underscoring Beltway thinking on national security priorities.

Digital activism that challenges excessive Pentagon spending, unfortunately, does not typically reach the most critical American constituencies. Sunjeev Bery, executive director of Freedom Forward, a human rights organization, shared with me that foreign policy reformers often "get seduced by the experience of generating public support and amplification" from those already sympathetic to their cause. Even if a tweet may be shared tens of thousands of times, that does not mean a significant number of voters hear the message, let alone in districts represented by members on the Armed Services Committees. To build a broad coalition, online activists must respect the thousands of high-paying defense jobs that are at the center of economic activity in many local communities, assuring those communities of their continued and vital role in building a twenty-first-century American defense. We also should acknowledge the importance of funding DARPA (only about $3.5 billion) and other defense-related research and development that has spawned entire new industries. Any proposed cuts should be narrowly targeted to go after waste, monopoly profits, excessive executive pay, and overseas interventions—not strategic initiatives or benefits for military families.

Bery believes a central challenge for true decentralizing foreign policy is to create online spaces that encourage nuanced public discussion with an understanding of local culture and local economies, not just broad-based Twitter pronouncements.

Nonetheless, online activism about bloated defense budgets is having an impact on Congress. In 2020, inspired by grassroots mobilization, Representatives Barbara Lee and Mark Pocan created the Defense Spending Reduction Caucus, committing to responsible cuts in the defense budget. An amendment introduced that year to cut the budget by 10 percent received ninety-three votes, which was nearly half of the House Democratic Caucus. Such amendments in prior years typically received fewer than thirty votes and from only the most progressive members.

The digital age has increased the scrutiny on defense contractors that rip off the American taxpayers by charging monopoly prices. The price-gouging lines the pockets of defense executives. The average CEO pay of major defense contractors is more than $20 million, and the average senior executive pay is $5 million, subsidized by our taxes. I led a bipartisan hearing on the House Oversight Committee with the support of Republicans Jim Jordan and Mark Meadows, two of Trump's closest allies, to demand that TransDigm reimburse the government for overcharging for military parts including cables, valves, rings, motors, and disks. TransDigm had a business model of acquiring smaller suppliers and then raising the price once they became a sole contractor. Unfortunately, this practice is common at the Department of Defense. A report found that the department "did not compete" in "67 percent of 183" major contracts for weapons and parts acquisition.

Matt Stoller, a fellow at the Open Markets Institute, called attention to TransDigm's transgressions based on the investigative work of the trade publication *Capitol Forum*. Congress would probably never have been aware of the misconduct if it were not for Stoller's advocacy to me and others. Journalists at the *Intercept* and activists also began to raise the issue publicly, putting pressure on the company to take responsibility. Embarrassed by the Congressional Oversight hearing, TransDigm agreed to reimburse the government $16.1 million, a fraction of their excess profits. The incident highlighted the potential investigations that defense contractors face in a world where information is hard to contain, and nontraditional journalists can disseminate the results of their work.

The goal for the defense budget should be to addresses the modern, safety needs of Americans. There certainly have been times this century when military force was required such as striking Al Qaeda in Afghanistan after 9/11 and preventing ISIS from establishing a caliphate in 2014. But we should not build nuclear weapons we do not need or overspend on defense contractors at the expense of broader national security priorities such as keeping us safe from pandemics. Our focus should also be on cybersecurity, which can be a source of new good-paying jobs in defense towns. While cybersecurity for our most sensitive weapon systems is now part of our national security strategy, we need an operational plan to address the cyberthreats that impact Americans in their daily life.

MANHATTAN PROJECT FOR CYBERSECURITY

As a former presidential appointee at the Commerce Department during the Obama administration, the 2020 SolarWinds cyberattack on our federal agencies caught my attention. SolarWinds is a public company that supports the IT operations and security for many large corporations and government agencies, and their system was hacked by suspected Russian spies who were able to read the emails of Commerce, Treasury, Justice, and Energy Department officials for months. The attackers added malware, a malicious software, to a SolarWinds product so that when the company offered a routine product update, many existing customers were compromised and the spies gained unauthorized access to their accounts. Although there are no reports that the attackers obtained classified information, they did see extensive correspondence, documents, files, and personnel information. The real danger is not just that they obtained sensitive information, but that they could have manipulated the data itself to confuse American policymakers.

If our federal government is this susceptible to cyberattacks, consider the broader vulnerability of the American public. We saw a glimpse of the potential devastation when the Colonial Pipeline in Texas was hacked by a Russian-based cyber-hacking group called DarkSide. This led to cars lining up at empty gas stations across the Southeast as gasoline shortages plagued our nation. It was reported that Colonial Pipeline ended up paying the hackers $5 million to get back online. Imagine if this was a government-linked hacking group, or an adversarial government itself, whose goal was not just money, but to destabilize and seriously harm our country.

Almost every American business fears cyberattacks, interrupting their ability to operate. While the U.S. military will protect Americans from a ground invasion or missile strikes, there is no cyber force to protect them from online attacks. No security force patrols the internet looking for hackers that threaten local communities or individual businesses. It is not possible, moreover, for the U.S. to bar potential adversaries from using encryption to access our networks. Unlike China, our constitutional values prohibit building a firewall against encrypted communication or banning it altogether. So American businesses are largely on their own to defend themselves in a world filled with online threats.

Technical solutions exist to protect against cyberattacks. Alex Aiken, one of the nation's leading computer scientists at Stanford University, argues that software verification can ensure that all points of vulnerability are protected through mathematical proof. Think about this way: Before moving into a home, we don't just test whether the doors have working locks, but we also rely on the verification provided by home inspectors of every structural element that prevents someone from easily breaking in. Similarly, when the entire structure of software is verified as secure and protocols are adopted for those interacting with the software, it drastically reduces the threat of a cyber invasion. Cutting-edge research for software verification is being sponsored by the Department of Defense, but currently is used in less than 1 percent of software given the cost. It also is typically used for only 100,000 lines of code when most elements of critical infrastructure such as a power plant or utility company require millions of lines of code. This is not an insurmountable burden but one that requires additional and meaningful investment in R&D.

Another notable cyberattack, the 2008 Buckshot Yankee one, compromised many military computers, for which the Defense Department implemented stringent cybersecurity standards for defense contractors as a result and set up a U.S. Cyber Command to enforce them. Herb Lin, an expert in cyber policy at Stanford, maintains that we need a stronger framework to protect other government agencies and private sector actors that currently do not have the Defense Department software standards. While they do not need to be as robust as the standards protecting our most sensitive weapons systems, the status quo is unacceptable.

President Biden should call for a Manhattan Project focused on cybersecurity. Five immediate reforms would help protect Americans online. First, any government contractor such as SolarWinds and any public company should be required to develop a cybersecurity plan consistent with the National Institute of Standards and Technology (NIST) framework, detail its implementation, and file it with the Department of Commerce. Currently the NIST guidelines are voluntary with no accountability for compliance. Second, when a cyber breach occurs, there must be civil liability for any company that does not live up to the terms of its NIST plan. A liability standard would incentivize companies to include cyber experts as part of software design teams as opposed to bringing them on as an afterthought after a product is completed. Third, the default setting in any software should have all the cyber protections active. Currently, when software is sold to customers, including to critical infrastructure companies or agencies, the cyber features are often turned off so they don't interfere with customer convenience or ease of use. With today's threats, security must take precedence over convenience. Fourth, we should allocate funding to the Department of Homeland Security for cutting-edge research on cybersecurity, including for safeguards against quantum computing which can break encryption. Finally, the Department of Commerce should provide small- and medium-sized businesses with grants and technical expertise to assist in developing and implementing cybersecurity plans. This basic vision for cybersecurity is foundational in a digital age when businesses and individuals are vulnerable to attacks with almost every online interaction.

MOBILIZING AGAINST ENDLESS WARS

Prominent cable news hosts who tweeted about the humanitarian catastrophe in Yemen during the day, privately apologized to me for not having segments about it on their news programs at night. I realized early on in my advocacy to end the U.S. involvement in the war in Yemen that it was far easier for me to get on television to discuss Trump's latest tweet or the intraparty Democratic squabbles than to discuss the millions of Yemeni civilians who were on the brink of famine. Producers told me that viewers changed the channel when images of American-made bombs dropped on school buses, or starving Yemeni children flashed on-screen. Most of the public education about Yemen thus took place online with grassroots organizations such as Just Foreign Policy, Win Without War, and MoveOn. They initiated petitions and email campaigns where hundreds of thousands of American citizens called on members of Congress to stop U.S. support for the Saudi bombing campaign in Yemen. Celebrity activists like Eve Ensler, Mark Ruffalo, and Alyssa Milano first learned about the Yemen disaster on social media, and then engaged in effective digital marketing to wake Congress up from our slumber.

Digital organizing changed American foreign policy in Yemen. As a freshman member of Congress back in 2017, I saw this unfold after introducing the Yemen War Powers Resolution to stop all military support to the Saudi-led coalition fighting a war in Yemen. At the time, no senior House Democrat wanted to touch the issue because it would have forced a vote when our caucus was split about the strategic value of the Saudi relationship: the Saudis hosted American bases, served as a check against Iran, and purchased American weapons. House Democrats also disagreed about whether providing military support to the Saudis constituted engaging in hostilities that required congressional authorization. Because of online organizing, we succeeded in getting a compromise resolution passed through the House recognizing the U.S.'s unauthorized role in the war. Often activists had more knowledge, gathered from online sources, about our involvement in Yemen than many of the members of Congress or their staff.

Successful passage of the compromise House resolution convinced Senator Bernie Sanders to introduce the War Powers Resolution in the Senate. Then, for a period of nearly two years, Senator Sanders and I introduced the Resolution time and again, as well as related amendments, slowly widening the coalition of supporters. Each effort saw more members of Congress and senators come aboard. While our staff, such as Geo Saba, Keane Bhatt, and Kate Gould, deserve credit for working the halls of Congress, they would be the first to attest it was targeted digital petitions and online outreach that convinced members to support our effort. As Stephen Miles, executive director of Win Without War, put it, "the internet supercharged our work for peace, making rapid mass mobilizations possible." Some online activists even supported primary challengers to those members who initially refused to take a strong stand against the Yemen war.

The dam protecting the U.S.-Saudi relationship finally broke after the high-profile murder of journalist and U.S. resident Jamal Khashoggi. The evidence suggests that the Saudi government plotted his assassination precisely because of his withering criticism of his government's war in Yemen, including as a columnist for *The Washington Post*. On the Hill, the outrage was bipartisan and swift. Too often, however, a surge of outrage in Washington gives way to returning to the status quo. The difference in this case was the digital and organizing infrastructure that Yemen activists had built. They were able to flood members' social media accounts and offices with viral images and articles about the suffering of Yemeni women and children at the hands of the Saudis. Digital platforms may have given thousands of activists a voice, but what made them effective is linking their advocacy with a sophisticated understanding of the traditional levers of power on the Hill.

Just a few weeks after assuming the speakership, Nancy Pelosi brought the War Powers Resolution to the House floor where it successfully passed. When the gavel dropped and the resolution passed, I couldn't help but think back to my fourteen-year-old self. My ninth-grade teacher probably would not have imagined that I would go from penning an op-ed addressed to the president about the Iraq War in 1991 to one day working with the speaker of the House and Congress to legally direct the president to remove U.S. military support from a war in the Middle East. This time my efforts certainly received the attention of the president. The legislation received President Trump's second veto of his presidency. Online organizing had broken through to the highest echelons of power with only a supporting role from mainstream newspapers, think tanks, foreign policy hands, or for that matter, politicians. Although President Trump vetoed the legislation, the administration voluntarily stopped refueling Saudi planes as a response to pressure from the Hill. Martin Griffiths, the United Nations special envoy for Yemen, believes that it paved the way for the cease-fire in Hodeida, a strategic port city in Yemen, and set us on the path to end U.S. involvement in the war. Digital organizing secured a place in modern history by standing up for human rights and establishing a precedent for influencing decision makers.

Online activism on matters of war and peace has also shattered conventional political alignments, resulting in my issue-based partnerships with Freedom Caucus members to prevent war in Iran and end the 1950–53 war in Korea. Some Republicans who I worked with are President Trump's staunchest allies and, to my dismay, voted against certifying the results of the 2020 election. Many pundits wonder how we manage to even converse, let alone work on legislation together. What I have found is that there is a passionate conservative base that believes our entanglements overseas have cost us lives, divert resources and attention from our focus on China, and prevent us from taking care of our needs at home. The foreign policy establishment that fumbled our way into a twenty-year war in Afghanistan and colossally blundered in Iraq faces a popular revolt from both the right and the left. Some of my most interesting and provocative Twitter threads are ones where I tagged Republican members about avoiding another Middle East war or bringing home our troops from Afghanistan. These rare moments pierced social media bubbles, where those who typically attacked me as a California progressive cheered on my advocacy for restraint and taking on bloated defense spending.

The amendment to the National Defense Authorization Act to restrict President Trump from waging war in Iran passed the House overwhelmingly with 251 votes, including 27 Republican members, in 2019. Even though the amendment was ultimately stripped in the defense bill that went to the president's desk, it served as a counterweight to the pressure that Trump was facing within his own administration from Secretary of State Mike Pompeo and National Security Advisor John Bolton to escalate the Iran conflict. A number of House Republicans had personally spoken with President Trump about our amendment, and Trump was well aware that support for another Middle East war was waning in Congress. The advocates for military restraint had come a long way from the days when a bipartisan Congress overwhelmingly gave both President Bushes authorization for their Iraq wars. I have no doubt that advocacy groups, which derive power from their email lists and digital organizing on social media, had an impact. On the Democratic side, Speaker Pelosi and House Armed Services chair Adam Smith both acknowledged the role of online organizing by Win Without War, MoveOn, and VoteVets in securing support from caucus members. On the Republican side groups such as Concerned Veterans for America, FreedomWorks, and the Koch-backed Americans for Prosperity launched online campaigns targeted at the Freedom Caucus to stand up for nonintervention. Although digital organizing, like canvassing or rallies, is sometimes driven by large financial investments and should not be misconstrued as an organic barometer of public opinion, it has undeniably provided millions of Americans a voice in foreign policy decisions that historically have been decided by an elite club inside the Beltway.

Before the pandemic struck, Representative Andy Biggs and I were supposed to travel to South Korea together to meet with President Moon Jae-in and strategize about a resolution to the conflict on the Korean Peninsula. Many Americans do not know that we have not formally ended the war with North Korea—we only have a cessation to the Korean War with an Armistice Agreement in 1953. Biggs and I supported both Moon's and Trump's call to have a formal peace agreement with North Korea, with a view that this would make North Korea feel less threatened and might allow for more collaboration and oversight on denuclearization measures. My approach was influenced by my conversation with former president Jimmy Carter. One of the honors of my life was traveling to Atlanta for a forty-five-minute meeting with Carter, where he recounted in precise detail his meeting with Kim Il-sung, Kim Jong-un's grandfather, in 1994 and a framework they proposed to bring peace and denuclearization. Carter recounted that he was "a submarine officer in the Pacific during the Korean War," and the issue was personal to him. His central thesis was that North Korea seeks respect and recognition by the U.S. He was initially hopeful about the Trump administration's efforts to engage them and encouraged me to travel to the Korean Peninsula with a Republican counterpart to bring more specificity and coherence to our efforts.

While leaders like President Carter provide the vision for a reimagined foreign policy toward North Korea, they have a mobilized online community to back them up with groups like Women Cross DMZ. Founded in 2014, the organization is a global online movement of women mobilizing for peace on the Korean Peninsula. They reached out to Biggs and me as well as scores of members of Congress to advocate for diplomacy. Through their efforts, we were able to secure fifty-one cosponsors, including Gregory Meeks, the new chair of the House Foreign Affairs Committee, for a House resolution calling for a formal end to the war. What online activism can do, especially when global and diverse in composition, is provide muscle behind dissenting and alternative approaches to foreign policy hotspots. There is, of course, danger that shallow populism or online conspiracies may subvert thoughtful foreign policy, which I will explore in the next section. For now, it is worth noting that citizen engagement can often challenge generational assumptions about conflicts. With grassroots support, members of Congress feel more comfortable crossing party lines and working toward outreach and diplomacy rather than defaulting to status quo thinking about the world's hot spots.

MULTIRACIAL AMERICA AND GLOBAL DIGNITY

It would be naive to assume that greater public involvement in foreign policy or more public exposure to people around the world, facilitated by the internet, will always translate into support for pluralistic democracy. In fact, the rise of nationalism and xenophobia casts doubt on whether decentralization of foreign policy will lead to a dignity-centered approach. The internet globalized parochial populism. It facilitated an international following and networks for Trump's movement decrying immigrants, touting traditional culture and religion, and rejecting international institutions. Trump's supporters found common cause with populists on the right like Bolsonaro, Netanyahu, Le Pen, Orban, Farage, and Modi, and are determined to subvert a cosmopolitan view of the world with a transnationalism that is, ironically, grounded in affirming and celebrating national identity. Steve Bannon, a chief strategist for Trump, has described this as a "global tea party movement" committed to "right-wing populist nationalism" that will take on the "party of Davos."

Tech utopianism that advanced the view that the internet would facilitate global peace and human rights underappreciated the need for nations to do the hard work of cultivating liberal, democratic values in their people. It is not just that states such as China, Iran, and Saudi Arabia abused technology to suppress human rights. Even within democracies, populist movements seek allies overseas keen to suppress minority culture and to maintain preeminence for their religion, race, or founding narrative. Internet platforms allow them to participate in transnational groups that reinforce their own prejudices and ignore people who challenge their interpretation of history or worldview. Exposure to difference has not led to respect of difference. The latter must be part of a nation's educational system, governance bodies, and civic and economic life.

The danger within the U.S. is that a decentralized foreign policy nudges us in the direction of isolationism. While public opinion is turning against endless wars, some of these same citizens challenge our engagement in any effort abroad. The America First movement calls into question foreign aid, supporting human rights in other nations, alliances, trade, international institutions, and multilateral treaties such as the Paris Climate Accords, the Intermediate-range Nuclear Forces Treaty, and the Open Skies Agreement, wondering if the U.S. should be part of the U.N., NATO, and even the World Health Organization during a once-in-a-century pandemic. One of my Republican colleagues in Congress whom I work with on ending forever wars won't cosponsor any legislation if it even mentions the U.N. Although President Biden is reversing Trump's approach and reentering these important global alliances, the success of Trump's movement and lingering appeal should make us vigilant about the fragility of America's multilateral commitments.

The isolationist strand in American foreign policy is in sharp contrast to an ideology of championing freedom, human rights, and self-determination around the world that is part of our rich history. FDR led our nation not only in defeating economic depression and tyranny, but also in advocating for a postcolonial world. His envoy to India, Colonel Louis Johnson, was the one who advocated for a timeline for Indian independence and Roosevelt repeatedly pressed British prime minister Winston Churchill on the matter. FDR's worldview was influenced by President Woodrow Wilson, in whose administration he served. As early as 1918, Wilson supported self-determination that inspired Indian freedom fighters like Gandhi and Nehru—which stood in stark contrast to his legacy of racism and support for segregation.

The narrative of the Indian freedom movement and other movements for justice and freedom around the world find themselves flowing through immigrants within our body politic. America is poised to become the first major multiracial democracy in human history. Consider that America's white (non-Hispanic) population is about 60.1 percent. This is much lower than Canada, which is easily more than 70 percent white. The United States' diversity also compares favorably with both Australia and the United Kingdom. About 85 percent of Australians today "are descendants of European settlers," mostly from Britain or Ireland. As of the last 2011 census, 87.2 percent of the population in Britain "were white British."

What is striking about America post-1965 is that the vast majority of immigrants, like my parents, have been non-European. This is the result of the Immigration Act of 1965 that removed discriminatory quotas for immigration from non-European countries. According to the Congressional Research Service, prior to 1965 the percentage of immigrants and their children who were of European descent was nearly 90 percent, and non-European immigrant families constituted less than a few percent of the total population. Post-1965, half of immigrants coming to the U.S. have been from Latin America and a quarter from Asia. Europeans make up only 15.5 percent of immigrant families. In fact, non-European immigrants and their children comprise nearly 70 million Americans, almost 22 percent of our population.

Given these demographic changes in the U.S., we now have the possibility that new voices might shape a foreign policy agenda that shows basic respect for the rights and aspirations of all human beings. A progressive foreign policy would recognize that the problems of the twenty-first century, whether climate change, pandemics, cybersecurity, or nuclear proliferation, do not lend themselves to going it alone. This vision is perhaps more attainable if we succeed in this book's central mission of spreading digital opportunity and connecting left-behind communities with thriving metropolises, diminishing the zeal for inward-looking nationalism.

Those involved in setting our foreign policy have a dearth of imagination about including diverse voices to help inform their decisions about different parts of the world. The exclusivity of the foreign policy elite would not be as acceptable in a domestic policy context. Today, we would not condone a situation where Black perspectives were not included in decision-making or where women did not have a seat at the table. Yet the foreign policy world suffers not just from a lack of diversity in senior appointees, but also with their outreach. Policymakers consult a handful of representatives from ethnic communities familiar to the Beltway instead of engaging broadly with diasporic communities. They don't seek out groups who challenge their ideology and rely too heavily on elites who no longer have a clear image of what life is like in a nation they may have left decades ago. This myopia applies when making policy about South Asia, China, Africa, Latin America, or the Middle East, leaving diasporas grumbling that their adopted nation is oblivious. Whether internet mobilization of America's diverse communities will pierce through the tightly guarded, self-perpetuating foreign policy priesthood remains an open question.

When I visited the American embassy in India as a law student is forever seared in my mind. An American embassy official shouted at me, "Get out of this line. You are not an American citizen." Extended family and overseas friends had told me stories about how embassy personnel could be arrogant, but this was the first time I experienced it while I was there to try to help my cousin. My cousin, a student in the States, had lost his green card, and my extended family thought that as a law student I could help. "No big deal, let's just stand in the long line," my cousin reassured me after witnessing the incident. "It's not worth a fight." He was right—who knows what retribution embassy officials may have exacted on my cousin or what they could have done to make my journey back home more complicated? So I swallowed my pride and stood in the line for noncitizens as an American citizen. Decades later, when I met the U.S. ambassador to India coleading a mission there as deputy assistant secretary of commerce, I recounted this incident in detail, except for the name of the official I couldn't remember who had insulted my dignity. As more Americans with experiences and cultural sensitivities similar to mine rise to positions of leadership, perhaps our face to the world will become kinder, more tolerant, and humbler. That is the hope. A multiracial America may be more committed to striving for Dr. Martin Luther King's vision that "we are all caught in an inescapable network of mutuality, tied in a single garment of destiny."

THE GLOBAL PROMISE OF DIGITAL MOVEMENTS

Although many are familiar with John Quincy Adams's warning that America "goes not abroad, in search of monsters to destroy," they overlook his preceding sentence that America's "heart, her benedictions and her prayers" are with freedom movements everywhere in the world. Adams was not an isolationist: he believed that America should strive to advance the principles of "equal justice" and "equal liberty" but was skeptical about using military force to achieve them. What Adams hoped for was that we could give voice to our ideals, that over time our example may lead to the spread of liberal democracy, that through trade, dialogue, and cultural exchange we could influence people to embrace liberty. The digital age makes Adams's vision of expressing nonviolent solidarity with democratic movements more possible.

We saw how powerful global solidary movements can be after George Floyd's murder. Black Lives Matter led protests across the U.S. and sparked "a movement around the world" with protests in many nations. The Floyd protests demonstrated that we are capable of promoting our ideals internationally by setting an example through domestic action. Our mobilizing for racial justice inspired those in Belgium to stand up against their colonial history, in the U.K. against police brutality and statues glorifying slaveholding, in South Africa against human rights abuses, and in Brazil against President Jair Bolsonaro's arbitrary exercise of power and state violence. It was also remarkable to see how much support the Black Lives Matter protests enjoyed within days from activists in almost every continent, including in Syria, where Aziz Asmar, an artist, painted a mural of George Floyd on a broken wall that was left standing from an air strike on his home. He wanted to express his solidarity with unarmed Black victims of police violence which reminded him of the helplessness of civilians in the brutal Syrian civil war. The internet has made it possible for mass multinational movements to emerge rapidly, without much planning when an incident or speech strikes an emotional chord. These moments provide an avenue to stand up for democratic values without using military force.

Online organizing, however, has not yet been able to overcome repressive regimes like the ones that rule China, Iran, North Korea, and Saudi Arabia. These countries engage in what legal scholar Tim Wu describes as "net nationalism," using the internet to "promote state propaganda" while banning sources of news or ideological perspectives that contradict state ideology. These authoritarian regimes prevented Black Lives Matter protests from taking hold on a mass scale in their nations or doing so in a way that led to substantive changes. Even democracies such as India have resorted to shutting down the internet to maintain stability and suppress protests. And there is always the use of brute force, where fledgling internet uprisings or expressions of solidarity that led to the Arab Spring in places like Syria stood little chance against President Bashar al-Assad's brutality, for example.

The philosopher Jürgen Habermas's hope that "spontaneous and egalitarian nature of unlimited communication [online] can have subversive effects under authoritarian regimes" is severely restricted by the countermobilization of illiberal regimes. China routinely blocks encrypted virtual private networks (VPNs) and prosecutes residents and visitors who use them to try to get around blocked websites. While some hold out hope for a wireless, space-based ISP that could allow users to bypass national detection, so far determined states are able to counter such innovations and suppress dissident voices.

We should not, however, despair that the digital age is antithetical to the aspirations of building a global community. There are promising large-scale movements that are organic and citizen based. For example, Purpose is a social impact agency with a mission of building movements for a more open, just, and habitable world, including organizing for racial equity, gun violence prevention, ending global poverty, tackling misinformation on Covid-19, and promoting clean energy and clean air. Its founder, New York–based Jeremy Heimans, previously cofounded Avaaz, a "the world's largest online citizens' movement," which has more than 60 million members and relies largely on petitions and email campaigns, partnering with MoveOn.org and other progressive organizations. Avaaz has mobilized support for the Paris Climate Accords, opposed global media mergers, and provided humanitarian aid to dissidents in Syria and natural disaster victims in Pakistan and Haiti. The group's advocacy, though, for a no-fly zone over Syria and Libya remains controversial given both would have committed the U.S. to more military intervention in the Middle East. Then there are organizations such as UNITE where I am a member, committed to ending infectious disease around the world, and Unite, founded by Special Olympics chairman Tim Shriver, that seeks to unite Americans with millions around the world to focus on tackling some of humanity's biggest problems. We need more investment and experimentation in the kind of online spaces that these organizations are creating.

One of the biggest challenges in fostering a global community is building digital infrastructure and capability across the world. While our primary duty is at home, human dignity does not end at our borders, and the inalienable rights of every person are not contingent on their nationality. It is appropriate to look after our loved ones, extended families, communities, and nation first. But we cannot be blind to our broader obligations to the world.

The U.S. should support the "Roadmap for Digital Cooperation," for example, spearheaded by United Nations secretary-general António Guterres, to build digital infrastructure and digital skills in developing nations. It is not just morally right, but strategically smart. It helps ensure that American values of an open internet are embedded in the global technology infrastructure. Supporting international digital development also makes it easier for people in difficult regions of the world to survive and flourish, especially if it improves economic opportunity which leads, in turn, to less extremism and more political stability. Our first focus must always be on issues of human rights and justice. We must be wary of tech-washing where nations tout their investments in a start-up culture or tech scene to cover up state-sanctioned violence, discrimination, or oppression. But we cannot leave out a conversation about modern economic rights when we discuss the marginalized and oppressed. As we expand our digital capacity in the U.S., we should participate in global efforts to foster innovation hubs for the next generation as a tool for economic empowerment and even conflict resolution.

ON CHINA

The hope that the spread of the digital economy may usher in peace runs into the hard reality of authoritarian China. We need a sober China strategy not clouded by tech utopianism. What the digital age enables is the decentralization of our China policy, giving ordinary citizens, including Asian Americans, a larger say in the bilateral relationship. American public opinion, when informed, is much more nuanced than the hawks who seek a new Cold War.

The American people are not naive. According to polls conducted by the Chicago Council on Global Affairs and the University of Texas at Austin, 55 percent of Americans view China as a "critical threat" and 54 percent said out of any other country, China poses the greatest threat. But only 41 percent support using military force against China in a hypothetical conflict, even though the majority of foreign policy opinion leaders do. Americans are tired of spending trillions preparing for potential war and then politicians turning around and saying we can't afford to pay for health care, education, and green infrastructure. A paramount objective, then, of our China strategy must be to strengthen diplomatic engagement to prevent conflicts with them in any of the world's hotspots.

There are seven key principles of a China policy that could enjoy broad public support. First, Americans support cooperation with China where it is in our strategic interest. We should work with China on problems like North Korea, Iran, climate change, and arms control. Washington could learn from the common sense of most Americans who can separate areas for discrete cooperation with China from those of rivalry and competition.

Second, nearly 90 percent of Americans across the political spectrum support standing up for human rights. The more the public has a say, the more human rights will be at the center of any bilateral conversations. The internment of more than one million Uighurs in detention camps, creating a system of slave labor, with some women being systematically raped, tortured, and sterilized, is one of the gravest human rights issues of our time. I've cosponsored legislation, the Uyghur Human Rights Policy Act, to sanction Chinese Communist Party officials violating Uighur human rights and block exports from the Xinjiang region made by Uighur slave labor. More than targeted sanctions, we should set an example by expediting Uighur refugees, which could convince other nations to also welcome them.

Third, many Americans understand the economic importance of continuing to protect freedom of navigation in the Asia-Pacific. Nearly $3.4 trillion in trade passes through the South China Sea each year. Any disruption to this trade would cause Americans to feel pain in their pocketbooks. China is setting up fake islands in the South China Sea and laying claim to many islands that regional Asian countries contend belong to them to extend their control over international waters. China knows that with more territory it can control more shipping lanes and international water, particularly in the South China Sea, which contains fishing and 11 billion barrels of untapped oil and 190 trillion cubic feet of natural gas. The U.S. should stand on the side of the facts, but should let a nonbiased international institution like the U.N. settle these disputes amongst the claimants. The U.S. can reduce our Freedom of Navigation exercises if China stops militarizing and reclaiming the disputed islands.

Fourth, if we are to be true to the public's desire to avoid military conflict, we must deter China from invading Taiwan, which supplies many of the advanced semiconductors that are essential to the critical infrastructure of our digital economy. The best way to do this is to help Taiwan with its investments in coastal defenses and antiship missiles to deter China from invading, especially given that some of Taiwan's more traditional surface ships and planes are no match for Chinese missiles. The Quincy Institute, a foreign policy think tank, also calls for the U.S. to help strengthen Taiwan's own industrial defense base so that it is not reliant on outside countries if China were to blockade the country. It recommends continuing to boost economic ties with Taiwan via a bilateral investment agreement and people-to-people exchanges and supporting its observer status and participation in international organizations like the WHO.

Fifth, the American public strongly supports strengthening our alliances. In addition to Taiwan, some of our strongest global allies are in China's backyard. We should strive to have better relations with Asian nations including India, Japan, the Philippines, South Korea, and Vietnam than China has with them. We have a unique advantage with our strong Asian diaspora. My district is the only majority-Asian district in the continental U.S. so I see how diasporas build these ties economically and culturally. We also should avoid pushing Russia and China into the same camp. We must remain vigilant against Russia's military incursions and human rights abuses—at the time of writing, critic of President Vladimir Putin and human rights and democracy defender Alexei Navalny had been sentenced to two and a half years in a labor camp. But we should work with Russia on issues of mutual interest like cyber arms control, and on nuclear arms agreements like extending New START, which President Biden did in his first days in office, and reinstating weapons treaties from which Trump withdrew, such as the Open Skies Agreement and the Intermediate-Range Nuclear Forces Treaty.

Sixth, we need a balanced economic relationship with China that considers the interests of both our producers and our exporters. For starters, we must prevent their abuses of IP theft, joint venture agreements, and unfair trade that have cost us millions of jobs. At the same time, we should continue to increase access to China's market that strengthens our agriculture, financial, technology, and entertainment industries and provides cheaper products for our manufacturers and consumers. We also should allow for waivers to IP laws so the developing world has access to life-saving drugs. One way to change China's unfair practices without triggering a harmful trade war is to condition lifting our existing tariffs and trade restrictions on benchmarks for reducing IP theft and dumping activity. Most important, we must reform the World Trade Organization to include more explicit prohibitions against state subsidies or forced technology transfers which have become hallmarks of China's foreign policy, as well as strengthen the dispute-resolution system to make it more effective and efficient. The U.S. has won many of the disputes it has brought before the WTO against China, but it needs to have the ability to aggressively bring more cases when our manufacturers are facing an uneven playing field. Our ability to strengthen the WTO and cast China as the outlier of the global trading system depends on coordinating with Europe, Canada, Japan, and India—our leverage is much higher if we act in concert with China's other major trading partners.

Finally, our real competition is one of technology leadership. Christopher Darby and Sarah Sewall, the CEO and vice president of In-Q-Tel, the CIA's investment arm, put it well in their recent *Foreign Affairs* article: "China's push for technological supremacy is not simply aimed at gaining a battlefield advantage; Beijing is changing the battlefield itself." China can win the next war without firing a shot, by exporting their technology around the globe, giving them access to data, and the power to set the rules for global communication. Darby and Sewall call for our country to increase investment to compete with China, including funding early-stage start-ups (up to $500 million more a year) and late-stage start-ups (up to $5 billion more a year), particularly in these breakthrough technologies like artificial intelligence, 5G, and synthetic biology. Our ability to win this new century may depend on whether visionary calls for smart public spending that bet on American talent and ingenuity gain sufficient currency in the public debate, versus xenophobic reactions like banning Chinese grad students and plotting for war which becomes a self-fulfilling prophecy.

UNIVERSAL DEMOCRATIC VALUES

My vision for the twenty-first century embraces Amartya Sen's vision of democracy as a "universal value." Instead of imposing an external label on Asian cultures from the perspective of an outsider with glaring cultural illiteracies, Sen seeks to work from within those cultures' traditions and canonical texts to show how they value democracy. If democracy is not simply a Western value but grounded in a respect for human dignity with roots in non-European cultures as well, then a widely shared aspiration for our age is to foster the rise of pluralistic democracies that cooperate across the world.

Digital technology should contribute to achieving this vision. We need an international forum that establishes common standards for an open internet free from government censorship that values privacy, free expression, fair competition, meaningful cross-cultural exchange, distributed opportunity, and protection against violence, misinformation, and human rights abuses. These are the building blocks of a modern, liberal democracy.

A good place to begin to achieve this international approach to the internet is to build upon the transatlantic Trade and Technology Council dialogue that European Commission president Ursula von der Leyen has proposed. The forum, though, should not only include Western nations, but also democratic ones from Asia, Africa, and Latin America. We need such a forum for practical reasons to counter the power of big tech, which has circumvented or brushed off EU enforcement, and prevent a race to the bottom that may undermine democratic ideals. It also must swiftly and decisively address gross abuses, such as a government shutting down the internet to suppress protesters or a governing body using the internet to aid genocide in Myanmar.

There is a deeper reason, however, to establish an international internet governance forum. Much like how properly designed digital platforms can contribute to healing divides within the U.S., they can also foster greater understanding among nations. There is admittedly far thicker institutional, cultural, and economic commonality within a nation-state than between nations partaking in constructive online dialogue and the camaraderie of shared work. Nonetheless, there are opportunities to mitigate the worst kinds of xenophobia online and to encourage the development of digital applications such as Google Scholar that build global communities by advancing shared pursuits. As Anurag Acharya, the inventor of Google Scholar, put it to me, "a smart young researcher in small-town India today can quickly find and learn all that her peers in Cambridge, Berkeley, and Geneva have discovered and can build on it."

Transnational bodies such as the EU or accords such as the Paris Agreement also would be strengthened with a compelling digital architecture that integrates social media platforms to facilitate dialogue on critical issues among working- and middle-class people across nations. The creation of inclusive, transnational digital spheres, with rich and diverse news sources and robust discussion, is critical to the success of international institutions and global projects. At the very least, ideas originating from an internet governance forum can help shape national public debate so that it is open to new voices and foreign media perspectives.

If one believes, as Habermas beautifully posits, that the act of rational communication itself suggests the possibility for mutual understanding, consensus, and peace, then we should be hopeful that the internet dramatically increases the possibility for constructive communication regardless of distance. Habermas recognizes that the real world of politics is messy, filled with bitter conflicts, self-interest, power struggles, vengeance, and scarcity. His modest hope is that vibrant public spheres, even transnational ones, can nudge government actors in a moral direction. Even as groups self-select online and potentially tune out contrary viewpoints, the digital age has opened up unprecedented opportunities to interact with people around the world. Younger Americans are talking to people in Western Europe, Mexico, India, Russia, and even China with an ease that would have been unimaginable for previous generations who might have received paper mail every few months from an overseas pen pal. Our task is to build, then, the cultural and institutional frameworks, both within our nations and beyond, to ensure that more global conversation moves us in the direction of a more democratic and just world.

10

DEMOCRATIC PATRIOTISM

One of the events I most look forward to is the monthly congressional Library of Congress dinner. This is one of the few modern remnants of the type of deliberative salons our founders hoped would find a place on the calendars of members of Congress, with guest speakers ranging from Bill Gates to Annette Gordon-Reed, a leading historian. David Rubenstein, one of the nation's most prominent philanthropists when it comes to funding civic projects to strengthen democracy in America, moderates these conversations. One dinner sticks out in my mind, when David Blight spoke to us about his masterful biography, *Frederick Douglass: Prophet of Freedom*. In an exchange I had with him afterward about what Douglass would have said about Asian Americans and recent incidents of hate, he referred me to Douglass's speech "Our Composite Nationality." The purpose of Douglass's 1869 speech was to passionately advocate for the inclusion of Chinese immigrants, while also offering perhaps the most compelling vision for a cohesive multiracial, multireligious America.

Here, drawing on Douglass's words, I lay out a theory for democratic patriotism that inspires citizens to accept a modern American identity not resigned to rigid tribalism or an attachment merely to the principles of liberalism. Democratic patriotism calls for citizens to have an equal opportunity to participate in building our national culture while embracing a spirit of civility to support a rich plurality of local cultures that make up the whole and to resolve differences based on the specific context and circumstances. Democratizing the digital economy—the central theme of this book—is critical to achieve this vision. We need to empower Americans like Alex Hughes, who is succeeding in a tech job in Paintsville, Kentucky, so that local cultures thrive instead of slipping away, and design digital platforms to be conducive for deliberation and cultural exchange so we can build a shared national purpose.

OUR DIVERSITY AS A BLESSING

What makes Douglass's vision extraordinary is his synthesis of pluralism and unity in our democracy. He begins by observing that America is "the most conspicuous example of a composite nationality," adding "our people defy all the ethnological and logical classifications." As if describing America today, he writes, "In races we range all the way from black to white, with intermediate shades." He argues it is a blessing that America is "composed of different races." No race or ethnic group is perfect, suggests Douglass, and the "whole of humanity" is "greater than a part." Our diversity allows us to harness the talents of different groups, challenges our ideas, pushes us to improve, and perhaps most important, checks the "arrogance and intolerance which are almost the inevitable concomitants of general conformity." The "greatness and grandeur" of our nation is a result of our dialectic engagement with diverse traditions and modes of thinking.

Douglass confronts directly our ugly legacy of racism. While grappling with the sin of "race pride" that enslaved him and undergirded America's shameful and unforgivable treatment of Black and Native Americans for generations, he is hopeful that our core principles allow different races and creeds to help shape our national story. What can bind us together as Americans is "a principle of perfect civil equality to the people of all races and of all creeds," and that people from "all quarters of the globe" share "a common aspiration for rational liberty as against caste, divine right Governments and privileged classes." Douglass pushes us further, arguing the American identity is defined by more than a commitment to these theoretical ideals. It is richer. He hopes for an America where we "vibrate with the same national enthusiasm" and "seek the same national ends." He imagines a society embracing a substantive vision of "our science and civilization," including music, arts, sports, customs, and moral commitments. For Douglass, the ambition to formulate a shared conception of equality and liberty is to be complemented with a broader ambition to formulate a shared national purpose.

In his defense of Chinese immigrants, Douglass argues that we can dismiss aspects of their worldview, but should respect the five-thousand-year-old culture of a people that makes up "one fifth of the population of the world" and contributed to the "progress in civilization" with key inventions such as paper, the compass, and printing. If we build a composite nation filled with immigrants from almost every nation, respecting and learning from each other, then we can be deeply proud and attached to the national culture that emerges.

CULTURAL FLUIDITY

A key attribute of democratic patriotism, building on Douglass's insights, is that our national "aims and ends" must continually evolve, remaining as fluid as the people comprising our nation, with room for an array of communities. There is no fixed national identity. Our national identity must be a radically democratic process subject to continual debate and examination. This framing also borrows from Habermas's insight that the public sphere must be open in a multiracial democracy to both new and previously marginalized citizens who "get a voice in public debates" and can shift national culture.

America is ideally defined by what gains cultural ascendancy over time provided that there is equal opportunity for participation in the creation of our identity. Our identity at any fixed point in time, moreover, should not undermine core democratic values, desecrate seminal texts, or rush to repudiate defining moments that shine through the centuries. Today we are characterized by many aspirations: curing cancer; starting businesses in garages; creating world-class movies, music, and art; exploring space; protecting national parks, farmland, forests, and ocean areas; honoring our troops and first responders; inspiring social movements; healing racial divides; achieving athletic excellence; reindustrializing; rewarding hard work; and uplifting local heroes and volunteers who serve their community.

Under a theory of democratic patriotism, the process of identity formation is admittedly fraught with challenges. It is rooted in an imperfect historical legacy, invariably distorted by the preferences of the rich and powerful, and weighted toward long-established narratives. The gradual process of changing culture over multiple generations can, in fact, be a source of comfort to many who are concerned about their way of life slipping away. The deck is, alas, stacked in favor of those who have been free and equal citizens in America the longest. But the task of a democratic society is to be vigilant, during any given time period, about the degree of access people of different backgrounds have to a nation's political, economic, civic, artistic, and intellectual life which all contribute to culture formation. This undertaking is not simply a matter for the law or for the state, but requires an engaged citizenry committed to pushing for inclusion in every sphere. This is why Douglass speaks of "civil equality."

In fact, Douglass takes great pains to emphasize that both equality and liberty must be predicates for our composite nation. His insight foreshadows John Rawls's powerful formulation that "the concept of justice is independent from and prior to the concept of goodness in the sense that its principles limit the conceptions of the good which are permissible." In the American context, active state promotion or failure to protect the free practice of a specific religion, for instance, violates our conception of both the liberty and the equality that are necessary for a just society. There are many gray areas about what legal, institutional, and even cultural guardrails must constrain the influence of the majority in developing the common good. Our culture's legitimacy depends ultimately on how well the ideals of liberty and equality are adopted and practiced in various facets of national life, including among the many groups and associations shaping it. We must reject practices that demean people because of their race, gender, or faith. The question of the legitimacy of any aspect of national culture at any period will be a source of vigorous debate.

COWORKER IN THE KINGDOM OF CULTURE

The hope for democratic patriotism, ultimately, is to inspire a "sentiment of patriotism" among all Americans in embracing a richer sense of national purpose that goes further than—while being consistent with—democratic institutions or constitutional norms. We can perhaps ask for more than a Rawlsian consensus among competing traditions about important principles of justice and hope for what he called "a social union of social unions" where different communities harmonize into a national whole and may even coalesce around national projects. Many of us may embrace an expansive national vision, even knowing our own preferences could temporarily lose out. We may share Douglass's belief that interacting with the "most diverse populations" is a blessing and that what emerges is preferable to living in a nation reluctant to stand for more than a thin, justice-based conception of the common good. A more wide-ranging and immersive American identity can inspire stronger identification and deeper attachment. Ours can be an energetic vision of "fusion" in defining a common purpose, allowing each of us, as W. E. B. Du Bois memorably puts it, "to be a co-worker in the kingdom of culture."

THRIVING LOCALITIES

As we navigate the difficult task of building a common national culture out of our diversity, the importance of allowing people to flourish in their hometowns becomes even more apparent. Today, a significant number of Americans fear that their culture is fading away, that their values and way of life could be replaced by something that is new and foreign. Over time some national change is inevitable with a changing citizenry, especially in an immigrant nation. Anxious Americans can feel more secure if they can continue to develop the culture they inherited from their grandparents and parents where they live. They need not become, as Arlie Hochschild memorably put it, "strangers in their own land." This is one reason why the economic revitalization of towns across America is so important. Digital technology allows these towns to come back without having to give up who they are. It allows them to keep their identity while not distancing themselves from modernity. It allows residents like Alex Hughes to develop a new community of coworkers that transcends region, but still maintain a strong connection to generations of the Hughes family who lived in Appalachia. By supporting vibrant local cultures that maintain traditions, we make it easier for Americans of all backgrounds to work toward Douglass's vision of a composite nationality.

SPIRIT OF CIVILITY

To build a composite nation with a rich plurality of cultures that are not in perpetual conflict requires more than the economic development of local communities. It requires that we embrace a spirit of civility toward ways of life that may not be our own. We lose little—and typically gain much—by respecting the diverse faiths, traditions, and philosophies of communities even if we do not wish to adopt them or advocate that they become part of our national culture. A *spirit* of civility for the life journey of our fellow citizens goes beyond Rawls's demand of a *duty* of civility whereby we must provide reasons and empirical data based on a shared public framework that others can accept to justify our political positions. It asks that we also respect what gives meaning to their life—even if that is different from our own understanding of the world. It calls on us to root for their flourishing as they define it provided their worldview is consistent with the first principles of justice, not a significant imposition, and neither violates our deep commitments nor constitutes something that we detest. We take joy in observing, or even sometimes partaking in, their approach to life. We view cultural differences as potentially enriching and elucidating our own experience as opposed to threatening it.

If we are to develop a genuine sense of justice, of fairness concerning the values and interests of others, as Rawls asks, then we must strive to truly understand their values. If our sense of justice is "continuous with the love of mankind," as Rawls affirms, then that deep commitment means that we will desire for others to flourish or "to advance the other person's good as this person's rational self-love would require." While love imposes obligations beyond justice, Rawls recognizes that justice itself is rooted in caring fairly about the well-being of others. This may require us to pay attention to more than their material condition or freedom in a democratic society—basic needs which we can respect by complying with theoretical principles.

Nonetheless, Rawls likely would have hesitated to impose a duty of rooting for other worldviews as a requirement of justice, recognizing that a person may believe even certain reasonable ones to be false and not what another's "rational" self should desire. How could a person be forced to cheer for something which they reject and wish to convert or change? Perhaps, for Rawls, bracketing differences in cultural or religious life and protecting these expressions from state interference is the most we can hope for in a pluralistic society. Joshua Cohen, a student of Rawls, argues that he was inspired by Bodin, who envisioned interlocutors of different faiths loving each other while agreeing to refuse to discuss religion after reaching an impasse. But this is a distant kind of love, walling off the things that matter most. An engaged love means striving to understand another person's journey and vulnerability in search of truth and appreciating the customs and practices they believe in, even when they do not map neatly on to our worldview.

A spirit of civility stems from intellectual humility—a recognition of the limitations of reason to resolve ultimate issues which creates in us space for openness about how others choose to live while maintaining our own firm convictions about what is good and true. It requires us to look for ways to honor traditions that are important to others unless they are fundamentally inconsistent with our beliefs, recognizing the fallibility of our own approach, and seeking to love that which is deeply important to someone else and, in turn, wishing to be loved in a holistic way. It inspires us to question our own convictions about what may be in someone else's good and examine if there is any room for engaging fellow citizens where they are at in their life journey as opposed to remaining firmly wedded to our own picture of how their lives should unfold, with all the social distance and distrust that brings. The challenge is when conflicts still arise.

In situations where cultural preferences are in tension, we may choose flexibility in accommodating the important practices of others instead of insisting foremost on strict parity if we come to appreciate the fairness, value for critical reflection, and beauty of a society with many strong traditions. This embrace and celebration of pluralism is a recurrent theme in Douglass's philosophy. A devout Christian, he teaches us that to "welcome all . . . of every shade of religious opinion" does not dilute our own faith. "I know of no church, however tolerant; of no priesthood, however enlightened, which could be safely trusted with the tremendous power which universal conformity would confer," Douglass observes, adding "religious liberty always flourishes best amid the clash and competition of rival creeds." To this we might add in the modern context in which we live that our faith is strengthened by learning about other traditions and reading their important works.

These are not theoretical issues for me. They speak to my family's lived experience. When we moved into my childhood home on Amsterdam Avenue in Holland, Pennsylvania, in the mid-1980s, there was chatter on the street about the Khannas. A handful of neighbors were concerned about an Indian family moving in. My father realized quickly what the fuss was about. Every Christmas Eve in Bucks County, our neighbors put out luminarias on their curb. Some thought my family would not, given our Hindu faith. If we did not, there would be a notable gap in the street's lighting. My father told the neighbors we would put out the candles, and that his faith taught him to respect other holy days. Mom and Dad, in turn, took joy in sharing our food and customs with neighbors and invited them to our own celebrations. They also defended our Jewish neighbors who moved in after us and felt differently about the luminaria.

Years later, this story came rushing back to me, when I was a legal intern for Maryland lieutenant governor Kathleen Kennedy Townsend. One of her senior aides observed my aptitude for policy. He volunteered enthusiastically that I should work on the Hill because I could never be elected as a Hindu. Not to worry though. I could have a brilliant career, he assured me, rising up the congressional staff ladder. I refrained from sending him a note after my election to Congress. But I remember talking to my mother about the incident when it happened, who made me promise then that I would never give up my faith. "That would dishonor your grandfather," she said. "But don't worry. It will not be a barrier."

Like my parents who put out luminarias, many Americans may decide to participate in traditions that residents of a town grew up with and cherish. A recent Pew study found that while fewer Americans consider being Christian or having been born here key to being "truly American," a majority on both the right and left believe it important to adopt the country's "customs and traditions." Each of us knows, deep down, what practices we will never adopt or give up. This balance is different for every individual, every family, and every community. That is why I have suggested that in multiracial, multireligious societies, these situations are highly context-specific and not resolvable based on theory alone. We may be more willing to accommodate, for instance, certain traditions locally than across a very diverse nation.

What matters for the success of the American experiment is the spirit with which we approach these matters and how that spirit is cultivated within us as a people. This is not to gloss over or to be Pollyannaish about the heated conflicts and rivalries that are inevitable in our democracy. Rather, my argument is that the spirit of civility is a principle that Americans of different backgrounds—whether recent immigrants or descendants of our founders—may come to recognize is worth embracing as an ideal that orients our politics. It is a spirit that is rooted in one of the quintessential American traditions of seeking to understand and nurture the different aspirations of freedom seekers from every region of the world who come to our shores.

THE TEXTURE OF NATIONAL IDENTITY

Douglass recognized that a national identity is, ultimately, forged through historical events with power struggles and existential conflicts. It makes little sense for Americans to speak abstractly about equality without understanding our founders' boldness to chart "a new and more noble course" at the Constitutional Convention, the battles for emancipation, or of what happened in more recent times to John Lewis on the Edmund Pettus Bridge. It is not possible to appreciate the depth of our commitment to freedom without engaging in spirited discussion about Stonewall, Ferguson, and Standing Rock, in addition to Valley Forge, Gettysburg, or Normandy. Nations are not simply philosophical postulates; they have a history of lived experiences that define their principles, traditions, and interests. To think of America as only a commitment to an idea or to hope that we can simply reason ourselves to justice is to miss the specific events, even with different interpretations, that bind people together and add texture to our identity. As Martha Nussbaum puts it, "patriotic emotion" which stirs allegiance to national stories and ideals is rooted concretely in "particular individuals" and "physical places." We must acknowledge the power of experiential bonds in shaping our understanding of national purpose, while being inclusive in who gets to participate in building them or writing about them.

THE DANGER OF DOMINANCE

There is likely a tension between having a robust national purpose or strong local cultures with certain traditions of hierarchy and fostering true equality for those citizens who live on the margins. What is robust must not become so dominant that it subordinates all our other identities. A central thought in my argument is that there is a wide spectrum in thickness of national or community purpose that may be appropriate for democratic societies. As we deliberate what America will stand for, what our national purpose will be, we should be on guard against drifting toward exclusion.

One danger of a thicker kind of nationalism, as political philosopher Jan-Werner Müller warns, is that the culture could become overbearing and xenophobic. We've seen this with the rise over the past half decade of right-wing nationalism now sweeping across the world. In the United States Congress, Representatives Marjorie Taylor Greene and Paul Gosar started an America First Caucus with a draft document calling for immigration to be "curtailed" to those who will assimilate to "Anglo-Saxon" culture and traditions. While condemned even by many Republican leaders including former speaker John Boehner and Representative Liz Cheney, it highlights the potential dangers of supporting a strong national identity. Müller touts constitutional patriotism—where we may not agree on much except constitutional values like freedom and equality—as a possible remedy against such nationalism. The problem is that abstract principles and political institutions in and of themselves may not kindle in a general population the breadth of emotions that shape a national identity.

Douglass answers the dangers of exclusion without dousing, as I have shown, the hope for a fuller American identity. Douglass makes clear that the "right of migration" is a human right that "belongs to no particular race," and that the Asian, Latin, Middle Eastern, and African races have an equal right, "now and forever," as the white race to come to the U.S. Most important, he argues that Chinese immigrants should have as equal a chance to contribute to national culture as the English, Africans, Native Americans, Irish, Germans, or French. Douglass argues that a "desire to come" to America is proof, at a fundamental level, of a person's capability of fitting into the culture and any immigrant's inegalitarian prejudices or old-world ideas will be subject to the "freer air of America." While immigrants will likely over time embrace some "popular" customs, they should have an absolute right to "religious liberty," and to dissent and live a life "true" to their "convictions." Douglass warns that a thick conception of the common good, nationally or locally, must never morph into ethnocentrism and subjugation.

EMPOWERING ALL OF US

Douglass's vision informs this book, which, at its heart, is an attempt to imagine how technology can advance democratic patriotism which is predicated on respecting the dignity of every American. The book shares Douglass's faith that we can be a composite nation—that we can embrace a holistic, resplendent American identity that is more than just a formal contract among citizens. It offers a blueprint for structuring the technology revolution to empower left-behind Americans, regardless of their background, so they have a stronger voice in our economic and political life, build thriving communities, and are on more equal footing to participate in the dynamic process of developing our national culture. It argues that we must be intentional about creating space for artists, retail shops, and local newspapers, as well as for introverted and marginalized citizens, to help shape who we are as a people. It suggests that joint economic projects online and reasoned exchange on digital platforms can help us appreciate and respect differences. We must reduce social distance in our modern economy across geography, race, gender, and class to increase the level of trust in our body politic.

I recognize that technology is just one lens into Douglass's profound vision, which also requires major structural changes to our political and economic institutions and the inculcation of basic national values. But democratizing the digital economy is an important step in making us equal "co-worker[s] in the kingdom of culture," building the American identity. Deep down, what inspires my work to spread tech opportunity, what animates my interest in putting forth an Internet Bill of Rights, is doing my part to help us become the inclusive multiracial, multireligious democracy that Douglass believes is our destiny.

Americans are understandably jaded about tech's promise. Tech companies are seen as manipulating our data to line their pockets. Those not part of the prosperity in Silicon Valley, Austin, Seattle, or Boston wonder what will become of their towns and what are the prospects for their kids. Tech is directly contributing to soaring income inequality. And QAnon and the Capitol invasion are stark reminders of the destructive impact that digital platforms can have on our democracy.

Yet Douglass teaches us not to give cynics the final word. Despite enduring some of the most inhumane treatment during his enslavement, he articulated the most hopeful vision any American has of what our nation can and should be. He dismissed as "gloomy prophets" those who thought that "this Republic has already seen its best days; that the historian may now write the story of its decline and fall." Douglass knew better. He knew that our journey to be this universal nation, a nation of all nations, was so exceptional that we were just at "the beginning of our ascent." And as America strives to become the first major pluralistic democracy in world history, I still believe that America is on the ascent.

I believe our incredible diversity makes us the innovation and entrepreneurship capital of the world. I believe we can distribute digital opportunities and new industries in ways that will unleash the potential of millions of Americans if coupled with investments in capabilities. I believe that when we prosper together and respect local communities, we can turn around some of the despair, alienation, and anxiety that grips our nation. And I believe that our digital platforms can be designed in ways that vindicate the power of communication to bridge divides and, at least, begin to address past wrongs. We have more tools and resources at our disposal than Douglass ever could have imagined. Our challenge is to design new markets that foster the productive and creative capability of everyone, not just of the elite who are currently driving the innovation economy. Instead of passively allowing tech royalty and their legions to lead the digital revolution and serve narrow financial ends before all others, we need to put it in service of our broader democratic aspirations. We need to steer the ship, call the shots, and write the chapter that we envision together about technology's role in the extraordinary American story.

Acknowledgments

Elijah Bacal, a high school student, is responsible for this book coming into existence. He persuaded Jim Levine, a highly respected literary agent, to reach out to me after reading some of my op-eds. Elijah and Jim then convinced me to sketch an outline for this book and assured me that they would take care of the rest. They were true to their word. Jim introduced me to Stephanie Frerich at Simon & Schuster, who spent hours along with Jim and Elijah helping me frame the book's narrative. In my case, my agent and editor were not simply packagers or tweakers of the work product, but key intellectual partners from the very beginning of the journey. I could not have done this without their encouragement, feedback, criticism, and support.

A few others also were involved at the project's inception. Vikas Khanna, my brother, who is one of my closest confidants, helped me formulate and refine the central thesis. Martha Nussbaum read a very early draft and offered suggestions that helped structure the entire book. She shared with me how different thinkers have understood dignity. Bruce Ackerman spent hours discussing the application of political philosophy to the digital divide, and he offered detailed edits on the manuscript accompanied with probing questions. Vivek Shaiva, my cousin and a leading IT executive, helped me understand many of the intricacies of the industry.

Many others engaged with the work. Jon Gruber read the entire manuscript and offered critical commentary. Thomas Pogge, Joshua

Cohen, and Michael Neblo engaged in extensive back-and-forth over email to help me understand John Rawls and Jürgen Habermas. Rafael Reif shaped the chapter on science and democracy. Jon Levin helped me with some of the key economic arguments, Joan Williams focused my attention on working-class issues, and Michael Lind politely challenged some of my liberal assumptions. Doug Burns has taught me more about rural America than anyone else. Others who generously read and commented on early drafts include Michael Sandel, Arlie Hochschild, Jan-Werner Müller, Max Schireson, Anthony Appiah, Drew Faust, Kent Walker, David Berger, Roberto Unger, Joshua Cohen, Eugene Volokh, Nadine Strossen, Evelyn Aswad, David Blight, David Goldstone, Mark Brown, Talat and Kamil Hasan, Annelle Sheline, Nathan Tarcov, and Jonathan Kanter.

My thinking has deepened, and my public service is possible, because I have the most extraordinary team. They have shaped so many of my public ideas and legislative proposals, challenged my assumptions, and enhanced my knowledge. Geo Saba is one of the most brilliant, well-read, effective, imaginative, and compassionate leaders in Washington. The sky is the limit for him. Kate Gould is a trailblazer for human rights and a meticulous and deep thinker on issues of foreign policy and economic policy. Cooper Teboe is a once-in-a-generation political mind who understands rural America. Others who have worked for me and shaped my thinking include: Heather Purcell, Julia Albertson, Will McKelvey, Kevin Fox, Emma Preston, Pete Spiro, David Perez, Tom Pyke, Asya Evelyn, Keisha Bryant, Simeone Chien, Swapanthi Mandalika, Hiep Nguyen, Selene Ceja, Nicole Mata, Nandini Narayan, Angela Valles, Erik Sperling, Keane Bhatt, Katie Thomas, Chris Schloesser, Cassandra Langer, Chris Moylan, Galen Boggs, Vanesa Carr, David Chen, Liz Bartolomeo, and Mason Fong. The Congressional Research Service and the Library of Congress are national treasures.

Producing a book is a team effort. Simon & Schuster has been phenomenal. Thanks to Jonathan Karp for believing in the book. Emily Simonson offered incredible feedback on many drafts. Julia Prosser executed the promotion of this book brilliantly. Fred Chase is the best copy editor an author could ask for. Others who made this book a priority include Dana Canedy, Irene Kheradi, Jon Cox, Maria Mendez, Jackie Seow, Kimberly Goldstein, Alicia Brancato, Phil Metcalf, Ruth Lee-Mui, Adly Elewa, Cat Boyd, and Stephen Bedford.

Most important, this book would not have been possible without the intellectual contributions and unconditional support of Ritu, my wife. I lost two races for Congress before marrying her, and it's no coincidence I won the first race right after we were married. She was brilliant, funny, and charming on the stump, and was instrumental in my serving in Congress, which has allowed me to learn about the aspirations and needs of communities across our nation. She also has always had an eye for talent and management and helped me surround myself with a remarkable team. On the book itself, a casual comment from her over breakfast or while we were on a walk with the kids would make me rethink entire sections and chapters. I may not have always admitted that to her! She can get to the heart of an issue, asks detailed questions, and isn't impressed with vague abstractions that don't have meaning in people's lives. I am very lucky to be married to someone who is smarter than me and challenges me to be better. She was also incredibly patient with my writing schedule, being an unbelievable mother and supportive wife while I was often writing or editing until 2:00 a.m. Marrying her has been the biggest blessing in my life.

My children, Soren and Zara, are the joy of my life. I don't know if they will ever read this book, and I certainly will never push it on them. If they ever do decide to glance at it, I hope they will think that their father did his small part to make our nation and world a little better.

Notes

Chapter 1: Democratizing the Digital Revolution

3   *Headlines followed:* Nancy Scola, "Silicon Valley Sends Ambassador to Trump's Coal Country," *Politico*, March 26, 2017, https://www.politico.com/story/2017/03/ trump-election-silicon-valley-ambassador-appalachia-ro-khanna-236486.

7   *Extreme global poverty:* Max Roser and Esteban Ortiz-Ospina, "Global Extreme Poverty," online at OurWorldInData.org, first published in 2013 and revised in 2019, https://ourworldindata.org/extreme-poverty.

7   *Even as GDP and production:* David H. Autor, David Dorn, and Gordon H. Hanson, "China Shock: Learning from Labor Market Adjustment to Large Changes in Trade," National Bureau of Economic Research, Working Paper 21906, January 2016, https://www.nber.org/papers/w21906.

7   *According to a 2019 Brookings report:* Robert D. Atkinson, Mark Muro, and Jacob Whiton, "The Case for Growth Centers: How to Spread Tech Innovation Across America," Brookings, December 9, 2019, https://www.brookings.edu/research/ growth-centers-how-to-spread-tech-innovation-across-america.

8   *Nearly 50 percent of digital service:* Mark Muro, "No Matter Which Way You Look at It, Tech Jobs Are Still Concentrating in a Few Cities," Brookings, March 3, 2020, https://www.brookings.edu/research/tech-is-still-concentrating.

8   *In contrast, nearly 63 of 100:* Ibid.

8   *those living in communities:* Clara Hendrickson, Mark Muro, and William A. Galston, "Countering the Geography of Discontent: Strategies for Left-Behind Places," Brookings, November, 2018, https://www.brookings.edu/research/coun tering-the-geography-of-discontent-strategies-for-left-behind-places.

8   *As they struggle to:* Levi Sumagaysay, "Silicon Valley Is Not Suffering a Tech Exodus, and Money Is Flowing in at Record Rate—For a Fortunate Few," market watch.com, February 19, 20201, https://www.marketwatch.com/story/silicon -valley-is-not-suffering-a-tech-exodus-and-money-is-flowing-in-at-record -rate-for-a-fortunate-few-11613760421.

9   *We need to seed digital jobs:* The 25 million number is the addition of the expected 13 million new digital jobs to the existing 12.1 million existing tech jobs.
Brad Smith, "Microsoft Launches Initiative to Help 25 Million People Worldwide Acquire the Digital Skills They Need in a Covid-19 Economy," *Official
Microsoft Blog*, June 30, 2020 (charts showing 149 million new technology jobs
globally by 2025 and 13 million *new* ones in the United States, https://blogs.mi
crosoft.com/blog/2020/06/30/microsoft-launches-initiative-to-help-25-million
-people-worldwide-acquire-the-digital-skills-needed-in-a-covid-19-economy/;
The Computing Technology Industry Association (CompTIA), *Cyberstates 2020*,
March 2020, https://www.cyberstates.org/pdf/CompTIA_Cyberstates_2020.pdf
(12.1 million tech jobs in 2020, which includes technology professionals employed across every industry sector plus business professionals employed by tech
companies) (median wage is $80,000, twice the national median).

9   *According to a Harris:* Arianne Cohen, "Should You Flee Your City? Almost 40%
Have Considered It During the Pandemic," May 4, 2020, https://www.fastcom
pany.com/90500696/should-you-flee-your-city-almost-40-have-considered-it
-during-the-pandemic.

11   *Consider that 38 percent:* Kim Parker, Juliana M. Horowitz, Anna Brown, Richard Fry, D'Vera Cohn, and Ruth Igielnik, "What United and Divides Urban,
Suburban, and Rural Communities," Pew Research Center, May 22, 2018,
pp. 46–48, https://www.pewresearch.org/social-trends/wp-content/uploads/
sites/3/2018/05/Pew-Research-Center-Community-Type-Full-Report-FINAL
.pdf.

11   *For all the punditry:* Samuel J. Abrams, "Urban-Rural Divide Isn't What it Seems,"
AEI, July 3, 2018, https://www.aei.org/articles/urban-rural-divide-isnt-what-it
-seems.

11   *"techno-fetishism":* Dan Breznitz, *Innovation in Real Places: Strategies for Prosperity in an Unforgiving World* (New York: Oxford University Press, 2021).

11   *But the multiplier effect:* Enrico Moretti has researched extensively the multiplier effect of tech jobs. "The Multiplier Effect of Innovation Jobs," *MIT Sloan
Management Review*, June 6, 2012, https://sloanreview.mit.edu/article/the-multi
plier-effect-of-innovation-jobs.

11   *Moreover, in an astounding:* Editorial, "Why Are Southside and Southwest So in
Favor of Amazon," *Roanoke Times*, December 18, 2018.

12   *"nearly 60 percent of Idaho's net migration":* Troy Senik, "No Californians Need
Apply: In Idaho, Resentment to the Golden State Diaspora Grows," *City Journal*,
November 14, 2019, https://www.city-journal.org/california-migration-idaho.

12   *"tolerant and positive":* "California Movers, Moving to Idaho from California:
Myths and Facts," https://californiamoversusa.com/resources/moving-to-idaho
-from-california.

12   *Most Americans understand:* An online survey conducted by GQR among 1,501
likely November 2020 voters (399 Michigan, 300 Minnesota, 502 Pennsylvania,

300 Wisconsin) from September 30 to October 6, 2020, found that voters were most interested in candidates who would help them prepare for future opportunities and that more than 70 percent did not think technology would cost them their jobs. See also Dr. Ismail White and Harin Contractor, "Racial Differences on the Future of Work: A Survey of the American Workforce," Joint Center for Political and Economic Studies, July 24, 2019, https://jointcenter.org/wp-con tent/uploads/2019/09/Joint-Center-Racial-Differences-on-the-Future-of-Work -A-Survey-of-the-American-Workforce_0.pdf (finding that by a margin of 3:1 Americans believe technology has created more opportunities than it has taken away).

12 *The alternative to competing:* Ryan Heath, "Why Silicon Valley Could Become Tomorrow's Detroit," *Politico*, December 28, 2020, https://www.politico.com/ news/2020/12/18/silicon-valley-bay-area-business-model-448065.

13 *Our digital economy needs:* Matt Dunne talks about the need for a national equilibrium in a panel we did together. Matt Dunne's remarks, "America's Rural Opportunity," Commonwealth Club, May 13, 2021, https://www.common wealthclub.org/events/2021-05-13/americas-rural-opportunity.

13 *As Isabel Wilkerson has described:* Isabel Wilkerson, *Caste: The Origin of Our Discontents* (New York: Random House, 2020).

14 *"waiting in a long line stretching up a hill":* Brad Plumer, "What a Liberal Sociologist Learned from Spending Five Years in Trump's America," *Vox*, October 25, 2016, https://www.vox.com/2016/9/6/12803636/arlie-hochschild-strangers-land -louisiana-trump.

14 *"women, refugees, public sector workers":* Ibid.

16 *They recognize, as the writer:* Michael Lind's memo to me offering commentary on the book on March 13, 2021.

16 *It no longer makes sense:* Ibid.

16 *Nearly 20 percent of computer:* Nick Kolakowski, "Facebook, Google, Microsoft, Apple Diversity Plans: Tracking Progress," *Dice*, September 16, 2020, https://in sights.dice.com/2020/09/16/facebook-google-microsoft-apple-diversity-plans -tracking-progress.

16 *These companies are:* Ibid.

17 *"digital skills":* Press briefing by press secretary Jen Psaki and Secretary of Commerce Gina Raimondo, July 22, 2021, https://www.whitehouse.gov/brief ing-room/press-briefings/2021/07/22/press-briefing-by-press-secretary-jen -psaki-and-secretary-of-commerce-gina-raimondo-july-22-2021/.

17 *"skills gap":* Ibid.

20 *"I want a home here not only for the negro":* Frederick Douglass, "Our Composite Nationality," 1869, https://teachingamericanhistory.org/library/document/our -composite-nationality.

PART I: TWENTY-FIRST-CENTURY ECONOMY

Chapter 2: Building Community

24 *"15,000 to 4,000"*: Mark Green, "One-on-One: Shaping Our Appalachian Region: Connectivity . . . then Progress," *The Lane Report*, July 5, 2016, https://www.lanereport.com/65077/2016/07/one-on-one-shaping-our-appalachian-region-connectivity-then-progress.

24 *"That cannot be done solely"*: Jared Arnett, "Deep Down We Are a Solution to Be Discovered, Not a Problem to Be Solved," *KentuckyToday*, July 22, 2019, https://www.kentuckytoday.com/stories/deep-down-we-are-a-solution-to-be-discovered-not-a-problem-to-be-solved,20650.

24 *Remarkably, Eastern Kentucky*: Jared Arnett, "Must Do Our Part to Keep Appalachia Open," *The Daily Independent*, March 31, 2020, https://www.dailyindependent.com/opinion/jared-arnett-must-do-our-part-to-keep-appalachia-open/article_0a0b7dce-a36e-11ea-b8e7-87080731efc2.html.

25 *"a teacher or a nurse"*: Green, "One-on-One."

25 *"reality is that you can do whatever you want"*: Ibid.

25 *"not necessarily a plan"*: Rachel Adkins, "SOAR Exec: Embrace Technology," *The Daily Independent*, May 1, 2017, https://www.dailyindependent.com/news/soar-exec-embrace-technology/article_67bfc7b8-2eaf-11e7-b76e-4b32b9e334f3.html.

25 *"strengthen entrepreneurial education"*: Shaping Our Appalachian Region (SOAR), "Blueprint for the Future of Appalachia," https://www.soar-ky.org/wp-content/uploads/2021/02/SOAR-Blueprint.pdf.

25 *"Interapt's hiring results"*: Kelsey Bolar, "$2 Million Obama Era Program Gets 17 People Jobs," *The Daily Signal*, July 21, 2017, https://www.dailysignal.com/2017/07/21/exclusive-2-million-government-program-gets-17-people-jobs.

25 *"a consortium of tech employers"*: Ibid.

26 *"technology is the economy"*: Green, "One-on-One."

26 *"wireless telephones and television"*: "Winston Churchill, "Fifty Years Hence," 1931, http://rolandanderson.se/Winston_Churchill/Fifty_Years_Hence.php.

26 *"it possible to separate"*: Ezra Klein, "Paul Krugman on Climate, Robots, Single-Payer, and So Much More," *Vox*, December 26, 2019, https://www.vox.com/podcasts/2019/12/26/21011830/paul-krugman-obam-climate-medicare-robots-single-payer-andrew-yang.

27 *Accordingly, as reported by Brookings*: Clara Hendrickson, Mark Muro, and William A. Galston, "Countering the Geography of Discontent: Strategies for Left-Behind Places," Brookings, November, 2018, https://www.brookings.edu/research/countering-the-geography-of-discontent-strategies-for-left-behind-places.

27 *This geographic inequity*: William H. Frey, "For the First Time on Record, Fewer

than 10% of Americans Moved in a Year," Brookings, November 22, 2019, https://www.brookings.edu/blog/the-avenue/2019/11/22/for-the-first-time-on-record-fewer-than-10-of-americans-moved-in-a-year.

27 *Fewer than 10 percent:* Ibid.

27 *"there is relatively little migration":* Ryan Nunn, Jana Parsons, and Jay Shambaugh, "Americans Aren't Moving to Economic Opportunity," Brookings, November 19, 2018, https://www.brookings.edu/blog/up-front/2018/11/19/americans-arent-moving-to-economic-opportunity/.

27 *"they were 'rooted' and preferred":* Theresa Agovino, "Americans Aren't Moving: The Decline in Worker Mobility Presents a Challenge for Employers in a Tight Labor Market," SHRM, February 8, 2020, https://www.shrm.org/hr-today/news/all-things-work/pages/americans-are-not-moving.aspx.

27 *Microsoft estimates that:* Brad Smith, "Microsoft Launches Initiative to Help 25 Million People Worldwide Acquire the Digital Skills They Need in a Covid-19 Economy," *Official Microsoft Blog*, June 30, 2020 (charts showing 149 million new technology jobs globally by 2025 and 13 million *new* ones in the United States), https://blogs.microsoft.com/blog/2020/06/30/microsoft-launches-initiative-to-help-25-million-people-worldwide-acquire-the-digital-skills-needed-in-a-covid-19-economy.

27 *That means the total:* U.S. Bureau of Labor Statistics, "All Employees, Manufacturing [MANEMP]," retrieved from FRED, Federal Reserve Bank of St. Louis, https://fred.stlouisfed.org/series/MANEMP, March 21, 2021 (as of December 2020 about 12.2 million manufacturing jobs); Raynor de Best, "Number of Employees in U.S. Construction 2000–2018," Statista, March 11, 2021 (as of March 2021, 11.2 million construction jobs), https://www.statista.com/statistics/187412/number-of-employees-in-us-construction.

28 *According to Glassdoor.com:* "50 Best Jobs in America for 2021," glassdoor.com, https://www.glassdoor.com/List/Best-Jobs-in-America-LST_KQ0,20.htm.

28 *It may not come:* "Why Computer Science?," https://code.org/promote (click sixth circle on bottom of chart).

28 *But what is striking:* "The Computing Technology Industry Association (CompTIA)," *Cyberstates 2020*, March 2020, https://www.cyberstates.org/pdf/Comp-TIA_Cyberstates_2020.pdf.

28 *"Apple, Facebook, Google, and Netflix":* Robert E. Lighthizer, "How to Make Trade Work for Workers: Charting a Path Between Protectionism and Globalism," *Foreign Affairs*, July/August 2020, https://www.foreignaffairs.com/articles/united-states/2020-06-09/how-make-trade-work-workers.

28 *"autoworkers could be taught to code":* Ibid.

28 *In fact the United Auto Workers bargains:* "UAW Ford Contract Summary: Hourly Workers, November 2019," p. 15, https://uaw.org/wp-content/uploads/2019/11/NUMBERS-CORRECTED_FRI-11-1_11140-AM_Hourly-graphics.pdf.

29 *In fact, although hybrid:* Erik Brynjolfsson and Avinash Collis, "How Should We

Measure the Digital Economy," *Harvard Business Review*, November-December 2019, https://hbr.org/2019/11/how-should-we-measure-the-digital-economy. Avinash Collis estimates that the total value of digital goods, including many free services, to *consumers* is about $1.2 trillion annually. According to Collis, the Bureau of Economic Analysis tracks the contribution of the digital economy to *producers*, and they estimated it to be around $1.35 trillion in 2017. U.S. Bureau of Economic Analysis, "Digital Economy Accounted for 6.9% of GDP in 2017," https://www.bea.gov/news/blog/2019-04-04/digital-economy-accounted-69-percent-gdp-2017. If you add up both of these numbers as Collis and Brynjolfsson believe is necessary to account for all the free services, the contribution of digital to GDP-B is about $2.5 trillion, which is comparable to the $2.1 trillion of manufacturing value.

29 *"geographically clustered"*: David A. Price, "Enrico Moretti," *Federal Reserve Bank of Richmond Econ Focus*, First Quarter, https://www.richmondfed.org/publica tions/research/econ_focus/2019/q1/interview.

29 *"the largest multiplier of all"*: The Multiplier Effect of Innovation Jobs," *MITSloan Management Review*, June 06, 2012, https://sloanreview.mit.edu/article/the-mul tiplier-effect-of-innovation-jobs.

29 *Even in Silicon Valley:* Silicon Valley Institute for Regional Studies, "Silicon Valley Employment Trends Through 2016," September 2017, pp. 10–11, https://joint venture.org/images/stories/pdf/sv-employment-trends-2017-09.pdf.

29 *There was more fuss:* Louise Story, "As Companies Seek Tax Deals, Governments Pay High Price," *New York Times*, December 1, 2012, https://www.nytimes .com/2012/12/02/us/how-local-taxpayers-bankroll-corporations.html.

30 *"In my reading of the history of innovation hubs"*: James Pethokoukis, "5 Questions for Enrico Moretti on Innovation and Cities," AEI, Novermber 28, 2019, https://www.aei.org/economics/5-questions-for-enrico-moretti-on-innovation -and-urban-development.

30 *"tried hard to sustain lagging regions"*: Klein, "Paul Krugman on Climate, Robots, Single-Payer, and So Much More."

30 *"is being undermined by powerful economic forces"*: Paul Krugman, "Getting Real About Rural America," *New York Times*, March 22, 2019, https://www.nytimes .com/2019/03/18/opinion/rural-america-economic-decline.html.

30 *"reviving declining regions"*: Ibid.

30 *"in an attempt to revive the former East Germany"*: Ibid.

30 *The massive German capital:* "Eastern Germany Is Western Germany's Trillion Euro Bet," *Deutsche Welle (DW)*, September 24, 2010, https://www.dw.com/en/ eastern-germany-is-western-germanys-trillion-euro-bet/a-6016271.

30 *Southern Italy also suffers:* Rachel Donadio, "Corruption Is Seen as a Drain on Italy's South," *New York Times*, October 8, 2012, https://www.nytimes .com/2012/10/08/world/europe/in-italy-calabria-is-drained-by-corruption .html.

30 *As the Economic Innovation:* "The New Map of Economic Growth and Recovery," *Economic Innovation Group,* May 2016, https://eig.org/wp-content/up loads/2016/05/recoverygrowthreport.pdf.

30 *Many new businesses:* Ibid.

31 *Krugman fairly points out:* Klein, "Paul Krugman on Climate, Robots, Single-Payer, and So Much More."

31 *"skilled professionals":* Alexander W. Bartik, Zoe Cullen, Edward L. Glaeser, Michael Luca, and Christopher Stanton, "What Jobs Are Being Done at Home During the Covid-19 Crisis? Evidence from Firm-Level Surveys," Working Paper 20-138, Harvard Business School, June 2020, https://www.hbs.edu/faculty/Pub lication%20Files/20-138_ec6ff0f0-7947-4607-9d54-c5c53044fb95.pdf.

32 *"has given us confidence":* Tyler Clifford, "Cisco CEO Chuck Robbins: The Future Post-Pandemic Workplace Will Be Based on a 'Hybrid Model,'" cnbc.com, May 13, 2020, https://www.cnbc.com/2020/05/13/cisco-ceo-sees-a-hybrid-model -in-the-future-post-pandemic-workplace.html.

32 *"permanent remote working":* Nina Nanji, "Facebook: Our Staff Can Carry on Working from Home After Covid," bbc.com, April 19, 2021, https://www.bbc .com/news/business-56759151.

32 *"distributed workforce":* Don Sweeney, "Pinterest Pays $89.5 Million to Cancel Lease for New San Francisco Offices," *Sacramento Bee,* August 30, 2020, https:// www.sacbee.com/news/california/article245363805.html.

32 *"the 9-to-5 workday is dead":* "Creating a Best Workplace from Anywhere, for Everyone," Salesforce, February 9, 2021, https://www.salesforce.com/news/sto ries/creating-a-best-workplace-from-anywhere.

32 *"virtual first":* Dropbox Team, "Dropbox Goes Virtual First," Dropbox, October 13, 2020, https://blog.dropbox.com/topics/company/dropbox-goes-virtual -first.

32 *"decentralized company, with no headquarters":* Brian Armstrong, "Coinbase Is a Decentralized Company, with No Headquarters," February 24, 2021, https:// blog.coinbase.com/coinbase-is-a-decentralized-company-with-no-headquar ters-a9762c02546.

32 *According to* The New York Times*:* Nellie Bowles, "They Can't Leave the Bay Area Fast Enough," *New York Times,* January 14, 2021, https://www.nytimes .com/2021/01/14/technology/san-francisco-covid-work-moving.html.

32 *As of the end:* Ryan Moran, "San Francisco Rent Plunges 35% as Tech Giants Flee Area," KTVU Fox 2, December 10, 2020, https://www.ktvu.com/news/san -francisco-rent-plunges-35-as-tech-giants-flee-area.

32 *The Milken Institute found:* Misael Galdamez, Charlotte Kesteven, and Aaron Melaas, "Best-Performing Cities 2021: Foundations for Growth and Recovery," Milken Institute, 2021, https://milkeninstitute.org/sites/default/files/reports -pdf/Best-Performing-Cities-2021.pdf.

33 *When it comes to software engineers:* Kim Hart, "Covid-19 Scatters Tech Hubs

for Young Talent," *Axios*, May 10, 2021, https://www.axios.com/tech-hub-cities-young-talent-819f5148-0470-460e-ac82-d75f74c6087f.html.

33   *Satya Nadella . . . cautions that most:* Dealbook Newsletter, "What Satya Nadella Thinks," *New York Times*, May 14, 2020, https://www.nytimes.com/2020/05/14/business/dealbook/satya-nadella-microsoft.html.

33   *Nadella also highlights:* Ibid.

33   *Sundar Pichai, Alphabet's CEO:* Jack Kelly, "Google CEO Sundar Pichai Calls for a Hybrid Work-from-Home Model," *Forbes*, September 28, 2020; Chip Cutter, "Companies Start to Think Remote Work Isn't So Great After All," *Wall Street Journal*, July 24, 2020, https://www.wsj.com/articles/companies-start-to-think-remote-work-isnt-so-great-after-all-11595603397.

33   *Google recently announced:* Jennifer Elias, "Google to Spend $7 Billion on Data Centers and Office Space in 2021," cnbc.com, March 18, 2021, https://www.cnbc.com/2021/03/18/google-to-spend-7-billion-in-data-centers-and-office-space-in-2021.html.

33   *"physical locations are going":* Video transcript, "Facebook Builds Out in NYC, Betting on In-Person Future," *yahoo!finance*, February 25, 2021; https://www.yahoo.com/lifestyle/facebook-builds-nyc-betting-person-103000556.html.

34   *Google, for example, expects about 20 percent:* Tripp Mickle, "Google Adopts Hybrid Workweek, with 20% of Its Employees to Work Remotely," *Wall Street Journal*, May 5, 2021, https://www.wsj.com/articles/google-shifts-to-hybrid-workweek-allowing-20-of-its-employees-to-work-remotely-11620240694.

34   *"comforts of home":* This idea that remote interactions can reduce prejudice is discussed in more detail in Yair Amichai-Hamburger and Katelyn Y. A. McKenna, "The Contact Hypothesis Reconsidered: Interacting via the Internet," *Journal of Computer-Mediated Communication* 11, no. 3 (April 1, 2006): 825–43, 829–30, https://academic.oup.com/jcmc/article/11/3/825/4617713.

34   *"subtle differences in manner of dress":* Ibid., p. 829.

35   *virtual teams with diversity face significant hurdles:* These articles discuss extensively the hurdles with virtual teams: Sarah Morrison-Smith and Jaime Ruiz, "Challenges and Barriers in Virtual Teams: A Literature Review," *SN Applied Science* 2, no. 1096 (May 20, 2020), https://doi.org/10.1007/s42452-020-2801-5; Pamela J. Hinds and Mark Mortensen, "Understanding Conflict in Geographically Distributed Teams: The Moderating Effects of Shared Identity, Shared Context, and Spontaneous Communication," *Organization Science* 16, no. 3 (June 1, 2005): 290–307, https://pubsonline.informs.org/doi/10.1287/orsc.1050.0122.

35   *"less and less mixing":* Peter Dizikes, "Q&A: Why Cities Aren't Working for the Working Class," *MIT News*, February 20, 2019, https://news.mit.edu/2019/why-cities-aren%E2%80%99t-working-working-class-0220.

35   *It takes thoughtful leadership and well-designed platforms:* Traci Carte and Laku Chidambram discuss strategies for overcoming the challenges of diversity on virtual teams: Traci Carte and Laku Chidambaram, "A Capabilities-Based Theory of

Technology Deployment in Diverse Teams: Leapfrogging the Pitfalls of Diversity and Leveraging Its Potential with Collaborative Technology," *Journal of the Association for Information Systems* 5, no. 11–12 (December 2004), https://core.ac.uk/download/pdf/301382932.pdf.

35 *instead of restricting them:* Cat Zekrewski reports on how a number of tech companies are restricting political speech at work, including on their digital platforms: Cat Zekrewski, "The Technology 202: Basecamp Restricts Talk of Politics and Social Issues at Work," *Washington Post*, April 27, 2021, https://www.washingtonpost.com/politics/2021/04/27/technology-202-software-company-basecamp-restricts-talk-politics-social-issues-work/.

35 *"if you're not just talking":* Private correspondence with Charles Taylor on May 22, 2020, where he sent *What's to Be Done: Re-uniting the People*, which was prepared for lectures he gave in Berlin in June 2019 about the crisis of democracy in the West. The lectures are still unpublished.

36 *"rural America represents 15 percent":* Policy Summit 2021, "Pathways to Economic Resilience in Our Communities," June 23–25, 2021, https://web.cvent.com/event/4e3c24fd-27f8-4819-9d14-2650df465ec6/websitePage:c4758031-7d9d-4c81-8ea2-503711a5b3b3.

37 *"younger workers":* James Heckman and Alan Krueger make the case that credentialing younger generations new to the workforce has a higher return: James J. Heckman and Alan B. Krueger, "Human Capital Policy," in *Inequality in America: What Role for Human Capital Policies* (Cambridge: MIT Press, 2005), p. 201.

37 *provide multiple options for modern-day careers:* MacGillis explains why couples choose to work in urban centers: Alec MacGillis, *Fulfillment: Winning and Losing in One-Click America* (New York: Farrar, Straus & Giroux, 2021), p. 10.

37 *"one biotech firm in Appalachia":* Abhijit V. Banerjee and Esther Duflo, *Good Economics for Hard Times* (New York: PublicAffairs, 2019), p. 47.

38 *"hub-and-spoke":* MIT economist Jon Gruber used this phrase in private correspondence with me after reading a draft of this chapter, February 2021.

38 *"bold, persistent experimentation":* Franklin D. Roosevelt, Address at Oglethorpe University in Atlanta, Georgia, May 22, 1932, https://www.presidency.ucsb.edu/documents/address-oglethorpe-university-atlanta-georgia.

39 *Studies show that parts of the country:* The following articles provide evidence for the positive economic impact of land grant universities: Shimeng Liu, "Spillovers from Universities: Evidence from the Land-Grant Program," *Journal of Urban Economics* 87 (2015), https://lusk.usc.edu/sites/default/files/Spillovers_from_Universities_Land_grant_Program.pdf.; Enrico Moretti, "Estimating the Social Return to Higher Education: Evidence from Longitudinal and Repeated Cross-Sectional Data," *Journal of Econometrics* 121 (2004): 175–212, https://www.sciencedirect.com/science/article/abs/pii/S0304407603002653.

40 *"industrial classes":* The Morrill Act of 1862 (12 Stat. 503; 7 U.S.C. 301 et seq.).

40 *71 percent of tech talent is employed in private industry:* Amy Burke, "Science and

Engineering Indicators," National Science Board, September 26, 2019, https://ncses.nsf.gov/pubs/nsb20198.

40   *"valued by employers"*: Heckman and Krueger, "Human Capital Policy," p. 188.

42   *China builds a new technology-focused university almost every week:* Andreas Schleicher, "China Opens a New University Every Week," bbc.com, March 16, 2016, https://www.bbc.com/news/business-35776555.

43   *"digital public infrastructure"*: Eli Pariser and Danielle Allen, "To Thrive, Our Democracy Needs Digital Public Infrastrucutre," *Politico*, January 5, 2021, https://www.politico.com/news/agenda/2021/01/05/to-thrive-our-democracy-needs-digital-public-infrastructure-455061. See also Ethan Zuckerman, "What Is Digital Public Infrastructure," *Center for Journalism and Liberty*, November 2020, https://static1.squarespace.com/static/5efcb64b1cf16e4c487b2f61/t/5fb41b6aac578321b0c50717/1605639019414/zuckerman-digital-infrastructure-cjl-nov2020.pdf.

43   *According to Code.org:* https://code.org/promote.

43   *However, only 47 percent of current high schools:* Ibid.

44   *"Find Something New"*: Josh Wingrove and Jennifer Jacobs, "Apple's Cook, IBM's Rometty, Ivanka Trump to Tout Job Training," BNN Bloomberg, July 14, 2020, http://www.bnnbloomberg.ca/apple-s-cook-ibm-s-rometty-ivanka-trump-to-tout-job-training-1.1465128.

44   *Computer science consistently ranks:* https://code.org/promote.

44   *According to a Microsoft survey:* Betsy Foresman, "There's a Shortage of K–12 Computer Science Education in the U.S., Microsoft Finds," *Edscoop*, December 4, 2018, https://edscoop.com/theres-a-shortage-of-k-12-computer-science-education-in-the-u-s-microsoft-survey-finds/.

44   *To achieve universal computer science education:* This article provides statistics on our acute computer science teacher shortage: Lucy Kosturko, "Computer Science Education Support Surging: But Who's Going to Teach It," *SAS*, December 6, 2018, https://blogs.sas.com/content/sascp/2018/12/06/working-computer-science-teacher-demand/.

45   *Tulsa, for example, found great success:* David Louie, "Would You Leave the Bay Area and Move to Oklahoma for $10,000? Hundreds of Remote Workers Are Trying To," abc7news.com, September 7, 2020, https://abc7news.com/6413039/?ex_cid=TA_KGO_FB&utm_campaign=trueAnthem%3A%20Trending%20Content&utm_medium=trueAnthem&utm_source=facebook&fbclid=IwAR1h7h62pcEvBagqIwyScWcsfxtL2ZC9zTsX9_p8fun0JWN9TvUb8LlJhzI.

45   *West Virginia has begun to offer $12,000:* Rachel Trent, "Remote Workers Can Get Paid $12,000 to Move to West Virginia," CNN Business, April 18, 2021, https://www.cnn.com/2021/04/18/us/west-virginia-move-incentive-remote-workers-trnd/index.html.

45   *Stripe . . . offers its employees a $20,000 incentive:* Alexis Benveniste, "Stripe Is Paying Employees $20,000 if They Leave Big Cities—but They'll Also Get a Pay

Cut," CNN Business, September 17, 2020, https://www.cnn.com/2020/09/16/business/stripe-employees-new-cities/index.html.

45 *In fact, polling done on Blind:* Blind Blog-Workplace Insights, "44% of Professionals Are Happy to Take a Pay Cut," September 14, 2020, https://www.teamblind.com/blog/index.php/2020/09/14/44-of-professionals-are-happy-to-take-a-pay-cut/.

46 *He is passionate about reversing the trend that David Autor:* Dizikes, "Q&A: Why Cities Aren't Working for the Working Class."

46 *"chicken and egg problem":* Banerjee and Duflo, *Good Economics for Hard Times,* p. 47.

46 *"Brothers and sisters: I want to tell you this":* Jamesan Gramme, "Roosevelt's Rural Electrification Speech—Gordon College," Archives Blog, Upson County Georgia, July 16, 2018, https://www.upsoncountyga.org/Blog.aspx?IID=10.

47 *"electricity is a modern necessity of life":* Ibid.

47 *Currently, about 21 million Americans lack affordable internet access:* Kathryn de Wit, "21 Million Americans Still Lack Broadband Connectivity," Pewtrusts.org; July 10, 2019, https://www.pewtrusts.org/en/research-and-analysis/fact-sheets/2019/07/21-million-americans-still-lack-broadband-connectivity. See also Federal Communications Commission Report FCC 18-181, December 26, 2018, https://docs.fcc.gov/public/attachments/FCC-18-181A1.pdf.

47 *A staggering 15 percent of households with children:* Monica Anderson and Andrew Perrin, "Nearly One-in-Five Teens Can't Finish Their Homework Because of the Digital Divide," Pew Research Center, October 26, 2018, https://www.pewresearch.org/fact-tank/2018/10/26/nearly-one-in-five-teens-cant-always-finish-their-homework-because-of-the-digital-divide/.

48 *As economist Stephan Weiler and his coauthors have demonstrated:* Stephan Weiler, Sarah Low, and Tessa Conroy, "Fueling Job Engines: Impacts of Small Business Loans on Establishment Births in Metropolitan and Nonmetro Counties," *Contemporary Economic Policy* 35, no. 3 (2017): 575–95, https://onlinelibrary.wiley.com/doi/pdfdirect/10.1111/coep.12214?casa_token=gBfXHr_xnUIAAAAA:XyK5zTmVuhjmnlWZAamKB6euqIhGhxgyT4yTMpFzCjJB9hFJe46Ddts9P1wui-QQ7ECKy1Ivx7xq.

48 *While California had nearly 4,000 VC deals:* National Venture Capital Association (NVCA), 2020 Yearbook, March 2020, p. 27, https://nvca.org/wp-content/uploads/2020/03/NVCA-2020-Yearbook.pdf.

48 *A state like Iowa:* Ibid.

48 *His pioneering fund, Rise of the Rest:* Alex Konrad, "AOL Founder Steve Case Launches Second $150 Million 'Rise of the Rest' Fund to Back Entrepreneurs Across the U.S.," *Forbes,* October 28, 2019, https://www.forbes.com/sites/alexkonrad/2019/10/28/steve-case-launches-second-rise-of-rest-fund-at-under-30-summit/?sh=11de54d26632.

49 *The venture model:* Dan Breznitz, *Innovation in Real Places: Strategies for Prosperity in an Unforgiving World* (New York: Oxford University Press, 2021).

49 *According to Weiler's research:* Stephan Weiler, Luke Petach, and Tessa Controy, "It's a Wonderful Loan: Community Banking and Regional Economic Resilience," *Journal of Banking and Finance*, forthcoming, https://www.sciencedirect .com/science/article/pii/S0378426621000352?casa_token=bQKqYaaRPx0AAA AA:DPOw5W1QVWP5FALNWJ2dUmcTBQsumsox9r9kasTLtZqDD60Y38wa nokpzB5EunFcEWeEB5k.

49 *Approximately half of the country's nearly five thousand community banks:* Banking Strategist, "Community Banks: Number by State and Asset Size," https:// www.bankingstrategist.com/community-banks-number-by-state-and-asset -size.

50 *"best science":* Daniel Kevles, "The National Science Foundation and the Debate over Postwar Research Policy, 1942–1945: A Political Interpretation of Science: The Endless Frontier," *Isis* 68, no. 1 (March 1977): 4–26, https://www.jstor.org/ stable/230370?seq=1.

50 *The U.S. claims eighteen of the top twenty spots:* National Academy of Inventors and Intellectual Property Owners Association, "Top 100 Worldwide Universities Granted U.S. Utility Patents 2018," https://academyofinventors.org/wp-content/ uploads/2019/06/Top-100-2018.pdf.

50 *We have more than 60 percent:* Jonathan R. Cole, "The Triumph of America's Research University," *The Atlantic*, September 20, 2016, https://www.theatlantic .com/education/archive/2016/09/the-triumph-of-americas-research-univer sity/500798/.

50 *Jonathan Gruber and Simon Johnson show:* Jonathan Gruber and Simon Johnson, *Jump-Starting America: How Breakthrough Science Can Revive Economic Growth and the American Dream* (New York: PublicAffairs, 2019).

51 *Their conclusion is similar to the Brookings report:* Robert D. Atkinson, Mark Muro, and Jacob Whiton, "The Case for Growth Centers: How to Spread Tech Innovation Across America," Brookings, December 9, 2019, https://www.brook ings.edu/research/growth-centers-how-to-spread-tech-innovation-across -america/.

52 *Our legislation empowers cities to choose the type of technologies:* This editorial notes that "'Good-paying green jobs' are probably not jobs for Pittsburgh, or Cleveland, or Toledo, or Youngstown." Editorial Board, "The Man and the Record," *Pittsburgh Post-Gazette*, October 31, 2020, https://www.post-gazette.com/ opinion/editorials/2020/10/31/editorial-donald-trump-joe-biden-mike-pence -kamala-harris-presidential-candidate-endorsement/stories/202010310021. See also Brandon Dixon, "Tech Training Programs Rely on Experts to Steer Them Away from Fields That Won't Produce Jobs," *Pittsburgh Post-Gazette*, August 17, 2017, https://www.post-gazette.com/local/region/2017/08/17/technical-colleges -pittsburgh-tech-jobs-allegheny-conference-community-development/sto ries/201708060019.

52 *"better, more reliable, and cheap enough":* Dan Breznitz, working draft for a

forum on reviving local prosperity in the *Boston Review* (to be published September 2021).

52   *"If you come to middle America"*: Marisa Schultz, "Rep. Ro Khanna's Big Idea: Bringing Silicon Valley Jobs to Rural America," Fox News, May 8, 2020 (comments section), https://www.foxnews.com/politics/rep-ro-khannas-big-idea -moving-silicon-valley-to-rural-america.

52   *"group in power"*: Li Zhou, "Andrew Young Told Asian Americans to Prove Their Americanness. Here's Why That's Wrong," *Vox*, April 3, 2020, quoting Damon Young, "The Definition, Danger, and Disease of Respectability Politics, Explained," *The Root*, March 21, 2016.

53   *In fact, Enrico Moretti and his colleague Chang-Tai Hsieh*: Chang-Tai Hsieh and Enrico Moretti, "How Local Housing Regulations Smother the U.S. Economy," *New York Times*, September 6, 2017, https://www.nytimes.com/2017/09/06/ opinion/housing-regulations-us-economy.html.

53   *To keep and attract new entrepreneurs*: San Jose mayor Sam Liccardo addresses the particular challenges that the Bay Area faces to retain tech: Sam Liccardo, "Silicon Valley's Exodus: Stop Blaming Tech," *San Francisco Chronicle*, February 6, 2021, https://www.sfchronicle.com/opinion/openforum/article/Silicon -Valley-s-exodus-Stop-blaming-tech-15928928.php.

Chapter 3: Racial and Gender Equity

61   *When Ozoma shared her experience on social media*: Julie Bort and Taylor Nicole Rogers, "Former Pinterest Employees Describe a Traumatic Workplace Where Managers Humiliate Employees Until They Cry," *Businessinsider*, June 20, 2020, https://www.businessinsider.com/pinterest-employees-toxic-workplace-black -fired-ben-silbermann-2020-6.

61   *Kara Swisher soon after detailed*: Kara Swisher, "Hitting the Glass Ceiling, Suddenly, at Pinterest," *New York Times*, August 14, 2020, https://www.nytimes .com/2020/08/14/opinion/pinterest-discrimination-women.html.

62   *"unfair behavior and treatment"*: Allison Scott, Freada Kapor Klein, and Urirdiakoghene Onovakpuri, "Tech Leavers Study," Kapor Center for Social Impact, April 27, 2017, https://mk0kaporcenter5ld71a.kinstacdn.com/wp-content/up loads/2017/08/TechLeavers2017.pdf.

62   *"It was the first time I realized what racism felt like"*: Nathaniel Popper, " 'Tokenized': Inside Black Workers' Struggles at the King of Crypto Start-ups," *New York Times*, November 27, 2020, https://www.nytimes.com/2020/11/27/technol ogy/coinbase-cryptocurrency-black-employees.html.

62   *Indeed, numerous studies show that companies*: Vivian Hunt, Dennis Layton, and Sara Prince, "Why Diversity Matters," McKinsey & Company, January 1, 2015, https://www.mckinsey.com/business-functions/organization/our-insights/why -diversity-matters; Vivian Hunt, Sara Prince, Sundiatu Dixon-Fyle, and Lareina Yee, "Delivering Through Diversity," McKinsey & Company, January 2018,

Document2https://www.mckinsey.com/~/media/mckinsey/business%20func tions/organization/our%20insights/delivering%20through%20diversity/deliv ering-through-diversity_full-report.ashx; Chloe Taylor, "Having More Female Leaders May Boost Companies' Share Price, Performance, Credit Suisse Says," cnbc.com, October 14, 2019, https://www.cnbc.com/2019/10/14/female-leaders -may-boost-share-price-performance-credit-suisse-says.html.

62 *Economists estimate that the racial wealth gap:* Nick Noel, Duwain Pinder, Shelley Stewart, and Jason Wright, "The Economic Impact of Closing the Racial Wealth Gap," McKinsey & Company, August 13, 2019, https://www.mckinsey.com/in dustries/public-and-social-sector/our-insights/the-economic-impact-of-clos ing-the-racial-wealth-gap.

63 *"entirely white social networks":* Christopher Ingraham, "Three Quarters of Whites Don't Have Any Non-White Friends," *Washington Post,* August 25, 2014.

64 *"despair":* Anne Case and Angus Deaton, *Deaths of Despair and the Future of Capitalism* (Princeton: Princeton University Press, 2020).

64 *They see parallels in William Julius Wilson's work:* William Julius Wilson, *The Truly Disadvantaged: The Inner City, the Underclass, and Public Policy* (Chicago: University of Chicago Press, 1987).

64 *"when you economically abandon a people":* Scott Kaufman, "Megyn Kelly De- mands Cornel West Explain Why #BlackLivesMatter Doesn't Protest Black-on -Black Violence," *Salon,* August 25, 2015, https://www.salon.com/2015/08/25/ megyn_kelly_demands_cornel_west_explain_why_blacklivesmatter_doesnt_ protest_black_on_black_violence/.

64 *Contrary to common perception:* Sean Illing, "Rural America Does Not Mean 'White America,'" *Vox,* April 24, 2017, https://www.vox.com/conversa tions/2017/4/24/15286624/race-rural-america-trump-politics-media.

64 *It is impossible to achieve equity:* Kimberlé Crenshaw, "Demarginalizing the In- tersection of Race and Sex: A Black Feminist Critique of Antidiscrimination Doctrine, Feminist Theory and Antiracist Politics," *University of Chicago Legal Forum,* Vol. 1989, Issue 1, 1989, https://chicagounbound.uchicago.edu/cgi/view -content.cgi?article=1052&context=uclf.

65 *"in many ways, technology rights are the new civil rights":* John Lewis and Ro Khanna, "The Intertwined Freedom Movements of Gandhi and Martin Lu- ther King Jr.," *Boston Globe,* April 6, 2018, https://www.bostonglobe.com/ opinion/2018/04/05/the-intertwined-freedom-movements-gandhi-and-martin -luther-king/BmVLzhgwgJZE1Oz4CWiF4M/story.html.

65 *Yes, women represent less than:* Blanca Myers, "Women and Minorities in Tech, by the Numbers," *Wired,* March 27, 2018, https://www.wired.com/story/com puter-science-graduates-diversity/.

66 *It is not a lack of capability or interest:* Staff Writers, "Women in Computer Sci- ence: Getting Involved in STEM," ComputerScience.org, May 5, 2021, https:// www.computerscience.org/resources/women-in-computer-science/.

66   *But Emily Chang shows in* Brotopia*:* Emily Chang, *Brotopia: Breaking Up the Boy's Club of Silicon Valley* (New York: Portfolio, 2018).

66   *In recent years, nearly half of women:* Sam Daley writes that "48% of women in STEM jobs report discrimination in the recruitment and hiring process." Sam Daley, "Women in Tech Stats Show the Industry Has a Long Way to Go," builtin .com, March 31, 2021, https://builtin.com/women-tech/women-in-tech-work place-statistics. Catherine Ashcraft and Sarah Blithe write about how women are far more likely to leave tech jobs midcareer: Catherine Ashcraft and Sarah Blithe, "Women in IT: The Facts," National Center for Women & Information Technology (NCWIT), 2009, https://www.wearethecity.com/wp-content/up loads/2014/12/Women-In-IT-The-Facts-NCWIT-October-2009.pdf.

66   *Similarly, in a Code2040 study:* Naomi Uwaka, "Five Myths Driving Racial Inequity in Tech," medium.com, August 15, 2018, https://medium.com/racial-equity -in-tech/five-myths-driving-racial-inequity-in-tech-db9201823e85.

66   *Consider that nearly 70 percent of Fortune 500 companies:* Hispanic Association of Corporate Responsibility, "Latinos on Corporate Boards, 2018," https://www .hacr.org/latinos-on-corporate-boards/.

66   *37 percent do not have a Black member:* J. Yo-Jud Cheng, Boris Groysberg, and Paul M. Healy, "Why Do Boards Have So Few Black Directors," *Harvard Business Review*, August 13, 2020, https://hbr.org/2020/08/why-do-boards-have-so-few -black-directors.

66   *The law has had an impact already:* Martha Groves, "How California's 'Women Quota' Is Already Changing Corporate Boards," *CalMatters*, December 16, 2019, https://calmatters.org/economy/2019/12/california-woman-quota-corporate -board-gender-diversity/.

66   *"Women in the Boardroom":* Deloitte Global Center for Corporate Governance, "Women in the Boardroom: A Global Perspective," fifth edition, p. 3, https:// www2.deloitte.com/gr/en/pages/risk/articles/women-in-the-boardroom5th -edition.html.

66   *"Delivering Through Diversity":* Hunt et al., "Delivering Through Diversity."

67   *"would never get near the C-suite":* Joan Williams, *White Working Class: Overcoming Class Cluelessness in America* (Boston: Harvard Business Review Press, 2020), p. 74.

69   *He can cite from memory:* Isheka N. Harrison, "Rodney Sampson's OHUB Partners with Morehouse College to Launch Virtual Coding School," *The Moguldom Nation*, April 03, 2020, https://moguldom.com/267962/rodney-sampsons-ohub -partners-with-morehouse-college-to-launch-virtual-coding-school/. See also Kelemwork Cook, Duwain Pinder, Shelley Stewart, Amaka Uchegbu, and Jason Wright, "The Future of Work in Black America," McKinsey & Company, October 4, 2019, https://www.mckinsey.com/featured-insights/future-of-work/the -future-of-work-in-black-america.

69   *food service roles:* Susan Lind, James Manyika, Liz Hilton Segel, Andre Dua,

Bryan Hancock, Scott Rutherford, and Brent Macon, "The Future of Work in America: People and Places, Today and Tomorrow," McKinsey Global Institute, July 11, 2019, https://www.mckinsey.com/featured-insights/future-of-work/the -future-of-work-in-america-people-and-places-today-and-tomorrow.

70 *"Black and Hispanic students were 1.5 and 1.7 times":* Blanca Myers, "Women and Minorities in Tech, by the Numbers," *Wired,* March 27, 2018, https://www.wired .com/story/computer-science-graduates-diversity/.

71 *Apple, under Lisa Jackson's leadership:* Michal Lev-Ram, "Apple Reveals How It Will Spend the $100 Million It Pledged in June Towards Racial Equity," *fortune .com*; January 13, 2021, https://fortune.com/2021/01/13/apple-diversity-racial -equity-100-million-hbcu-harlem-capital/.

71 *Netflix CEO Reed Hastings:* Jessica Bursztynsky, "Netflix CEO Reed Hastings Do- nating $120 Million to Historically Black Institutions," cnbc.com, June 17, 2020, https://www.cnbc.com/2020/06/17/netflix-ceo-hastings-donating-120-million -to-historically-black-institutions.html.

73 *A gadget is not a substitute:* Julian P. Cristia, Pablo Ibarraran, Santiago Cueto, Ana Santiago, and Eugenio Severin, "Technology and Child Development: Evidence from the One Laptop per Child Program," Inter-American Development Bank, 2012, pp. 14–15, https://publications.iadb.org/publications/english/document/ Technology-and-Child-Development-Evidence-from-the-One-Laptop-per -Child-Program.pdf.

73 *The federal government should establish:* "Stanford Students Start Program to Provide Free Laptops to Homeless, Low-Income Students During Pandemic," abc7news.com, December 3, 2020, https://abc7news.com/free-computers -bridging-tech-stanford-used-laptops-online-school/8471438/.

73 *Representative Alexandria Ocasio-Cortez put forward:* Natalie Marchant, "This Online Scheme Gives Parents Help with Their Kids' Homework," weforum.org, December 16, 2020, https://www.weforum.org/agenda/2020/12/homework -helpers-alexandria-ocasio-cortez/.

73 *The program was so popular:* Alexanderia Ocasio Cortez website, https://act.oca siocortez.com/signup/homework-helpers/.

74 *Her organization provided more than 300,000:* https://girlswhocode.com/.

74 *While this is progress:* Mark J. Perry, "Chart of the Day: The Declining Female Share of Computer Science Degrees from 28% to 18%," AEI, December 6, 2018, https://www.aei.org/carpe-diem/chart-of-the-day-the-declining-female-share -of-computer-science-degrees-from-28-to-18/?utm_source=feedburner&utm_ medium=feed&utm_campaign=Feed%3A%20aei-ideas%2Fposts%20 %28AEIdeas%20Posts%29.

75 *Black, Latino, and women entrepreneurs receive:* "US Venture Capital Investment Surpasses $130 Billion in 2019 for Second Consecutive Year," January 14, 2020, https://nvca.org/pressreleases/us-venture-capital-investment-surpasses-130-bil lion-in-2019-for-second-consecutive-year/; http://breakingthemold.openmic

.org. Megan Rose Dickey's article highlights how small a fraction goes to women and Black and Brown founders: Megan Rose Dickey, "The Future of Diversity and Inclusion in Tech," techcrunch.com, June 17, 2019, https://techcrunch .com/2019/06/17/the-future-of-diversity-and-inclusion-in-tech/.

75 *Only 11 percent of venture capital partners are women:* Johannes Lenhard, "Inside VC Firms: The Gender Divide," crunchbase.com, August 14, 2019, https://news .crunchbase.com/news/inside-vc-firms-the-gender-divide/.

75 *less than one percent are Black or Latino:* Hadiyah Mujhid, "The Underrepresentation of Black and Latinx People in Venture Capital Is an American Problem," HBCUvc, December 4, 2018, https://blog.hbcu.vc/the-underrepresen tation-of-black-and-latinx-people-in-venture-capital-is-an-american-problem -f09129cfbd65.

76 *A Stanford study concluded:* Melissa De Witte, "Venture Capital Funds Led by People of Color Face More Bias the Better They Perform, Stanford Researchers Find," *Stanford News*, August 12, 2019, https://news.stanford.edu/2019/08/12/ race-influences-professional-investors-judgments/.

76 *According to a Harlem Capital report:* Harlem Capital Partners, "200 Black & Latino Founders That Have Raised $1mm+," 2019 Diversity Report, February 2020, https://harlem.capital/wp-content/uploads/2020/08/2019-Diverse-Founder-Ad endum_v28-1.pdf.

77 *In fact, a 2016 Stanford study:* Robert Fairlie, Alicia Robb, and David T. Robinson, "Black and White: Access to Capital Among Minority-Owned Startups," *Stanford Institute for Economic Policy Research*, December 15, 2016, p. 710, https://siepr .stanford.edu/sites/default/files/publications/17-003.pdf.

78 *Latino entrepreneurs, according to a Kauffman report:* "Kauffman Compilation: Research on Race and Entrepreneurship," Ewing Marion Kauffman Foundation, December 2016, p. 3. https://www.kauffman.org/wp-content/uploads/2019/12/ kauffman_compilation_race_entrepreneurship.pdf.

78 *This should be coupled:* Kimberly Mlitz, "U.S. Federal Government IT Expenditure 201–2021, statista.com, June 28, 2021.

78 *Although most people in Silicon Valley have never:* Ryan Hurst, "Freedmen's Savings and Trust Company (1865–1874)," *BlackPast*, January 19, 2009, https:// www.blackpast.org/african-american-history/freedmen-s-savings-and-trust -company-1865-1874/.

78 *CDFIs have less than one percent:* "FDIC's Investing in the Future of Mission-Driven Banks," Federal Deposit Insurance Corporation (October 2020), pp. 2–4, https://www.fdic.gov/regulations/resources/minority/mission-driven/guide.pdf.

79 *"health and beauty simple for people of color":* Cromwell Schubarth, "Tristan Walker Sells His 'Ethnic Beauty' Startup to Procter & Gamble," *Silicon Valley Business Journal*, December 12, 2018, https://www.bizjournals.com/sanjose/ news/2018/12/12/tristan-walker-sells-hisethnic-beauty-startup-to.html.

79 *According to a McKinsey study:* Te-Ping Chen, "The New Push for Corporate

Diversity Comes with an Atlanta Address," *Wall Street Journal*, March 20, 2021, https://www.wsj.com/articles/to-attract-black-employees-companies-move-to-them-11616212810.

79 *Much of its success can be attributed to its Black users:* Salvador Rodriguez, "How Black Users Are Saving Clubhouse from Becoming a Drab Hangout for Tech Bros," cnbc.com, January 10, 2021, https://www.cnbc.com/2021/01/10/black-users-turned-social-app-clubhouse-from-drab-to-fun.html.

79 *Clubhouse today may not be rife with sexism and racism:* Olivia Smith, "On Clubhouse, Women and People of Color Face Abuse," *Grit Daily*, January 16, 2021, https://gritdaily.com/on-clubhouse-women-and-people-of-color-face-abuse/.

81 *The U.S. accounts for 25 percent of:* The Last Mile, https://thelastmile.org.

81 *has a recidivism rate of over 50 percent:* The Healthy People 2020, "Social Determinants of Health," HealthyPeople.gov, https://www.healthypeople.gov/2020/topics-objectives/topic/social-determinants-health/interventions-resources/incarceration#34.

81 *Mass incarceration disproportionately impacts:* Matt Vogel and Lauren C. Porter, "Toward a Demographic Understanding of Incarceration Disparities: Race, Ethnicity, and Age Structure," *Journal of Quantitative Criminology*, September 12, 2015, https://www.ncbi.nlm.nih.gov/pmc/articles/PMC5106500/#Fn1.

81 *Not a single graduate has returned:* Monica Humphries, "People in Prisons Are Learning to Code and It Might Alter the Course of Their Lives," Nationswell, May 15, 2019, https://nationswell.com/prisoners-learning-to-code/.

82 *As economist Raj Chetty discovered:* David Leonhardt, Amanda Cox, and Claire Cain Miller, "An Atlas of Upward Mobility Shows Paths Out of Poverty," *New York Times*, May 4, 2015, https://www.nytimes.com/2015/05/04/upshot/an-atlas-of-upward-mobility-shows-paths-out-of-poverty.html.

82 *Alana Semuels writes powerfully:* Alana Semuels, "Chicago's Awful Divide," *The Atlantic*, March 28, 2018, https://www.theatlantic.com/business/archive/2018/03/chicago-segregation-poverty/556649/.

82 *"40 percent of Black 20-to-24-year-olds":* Ibid.

83 *"elite schools or fitness centers":* Enrico Berkes and Ruben Gaetani, "Income Segregation and Rise of the Knowledge Economy," Rotman School of Management Working Paper No. 3423136, July 19, 2019, https://papers.ssrn.com/sol3/papers.cfm?abstract_id=3423136.

83 *Richard Florida, an urban theorist, writes extensively:* Richard Florida, "Why America's Richest Cities Keep Getting Richer," *The Atlantic*, April 12, 2017, https://www.theatlantic.com/business/archive/2017/04/richard-florida-winner-take-all-new-urban-crisis/522630/.

83 *"finding ways to mitigate":* Richard Florida, "How Innovation Leads to Economic Segregation," Bloomberg.com, October 24, 2017, https://www.bloomberg.com/news/articles/2017-10-24/the-disturbing-link-between-innovation-and-segregation.

83 *Tech progressives often talk a big game:* @ezraklein tweet February 11, 2021, https://twitter.com/ezraklein/status/1359924294730452996.

84 *They set up successful tech centers:* The Upshot, "The Best and Worst Places to Grow Up: How Your Area Compares," *New York Times*, May 4, 2015, https://www.nytimes.com/interactive/2015/05/03/upshot/the-best-and-worst-places-to-grow-up-how-your-area-compares.html.

Chapter 4: Empowering Workers

89 *Courtney Brown was invisible to the customers:* Courtney shared her entire story on this digital panel where Senator Warren, Ai-jen Poo, and I participated: https://www.youtube.com/watch?v=YSzt6XmFY-4, April 29, 2020.

89 *And while Amazon gave a $2 raise:* Isobel Asher Hamilton, "Amazon Drops $2 Coronavirus Pay Raise for Warehouse Workers as CEO Jeff Bezos' Fortune Nears $150 Billion," *businessinsider.com*, June 3, 2020, https://www.businessinsider.com/amazon-cuts-2-dollar-hazard-pay-bezos-150-billion-2020-6.

89 *As she put it:* https://www.youtube.com/watch?v=YSzt6XmFY-4, April 29, 2020.

90 *"all labor has dignity":* Martin Luther King Jr., "All Labor Has Dignity," March 18, 1968, speech at Bishop Charles Mason Temple of the Church of God in Christ in Memphis, Tennessee.

90 *As Josh Bivens and Lawrence Mishel at the Economic Policy Institute:* Josh Bivens and Lawrence Mishel, "Understanding the Historic Divergence Between Productivity and a Typical Worker's Pay," Economic Policy Institute, September 2, 2015, https://www.epi.org/publication/understanding-the-historic-divergence-between-productivity-and-a-typical-workers-pay-why-it-matters-and-why-its-real/.

90 *Carter C. Price and Kathryn Edwards:* Carter C. Price and Kathryn Edwards, "Trends in Income from 1975 to 2018," RAND Corporation, September 2020, https://www.rand.org/pubs/working_papers/WRA516-1.html.

90 *"full income distribution":* Ibid., p. 1.

90 *But after 1975, the gains:* Ibid.

90 *"had income growth remained as equitable":* Ibid.

91 *Apple, located in my district, reached:* Jack Nicas, "Apple Reaches $2 Trillion, Punctuating Big Tech's Grip," *New York Times*, August 19, 2020, https://www.nytimes.com/2020/08/19/technology/apple-2-trillion.html.

91 *In fact, in the last five years:* Bill Hobbs, "FAANG Stands for Five Very Successful Tech Companies That Can Move the Stock Market—Here's What to Know About Investing in Them," *businessinsider.com*, November 6, 2020, https://www.businessinsider.com/what-is-faang.

91 *A University of Chicago study:* Jonathan Dingel and Brent Neiman, "How Many Jobs Can Be Done at Home," Becker Friedman Institute for Economics at the University of Chicago, June 19, 2020, https://bfi.uchicago.edu/working-paper/how-many-jobs-can-be-done-at-home/.

92 *"What is that?"*: "Digital Rally for Essential Workers with Senator Eliza-beth Warren, Rep. Ro Khanna, and Ai-jen Poo," https://www.youtube.com/watch?v=YSzt6XmFY-4, April 29, 2020.

93 *During the worst months of the pandemic*: Chuck Collins, "Updates: Billionaire Wealth, U.S. Job Losses and Pandemic Profiteers," Inequality.org, April 15, 2021, https://inequality.org/great-divide/updates-billionaire-pandemic/.

93 *According to Inequality.org, while many businesses*: Ibid.

94 *"rose in step with productivity"*: Dean Baker, "What the Minimum Wage Would Be if It Kept Pace with Productivity," *CounterPunch*, January 24, 2020, https://www.counterpunch.org/2020/01/24/what-the1-minimum-wage-would-be-if-it-kept-pace-with-productivity/.

94 *If that trend continued*: Ibid.

94 *This is assuming, as Ryan Bourne at Cato astutely points out*: Ryan Bourne, "Ro Khanna and the $23 Minimum Wage," Cato Institute, February 25, 2021, https://www.cato.org/blog/ro-khanna-23-minimum-wage.

94 *In their famous paper, economists*: David Card and Alan B. Krueger, "Minimum Wages and Employment: A Study of the Fast Food Industry in New Jersey and Pennsylvania," National Bureau of Economic Research, October 1993, https://www.nber.org/papers/w4509.

94 *"the employment effects are small"*: Arindrajit Dube, "Impacts of Minimum Wages: Review of the International Evidence," *National Bureau of Economic Research*, November 2019, p. 3, https://assets.publishing.service.gov.uk/government/uploads/system/uploads/attachment_data/file/844350/impacts_of_minimum_wages_review_of_the_international_evidence_Arindrajit_Dube_web.pdf.

94 *A couple of recent studies caution*: Grace Lordan and David Neumark, "People Versus Machines: The Impact of Minimum Wages on Automatable Jobs," National Bureau of Economic Research, August 2017, https://www.nber.org/papers/w23667. See also Ekaterina Jardim, Mark C. Long, Robert Plotnick, Emma van Inwegen, Jacob Vigdor, and Hilary Wething, "Minimum Wage Increases, Wages, and Wage Employment: Evidence from Seattle," National Bureau of Economic Research, June 2017, https://www.nber.org/papers/w23532.

94 *"employers to adjust to the new standard"*: Ben Zipperer, "Gradually Raising the minimum Wage to $15 Would Be Good for Workers, Good for Businesses, and Good for the Economy," Economic Policy Institute, February 7, 2019, https://www.epi.org/publication/minimum-wage-testimony-feb-2019/.

94 *Interestingly, some of the most recent studies*: Jeffrey Clemens, Lisa B. Kahn, and Jonathan Meer, "Dropouts Need Not Apply? The Minimum Wage and Skill Up-grading," National Bureau of Economic Research, May 2020, https://www.nber.org/papers/w27090.

95 *Nearly 90 percent of Americans over eighteen*: "Percentage of the Population in the

United States Who Have Completed High School or More from 1960 to 2019, by Gender," *statista*, https://www.statista.com/statistics/184266/educational-attainment-of-high-school-diploma-or-higher-by-gender/.

95 *Studies show that towns:* Jose Azar, Emiliano Huet-Vaughn, Ioana Marinescu, Bledi Taska, and Till von Wachter, "Minimum Wage Employment Effects and Market Concentration," National Bureau of Economic Research, July 2019, https://www.nber.org/papers/w26101.

95 *When employers have market power:* Ibid.

95 *Within a month of introducing the legislation:* We introduced the Stop BEZOS Act on September 5, 2018, and Amazon announced its wage raise to $15 on October 2, 2018. Caroline Kelly, "Bernie Sanders Praises Jeff Bezos on Amazon $15 Minimum Wage," *CNN Politics*, October 2, 2018, https://www.cnn.com/2018/10/02/politics/bernie-sanders-jeff-bezos-minimum-wage/index.html.

95 *In a tweet, Bezos thanked:* Ibid.

96 *Even before the pandemic:* "Number of Amazon.com Employees from 2007 to 2020," statista, https://www.statista.com/statistics/234488/number-of-amazon-employees/.

96 *By 2020, they were already:* Ibid.

96 *They simply did not replace their workers:* Jason Del Rey, "How Robots Are Transforming Amazon Warehouse Jobs—for Better and Worse," recode.com, December 11, 2019, https://www.vox.com/platform/amp/recode/2019/12/11/20982652/robots-amazon-warehouse-jobs-automation.

96 *"chasing the Holy Grail":* Ibid.

96 *In fact, Amazon's stock was about:* "Amazon-24 Year Stock Price History," *AMZN, Macrotrends*, https://www.macrotrends.net/stocks/charts/AMZN/amazon/stock-price-history.

96 *It should come as no surprise that Amazon's profitability:* Ken Berman and Gorilla Trades report on Amazon's $55 billion cash on hand: Ken Berman and Gorilla Trades, "Big Tech's AAA Balance Sheets," *Forbes*, May 5, 2020, https://www.forbes.com/sites/kenberman/2020/05/05/big-techs-aaa-balance-sheets/?sh=47686edb9118. Jeremy Owens reports that Amazon had profits of $21.3 billion in 2020: Jeremy C. Owens, "Jeff Bezos to Step Down as Amazon CEO After Record-Smashing 2020," *marketwatch.com*, February 2, 2021, https://www.marketwatch.com/story/bezos-to-step-down-as-amazon-ceo-after-record-smashing-2020-ends-with-first-100-billion-quarter-11612300679.

96 *Finally, thoughtful critics raised:* Catherine Rampell, "Tax Bezos. Help Workers. But Not Like This," *Washington Post*, September 6, 2018, https://www.washingtonpost.com/opinions/tax-bezos-help-workers-but-not-like-this/2018/09/06/9ebd64ae-b20d-11e8-aed9-001309990777_story.html.

96 *Gary Becker, the late Nobel Laureate in economics, showed:* Gary S. Becker, "Crime and Punishment: An Economic Approach," in Gary S. Becker and William M.

Landes, eds., "Essays in the Economics of Crime and Punishment," National Bureau of Economic Research, 1974, pp. 1–54, https://www.nber.org/system/files/chapters/c3625/c3625.pdf.

97 *While they increased their minimum wage:* Eugene Kum, "Amazon's Hourly Workers Lose Monthly Bonuses and Stock Awards as Minimum Wage Increases," cnbc.com, October 3, 2018.

97 *Whatever their motives, research:* Ellora Derenoncourt, Clemens Noelke, and David Weil, "Spillover Effects from Voluntary Employer Minimum Wages," February 28, 2021, https://papers.ssrn.com/sol3/papers.cfm?abstract_id=3793677.

97 *Many of these firms emulated:* Ibid.

97 *For instance, Target recently raised:* Melissa Repko, "Target Raises Minimum Wage to $15 an Hour Months Before Its Deadline," cnbc.com, June 17, 2020, https://www.cnbc.com/2020/06/17/target-raises-minimum-wage-to-15-an-hour-months-before-its-deadline.html.

98 *Recognizing that we will not have Republican votes:* Manu Raju, "Progressive House Democrats Pressure Harris to Invoke Rarely Employed Move to Ignore Parliamentarian Decision on Wage Hike," *CNN Politics*, March 1, 2021, https://www.cnn.com/2021/03/01/politics/house-democrats-kamala-harris-wage-hike/index.html.

98 *Jesse Rothstein . . . finds that roughly 70 percent:* "Is the EITC as Good as an NIT Conditional Cash Transfers and Tax Incidence," *American Economic Journal*, February 2010, https://eml.berkeley.edu/~saez/course/rothsteinAEJ10.pdf.

98 *In 2017, Senator Sherrod Brown and I:* Chuck Marr, Emily Horton, and Brendan Duke, "Brown-Khanna Proposal to Expand EITC Would Raise Incomes of 47 Million Working Households," Center on Budget and Policy Priorities, October 10, 2017, https://www.cbpp.org/research/federal-tax/brown-khanna-proposal-to-expand-eitc-would-raise-incomes-of-47-million-working.

99 *More than half of the recipients of the EITC:* Ibid.

99 *Studies show that most families would use:* Ibid.

99 *Apple, in my district, received:* Daisuke Wakabayashi and Brian X. Chen, "Apple, Capitalizing on New Tax Law, Plans to Bring Billions in Cash Back to U.S.," *New York Times*, January 17, 2018, https://www.nytimes.com/2018/01/17/technology/apple-tax-bill-repatriate-cash.html.

99 *Much of this money went:* Matt Phillips, "Trump's Tax Cuts in Hand, Companies Spend More on Themselves Than on Wages," *New York Times*, February 26, 2018, https://www.nytimes.com/2018/02/26/business/tax-cuts-share-buybacks-corporate.html.

99 *What is even more shocking is that Amazon:* Matthew Gardner, Steve Wamhaff, Mary Martellotta, and Lorena Roque, "Corporate Tax Avoidance Remains Rampant Under New Tax Law," Institute of Taxation and Economic Policy, April 2019, //itep.sfo2.digitaloceanspaces.com/04119-Corporate-Tax-Avoidance-Remains-Rampant-Under-New-Tax-Law_ITEP.pdf.

99 *Real average hourly wages stalled:* Michael Madowitz and Seth Hanlon, "GDP Is Growing, but Workers' Wages Aren't," Center for American Progress, July 26, 2018, https://www.americanprogress.org/issues/economy/reports/2018/07/26/454087/gdp-growing-workers-wages-arent/.

100 *As Deaton and Case have shown:* Anne Case and Angus Deaton, *Deaths of Despair and the Future of Capitalism* (Princeton: Princeton University Press, 2020).

100 *If health care family premiums can cost:* Ibid.

101 *The standard was set forth by:* National Labor Relations Board, 153 N.L.R.B. 1488 (N.L.R.B. 1965), July 19, 1965, https://casetext.com/admin-law/the-greyhound-corp-4.

101 *This standard was changed in 1984:* National Labor Relations Board, 271 N.L.R.B 798 (N.L.R.B 1984), July 31, 1984, https://casetext.com/admin-law/tli-inc-263. See also National Labor Relations Board, 269 N.L.R.B 324 (N.L.R.B 1984), March 21, 1984, https://www.nlrb.gov/cases-decisions.

102 *At the beginning of this year:* Kate Conger, "Hundreds of Google Employees Unionize, Culminating Years of Activism," *New York Times*, January 4, 2021, https://www.nytimes.com/2021/01/04/technology/google-employees-union.html.

102 *The union, affiliated with the well-known:* Alphabet Workers Union, https://alphabetworkersunion.org/.

102 *Although it is a minority union:* Conger, "Hundreds of Google Employees Unionize, Culminating Years of Activism."

102 *In 2019, the House of Representatives passed:* Don Gonyea, "House Democrats Pass Bill That Would Protect Worker Organizing Efforts," NPR, March 9, 2021, https://www.npr.org/2021/03/09/975259434/house-democrats-pass-bill-that-would-protect-worker-organizing-efforts.

102 *Even so, Congress can require:* While we passed sick leave as part of Covid relief, we exempted employers with over 500 employees, leaving 60 million Americans without guaranteed paid leave. Our future legislation on paid family and sick leave should not exempt large employers that can meet the requirement most easily. Steven Findlay, "Congress Left Big Gaps in the Paid Sick Days and Paid Leave Provisions of the Coronavirus Emergency Legislation," Healthaffairs.org, April 29, 2020, https://www.healthaffairs.org/do/10.1377/hblog20200424.223002/full/.

102 *For the purposes of illustration:* Greg Bensinger, "Uber: The Ride-Hailing App That Says It Has 'Zero' Drivers," *Washington Post*, October 14, 2019, https://www.washingtonpost.com/technology/2019/10/14/uber-ride-hailing-app-that-says-it-has-zero-drivers/.

103 *The proposition is absurd:* Bobby Allyn, "California Judge Orders Uber and Lyft to Consider All Drivers Employees," NPR, August 10, 2020, https://www.npr.org/2020/08/10/901099643/california-judge-orders-uber-and-lyft-to-consider-all-drivers-employees.

103 *The company then, in coalition:* "Prop 22: Uber Drivers Sue Over Alleged

'Pressure' to Vote, Advocate for Ballot Measure," *CBS SF BayArea*, October 23, 2020, https://sanfrancisco.cbslocal.com/2020/10/23/prop-22-uber-drivers-sue-over-alleged-pressure-to-vote-advocate-for-ballot-measure/.

103 *Uber sits on more than $5 billion:* yahoo!finance, https://finance.yahoo.com/quote/UBER/key-statistics/.

103 *It can afford the additional $500 million:* "Bay City News, Lawsuit Accuses Uber of Saving $500M Annually by Misclassifying Drivers," *NBC Bay Area*, September 13, 2018, https://www.nbcbayarea.com/news/local/lawsuit-accuses-uber-of-saving-500m-annually-by-misclassifying-drivers/208431/.

104 *For example, under current law:* Integrity Data, https://www.integrity-data.com/blog/affordable-care-act-insurance-for-part-time-employees-what-employers-need-to-know/.

104 *Studies show that 45 percent:* Nari Rhee and Illana Boivie, "The Continuing Retirement Savings Crisis," National Institute on Retirement Security, March 2015, https://www.nirsonline.org/wp-content/uploads/2017/07/final_rsc_2015.pdf.

105 *"For most, the dignity work affords":* Joan Williams, *White Working Class: Overcoming Class Cluelessness in America* (Boston: Harvard Business Review Press, 2020), p. 31.

105 *Senator Warren has a detailed plan:* Elizabeth Warren, "Expanding Social Security," medium.com, September 12, 2019.

106 *Because of economic insecurity:* Zhe Li, "The Social Security Retirement Age," Congressional Research Service (Figure 2), "https://www.crs.gov/Reports/R44670?source=search&guid=6a77d9f3053141c9880eac9b2adef7ab&index=0.

106 *They already pay it on every dollar:* Howard Perlman, "Social Security Wage Base Rises to $142,800 for 2021," bloombergtax.com, October 13, 2020, https://news.bloombergtax.com/payroll/social-security-wage-base-rises-to-142-800-for-2021.

106 *Berkeley economist Danny Yagan shows:* Danny Yagan, "Capital Tax Reform and the Real Economy: The Effects of the 2003 Dividend Tax Cut," *American Economic Review* (2015), https://eml.berkeley.edu/~yagan/DividendTax.pdf.

106 *In addition to expanding Social Security:* Gene Sperling, *Economic Dignity* (New York: Penguin, 2020), pp. 200–204.

106 *As Sperling argues:* Ibid.

107 *"Good work finds the way between pride and despair":* Wendell Berry, "What Are People For?," July 18, 2016, https://www.dailygood.org/story/1324/wendell-berry-what-are-people-for-/.

108 *"physically and emotionally taxing":* Annie Lowrey, "Low-Skill Workers Aren't a Problem to Be Fixed," *The Atlantic*, April 23, 2021, https://www.theatlantic.com/ideas/archive/2021/04/theres-no-such-thing-as-a-low-skill-worker/618674/.

108 *"been growing much more slowly than in the past":* Paul Krugman, "Democrats Avoid the Robot Rabbit Hole," *New York Times*, October 17, 2019, https://www.nytimes.com/2019/10/17/opinion/democrats-automation.html.

109 *"arbitrary authority"*: Joshua Cohen, "Good Jobs," MIT Work of the Future, http://workofthefuture.mit.edu/wp-content/uploads/2020/10/2020-Research -Brief-Cohen.pdf.

109 *"a very complex algorithm"*: Eileen Guo and Karen Hao, "This Is the Stanford Vaccine Algorithm That Left Out Frontline Doctors," *MIT Technology Review*, December 21, 2020, https://www.technologyreview.com/2020/12/21/1015303/ stanford-vaccine-algorithm/.

110 *"high road"*: Joel Rogers, "What Does "High Road" Mean?" (1990), https://cows .org/wp-content/uploads/sites/1368/2020/05/1990-What-does-22high-road22 -mean.pdf.

110 *Private industry and union leaders:* UC Berkeley Labor Center, "Taking the High Road," May 1, 2020, https://laborcenter.berkeley.edu/taking-the-high-road/.

110 *Economists have found that when:* Simon Jager, Benjamin Schoefer, and Jorg Heining, "Labor in the Boardroom," *The Quarterly Journal of Economics* 136, no. 2 (May 2021): 669–725, https://academic.oup.com/qje/article/136/2/669/594 4124?login=true.

111 *"excessive automation"*: Daron Acemoglu, "Remaking the Post-Covid World," International Monetary Fund, Spring 2021, https://www.imf.org/external/pubs/ft/ fandd/2021/03/COVID-inequality-and-automation-acemoglu.htm.

111 *"many automation technologies"*: Ibid.

111 *Acemoglu points out that labor:* Ibid.

111 *For example, studies have found that:* Sophia Harris, "A Crime of Opportunity: Why Some Shoppers Steal at Self-Checkout," CBC News, November 17, 2019, https://www.cbc.ca/news/business/self-checkout-shoplifting-retail-theft-1 .5361316.

112 *When employees worked from home during the pandemic:* Cyrus Farivar, "Big Tech Has Largely Left Silicon Valley—and Left Its Blue-Collar Workers Behind," *yahoo!news*, November 12, 2020, https://news.yahoo.com/silicon-valleys-blue -collar-workers-170000865.html.

113 *Amazon's A2Tech:* Neal Karlinsky, "A Tech Job Without College," Amazon, October 15, 2018, https://www.aboutamazon.com/news/operations/a-tech-job-with out-college.

114 *Google and Facebook were explicit that:* Sam Dean, "Google, Facebook Offer Paid Leave to Parents Amid Coronavirus School closures," *Los Angeles Times*, March 31, 2020, https://www.latimes.com/business/technology/story/2020-03 -31/coronavirus-google-facebook-paid-leave-school-closures.

114 *The financial cost of child care to American families:* Sean Fleming, "These Countries Have the Most Expensive Childcare," World Economic Forum, April 23, 2019, https://www.weforum.org/agenda/2019/04/these-countries-have-the-most -expensive-childcare/.

114 *This is higher than in any EU country:* Ibid.

115 *"part of the basic infrastructure of this nation"*: Chabeli Carrazana, "Elizabeth

Warren Put Child Care Front and Center at the DNC," *the 19th*, August 20, 2020, https://19thnews.org/2020/08/elizabeth-warren-put-child-care-front-and-center-at-the-dnc/.

115 *She envisions these services:* Elizabeth Warren, "My Plan for Universal Child Care," medium.com, February 19, 2019, https://medium.com/@teamwarren/my-plan-for-universal-child-care-762535e6c20a.

115 *Biden's proposal calls for giving:* Carmen Reinicke, "Biden Tax Plan Could Save Some Families Nearly $15,000 a Year on Child Care," cnbc.com, April 28, 2021, https://www.cnbc.com/2021/04/28/biden-plan-could-save-families-nearly-15000-a-year-on-child-care.html.

115 *Consider that the average rent:* Adam Brinklow, "Silicon Valley Has the Highest Housing Costs in the U.S.," *Curbed San Francisco*, February 19, 2019, https://sf.curbed.com/2019/2/19/18229922/silicon-valley-index-2019-housing-gentrification-wealth-gap.

116 *"extremely rent-burdened":* "Soaring Rents, Falling Wages," Working Partnerships USA, https://siliconvalleyrising.org/files/SoaringRentsFallingWages.pdf.

117 *Again, Senator Warren has one of the best proposals:* Elizabeth Warren, "My Housing Plan for America," medium.com, March 16, 2019, https://medium.com/@teamwarren/my-housing-plan-for-america-20038e19dc26.

Chapter 5: Progressive Capitalism

122 *"one to n":* Peter Thiel and Blake Masters, *Zero to One: Notes on Startups, or How to Build the Future* (Westminster, MD: Currency, 2014).

123 *Mark Zuckerberg's parents hired a computer science:* Jose Antonio Vargas, "The Face of Facebook," *New Yorker*, September 20, 2010, https://www.newyorker.com/magazine/2010/09/20/the-face-of-facebook.

123 *His parents also sent him to an elite:* Ibid.

123 *Bill Gates attended a private school in Seattle:* Zameena Mejia, "Bill Gates Learned What He Needed to Start Microsoft in High School," cnbc.com, May 24, 2018;https://www.cnbc.com/2018/05/24/bill-gates-got-what-he-needed-to-start-microsoft-in-high-school.html.

123 *"If there had been no Lakeside, there would have been no Microsoft":* Ibid.

123 *"the true source of the wealth of a nation":* Joseph Stiglitz, "Progressive Capitalism Is Not an Oxymoron," *New York Times*, April 19, 2019, https://www.nytimes.com/2019/04/19/opinion/sunday/progressive-capitalism.html.

124 *"substantive freedoms":* Amartya Sen, *Development as Freedom* (New York: Anchor, 1999), p. 1.

124 *"have reason to value":* Ibid., p. 10.

124 *"substantive freedoms":* Ibid., p. 1.

124 *"true individual freedom":* Franklin Roosevelt, Message to Congress, January 11, 1944, https://fdrlibrary.tumblr.com/post/185749479859/true-individual-freedom-cannot-exist-without.

125 *Amartya Sen, who rejects GDP as our north star:* Sen, *Development as Freedom*, pp. 294–95.

125 *"how extensively and effectively people invest in themselves":* Gary S. Becker, "The Age of Human Capital," in Edward P. Lazear, *Education in the Twenty-First Century* (Palo Alto: Hoover Institution Press, 2002), pp. 3–8, https://www.hoover.org/sites/default/files/uploads/documents/0817928928_3.pdf.

125 *"schooling, on-the-job training":* Ibid., p. 3.

125 *"over 70 percent of the total capital in the United States":* Ibid.

126 *"more educated and healthier populations":* Ibid., p. 5.

126 *"social exclusion":* Amartya Sen, "Inequality, Unemployment and Contemporary Europe," *International Labour Review* 136, no. 2 (1997): 160, http://ilo.org/public/english/revue/download/pdf/sen.pdf.

126 *"because of a wastage of productive power":* Ibid.

126 *"being able to work as a human being":* Martha C. Nussbaum, *Creating Capabilities* (Cambridge: Belknap Press, 2011), p. 34.

126 *Sen suggests that every society should:* Sen, *Development as Freedom*, pp. 30–34.

126 *Nussbaum argues that societies can debate the amount:* Nussbaum, *Creating Capabilities*, pp. 33–34, 73–76.

128 *Numerous other developed countries have:* Amartya Sen, "Universal Healthcare: The Affordable Dream," *The Guardian*, January 6, 2015, https://www.theguardian.com/society/2015/jan/06/-sp-universal-healthcare-the-affordable-dream-amartya-sen.

128 *"can certainly afford to provide healthcare":* Ibid.

128 *Currently the U.S. will need:* Rayna M. Letourneau, "Amid a Raging Pandemic, the US Faces a Nursing Shortage. Can We Close the Gap?," *The Conversation*, November 20, 2020, https://theconversation.com/amid-a-raging-pandemic-the-us-faces-a-nursing-shortage-can-we-close-the-gap-149030; "New Findings Confirm Predictions on Physician Shortage," AAMC, April 23, 2019, https://www.aamc.org/news-insights/press-releases/new-findings-confirm-predictions-physician-shortage.

128 *Studies suggest that a single payer system:* Tsung-Mei Cheng, "Health Care Spending in the US and Taiwan: A Response to It's Still the Prices, Stupid, and a Tribute to Uwe Reinhardt," *HealthAffairs*, February 6, 2019, Document2https://www.healthaffairs.org/do/10.1377/hblog20190206.305164/full/.

128 *"a strong relationship":* Sen, "Universal Healthcare."

128 *Sen points to Japan, South Korea:* Ibid.

129 *In fact, Deaton and Case . . . have shown:* Anne Case and Angus Deaton, *Deaths of Despair and the Future of Capitalism* (Princeton: Princeton University Press, 2020).

129 *In a widely read study:* Brigitte C. Madrian, "Employment-Based Health Insurance and Job Mobility: Is There Evidence of Job-Lock," *Quarterly Journal of Economics* 109 (February 1994): 27–54, https://econpapers.repec.org/article/oupqjecon/v_3a109_3ay_3a1994_3ai_3a1_3ap_3a27-54..htm.

130 *"cut back on healthcare"*: Chelsey Ledue, "More than Half of Americans Say Family Skimped on Medical Care Due to Costs," *Healthcare Finance*, February 25, 2009. https://www.healthcarefinancenews.com/news/more-half-americans-say-family-skimped-medical-care-due-costs.

131 *"European examples richly illustrate"*: Sen, "Universal Healthcare."

131 *Taiwan's experience supports this point:* Tsung-Mei Cheng, "Taiwan's New National Health Insurance Program: Genesis and Experience So Far," *HealthAffairs*, May/June 2003, https://www.healthaffairs.org/doi/pdf/10.1377/hlthaff.22.3.61.

131 *Contrary to critics' fears about rising costs:* Ronald Brownstein, "Can Warren Actually Avoid Taxing the Middle Class?," *The Atlantic*, November 3, 2019, https://www.theatlantic.com/politics/archive/2019/11/warren-medicare-all-taxes/601315/.

131 *Studies further show that Medicare for All:* William H. Shrank, Teresa L. Rogstad, and Natasha Parekh, "Waste in the US Health Care System," *JAMA*, October 7, 2019, https://jamanetwork.com/journals/jama/article-abstract/2752664.

132 *Find Something New:* David Knowles, "Ivanka Trump Tells Workers to 'Find Something New'—Because Old Jobs Aren't Coming Back," *yahoo!news*, July 14, 2020, https://news.yahoo.com/ivanka-trump-tells-workers-to-find-something-new-because-old-jobs-arent-coming-back-183756343.html.

132 *"App Development with Swift 4.2":* Michelle Singletary, "Ivanka Trump's Find Something New Career Campaign Is More Hype than Help," *Washington Post*, July 24, 2020, https://www.washingtonpost.com/business/2020/07/24/ivanka-trump-find-something-new/.

133 *Mike Konczal, a fellow at the Roosevelt Institute:* Mike Konczal, "Only 1.4% of Free College Spending Would Go to Children of Millionaires and Billionaires," medium.com, November 20, 2019, https://medium.com/@rortybomb/only-1-4-of-free-college-spending-would-go-to-children-of-millionaires-and-billionaires-39c0d2c2fa1b.

134 *If you only provided free college to those making:* Ibid.

134 *"means-testing college tuition relief doesn't save much money":* Ezra Klein, "Paul Krugman on Climate, Robots, Single-Payer, and So Much More," *Vox*, December 26, 2019, https://www.vox.com/podcasts/2019/12/26/21011830/paul-krugman-obam-climate-medicare-robots-single-payer-andrew-yang.

134 *"it makes the program simpler and the base of support stronger":* Ibid.

134 *If you still have grave concerns:* Kimberly Amadeo, "Afghanistan War Cost, Timeline, and Economic Impact," *the balance*, February 23, 2021, https://www.thebalance.com/cost-of-afghanistan-war-timeline-economic-impact-4122493.

134 *Nobel Laureate James Heckman has shown:* James Heckman, "The Economics of Human Potential," https://heckmanequation.org/.

135 *An immersive program for children:* James Heckman, "Return on Investment in Birth-to-Three Early Childhood Development Program," heckmanequation.org,

September 6, 2018, https://heckmanequation.org/www/assets/2018/09/F_ROI
-Webinar-Deck_birth-to-three_091818.pdf.

135 *"coordinate these early childhood resources":* James Heckman, "There's More to
Gain by Taking a Comprehensive Approach to Early Childhood Development,"
heckmanequation.org., https://heckmanequation.org/www/assets/2017/01/F_
Heckman_CBAOnePager_120516.pdf.

136 *The problem is that the cutoff:* Eligibility Guidelines, Santa Clara County Office
of Education, https://www.sccoe.org/depts/students/early-learning-services/
Pages/ELS-Eligibility.aspx.

136 *Even more shocking is:* Santa Clara County Office of Education, Annual Report
2019-2020, p. 7, https://headstart.sccoe.org/Documents/Annual_Report.pdf.

138 *When Congress passed the:* "Huffman Leads Bipartisan Request for Full IDEA
Funding," April 3, 2020, https://huffman.house.gov/media-center/press-releases/
huffman-leads-bipartisan-request-for-full-idea-funding.

138 *Today, federal funding covers:* Ibid.

138 *According to Senator Warren's estimates:* Elizabeth Warren, "A Great Public
School Education for Every Student," medium.com, October 21, 2019, https://
medium.com/@teamwarren/a-great-public-school-education-for-every-stu
dent-6d306f7f986b.

138 *The current average salary for teachers:* Cindy Long, "Average Teacher Salary
Down 4.5% Over Past Decade," *NEA News,* April 29, 2019, https://www.nea.org/
advocating-for-change/new-from-nea/average-teacher-salary-down-45-over
-past-decade.

138 *"the largest-ever one-time federal investment in K–12 education":* Nicholas Johnson and Victoria Jackson, "American Rescue Plan Act Includes Much-Needed
K–12 Funding," Center on Budget and Policy Priorities, March 15, 2021, https://
www.cbpp.org/research/state-budget-and-tax/american-rescue-plan-act-in
cludes-much-needed-k-12-funding.

139 *Yet, it is bewildering that a society:* "Hunger in America," Feeding America,
https://www.feedingamerica.org/hunger-in-america.

140 *We know that children lacking food:* Council on Community Pediatrics and Committee on Nutrition, "Promoting Food Security for all Children," *Pediatrics,* November 2015, https://pediatrics.aappublications.org/content/136/5/e1431.

140 *Studies, moreover, show that poor nutrition:* Lauren Weber, "Healthier Workers
Are More Productive, Study Finds," *Wall Street Journal,* August 8, 2017, https://
www.wsj.com/articles/healthy-workers-are-more-productive-study-finds
-1502219651.

140 *Senator Bernie Sanders and Representative Ilhan Omar:* Ayelet Sheffey, "Bernie
Sanders, Ilhan Omar Push for Permanent Free School Lunch," *Business Insider,*
May 10, 2021, https://www.businessinsider.com/universal-school-meals-bernie
-sanders-ilhan-omar-free-lunch-hunger-2021-5.

140 *President Biden's American Rescue Plan:* "USDA Increases SNAP Benefits Up to $100 Per Household with Funding from American Rescue Plan," U.S. Department of Agriculture, March 22, 2021, https://www.usda.gov/media/press-releases/2021/03/22/usda-increases-snap-benefits-100-household-funding-american-rescue.

141 *Currently, as Gene Sperling has observed:* Gene Sperling, *Economic Dignity* (New York: Penguin, 2020), pp. 142–43.

141 *But according to his calculations:* Ibid.

141 *Sperling calls for a more accessible:* Ibid., pp. 142–44.

142 *As Banerjee and Duflo show:* Abhijit V. Banerjee and Esther Duflo, *Good Economics for Hard Times* (New York: PublicAffairs, 2019), p. 283.

143 *One of the historic achievements of this:* Carmen Reinicke, "Keeping the Expanded Child Tax Credit Would Help 65.6 Million American Kids," cnbc.com, May 26, 2021, https://www.cnbc.com/2021/05/26/keeping-expanded-child-tax-credit-would-help-65point6-million-american-kids.html.

143 *Arlie Hochschild's scholarship has shown:* Arlie Russell Hochschild, *Strangers in Their Own Land* (New York: The New Press, 2016).

144 *Still, nearly half of Americans support:* "Little Public Support for Reductions in Federal Spending," Pew Research Center, April 11, 2019, https://www.pewresearch.org/politics/2019/04/11/little-public-support-for-reductions-in-federal-spending/.

144 *"Jesus said that nations would be judged":* Christen McCurdy, "William J. Barber II Calls for a Moral America," *streetroots*, November 8, 2019. https://www.streetroots.org/news/2019/11/08/william-j-barber-ii-calls-moral-america.

144 *One of my most popular proposals:* Leada Gore, "Ohio's Tim Ryan, Another Lawmaker Propose $2,000 Monthly Stimulus Check," *Pittsburgh Post-Gazette*, April 15, 2020, https://www.post-gazette.com/news/politics-nation/2020/04/15/2000-a-month-Americans-proposed-bill-House-Democrats-stimulus-check-coronavirus/stories/202004150168.

145 *More broadly, we can commit to stopping our endless:* "United States Budgetary Costs and Obligations of Post 9/11 Wars Through FY2020: 6.4 Trillion," Watson Institute International & Public Affairs, November 13, 2019, https://watson.brown.edu/costsofwar/files/cow/imce/papers/2019/US%20Budgetary%20Costs%20of%20Wars%20November%202019.pdf.

145 *What is unjustifiable is that the IRS:* Jesse Eisinger and Paul Kiel, "Why the Rich Don't Get Audited," *New York Times*, May 3, 2019, https://www.nytimes.com/2019/05/03/sunday-review/tax-rich-irs.html.

146 *Sarin and Summers estimate that:* Natasha Sarin and Lawrence H, Summers, "Shrinking the Tax Gap: Approaches and Revenue Potential," National Bureau of Economic Research, November 2019, https://www.nber.org/system/files/working_papers/w26475/w26475.pdf.

146 *It is outrageous that many of the richest corporations*: Anna Akins highlights that tech companies in the S&P 500 pay an effective tax rate of 14.5 percent, with big tech some of the worst offenders: Anna Akins, "What Joe Biden's U.S. Tax Plan Could Mean for Big Tech," S&P Global, October 6, 2020, https://www.spglobal .com/marketintelligence/en/news-insights/latest-news-headlines/what-joe -biden-s-us-tax-plan-could-mean-for-big-tech-60549176.

146 *These special tax breaks need*: Matthew Gardner and Steve Wamhoff, "Biden's Minimum Corporate Tax Proposal: Yes, Please Limit Amazon's Tax Break," ITEP, July 19, 2020, https://itep.org/bidens-minimum-corporate-tax-proposal-yes -please-limit-amazons-tax-breaks/.

147 *Nicholas Kristof . . . recently observed*: Nicholas Kristof, "We're No. 28! And Dropping!," *New York Times*, September 9, 2020, https://www.nytimes.com/2020/09/09/ opinion/united-states-social-progress.html.

147 *He also cites research showing*: Nicholas Kristof, "U.S.A., Land of Limitations?," *New York Times*, August 8, 2015, https://www.nytimes.com/2015/08/09/opinion/ sunday/nicholas-kristof-usa-land-of-limitations.html.

147 *In an important paper looking*: James J. Heckman and Rasmus Landersø. "Lessons from Denmark About Inequality and Social Mobility," National Bureau of Economic Research, Working Paper No. 28543 (2021), https://www.nber.org/ papers/w28543.

PART II: TWENTY-FIRST-CENTURY CITIZENSHIP

Chapter 6: Internet Bill of Rights

151 *"Congressman, iPhone is made by a different company"*: "'iPhone is made by a different company' Google CEO says to Rep. King," YouTube video, https://www .youtube.com/watch?v=wmuROTmazco.

151 *"not by default"*: Minda Zetlin, "Google CEO Sundar Pichai Spent 3 ½ Hours Before Congress. Here Are the Strangest Things They Asked," *Inc.*, https://www .inc.com/minda-zetlin/google-ceo-sundar-pichai-congress-representatives -hearings-funny-stupid-questions.html.

151 *"$100 million a year"*: Ibid.

151 *"Senator, we run ads"*: "Senator Asks How Facebook Remains Free, Mark Zuckerberg Smirks: 'We Run Ads,'" Youtube video, https://www.youtube.com/ watch?v=n2H8wx1aBiQ.

152 *"the world with pamphlets and books"*: Ann Blair, "Information Overload, the Early Years," *Boston Globe*, November 28, 2010, http://archive.boston.com/bostonglobe/ ideas/articles/2010/11/28/information_overload_the_early_years/?page=2.

153 *Every time we participate in*: Evelyn Aswad, "Losing the Freedom to Be Human," *Columbia Human Rights Law Review* 52 (2020), https://papers.ssrn.com/sol3/ papers.cfm?abstract_id=3635701.

153 *"track users across the internet"*: Nathalie Maréchal, Rebecca Mackinnon, and
Jessica Dheere, "Getting to the Source of Infodemics: It's the Business Model,"
New America, May 2020, pp. 32–33, https://d1y8sb8igg2f8e.cloudfront.net/docu
ments/Getting_to_the_Source_of_Infodemics_Its_the_Business_Model_2020
-05.pdf.

153 *"If we accept as normal"*: 2019 Commencement Address by Apple CEO Tim
Cook, June 16, 2019, https://news.stanford.edu/2019/06/16/remarks-tim-cook
-2019-stanford-commencement/.

153 *Drawing on Cook's profound words*: Aswad, "Losing the Freedom to Be Human."

154 *"64% of all extremist group joins"*: Ibid. Aswad cited a *Wall Street Journal* article
for this quote: Jeff Horwitz and Deepa Seetharaman, "Facebook Executives Shut
Down Efforts to Make the Site Less Divisive," *Wall Street Journal*, May 26, 2020,
https://www.wsj.com/articles/facebook-knows-it-encourages-division-top-ex
ecutives-nixed-solutions-11590507499.

154 *The QAnon conspiracy theory*: Roger McNamee, "Facebook Drove QAnon's Mad
Growth and Enhanced Its Power to Poison Elections," *Los Angeles Times*, September 30, 2020, https://www.latimes.com/opinion/story/2020-09-30/facebook
-qanon-conspiracy-social-media-election.

154 *Twitter also recommended QAnon tweets*: Ibid.

154 *QAnon also thrived on YouTube*: Kevin Roose, "YouTube Cracks Down on
QAnon Conspiracy Theory, Citing Offline Violence," *New York Times*, October 15, 2020, https://www.nytimes.com/2020/10/15/technology/youtube-bans
-qanon-violence.html.

154 *Because of the advocacy from people*: Salvador Rodriguez, "Facebook Will Stop
Recommending Political Groups Permanently," cnbc.com, January 27, 2021,
https://www.cnbc.com/2021/01/27/facebook-will-stop-recommending-politi
cal-groups-permanently.html.

154 *It took the January 6 Capitol attack*: Ibid.

155 *Concerned about the dangers tech poses for democracy*: Kara Swisher, "Introducing the Internet Bill of Rights," *New York Times*, October 4, 2018, https://www
.nytimes.com/2018/10/04/opinion/ro-khanna-internet-bill-of-rights.html.

156 *Regulations should also restrict the possibility*: Daniel J. Solove, "Privacy Self-
Management and the Consent Dilemma," *Harvard Law Review* (2013), https://
papers.ssrn.com/sol3/papers.cfm?abstract_id=2171018.

156 *And they should limit the number of items*: Ibid.

157 *If users want, they should be given*: Stephen Wolfram, "Testifying at the Senate
about A.I.—Selected Content on the Internet," June 25, 2019, https://writings
.stephenwolfram.com/2019/06/testifying-at-the-senate-about-a-i-selected-con
tent-on-the-internet/.

157 *Dorsey wants users to have more options*: Jacob Kastrenakes, "Twitter's Jack
Dorsey Wants to Build an App Store for Social Media Algorithms," *theverge*,

February 9, 2021, https://www.theverge.com/2021/2/9/22275441/jack-dorsey-decentralized-app-store-algorithms.

158 *"similar characteristics or behaviors":* Dirk Bergemann, Alessandro Bonatti, and Tan Gan, "The Economics of Social Data," Cowles Foundation for Research in Economics, July 26, 2020, https://cowles.yale.edu/sites/default/files/files/pub/d22/d2203-r2.pdf.

158 *In fact, tech companies like Google:* Paper, Fox Business, March 16, 2020, https://www.foxbusiness.com/technology/google-market-share-europe-gdpr.

158 *Most concerning, the big tech companies were successful:* Soheil Human and Florian Cech, "A Human-Centric Perspective on Digital Consenting: The Case of GAFAM," in Alfred Zimmerman, Robert J. Howlett, and Lakhmi C. Jain, *Human Centered Intelligent Systems* (Singapore: Springer, 2020), https://link.springer.com/chapter/10.1007/978-981-15-5784-2_12.

159 *Both banned the use of X-Mode:* Byron Tau, "Apple and Google to Stop X-Mode from Collecting Location Data from Users' Phones," *Wall Street Journal*, December 9, 2020; https://www.wsj.com/articles/apple-and-google-to-stop-x-mode-from-collecting-location-data-from-users-phones-11607549061.

159 *Apple took additional, constructive steps:* "Data Privacy Day at Apple: Improving Transparency and Empowering Users," Apple Newsroom, January 27, 2021, https://www.apple.com/newsroom/2021/01/data-privacy-day-at-apple-improving-transparency-and-empowering-users/.

159 *Facebook knew that Cambridge Analytica:* "Zuckerberg: Facebook Believed Cambridge Analytica Deleted Private Data," video, *Guardian*, April 10, 2018, https://www.theguardian.com/us-news/video/2018/apr/10/zuckerberg-facebook-believed-cambridge-analytica-deleted-private-data-video.

159 *Instead, it confronted Cambridge Analytica privately:* Ibid.

160 *"accept or reject a letter to the editor":* Daphne Keller, "CDA 230 Reform Grows Up: The Pact Act Has Problems but It Is Talking About the Right Things," The Center for Internet and Society, http://cyberlaw.stanford.edu/blog/2020/07/cda-230-reform-grows-pact-act-has-problems-it%E2%80%99s-talking-about-right-things.

160 *California's recent privacy law gives consumers:* David Kessler and Anna Rudawski, "CCPA Extends 'Right to Deletion' to California Residents," Norton Rose Fulbright blog network, September 27, 2018, https://www.dataprotectionreport.com/2018/09/ccpa-extends-right-to-deletion-to-california-residents/.

160 *There are limited exceptions:* https://carnaclaw.com/news-and-events/commercial-business-litigation/california-right-to-be-forgotten-law/; https://www.mondaq.com/unitedstates/privacy-protection/831300/ccpa-the-qualified-right-to-deletion.

161 *Her scholarship:* Danielle Keats Citron, *Hate Crimes in Cyberspace* (Cambridge: Harvard University Press, 2014).

161 *The rampant racism and misogyny online:* Rachelle Hampton, "The Black Feminists Who Saw the Alt-Right Threat Coming," *slate.com*, April 23, 2019, https://slate.com/technology/2019/04/black-feminists-alt-right-twitter-gamergate.html.

161 *"doxxing content":* "Remove Your Personal Information from Google," https://support.google.com/websearch/troubleshooter/3111061?hl=en.

162 *According to* Wired, *Equifax knew:* Lily Hay Newman, "Equifax Officially Has No Excuses," *Wired,* September 14, 2017, https://www.wired.com/story/equifax-breach-no-excuse/.

162 *Currently, according to Hayley Tsukayama:* Hayley Tsukayama, "Why It Can Take So Long for Companies to Reveal Their Data Breaches," *Washington Post,* September 8, 2017, https://www.washingtonpost.com/news/the-switch/wp/2017/09/08/why-it-can-take-so-long-for-companies-to-reveal-their-data-breaches/.

165 *"the data rates had been reduced to 1/200":* Mozilla v. FCC, Case No. 18-1051, Declaration of Anthony Bowden filed August 20, 2018, https://assets.documentcloud.org/documents/4780226/VerizonFireDeclaration.pdf.

165 *Although we have not seen the most:* Lindsey Stern, "Broadband Providers Are Quietly Taking Advantage of an Internet Without Net Neutrality Protections," *Public Knowledge,* January 29, 2019, https://www.publicknowledge.org/blog/broadband-providers-are-quietly-taking-advantage-of-an-internet-without-net-neutrality-protections/.

166 *Americans pay almost twice as much:* Philllip Dampier, "Great North American Ripoff: Canada, U.S. Pay Double What Europe, Asia Pays, Stop the Cap!," September 26, 2017, https://stopthecap.com/2017/09/26/great-north-american-broadband-ripoff-canada-u-s-pay-double-europe-asia-pays/.

166 *Most Americans either have no choice:* Jon Brodkin, "US Broadband: Still No ISP Choice for Many, Especially at Higher Speeds," August 10, 2016, arstechnica.com, https://arstechnica.com/information-technology/2016/08/us-broadband-still-no-isp-choice-for-many-especially-at-higher-speeds/.

167 *Amazon has a favorable rating of:* https://accountabletech.org/wp-content/uploads/Accountable-Tech-January-2021-Polling.pdf.

167 *Even Facebook, the outcast in terms of approval:* Ibid.

167 *Barry Lynn and Matt Stoller:* Barry Lynn, *Liberty from All Masters: The New American Autocracy vs. the Will of the People* (New York: St. Martin's Press, 2020). See also Matt Stoller, *Goliath: The 100 Year War Between Monopoly Power and Democracy* (New York: Simon & Schuster, 2020); Zephyr Teachout, *Break 'Em Up: Recovering Our Freedom from Big Ag, Big Tech, and Big Money* (New York: All Points Books, 2020).

168 *"information fiduciaries":* Jack M. Balkin and Jonathan Zittrain, "A Grand Bargain to Make Tech Companies Trustworthy," *The Atlantic,* October 3, 2016, https://www.theatlantic.com/technology/archive/2016/10/information-fiduciary/502346/.

169 *Apple and Google design the basic architecture:* James Vincent, "99.6 Percent of New Smartphones Run Android or iOS," *The Verge*, February 16, 2017, https:// www.theverge.com/2017/2/16/14634656/android-ios-market-share-blackberry -2016.

170 *In Ireland, nearly 30 percent of the country:* "Ireland Dominates the World's Most Successful Contact Tracing App to the Linux Foundation," *nearform*, July 20, 2020, https://www.nearform.com/blog/ireland-donates-contact-tracing-app-to -linux-foundation/. See also "Loved or Loathed? How Germany's Coronavirus Tracking App Is Faring," dw.com, June 26, 2020, https://www.dw.com/en/loved -or-loathed-how-germanys-coronavirus-tracking-app-is-faring/a-53959165 .Document2.

170 *The U.S. adoption rates were dramatically lower:* "Few Adopting Apple Google Covid-19 Exposure apps," *Modern Healthcare*, December 6, 2020, https://www .modernhealthcare.com/technology/few-adopting-apple-google-covid-19-ex posure-apps.

170 *Google pays Apple between $8–12 billion:* Daisuke Wakabayashi and Jack Nicas, "Apple, Google and a Deal That Controls the Internet, *New York Times*, October 25, 2020, https://www.nytimes.com/2020/10/25/technology/apple-google -search-antitrust.html.

171 *The allegation is that this perpetuates Google's dominance:* "How Google Retains More than 90 Percent of Market Share," *Business Insider*, April 23, 2018, https:// www.businessinsider.com/how-google-retains-more-than-90-of-market-share -2018-4.

171 *The House Antitrust Subcommittee issued a scathing:* Subcommittee on Antitrust, "Commercial and Administrative Law of the Committee on the Judiciary, Majority Staff Report and Recommendations, Investigation of Competition in Digital Markets" (2020), https://assets.documentcloud.org/documents/7222833/House -Tech-Antitrust-Report.pdf.

172 *"dominant position":* "Competition Policy," European Commission, https:// ec.europa.eu/competition-policy/consumers/what-competition-policy_en.

172 *"people don't use Google because":* Kent Walker, "A Deeply Flawed Lawsuit That Would Do Nothing to Help Consumers," Google Public Policy, October 20, 2020, https://blog.google/outreach-initiatives/public-policy/response-doj.

172 *"in a matter of seconds":* Ibid.

173 *Google makes a serious argument:* Ibid.

173 *Microsoft's antitrust settlement from 2001:* Department of Justice press release, "Department of Justice and Microsoft Corporation Reach Effective Settlement on Antitrust Lawsuit," November 2, 2001, https://www.justice.gov/archive/atr/ public/press_releases/2001/9463.htm.

173 *The company grew from a market cap:* Taylor Soper, "Microsoft on Verge of Reaching $2 Trillion Market Cap Milestone Following This Week's Earnings Report," *GeekWire*, April 26, 2021, https://www.geekwire.com/2021/micro

soft-verge-passing-2-trillion-market-cap-milestone-following-weeks-earnings
-report/.

173 *Amazon controls more than 50 percent:* Lina M. Khan, "The Separation of Platforms and Commerce," *Columbia Law Review* 119 (2019), https://columbialaw
review.org/content/the-separation-of-platforms-and-commerce/.

173 *"Buy Box":* Ibid.

173 *The Buy Box is what allows customers:* Ibid.

174 *Khan, moreover, argues that Amazon's practice:* Ibid.

174 *What may be most problematic:* Ibid.

174 *"Facebook has a right to control its product":* Sambreel Holdings LLC v. Facebook,
Inc. (S.D. Cal. 2012).

175 *Under European law:* Vassilis Hatzopoulos, "The EU Essential Facilities Doctrine," Research Papers in Law, *European Legal Studies,* June 2006, http://aei.pitt
.edu/44287/1/researchpaper_6_2006_hatzopoulos.pdf.

176 *"limited interoperability":* Competition & Markets Authority, "Online Platforms
and Digital Advertising: Market Study Final Report," July 1, 2020, https://assets
.publishing.service.gov.uk/media/5efc57ed3a6f4023d242ed56/Final_report_1_
July_2020_.pdf.

177 *Most big tech companies will place many:* Paola Rosa-Aquino, "Fix, or Toss? The
'Right to Repair' Movement Gains Ground," *New York Times,* October 23, 2000,
https://www.nytimes.com/2020/10/23/climate/right-to-repair.html.

178 *According to the American Antitrust Institute:* Diana L. Moss, "The Record of
Weak U.S. Merger Enforcement in Big Tech," American Antitrust Institute,
July 8, 2019, https://www.antitrustinstitute.org/wp-content/uploads/2019/07/
Merger-Enforcement_Big-Tech_7.8.19.pdf.

178 *The report finds Google did 234:* Ibid.

178 *"the Google–ITA Software, Inc. matter":* Ibid.

178 *Those who follow Silicon Valley deals:* Sarah Frier, *No Filter: The Inside Story of
Instagram* (New York: Simon & Schuster, 2020).

180 *Senator Amy Klobuchar has introduced:* Reuters Staff, "Klobuchar Bill Would
Help U.S. Antitrust Enforcers Stop Mergers," reuters.com, February 4, 2021,
https://www.reuters.com/article/usa-antitrust-klobuchar/klobuchar-bill-would
-help-u-s-antitrust-enforcers-stop-mergers-idUSL1N2K93M8.

180 *According to Scott Sher:* Scott Sher, an antitrust attorney at Wilson Sonsini Good-
rich & Rosati, analyzed FTC and DOJ from 2017 to 2019 and concluded that only
about 2.2 percent of mergers were "mega deals" worth more than $5 billion.

181 *Look at what happened to Stockton mayor:* Anita Chabria, "Rising Democratic
Star Michael Tubbs Risks Reelection Defeat, Thanks in Part to a Stockton Blog,"
Los Angeles Times, November 6, 2020, https://www.latimes.com/california/
story/2020-11-06/stockton-mayor-election-michael-tubbs-risks-defeat.

181 *More generally, studies show local:* PEN America, "Losing the News: The Deci-
mation of Local Journalism and the Search for Solutions," https://pen.org/

wp-content/uploads/2019/12/Losing-the-News-The-Decimation-of-Local-Journalism-and-the-Search-for-Solutions-Report.pdf.

181 *"depriving the content creators of digital ad revenue"*: Gary Abernathy, "How Small News Outlets Are Pushing Back Against Big Tech," *Washington Post*, June 25, 2021, https://www.washingtonpost.com/opinions/2021/06/25/how-small-news-outlets-are-pushing-back-against-big-tech/.

182 *PEN America, a community of writers*: PEN America, "Losing the News," p. 66.

182 *They propose a 2 percent*: Ibid.

182 *"National Endowment for Journalism"*: Bruce Ackerman and Ian Ayres, "A National Endowment for Journalism," *The Guardian*, February 13, 2009, https://www.theguardian.com/commentisfree/cifamerica/2009/feb/12/newspapers-investigative-journalism-endowments.

182 *"band together"*: Enquirer Editorial Board, "Editorial: Google, Facebook Profit from Local News Without Paying for It. That Must End," *The Enquirer*, May 13, 2021, https://www.cincinnati.com/story/opinion/2021/05/13/editorial-congress-must-pass-journalism-competition-and-preservation-act/5071935001/.

183 *Technology writer Kevin Roose has*: Kevin Roose, "Buy This Column on the Blockchain!," *New York Times*, March 24, 2021, https://www.nytimes.com/2021/03/24/technology/nft-column-blockchain.html.

183 *"the internet has the potential to expand choice"*: Neil Turkewitz, "Dissonant Intervals & Bittersweet Symphonies: Music's Past, Present & Future," medium.com, May 16, 2018, https://medium.com/@nturkewitz_56674/dissonant-intervals-bittersweet-symphonies-musics-past-present-future-d2cacc4f4f82.

183 *In 2020, more than fifteen thousand stores closed*: Walter Loeb, "More than 15,500 Are Closing in 2020 So Far—A Number That Will Surely Rise," *Forbes*, July 6, 2020, https://www.forbes.com/sites/walterloeb/2020/07/06/9274-stores-are-closing-in-2020—its-the-pandemic-and-high-debt—more-will-close/?sh=65146bb0729f.

Chapter 7: Deliberation Online

186 *Across the Middle East, citizens*: Ishaan Tharoor, "In a World of Crisis, Tunisia Democracy Marches On," *Washington Post*, November 5, 2019, https://www.washingtonpost.com/world/2019/11/05/world-crisis-tunisias-democracy-marches/.

186 *This was the context in which*: Eric Schmidt and Jared Cohen, *The New Digital Age: Reshaping the Future of People, Nations and Business* (New York: Alfred A. Knopf, 2013).

187 *"organize"*: Ibid.

187 *"everyone"*: Ibid.

188 *In a seminal report titled*: Muslim Advocates, "Complicit: The Human Cost of Facebook's Disregard for Human Life," October 21, 2020, https://muslimadvocates.org/wp-content/uploads/2020/10/Complicit-Report.pdf.

188 *According to the report, more than 25,000:* Ibid.

188 *"determining role":* Ibid.

188 *In 2017, amid protests surrounding:* John Bonazzo, "Facebook Removes White Nationalist Group Pages After Charlottesville Attack," *Observer*, August 16, 2017, https://observer.com/2017/08/charlottesville-facebook-removes-racist-pages/.

188 *"take up arms":* Russell Brandom, "Facebook Takes Down 'Call to Arms' Event After Two Shot Dead in Kenosha," *The Verge*, August 26, 2020, https://www.theverge.com/2020/8/26/21402571/kenosha-guard-shooting-facebook-deplatforming-militia-violence.

189 *"civil war":* Parler LLC v. Amazon Web Services, Inc., Amazon's Opposition to Parler's Motion for Temporary Restraining Order, January 12, 2021, https://www.courtlistener.com/recap/gov.uscourts.wawd.294664/gov.uscourts.wawd.294664.10.0_1.pdf.

190 *"I don't feel responsible for any of this":* Kara Swisher, "If You Were on Parler, You Saw the Mob Coming," *New York Times*, January 11, 2021, https://www.nytimes.com/2021/01/07/opinion/sway-kara-swisher-john-matze.html.

190 *"Stop the Steal":* Rebecca Heilweil and Shirin Ghaffary, "How Trump's Internet Built and Broadcast the Capitol Insurrection," *recode*, January 8, 2021, https://www.vox.com/recode/22221285/trump-online-capitol-riot-far-right-parler-twitter-facebook.

190 *"Red-State Succession":* Ibid.

190 *"In* An Ugly Truth*":* Sheera Frenkel and Cecilia Kang, *An Ugly Truth* (New York: Harper, 2021).

190 *Twitter appropriately prioritizes the ability:* Twitter Inc., "Permanent suspension of @realDonaldTrump," January 8, 2021, https://blog.twitter.com/en_us/topics/company/2020/suspension.html.

191 *Facebook decided to maintain the ban:* Adi Robertson and Alex Heath, "Facebook Gives Trump a 2-Year Suspension, Changes Rules for Politicians," *The Verge*, June 4, 2021, https://www.theverge.com/2021/6/4/22519073/facebook-trump-ban-2-year-oversight-board-decision-political-figures-newsworthiness.

191 *As far as what federal regulations:* Brandenburg v. Ohio, 395 U.S. 444 (1969), https://www.law.cornell.edu/supremecourt/text/395/444.

191 *"very near future":* Kent Greenwalt, *Speech, Crime, and the Uses of Language* (New York: Oxford University Press, 1989).

192 *To avoid going down a road:* Nadine Strossen, *Hate: Why We Should Resist It with Free Speech, Not Censorship* (Oxford: Oxford University Press, 2018).

192 *A report from CounterAction about:* CounterAction, "Social Media in 2020 Incitement," November 25, 2020, https://counteraction.com/incitement.pdf.

193 *Currently, victims abroad have little recourse:* Poppy McPherson, "Facebook Says It Was "Too Slow" to Fight Hate in Myanmar," reuters.com, August 16, 2018, https://www.reuters.com/article/us-myanmar-facebook-rohingya/facebook-says-it-was-too-slow-to-fight-hate-speech-in-myanmar-idUSKBN1L1066.

195 *"de-amplification, de-monetization"*: "United Nations Strategy and Plan of Action on Hate Speech," September 20, p. 39, https://www.un.org/en/genocidepreven tion/documents/UN%20Strategy%20and%20PoA%20on%20Hate%20Speech_ Guidance%20on%20Addressing%20in%20field.pdf.

197 *But despite the prominence of right-wing news:* Paul M. Barrett and J. Grant Sims, "False Accusation: The Unfounded Claim that Social Media Companies Censor Conservatives," NYU Stern Center for Business and Human Rights, February 2021, https://bhr.stern.nyu.edu/bias-report-release-page.

197 *"racially biased censorship"*: Coalition Letter to Joel Kaplan, Facebook Director of Global Policy, January 18, 2017, https://s3.amazonaws.com/s3.sumofus.org/ images/Response_to_Joel_Kaplan__77_organizations-3.pdf.

198 *According to an MIT study:* Peter Dizikes, "Study: On Twitter, False News Travels Faster than True Stories," MIT News Office, March 8, 2018, https://news.mit .edu/2018/study-twitter-false-news-travels-faster-true-stories-0308.

198 *"economic, cultural, or spiritual"*: David Brooks, "The Rotting of the Republican Mind," *New York Times*, November 26, 2020, https://www.nytimes .com/2020/11/26/opinion/republican-disinformation.html.

199 *Although recent academic literature has:* Matthew Gentzkow and Jesse M. Shapiro, "Ideological Segregation Online and Offline," *Quarterly Journal of Economics* 126, no. 4 (November 2011). See also Richard Fletcher, "The Truth Behind Filter Bubbles: Bursting Some Myths," RISJ Business and Practice of Journalism Seminar Series, Green Templeton College, Oxford, January 22, 2020, https:// reutersinstitute.politics.ox.ac.uk/risj-review/truth-behind-filter-bubbles-burst ing-some-myths.

199 *". . . extreme"*: Carolyn E. Schmitt, "Network Propaganda," *Harvard Gazette*, October 25, 2018, https://news.harvard.edu/gazette/story/2018/10/network-propa ganda-takes-a-closer-look-at-media-and-american-politics/.

199 *The federal government is limited: United States v. Alvarez,* 567 U.S. 709 (2012), https://supreme.justia.com/cases/federal/us/567/709/.

200 *Facebook already puts out a high-level:* "Facebook Community Standards Enforcement Report," https://transparency.facebook.com/community-standards -enforcement.

201 *"third-party accountability"*: Elizabeth Kivowitz and Melissa Abraham, "Are We Using Technology or Are We Being Used? Q&A with UCLA's Ramesh Srinivasan," UCLA Newsroom, January 13, 2021, https://newsroom.ucla.edu/stories/ are-we-using-technology-or-are-we-being-used.

201 *"building towards a common understanding"*: @jack January 13, 2021, https:// twitter.com/jack/status/1349510783432941568.

201 *"supportive," "safe," "informed," "inclusive"*: Bryan Clark, "Zuckerberg's Epic Manifesto Details Facebook's Plan to Save the World," *The Next Web*, February 17, 2017, https://thenextweb.com/news/zuckerbergs-epic-manifesto-details-facebooks -plan-to-save-the-world.

201 *Pushing opposing material to users:* Christopher A. Bail et al., "Exposure to Opposing Views on Social Media Can Increase Political Polarization," *Proceedings of the National Academy of Sciences*, September 2018, https://www.pnas.org/content/115/37/9216.

202 *"commercial basis":* Jürgen Habermas, Sara Lennox, and Frank Lennox, "The Public Sphere: An Encyclopedia Article (1964)," *New German Critique* 3 (1974): 49–55, https://www.unige.ch/sciences-societe/socio/files/2914/0533/6073/Habermas_1974.pdf.

202 *"commercialized":* Ibid.

203 *Government could fund a national platform:* Eli Pariser and Danielle Allen, "To Thrive, Our Democracy Needs Digital Public Infrastructure," *Politico*, January 5, 2021, https://www.politico.com/news/agenda/2021/01/05/to-thrive-our-democracy-needs-digital-public-infrastructure-455061.

204 *"killing people":* Kathryn Watson, "Biden Softens Comment About Facebook 'Killing People' Because of Covid Misinformation," cbsnews.com, July 19, 2021, https://www.cbsnews.com/news/biden-facebook-covid-killing-people/.

205 *According to a fascinating study:* Gordon Pennycook and David G. Rand, "Fighting Misinformation on Social Media Using Crowdsourced Judgments of News Source Quality," *Proceedings of the National Academy of Sciences*, February 2019, https://www.pnas.org/content/116/7/2521.short.

206 *Facebook's internal data shows:* Craig Silverman and Ryan Mac, "Facebook's Internal Data Show That: Facebook Knows That Adding Labels to Trump's False Claims Does Little to Stop Their Spread," *Buzzfeed*, November 16, 2020, https://www.buzzfeednews.com/article/craigsilverman/facebook-labels-trump-lies-do-not-stop-spread.

206 *At least 5 percent of Facebook:* Jack Nicas, "Why Can't the Social Networks Stop Fake Accounts," *New York Times*, December 8, 2020, https://www.nytimes.com/2020/12/08/technology/why-cant-the-social-networks-stop-fake-accounts.html.

206 *a staggering 45 percent of tweets concerning Covid-19:* Bobby Allyn, "Researchers: Nearly Half of Accounts Tweeting About Coronavirus Are Likely Bots," NPR, May 20, 2020, https://www.npr.org/sections/coronavirus-live-updates/2020/05/20/859814085/researchers-nearly-half-of-accounts-tweeting-about-coronavirus-are-likely-bots.

206 *"suspected of being bots":* Corbin Hiar, "Twitter Bots Are a Major Source of Climate Disinformation," *E&E News*, January 22, 2021, https://www.scientificamerican.com/article/twitter-bots-are-a-major-source-of-climate-disinformation/.

207 *An Indiana University study that analyzed:* Chengcheng Shao et al., "The Spread of Low-Credibility Content by Social Bots," *Nature Communications*, November 2018, https://www.nature.com/articles/s41467-018-06930-7.

207 *"over 86% of shares":* Trevor Davis, Steven Livingston, and Matt Hindman, "Suspicious Election Campaign Activity on Facebook," School of Media & Public Affairs,

The George Washington University, July 2019, https://smpa.gwu.edu/sites/g/files/zaxdzs2046/f/2019-07-22%20-%20Suspicious%20Election%20Campaign%20Activity%20White%20Paper%20-%20Print%20Version%20-%20IDDP.pdf.

207 *As Carnegie Mellon Computer Science professor Kathleen Carley*: "Human Voices, Bot Networks and the Spread of Disinformation Ft Professor Kathleen Carley," https://podcasts.apple.com/us/podcast/human-voices/id1520755784?i=1000481646960.

208 *"Not a real video. It's doctored"*: Olivia Messer, " 'Fox & Friends' Admit Diamond & Silk Mocked Doctored Video of 'Crazy Nancy,' " *Daily Beast*, May 24, 2019, https://www.thedailybeast.com/fox-and-friends-admit-diamond-and-silk-mocked-doctored-video-of-crazy-nancy-pelosi.

209 *"barbs and fiery accusations"*: Barbara Richter, "Benjamin Franklin and the Pamphlet Wars," *Humanities*, March 17, 2020, https://www.neh.gov/article/benjamin-franklin-and-pamphlet-wars.

210 *"Making the comparison between the Internet"*: Stephen Marche, "How We Solved Fake News the First Time," *The New Yorker*, April 23, 2018, https://www.newyorker.com/culture/cultural-comment/how-we-solved-fake-news-the-first-time.

210 *"adopting the best practices for civil discourse"*: Contract for the Web: https://contractfortheweb.org/.

210 *Finland is a constant victim of Russian disinformation*: Emma Charlton, "How Finland Is Fighting Fake News—in the Classroom," World Economic Forum, May 21, 2019, https://www.weforum.org/agenda/2019/05/how-finland-is-fighting-fake-news-in-the-classroom/.

211 *Such classes could be offered*: "Nina Jankowicz Testifies Before Congress on Tech & Information Warfare: The Competition for Influence and the DOD," April 30, 2021, hearing, https://www.wilsoncenter.org/video/nina-jankowicz-testifies-congress-tech-information-warfare-competition-influence-and-dod.

211 *"security theater"*: J. M. Porup, "5 Examples of Security Theater and How to Spot Them," *CSO*, May 27, 2020, https://www.csoonline.com/article/3544293/5-examples-of-security-theater-and-how-to-spot-them.html.

211 *Living Room Conversations is a nonprofit*: Living Room Conversations, https://livingroomconversations.org/.

212 *When it comes to limiting screen time*: Caroline Knorr, "Tips and Scripts for Managing Screen Time When School Is Online," Common Sense Media, https://www.commonsensemedia.org/blog/tips-and-scripts-for-managing-screen-time-when-school-is-online-0. See also "Take Control," Center for Humane Technology, https://www.humanetech.com/take-control.

212 *A study found that a staggering*: Katie Canales, "40% of Kids Under 13 Already Use Instagram and Some Are Experiencing Abuse and Sexual Solicitation, a Report Finds, as the Tech Giant Considers Building an Instagram App for Kids," *Business Insider*, May 13, 2021, https://www.businessinsider.com/kids-under-13-use-facebook-instagram-2021-5.

213 *Ryan Kaji is a ten-year-old:* Vicky McKeever, "This Eight-Year-Old Remains Youtube's Highest-Earner, Taking Home $26 Million in 2019, cnbc.com, December 20, 2019, https://www.cnbc.com/2019/12/20/ryan-kaji-remains-youtubes-highest-earner-making-26-million-in-2019.html.

213 *"harmful to minors":* Theresa Chmara, "Do Minors Have First Amendment Rights," *Knowledge Quest,* September–October 2015, http://www.ala.org/advocacy/sites/ala.org.advocacy/files/content/Do%20Minors%20Have%20First%20Amendment%20Rights%20in%20Schools.pdf.

214 *She helped institute two government-led initiatives:* Audrey Tang, "A Strong Democracy Is a Digital Democracy," *New York Times,* October 15, 2019, https://www.nytimes.com/2019/10/15/opinion/taiwan-digital-democracy.html?auth=login-email&login=email.

215 *"America in One Room":* James Fishkin and Larry Diamond, "This Experiment Has Some Great News for Our Democracy," *New York Times,* October 2, 2019, https://www.nytimes.com/2019/10/02/opinion/america-one-room-experiment.html.

215 *This program, which was the brainchild:* Ibid.

215 *Connecting to Congress:* https://connectingtocongress.org/.

215 *Surprisingly, an award-winning political science study:* Michael A. Neblo, Kevin M. Esterling, Ryan P. Kennedy, David M. J. Lazer, and Ananad E. Sokhey, "Who Wants to Deliberate—And Why?," *The American Political Science Review* 104, no. 3 (August 2010): 566–83, https://www.jstor.org/stable/40863769?seq=1.

216 *When it comes to Facebook:* Pew Research Center, "Social Media Fact Sheet," April 7, 2021, https://www.pewresearch.org/internet/fact-sheet/social-media/.

216 *David Lazer, a leading computational social scientist:* Lazer sent me this memo, which was not published as of the book's publication. Stefan McCabe, Jon Green, and David Lazer, "How Representative Are the Represented? Who Follows Which Members of Congress on Twitter?," May 2, 2021.

217 *Two of my signature bills:* Tal Kopan, "Democrat Most Likely to Succeed with Trump? Bay Area Progressive Ro Khanna," *San Francisco Chronicle,* December 4, 2020, https://www.sfchronicle.com/politics/article/Democrat-most-likely-to-succeed-with-Trump-Bay-15774250.php.

218 *"noncoercive coercion of the better argument":* Jürgen Habermas, *Between Facts and Norms: Contributions to a Discourse Theory of Law and Democracy* (Cambridge: MIT Press, 1996).

Chapter 8: Science in Democracy

221 *"constructive public engagement":* Mark B. Brown, "Expertise and Deliberative Democracy," in *Deliberative Democracy Issues and Cases* (edited by Stephen Elstub and Peter McLaverty) (Edinburgh: Edinburgh University Press, 2014), https://www.csus.edu/faculty/b/brownm/docs/brown%202014%20expertise%20in%20deliberative%20democracy.pdf.

221 *"public deliberation":* Ibid.

221 *"ecological reflexivity"*: Jen Iris Allan, "The Politics of the Anthropocene," *Ethics & International Affairs*, December 2009, https://www.ethicsandinternation alaffairs.org/2019/the-politics-of-the-anthropocene/.

221 *"principles for collective action"*: Ibid.

221 *Elizabeth Anderson, a leading philosopher*: Elizabeth S. Anderson, "Democracy, Public Policy, and Lay Assessment of Scientific Testimony," *Episteme*, June 2011, pp. 144–64, https://www.researchgate.net/publication/231767933_Democracy_ Public_Policy_and_Lay_Assessment_of_Scientific_Testimony.

223 *"grow the economy"*: Matthew Nisbet, "Knowledge into Action: Framing the Debates over Climate Change and Poverty," December 1, 2009, https://web .northeastern.edu/matthewnisbet/2009/12/01/knowledge-into-action-framing -the-debates-over-climate-change-and-poverty/.

223 *Republicans attacking the plan have alleged*: Zack Colman, "The Bogus Number at the Center of the GOP's Green New Deal Attacks," *Politico*, March 10, 2019, https://www.politico.com/story/2019/03/10/republican-green-new-deal-attack -1250859.

224 *This is the project that John Kerry*: John Kerry and Ro Khanna, "Don't Let China Win the Green Race," *New York Times*, December 9, 2019, https://www.nytimes .com/2019/12/09/opinion/china-renewable-energy.html.

224 *"We need a Marshall Plan for Middle America"*: William Peduto, Jamael Tito Brown, Nan Whaley, Andrew Ginther, John Cranley, Steve Williams, Ron Dulaney Jr., and Greg Fischer, "We Need a Marshall Plan for Middle America," *Washington Post*, November 22, 2020, https://www.washingtonpost.com/opin ions/2020/11/22/marshall-plan-middle-america-eight-mayors/.

225 *"Jobs, Jobs, Jobs, and More Jobs"*: Saul Griffith and Sam Calisch, "Mobilizing for a Zero Carbon America: Jobs, Jobs, Jobs, and More Jobs," *Rewiring America*, July 2020, https://www.rewiringamerica.org/jobs-report.

225 *"highly distributed geographically and difficult to offshore"*: Ibid.

226 *According to the Center on Global Energy*: Varun Sivaram, Colin Cunliff, David Hart, Julio Friedmann, and David Sandalow, "Energizing America," Columbia SIPA Center on Global Energy Policy (September 2020), https://spark.adobe .com/page/Azf8uWSlPJOo9/.

226 *To achieve this, Bill Gates*: Bill Gates, "Here's How the U.S. Can Lead the World on Climate Change Innovation," *Gates Notes*, December 3, 2020, https://www .gatesnotes.com/Energy/How-the-US-can-lead-on-climate-change-innovation.

226 *There's a reason why Lockheed Martin*: Aaron Gregg, "Bernie Sanders Blasts Defense Contractors over Soaring Costs, Vows Tougher Oversight," *Washington Post*, May 12, 2021, https://www.washingtonpost.com/business/2021/05/12/ bernie-sanders-defense-spending/.

226 *Nearly 22 percent of greenhouse gas*: "Sources of Greenhouse Gas Emissions," United States Environmental Protection Agency, https://www.epa.gov/ghgemis sions/sources-greenhouse-gas-emissions.

228 *China produces about 60 percent:* Kerry and Khanna, "Don't Let China Win the Green Race."

228 *"transmissions, exhaust systems, and fuel systems":* UAW Research Department, "Taking the High Road: Strategies for a Fair EV Future," https://uaw.org/wp-con tent/uploads/2019/07/190416-EV-White-Paper-REVISED-January-2020-Final .pdf.

230 *"remove environmentally sensitive land from agriculture production":* Conserva- tion Reserve Program, Farm Service Agency, U.S. Department of Agriculture, https://www.fsa.usda.gov/programs-and-services/conservation-programs/con servation-reserve-program/.

230 *I helped Iowa State researchers:* Art Cullen, "Can a California Democrat Con- nect the Coasts with the Heartland?," *Washington Post,* February 8, 2021, https:// www.washingtonpost.com/opinions/2021/02/08/can-california-democat-con nect-coasts-with-heartland/.

231 *"Obviously, the situation in the Middle East implicates our energy security":* Ari Shapiro, "Obama Aims to Reduce Foreign Oil Reliance," *All Things Considered,* NPR, March 30, 2011, https://www.npr.org/2011/03/30/134987903/obama -aims-to-reduce-foreign-oil-reliance.

231 *This requirement passed in the 2007:* "Department of Defense Announces Bil- lions of Dollars in Opportunities for Renewable Energy and Energy Efficiency Companies," *JDSUPRA,* August 18, 2011, https://www.jdsupra.com/legalnews/ department-of-defense-announces-billions-53822/.

231 *The Navy already has exceeded:* Office of the Assistant Secretary of Defense for Sus- tainment, Department of Defense Annual Energy Management and Resilience Re- port (2018), https://www.acq.osd.mil/eie/Downloads/IE/FY%202018%20AEMR .pdf.

232 *As Mark Brown told me:* Pew Research Center, "Two-Thirds of Americans Think Government Should Do More on Climate," June 23, 2020, https://www.pew research.org/science/2020/06/23/two-thirds-of-americans-think-government -should-do-more-on-climate/.

232 *PricewaterhouseCoopers has an outstanding report:* PwC, "Sizing the Prize, PwC's Global Artificial Intelligence Study: Exploiting the AI Revolution" (2017), https://www.pwc.com/gx/en/issues/analytics/assets/pwc-ai-analysis-sizing-the -prize-report.pdf.

233 *"advance of science and technology":* Consortium for Science, Policy & Outcomes at Arizona State University, "Vision and Mission," https://cspo.org/about-cspo/ vision-and-mission/.

233 *"high-risk":* Wonks and Techies, "Input on the European Commission White Paper 'On Artificial Intelligence—A European Approach to Excellence and Trust,'" June 15, 2020, https://hai.stanford.edu/sites/default/files/2020-07/HAI_ WhitePaper_v4B.pdf.

233 *We know facial recognition programs:* Tom Simonite, "The Best Algorithms

Struggle to Recognize Black Faces Equally," *wired.com*, July 22, 2019, https://www.wired.com/story/best-algorithms-struggle-recognize-black-faces-equally/.

234 *This fact was most strikingly demonstrated:* Jacob Snow, "Amazon's Face Recognition Falsely Matched 28 Members of Congress with Mugshots," ACLU, July 26, 2018, https://www.aclu.org/blog/privacy-technology/surveillance-technologies/amazons-face-recognition-falsely-matched-28.

234 *At the time, 20 percent:* Ibid.

234 *This led to a hearing on the House Oversight:* House Committee on Oversight and Reform, "Facial Recognition Technology: Its Impact on Our Civil Rights and Liberties," May 22, 2019, https://oversight.house.gov/legislation/hearings/facial-recognition-technology-part-1-its-impact-on-our-civil-rights-and.

234 *A groundbreaking Brookings report recommends:* Nicol Turner Lee, Paul Resnick, and Genie Barton, "Algorithmic Bias Detection and Mitigation: Best Practices and Policies to Reduce Consumer Harms," Brookings, May 22, 2019, https://www.brookings.edu/research/algorithmic-bias-detection-and-mitigation-best-practices-and-policies-to-reduce-consumer-harms/.

234 *The Algorithmic Accountability Act:* Adi Robertson, "A New Bill Would Force Companies to Check Their Algorithms for Bias," *The Verge*, April 10, 2019, https://www.theverge.com/2019/4/10/18304960/congress-algorithmic-accountability-act-wyden-clarke-booker-bill-introduced-house-senate.

234 *The McKinsey Global Institute's pioneering report:* James Manyika et al., "Jobs Lost, Jobs Gained: Workforce Transitions in a Time of Automation," McKinsey Global Institute, December 2017, https://www.mckinsey.com/~/media/mckinsey/industries/public%20and%20social%20sector/our%20insights/what%20the%20future%20of%20work%20will%20mean%20for%20jobs%20skills%20and%20wages/mgi%20jobs%20lost-jobs%20gained_report_december%202017.pdf.

235 *Currently, the federal government spends:* Ibid. (Exhibit E9).

235 *We also need federal regulations to ensure:* Will Douglas Heaven, "AI Needs to Face Up to Its Invisible-Worker Problem," *MIT Technology Review*, December 11, 2020, https://www.technologyreview.com/2020/12/11/1014081/ai-machine-learning-crowd-gig-worker-problem-amazon-mechanical-turk/.

235 *Saiph Savage, director of the Civic A.I. lab:* Ibid.

235 *Corporations such as Amazon:* Ibid

235 *"call themselves tech workers":* Ibid.

236 *"responsible":* "DOD Adopts Ethical Principles for Artificial Intelligence," U.S. Department of Defense, February 24, 2020, https://www.defense.gov/Newsroom/Releases/Release/Article/2091996/dod-adopts-ethical-principles-for-artificial-intelligence/.

237 *Unfortunately, a bipartisan paper authored in 2020:* Bipartisan Policy Center, "Cementing American Artificial Intelligence Leadership: AI Research & Development," August 6, 2020, https://bipartisanpolicy.org/report/ai-research-development/.

237 *Our private spending on AI, however:* Ibid.

237 *That is why the report recommends:* Ibid.

238 *As President Biden often emphasizes:* Brandi Vincent, "The President Referenced Infrastructure, Immigration, Quantum Computing and Much More in His First Formal Press Conference," nextgov.com, March 25, 2021, https://www.nextgov .com/cio-briefing/2021/03/biden-commits-investing-closer-2-gdp-science-re search/172933/.

238 *MIT economists Jon Gruber and Simon Johnson:* "Jump-Starting America: New Book by MIT's Jonathan Gruber and Simon Johnson Argues That Public Investment in Science Is Key to Revving Up the U.S. Growth Engine," MIT Sloan Office of Media Relations, April 9, 2019, https://mitsloan.mit.edu/press/jump-starting -america-new-book-mits-jonathan-gruber-and-simon-johnson-argues-public -investment-science-key-to-revving-u-s-growth-engine.

238 *China is, at least, at:* Gruber estimates China's R&D is more than what the OECD reports. Jonathan Gruber and Matt Hourihan, "How Much New Public R&D Spending is in the United States Innovation and Competition Act of 2021," June 11, 2021 (not published).

240 *Huawei spends more than $20 billion:* Sean, "Huawei Working Around the Clock, R&D Budget Increased to $20 Billion: CEO," gizmochina.com, March 26, 2020, https://www.gizmochina.com/2020/03/26/huawei-working-around-the-clock -rd-budget-increased-to-20-billion-ceo/.

240 *The United States continues to lead:* "2020 State of the U.S. Semiconductor Industry," Semiconductor Industry Association (2020), https://www.semiconductors .org/wp-content/uploads/2020/06/2020-SIA-State-of-the-Industry-Report.pdf.

241 *The challenge for our nation is that currently:* Ibid.

242 *"Bio-Belt":* John Cumbers, "The Bio-Belt: Growing the Future in Rural America," *Forbes,* July 15, 2019, https://www.forbes.com/sites/johncumbers/2019/07/15/ the-bio-belt-growing-the-future-in-rural-america/?sh=58bef3035461.

242 *The truth is the U.S. was the first:* Todd Kuiken, "U.S. Trends in Synthetic Biology Research Funding," Wilson Center, September 15, 2015, https://www.wilsoncen ter.org/publication/us-trends-synthetic-biology-research-funding.

Chapter 9: Decentralizing Foreign Policy

245 "What would make you": @RoKhanna, December 16, 2020, https://twitter.com/ rokhanna/status/1339324929066536960?lang=en.

246 *less than a quarter of what the Pentagon:* Ellen Mitchell, "The Pentagon's Battle of the Bands," *Politico,* May 5, 2016, https://www.politico.com/story/2016/05/ pentagons-bands-battle-223435.

246 the $16 trillion that the pandemic: David M. Cutler and Lawrence H. Summers, "The Covid-19 Pandemic and the $16 Trillion Virus," *JAMA,* October 20 2020, https://jamanetwork.com/journals/jama/fullarticle/2771764.

247 *According to* Time *magazine, Professor Zhang Yongzhen:* Carlie Campbell, "The

Chinese Scientist Who Sequenced the First Covid-19 Genome Speaks Out About the Controversies Surrounding His Work," *Time*, August 24, 2020, https://time.com/5882918/zhang-yongzhen-interview-china-coronavirus-genome/.

247 *He collaborated with Professor Edward Holmes:* Ibid.

248 *We currently have about eight hundred military:* "U.S. Military Bases Overseas: The Facts," https://www.overseasbases.net/fact-sheet.html.

248 *slush fund:* Mick Mulvaney, "Mulvaney, Van Hollen, Lee, Sanford Amendment Helps Prevent Abuse of OCO Slush Fund," *Vote Smart Facts Matter*, https://justfacts.votesmart.org/public-statement/1100038/mulvaney-van-hollen-lee-sanford-amendment-helps-prevent-abuse-of-oco-slush-fund.

248 *We've spent almost $2 trillion:* Congressional Research Service, "Overseas Contingency Operations Funding: Background and Status," September 6, 2019, https://crsreports.congress.gov/product/pdf/R/R44519#page=2.

248 *OCO is almost $70 billion:* "OCO Once Against Federal Government's 4th Largest 'Agency' in Discretionary Budget," Taxpayers for Common Sense, February 14, 2018, https://www.taxpayer.net/national-security/oco-federal-governments-4th-largest-agency-discretionary-budget/.

248 *The U.S. plans to spend more than a trillion:* Congressional Budget Office, "Approaches for Managing the Costs of U.S. Nuclear Forces, 2017 to 2046," October 31, 2017, https://www.cbo.gov/publication/53211#:~:text=CBO%20estimates%20that%20the%20most,upgrade)%20nuclear%20forces%20and%20about.

248 *According to the Department of Defense's public statements:* "America's Nuclear Triad," US Department of Defense, https://www.defense.gov/Experience/Americas-Nuclear-Triad/.

249 *The Air Force plans to do away with:* Steve Fetter and Kingston Reif, "A Cheaper Nuclear Sponge," warontherocks.com, October 18, 2019, https://warontherocks.com/2019/10/a-cheaper-nuclear-sponge/.

249 *Instead of making new ICBMs:* Kingston Reif, CBO: Nuclear Arsenal to Cost $1.2 Trillion, *Arms Control Association*, December 2017; https://www.armscontrol.org/act/2017-12/news/cbo-nuclear-arsenal-cost-12-trillion.

250 *An amendment introduced that year to cut:* Derek Major, "Ninety-Three Members of the House and 23 Senators Voted to Cut the Pentagon Budget," *Black Enterprise*, July 23, 2000, https://www.blackenterprise.com/ninety-three-members-of-the-house-and-23-senators-voted-to-cut-the-pentagon-budget/.

250 *The average CEO pay of major defense:* Sarah Anderson, "The Threat of War Inflates Stock Holdings of Military Contractor CEOs," *Inequality.org*, January 5, 2020; https://inequality.org/great-divide/war-profit-military-contractor-ceos/, This site has salaries of defense contractor executive officers; https://www.salary.com/personal/executive-salaries/.

250 *"did not compete:"* GAO, A Report to Congressional Committees Weapon Systems Annual Assessment, May 2019, p. 2; https://www.gao.gov/assets/gao-19-336sp.pdf; *"67 percent of 183:"* Ibid.

250 *Embarrassed by the Congressional Oversight hearing:* David Dayen, "How Rep. Ro Khanna Got a Price-Gouging Defense Contractor to Return $16.1 Million to the Pentagon," *Intercept*, May 28, 2019, https://theintercept.com/2019/05/28/ro -khanna-transdigm-refund-pentagon/.

252 *It was reported that Colonial Pipeline:* Michael Shear, Nicole Perlroth, and Clifford Krauss, "Colonial Pipeline Paid Roughly $5 Million in Ransom to Hackers," *New York Times*, May 13, 2021, https://www.nytimes.com/2021/05/13/us/poli tics/biden-colonial-pipeline-ransomware.html.

258 *"a submarine officer in the Pacific during the Korean war":* "Remarks by Former U.S. President Jimmy Carter at Korea University, Seoul, Korea," The Carter Center, March 22, 2010, https://www.cartercenter.org/news/editorials_speeches/ jimmy-carter-speech-korea-university.html.

259 *"global tea party movement":* Will Europe's Nationalists Welcome Bannon's Attempt to Unite the Right?," *France 24*, August 18, 2018, https://www.france24 .com/en/20180814-europe-nationalists-populists-bannon-unite-far-right-wing -movement-brussels-eu.

260 *His envoy to India, Colonel Louis Johnson:* Meenakshi Ahamed, *A Matter of Trust: India-US Relations from Truman to Trump* (New York: HarperCollins, 2021), pp. 22–25.

261 *Consider that America's white (non-Hispanic):* United States Census Bureau; https://www.census.gov/quickfacts/fact/table/US/RHI825219. See also William H. Frey, "The Nation Is Diversifying Even Faster than Predicted, According to New Census Data," Brookings, July 1, 2020, https://www.brookings.edu/ research/new-census-data-shows-the-nation-is-diversifying-even-faster-than -predicted/.

261 *Canada, which is easily more than 70 percent:* Census Profile, 2016 Census: "Clicking on Rates for Not a Visible Minority Shows 77.7 percent," https://www12.stat can.gc.ca/census-recensement/2016/dp-pd/prof/details/page.cfm?Lang=E&Geo 1=PR&Code1=01&Geo2=PR&Code2=01&Data=Count&SearchText=Canada& SearchType=Begins&SearchPR=01&B1=Visible%20minority&TABID=1.

261 *About 85 percent of Australians:* "Geographical Structure and Differential Natural Selection Among North European Populations," May 19, 2019, https://genepi .qimr.edu.au/contents/p/staff/McEvoyGenRespublsiehd.pdf. See also Sieni Kimalainen, "Top 5 Countries with the Largest White Population Outside of Europe," *insidermonkey*, September 13, 2020, https://www.insidermonkey.com/blog/top -5-countries-with-the-largest-white-population-outside-of-europe-876492/. Kimalainen writes that Australia is 92 percent white.

261 *"were white British":* Aaron O'Neil, "United Kingdom," statista, April 15, 2021, https://www.statista.com/statistics/270386/ethnicity-in-the-united-kingdom/.

261 *According to the Congressional Research Service:* Jill H. Wilson, "The Foreign-born and Second-Generation Population and Their Origins of Birth, 1900–2020," Congressional Research Service, February 9, 2021, https://khanna.house

.gov/sites/khanna.house.gov/files/Khanna%20memo%20on%20second%20
gen_FINAL.pdf.

261 *Post-1965, half of immigrants coming:* Ibid.

261 *In fact, non-European immigrants:* Ibid.

263 *"we are all caught in an inescapable network of mutuality":* Dr. Martin Luther
King, Remaining Awake Through a Great Revolution, Commencement Address
for Oberlin College, June 1965,https://www2.oberlin.edu/external/EOG/Black
HistoryMonth/MLK/CommAddress.html.

263 *"goes not abroad, in search of monsters to destroy":* John Quincy Adams's Warning
Against the Search for "Monsters to Destroy," 1821, https://www.mtholyoke.edu/
acad/intrel/jqadams.htm#:~:text=Wherever%20the%20standard%20of%20
freedom,vindicator%20only%20of%20her%20own.

263 *"equal justice":* Ibid.

263 *"a movement around the world":* Jen Kirby, " 'Black Lives Matter' Has Become a
Global Rallying Cry Against Racism and Police Brutality," *Vox,* June 12, 2020,
https://www.vox.com/2020/6/12/21285244/black-lives-matter-global-protests
-george-floyd-uk-belgium.

263 *Our mobilizing for racial justice inspired those:* CIGH Exeter, "A Law to End De-
colonizing Debates," Imperial and Global Forum, June 1, 2021; https://imperi-
alglobalexeter.com/2021/06/01/a-law-to-end-decolonising-debates/. See also
Kirby, " 'Black Lives Matter' Has Become a Global Rallying Cry Against Racism
and Police Brutality."

264 *It was also remarkable to see how much:* "In Solidarity and as a Symbol of Global
Injustices, a Syrian Artist Painted a Mural to George Floyd on a Bombed Idlib
Building," *Time,* June 6, 2020, https://time.com/5849444/george-floyd-mural
-idlib-syria/.

264 *"net nationalism":* Tim Wu, "A TikTok Ban Is Overdue," *New York Times,* August 18, 2020, https://www.nytimes.com/2020/08/18/opinion/tiktok-wechat-ban
-trump.html.

264 *Even democracies such as India:* Darrell M. West, "Shutting Down the Internet," Brookings, February 5, 2021, https://www.brookings.edu/blog/tech
tank/2021/02/05/shutting-down-the-internet/.

264 *"spontaneous and egalitarian nature":* Stuart Jeffries, "A Rare Interview with Jürgen Habermas," *Financial Times,* April 30, 2010, https://www.ft.com/content/
eda3bcd8-5327-11df-813e-00144feab49a.

265 *For example, Purpose is:* purpose.com.

265 *"the world's largest online citizens' movement":* Jeremy Heimans, "Thinkers Radar
Class of 2019," https://thinkers50.com/radar-2019/jeremy-heimans/.

265 *Then there are organizations such as:* UNITE, unitenetwork.org; Unite, unite.us.

265 *"Roadmap for Digital Cooperation":* Report of the Secretary-General Roadmap
for Digital Cooperation, June 2020, https://www.un.org/en/content/digital-co
operation-roadmap/.

266 *"critical threat"*: "Americans overwhelmingly see China as the greatest foreign challenger to the United States," Mapping The Future of U.S. China Policy, Center for Strategic & International Studies, https://chinasurvey.csis.org/analysis/americans-see-china-greatest-challenger/.

266 *But only 41 percent support*: Craig Kafura, Dina Smeltz, Joshua Busby, Joshua Kertzer, and Jonathan Monten, "Divisions on US-China Policy: Opinion Leaders and the Public," The Chicago Council On Global Affairs, February 1, 2021, https://www.thechicagocouncil.org/research/public-opinion-survey/divisions-us-china-policy-opinion-leaders-and-public.

267 *First, Americans support cooperation with China:* Ibid.

267 *Second, nearly 90 percent of Americans:* Ibid.

267 *The internment of more than one million Uighurs:* Matthew Hill, David Campanale, and Joel Gunter, [[this cite is using guillemets, not quotes]] 'Their Goal Is to Destroy Everyone' Uighur Camp Detainees Allege Systematic Rape, *bbc.com*, February 2, 2020, https://www.bbc.com/news/world-asia-china-55794071.

267 *More than targeted sanctions:* Olivia Enos and Hardin Lang, "The United States Should Give Fleeing Uighurs a Home," *Foreign Policy*, February 12, 2021, https://foreignpolicy.com/2021/02/12/united-states-uighurs-persecution-china-refugees-resettlement/.

267 *Third, many Americans understand the economic:* Policy Recommendations, "Mapping the Future of U.S. China Policy," Center for Strategic & International Studies, https://chinasurvey.csis.org/policy-recommendations/.

267 *Nearly $3.4 trillion dollars in trade:* Congressional Research Service, "U.S.-China Strategic Competition in South and East China Seas: Background and Issues for Congress," March 18, 2021, https://fas.org/sgp/crs/row/R42784.pdf.

267 *11 billion barrels of untapped oil:* Territorial Disputes in the South China Sea," Council on Foreign Relations, https://www.cfr.org/global-conflict-tracker/conflict/territorial-disputes-south-china-sea#:~:text=China's%20sweeping%20claims%20of%20sovereignty,Philippines%2C%20Taiwan%2C%20and%20Vietnam.

268 *The best way to do this is to help:* Michael D. Swaine, Jessica J. Lee, and Rachel Esplin Odell, "Toward an Inclusive & Balanced Regional Order: A New U.S. Strategy in East Asia," QI, January 11, 2021, https://quincyinst.org/2021/01/11/toward-an-inclusive-balanced-regional-order-a-new-u-s-strategy-in-east-asia/.

268 *Quincy . . . also calls for the U.S.:* Ibid.

268 *Fifth, the American public strongly supports:* "An overwhelming majority of U.S. thought leaders want to work with allies and partners to respond to the challenge from China even if it hurts relations with Beijing," Mapping The Future of U.S. China Policy, https://chinasurvey.csis.org/analysis/thought-leaders-support-working-with-allies/.

269 *At the same time, we should continue to increase:* Eric Levitz, "Only the Left Can Save Globalization Now," *New York Intelligencer*, February 9, 2021, https://

nymag.com/intelligencer/2021/02/only-the-left-can-save-globalization-now
.html.

269 *"China's push for technological supremacy"*: Christopher Darby and Sarah Sewall, "America's Eroding Technological Advantage," *Foreign Affairs*, March/April 2021, https://www.foreignaffairs.com/articles/united-states/2021-02-10/technology -innovation-wars.

269 *China can win the next war*: Ibid.

269 *Darby and Sewall call for our country*: Ibid.

270 *"universal value"*: Amartya Sen, "Democracy as a Universal Value," *Journal of Democracy* 10, no. 3 (1999): 3–17, https://www.unicef.org/socialpolicy/files/De mocracy_as_a_Universal_Value.pdf.

Chapter 10: Democratic Patriotism

273 *Frederick Douglass: Prophet of Freedom*: David W. Blight, *Frederick Douglass: Prophet of Freedom* (New York: Simon & Schuster, 2018).

273 *"Our Composite Nationality"*: Frederick Douglass, "Our Composite Nationality," 1869, https://teachingamericanhistory.org/library/document/our-composite -nationality/.

275 *"aims and ends"*: Ibid.

275 *"get a voice in public debates"*: Jürgen Habermas, "Multiculturalism and the Liberal State," *Stanford Law Review* 47, no. 5 (May 1995): 849–53.

276 *"civil equality"*: Douglass, "Our Composite Nationality."

276 *"the concept of justice is independent from"*: John Rawls, "Justice as Fairness: Political Not Metaphysical," in Shaun P. Young, *Political Liberalism* (Albany: State University of New York Press, 2004), pp. 25–53.

277 *"sentiment of patriotism"*: Douglass, "Our Composite Nationality."

277 *"a social union of social unions"*: John Rawls, *A Theory of Justice* (Cambridge: Belknap Press, 1971).

277 *"most diverse populations"*: Douglass, "Our Composite Nationality."

277 *"to be a co-worker in the kingdom of culture"*: W. E. B. Du Bois, *The Souls of Black Folk* (New York: Penguin, 2020).

278 *"strangers in their own land"*: Arlie Russell Hochschild, *Strangers in Their Own Land* (New York: The New Press, 2016).

279 *"continuous with the love of mankind"*: John Rawls, *A Theory of Justice* (Cambridge: Belknap Press, 1971), p. 417, "to advance the other person's good as this person's rational self-love would require": Ibid. at p. 166.

279 *Joshua Cohen, a student of Rawls*: John Rawls, Joshua Cohen, and Robert Adams, *A Brief Inquiry into the Meaning of Sin and Faith*, edited by Thomas Nagel (Cambridge: Harvard University Press, 2009).

280 *"welcome all"*: Douglass, "Our Composite Nationality."

281 *"truly American"*: Aidan Connaughton, "In Both Parties, Fewer Now Say Being Christian or Being Born in U.S. Is Important to Being 'Truly American,'" Pew

Research Center, May 25, 2021, https://www.pewresearch.org/fact-tank/2021/05/25/in-both-parties-fewer-now-say-being-christian-or-being-born-in-u-s-is-important-to-being-truly-american/.

282 *"a new and more noble course"*: The Federalist Papers, No. 14, https://press-pubs.uchicago.edu/founders/documents/v1ch4s22.html.

282 *"patriotic emotion"*: Martha C. Nussbaum, *Political Emotions* (Cambridge: Belknap Press, 2013), p. 214.

282 *"particular individuals"*: Ibid., p. 215.

282 *"physical places"*: Ibid.

283 *One danger of a thicker:* Jan-Werner Müller, *Constitutional Patriotism* (Princeton: Princeton University Press, 2008).

283 *"curtailed"*: America First Caucus Policy Platform, "Anglo-Saxon," https://punchbowl.news/wp-content/uploads/America-First-Caucus-Policy-Platform-FINAL-2.pdf.

283 *"right of migration"*: Douglass, "Our Composite Nationality."

285 *"gloomy prophets"*: Ibid.

Index

About the Author

RO KHANNA represents Silicon Valley in Congress. He has taught economics at Stanford, served as Deputy Assistant Secretary of Commerce in the Obama administration, and represented tech companies and start-ups in private practice. He enjoys spending time with his wife and two young children as well as his large extended family.